T0332618

# HANDBOOK OF MACHINE LEARNING

### Volume 1: Foundation
### of Artificial Intelligence

# HANDBOOK OF MACHINE LEARNING

## Volume 1: Foundation of Artificial Intelligence

### Tshilidzi Marwala

University of Johannesburg, South Africa

**World Scientific**

NEW JERSEY · LONDON · SINGAPORE · BEIJING · SHANGHAI · HONG KONG · TAIPEI · CHENNAI · TOKYO

*Published by*

World Scientific Publishing Co. Pte. Ltd.
5 Toh Tuck Link, Singapore 596224
*USA office:* 27 Warren Street, Suite 401-402, Hackensack, NJ 07601
*UK office:* 57 Shelton Street, Covent Garden, London WC2H 9HE

**Library of Congress Cataloging-in-Publication Data**
Names: Marwala, Tshilidzi, 1971–    author.
Title: Handbook of machine learning / by Tshilidzi Marwala (University of
    Johannesburg, South Africa).
Description: New Jersey : World Scientific, 2018- | Includes bibliographical references
    and index. Contents: volume 1. Foundation of artificial intelligence
Identifiers: LCCN 2018023989 | ISBN 9789813271227 (hc : alk. paper : v. 1)
Subjects: LCSH: Machine learning. | Artificial intelligence.
Classification: LCC Q325.5 .M3688 2018 | DDC 006.3/1--dc23
LC record available at https://lccn.loc.gov/2018023989

**British Library Cataloguing-in-Publication Data**
A catalogue record for this book is available from the British Library.

For any available supplementary material, please visit
https://www.worldscientific.com/worldscibooks/10.1142/11013#t=suppl

Desk Editors: Herbert Moses/Yu Shan Tay

Typeset by Stallion Press
Email: enquiries@stallionpress.com

Printed in Singapore

# Preface

*Handbook of Machine Learning: Foundation of Artificial Intelligence — Vol. 1 —* is the first of two volumes. It discusses concepts and applications of artificial intelligence. The artificial intelligence techniques that are studied include multi-layer networks, radial basis function, automatic relevance determination, Bayesian networks, support vector machines, fuzzy logic, rough sets, Gaussian mixture model, hidden Markov models, incremental learning, auto-associative network and hybrid systems. In addition, this book explores signal processing techniques, and these are the time domain, time–frequency domain and fractals approaches. This book also studies the difficult problem of causality.

These techniques are used to solve interesting problems such as modelling inflation, condition monitoring, speaker recognition, modelling interstate conflict, wine recognition, optimal character recognition, finance, artificial beer taster and modelling HIV.

This book is an interesting reference for graduate students, researchers and artificial intelligence practitioners.

*Tshilidzi Marwala, PhD*

March 2018
University of Johannesburg

# About the Author

 **Tshilidzi Marwala** is the Vice-Chancellor and Principal of the University of Johannesburg from 1st January 2018. From 2013 to 2017, he was the Deputy Vice-Chancellor for Research and Internationalization, and from 2009 to 2013 he was the Executive Dean of the Faculty of Engineering and the Built Environment, both at the University of Johannesburg. From 2003 to 2008, he progressively held the positions of Associate Professor, full Professor, the Carl and Emily Fuchs Chair of Systems and Control Engineering, as well as the SARChI Chair of Systems Engineering at the Department of Electrical and Information Engineering at the University of the Witwatersrand. From 2001 to 2003, he was the Executive Assistant to the technical director at South African Breweries. From 2000 to 2001 he was a post-doctoral research associate at Imperial College (then University of London). He received a Bachelor of Science in Mechanical Engineering (*magna cum laude*) from Case Western Reserve University (USA) in 1995, a Master of Mechanical Engineering from the University of Pretoria in 1997 and a PhD specializing in Artificial Intelligence and Engineering from the University of Cambridge in 2000. Marwala completed the Advanced Management Program (AMP) at Columbia University Businesses School in 2017 and completed a Program for Leadership Development (PLD) at Harvard Business School in 2007. Tshilidzi is a registered Professional Engineer, a Fellow of TWAS (The World Academy of Sciences), the Academy of Science of South Africa, the African Academy of Sciences and the South African Academy of Engineering. He is a Senior Member of the IEEE (Institute of Electrical and Electronics Engineering) and a distinguished member of the ACM

(Association for Computing Machinery). His research interests are multidisciplinary and include the Theory and Application of Artificial Intelligence to Engineering, Computer Science, Finance, Social Science and Medicine. He has an extensive track record in human capacity development having supervised 47 Master's and 28 Doctoral students to completion. Some of these students have proceeded with their doctoral and post-doctoral studies at leading universities such as Harvard, Oxford, Cambridge, British Columbia, Rutgers, Purdue, Chiba and Waseda. He has published 13 books in artificial intelligence, one of which has been translated into Chinese, over 300 papers in journals, proceedings, book chapters and magazines and holds four patents. He is an Associate Editor of the *International Journal of Systems Science* (Taylor and Francis Publishers). He has been a Visiting Scholar at Harvard University, University of California at Berkeley, Wolfson College of the University of Cambridge and Nanjing Tech University as well as a Member of the Programming Council of the Faculty of Electrical Engineering at the Silesian University of Technology in Poland. He has received more than 45 awards including the Order of Mapungubwe and was a delegate to the 1989 London International Youth Science Fortnight (LIYSF) when he was in high school. His writings and opinions have appeared in the magazines: *New Scientist*, *The Economist* and *Time Magazine*.

# Acknowledgements

I would like to thank the following former and current graduate students for their contribution to this manuscript: Michael Pires, Msizi Khoza, Ishmael Sibusiso Msiza, Nadim Mohamed, Lindokuhle Mpanza, Unathi Mahola, Dr. Brain Leke, Dr. Sizwe Dhlamini, Geg Hulley, Dr. Collins Leke, Thando Tettey, Bodie Crossingham, Professor Fulufhelo Nelwamondo, Dr. Vukosi Marivate, Dr. Shakir Mohamed, Dr. Bo Xing, Dr. David Starfield, Dr. Pretesh Patel, Dr. George Anderson, Dr. Mlungisi Duma, Dr. Dalton Lunga, Dr. Linda Mthembu, Dr. Craig Boesack, Dr. Bolanle Abe, Dr. Evan Hurwitz, Dr. Linda Mthembu, Dr. Marcos Alvares, Dr. Pramod Parida, Dr. Ali Hasan, Dr. Ilyes Boulkaibet, Dr. Satyakama Paul, Dr. Meir Perez, Dr. Megan Russell and Dr. Busisiwe Vilakazi.

I also thank colleagues and practitioners who have collaborated directly and indirectly to writing of the manuscript. I thank my supervisors Dr. Hugh Hunt, Professor Stephan Heyns and Professor Philippe de Wilde.

I dedicate this book to Dr. Jabulile Manana as well as my daughter Mbali Denga and sons Lwazi Thendo and Nhlonipho Khathutshelo.

*Tshilidzi Marwala*

March 2018
University of Johannesburg

# Contents

# Chapter 1

# Introduction

**Abstract.** This chapter introduces this book. It describes the representation of data in the time, frequency and time–frequency domains. It also describes how fractal characteristics can be extracted from data in the time (or space) domain. It then describes the common mistakes encountered when applying artificial intelligence methods. Finally, it describes machine-learning techniques that are studied in this book. These are the multi-layer perceptron, radial basis function, automatic relevance determination, support vector machines, fuzzy logic, rough sets, auto-associative network, Bayesian networks, hybrid models, online learning, causality, Gaussian mixture models, Hidden Markov models and reinforcement learning.

## 1.1 Introduction

Machine learning requires data to make decisions. The type of dataset, its values, how it is scaled, the amount of noise in the data, its sensitivity with respect to the outcome and how features are selected are all important in the effectiveness of machine learning. This chapter introduces data handling methods as well as artificial intelligence methods described in this book. The data handling methods introduced in this book are the domains in which data should be represented, and these are the time (or space) domain, frequency domain and time (or space)–frequency domain. These domains are important because, for example, in finger print recognition problems, the frequency domain methods are more effective than the time domain methods. Another example where frequency domain methods are more effective than the time domain methods is in condition monitoring of mechanical structures using vibration data (Marwala, 2012). It has been found that for non-stationary data, the time–frequency techniques are more viable than the frequency domain methods (Marwala, 2012). Some of the time domain methods explored are data processed using averages, variances and kurtosis (Marwala, 2013). The frequency domain methods are obtained using the Fourier transform. Fourier discovered many years ago that a signal can be represented in terms of sinusoids of varying frequencies and amplitudes. He then discovered that those frequencies are the natural frequencies of the structure or system under consideration. There are many types of the time–frequency analysis and these include Wigner–Ville distribution, short-time Fourier transform and the wavelet transform. This chapter also describes the fractal methods which have been found to be useful in stock market prediction (Lunga and Marwala, 2006a; Lunga, 2007). The chapter describes some important data handling methods such as scaling and accuracy measurements (Hurwitz and Marwala, 2012). This chapter also describes artificial intelligence methods studied in this book, and these include the multi-layer perceptron (MLP), radial basis function (RBF), automatic relevance determination (ARD), support vector machines (SVM), fuzzy logic, rough sets, auto-associative network, Bayesian networks, hybrid models, online learning, causality, Gaussian mixture models, Hidden Markov models and reinforcement learning.

## 1.2  Time Domain Data

Time domain representation of data is called time series data. It is called this because it is presented as a function of time. Marwala (2013) presented the quarterly GDP of the United States as a function of time, and this is shown in Figure 1.1. We observe in this figure that the GDP has grown as a function

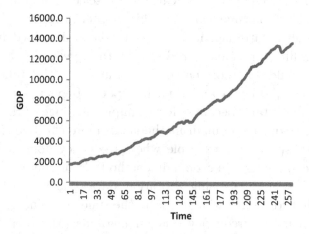

**Figure 1.1**   The quarterly GDP of the United States from 1947 to 2012.

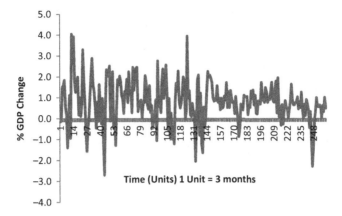

**Figure 1.2**  The percentage change of GDP of the United States from 1947 to 2012.

of time. Several statistical parameters can be derived from this dataset, and these include the average, variance and kurtosis (Marwala, 2007). Marwala expressed the data in Figure 1.1 in terms of percentage change of GDP, and this is given in Figure 1.2.

### 1.2.1 Average

The average is the quantification of the central tendency of data. For $N$ data points, the average $\bar{x}$ of series $x_1, x_2, \ldots, x_N$ is as follows (Hand, 2008; Marwala, 2013):

$$\bar{x} = \frac{1}{N} \sum_{i}^{N} x_i. \tag{1.1}$$

The use of averages includes studying the financial crisis (Ni *et al.*, 2013), portfolio selection (Pavlov and Hurn, 2012) and in double action market (Chiarella *et al.*, 2012).

### 1.2.2 Variance

Variance is the measure of the spread of the data and is estimated by calculating the difference between the average value of the sum-of-squares and the square of the sum of averages. This is written as follows (Hand, 2008; Marwala, 2013):

$$\mathrm{Var}x = \frac{1}{N} \sum_{i}^{N} (x_i)^2 - \left( \frac{1}{N} \sum_{i}^{N} (x_i) \right)^2. \tag{1.2}$$

This has been used to estimate the income variance in cross-sectional data (Uematsu *et al.*, 2012), the rise and fall of S&P500 variance futures (Chang *et al.*, 2013), to analyse the relationship between accruals, cash flows and equity returns (Clatworthy *et al.*, 2012) and to estimate risk in commodity markets (Prokopczuk *et al.*, 2017). Marwala (2013) transformed the data in Figure 1.2 into the 6-time unit moving average and variance and this results are shown in Figures 1.3 and 1.4, respectively.

In this figure, it is observed that in the earlier years, the growth of the GDP was more volatile than in the later years.

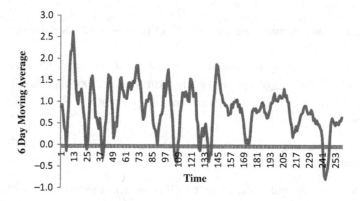

**Figure 1.3**   The 6-unit period moving average of the percentage change of GDP of the United States from 1947 to 2012.

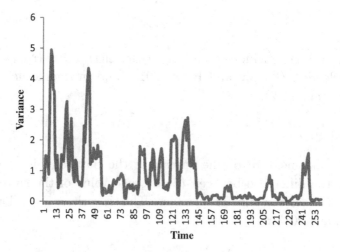

**Figure 1.4**   The 6-unit period moving variance of the percentage change of GDP of the United States from 1947 to 2012.

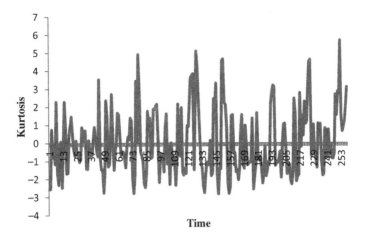

**Figure 1.5**  The 6-unit period moving kurtosis of the percentage change of GDP of the United States from 1947 to 2012.

### 1.2.3  Kurtosis

To analyse a situation where there is occasional spiking of data, we use kurtosis. Kurtosis has been successfully used to study the information content prior to earnings announcements for stock and option returns (Diavatopoulos *et al.*, 2012), in portfolio rankings (di Pierro and Mosevichz, 2011), in hedging (Angelini and Nicolosi, 2010), in risk estimation (Dark, 2010), in rolling bearing elements (Liu *et al.*, 2018) and financial time series (Xu and Shang, 2018). The calculated kurtosis value is usually normalized by the square of the second moment. A high value of kurtosis shows a sharp distribution peak. It indicates that the signal is impulsive in character. Marwala (2013) transformed the data in Figure 1.2 into kurtosis, the results in Figure 1.5 were obtained. Kurtosis is written as follows (Hand, 2008; Marwala, 2013):

$$K = \frac{1}{N} \sum_{i=1}^{N} \frac{(x_i - \bar{x})^4}{\sigma^4}, \tag{1.3}$$

where $\bar{x}$ is the mean and $\sigma$ is the variance.

### 1.3  Frequency Domain

The frequency domain analysis is based on the Fourier series. The Fourier series states that every periodic function can be estimated using a Fourier series expressed in terms of sines and cosines (Marwala, 2013). This implies that each signal is represented in terms of a series of cycles with different amplitudes and frequencies. The function $f(x)$ can be estimated using the Fourier series as follows (Moon and Stirling, 1999; Marwala, 2013):

$$f(x) \approx \frac{a_0}{2} + \sum_{n=1}^{N}(a_n \cos(nx) + b_n \sin(nx)), \quad N \geq 0, \qquad (1.4)$$

where

$$a_n = \frac{1}{\pi}\int_{-\pi}^{\pi} f(x) \cos(nx)dx, \quad n \geq 0, \qquad (1.5)$$

and

$$b_n = \frac{1}{\pi}\int_{-\pi}^{\pi} f(x) \sin(nx)dx, \quad n \geq 1. \qquad (1.6)$$

Marwala (2013) used this procedure in Equations (1.4)–(1.6) to estimate Figure 1.2 and this results in Figure 1.6.

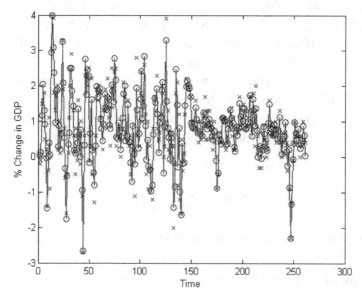

**Figure 1.6**  The Fourier series reconstruction of the percentage change of GDP of the United States from 1947 to 2012. Key: ×: 10 terms ○: 100 terms.

The representation of a signal using sine and cosine functions implies that we can transform a time domain signal into the frequency domain. This we achieve by applying the fast Fourier transform (FFT), which is a computationally efficient technique for estimating the Fourier transform through exploiting the symmetrical relationship of the Fourier transform. If the FFT is applied to the function, $x(t)$, can be written as follows (Moon and Stirling, 1999; Marwala, 2013):

$$X(\omega) = \frac{1}{2\pi} \int_{-\infty}^{\infty} x(t)e^{-i\omega t}dt, \tag{1.7}$$

where $\omega$ is the frequency and $t$ is the time. This relationship can be written as follows in the discrete form:

$$X_k = \sum_{n=0}^{N-1} x_n e^{-i2\pi k \frac{n}{N}}, \quad k = 0, \ldots, N-1. \tag{1.8}$$

Marwala (2013) used the Fourier to transform Figure 1.2 into Figure 1.7. The peaks in this figure correspond to the cycles, and phase plot indicates the time lag. Successful application of frequency domain analysis includes

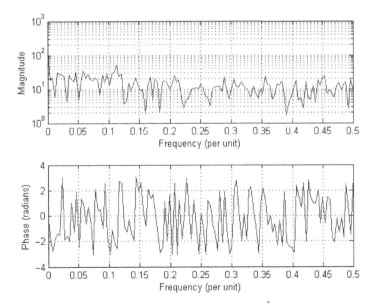

**Figure 1.7**   The magnitude and phase from the percentage change of GDP of the United States from 1947 to 2012.

in exchange rate misalignment (Grossmann and Orlov, 2012), in causality between producers' and consumers' price indices (Tiwari, 2012), in causality between the consumer price index and the wholesale price index (Shahbaz et al., 2012), in analysis of foreign exchange order flows (Gradojevic, 2012) and to study hearing aids (Pradhan et al., 2018).

## 1.4  Time–Frequency Domain

In the time–frequency domain methods, it is possible to see both the time and frequency domains at the same time (Marwala, 2013). Time–frequency domain methods include the short-time Fourier transform, wavelet transform, bilinear time–frequency distribution function (e.g. Wigner distribution function), modified Wigner distribution function, and Gabor–Wigner distribution function (Goupillaud et al., 1984; Delprat et al., 1992; Cohen, 1995; Flandrin, 1999; Papandreou-Suppappola, 2002; Marwala, 2013).

Successful applications of wavelet include detecting singularities in traffic and data (Zheng and Washington, 2012), to study business cycles (Caraiani, 2012), in option pricing (Haven et al., 2012), in mortality and economics (Svensson and Krüger, 2012), in stock market (Dajcman et al., 2012) as well as interest and exchange rates (Hacker et al., 2012). The Morlet wavelet is as follows (Goupillaud et al., 1984; Marwala, 2013):

$$\Phi_\sigma(t) = c_\sigma \pi^{-\frac{1}{4}} e^{-\frac{1}{2}t^2} (e^{i\sigma t} - \chi_\sigma). \tag{1.9}$$

Here, $\chi_\sigma = e^{-\frac{1}{2}\sigma^2}$ and it is the admissibility criterion while the normalization constant is

$$c_\sigma = \left( 1 + e^{-\sigma^2} - 2e^{-\frac{3}{4}\sigma^2} \right)^{-\frac{1}{2}}. \tag{1.10}$$

The Fourier transform of the Morlet wavelet is as follows (Goupillaud et al., 1984; Marwala, 2013):

$$\Phi_\sigma(\omega) = c_\sigma \pi^{-\frac{1}{4}} \left( e^{-\frac{1}{2}(\sigma-\omega)^2} - \chi_\sigma e^{-\frac{1}{2}\omega^2} \right). \tag{1.11}$$

The variable $\sigma$ controls the trade-off between time and frequency resolutions. Marwala (2013) applied Morlet wavelet analysis to transform Figure 1.2 to obtain Figure 1.8 (Chui, 1992; Kingsbury, 2001).

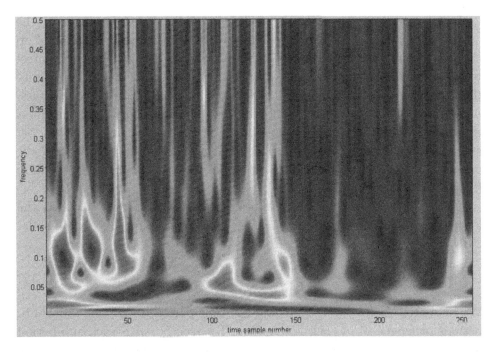

**Figure 1.8** The wavelet transform of the percentage change of GDP of the United States from 1947 to 2012.

## 1.5 Fractals

Fractal analysis is a procedure for defining complex shapes (Marwala, 2013). Fractal dimensions of an object indicate the degree to which the object occupies space (Lunga, 2007; Lunga and Marwala, 2006a; Marwala, 2012). A fractal dimension of a time series articulates how turbulent the time series is and quantifies the level to which the time series is scale-invariant (Lunga and Marwala, 2006a; Lunga, 2007; Marwala, 2013). Rescaled range (R/S) analysis approximates fractal dimensions using the Hurst exponent for a time series (Hurst, 1951; Marwala, 2013). Successful applications of fractal theory include in the stock market (Lunga and Marwala, 2006a), condition monitoring (Nelwamondo *et al.*, 2006a), speaker identification (Nelwamondo *et al.*, 2006b). They applied a multi-scale fractal dimension for speaker identification systems. Other applications of fractals include in financial markets (Kristoufek, 2012), to study the efficiency of capital markets (Krištoufek and Vošvrda, 2012), in manufacturing systems and in face recognition (Tang *et al.*, 2018).

Lunga and Marwala (2006b) used a technique for approximating the quality of a time series signal to identify the intervals that are vital to classify a time signal. Hurst (1951) proposed the R/S analysis to control reservoir on the Nile River dam. The goal of this problem was to identify the optimal design of a reservoir from data of measured river discharges. A desirable reservoir does not run dry or overflow. Hurst proposed the Hurst exponent ($H$) which is applied to categorize time series signals into random and non-random series. The R/S analysis identifies the average non-periodic cycle and the measure of persistence in trends because of long memory effects (Skjeltorp, 2000; Marwala, 2013).

In the R/S analysis, with a time series of length $M$ we calculate the logarithm of a ratio with length $N = M-1$ as follows (Lunga, 2007; Marwala, 2013):

$$N_i = \log\left(\frac{M_{i+1}}{M_i}\right), \quad i = 1, 2, 3, \ldots, (M-1). \tag{1.12}$$

We estimate the average by splitting the time period into $T$ adjoining sub-periods of length $j$, in such a way that $T * j = N$, with each sub-period named $I_t$, with $t = 1, 2, \ldots, T$ and each element in $I_t$ named $N_{k,t}$ such that $k = 1, 2, \ldots, j$. We write this average as follows (Lunga and Marwala, 2007; Lunga, 2007; Marwala, 2013):

$$e_t = \frac{1}{j}\sum_{k=1}^{j} N_{k,t}. \tag{1.13}$$

Here, $e_t$ is the average value of the $N_i$ enclosed in sub-period $I_t$ of length $j$. We calculate the time series of data $X_{k,t}$ from the mean for each sub-period $I_t$, as follows (Lunga, 2007; Marwala, 2013):

$$X_{k,t} = \sum_{i=1}^{k} (N_{k,t} - e_t), \quad k = 1, 2, 3, \ldots, j. \tag{1.14}$$

We write the range of the time series in relation to the mean within each sub-period as follows (Lunga, 2007; Marwala, 2013):

$$R_{T_t} = \max(X_{k,t}) - \min(X_{k,t}), \quad 1 < k < j. \tag{1.15}$$

We calculate the standard deviation of each sub-period as follows (Lunga, 2007; Marwala, 2013):

$$S_{I_t} = \sqrt{\frac{1}{j}\sum_{i=1}^{k} (N_{i,t} - e_t)^2}. \tag{1.16}$$

We rescale the range of each sub-period $R_{Tt}$ by the respective standard deviation $S_{It}$ for all the $T$ sub-intervals in the series to obtain the average R/S value as (Lunga, 2007; Marwala, 2013):

$$e_t = \frac{1}{T} \sum_{t=1}^{T} \left( \frac{R_{It}}{S_{It}} \right). \tag{1.17}$$

We can repeat the computation in Equations (1.12)–(1.17) for different time ranges. We realize this by sequentially increasing $j$ and reiterating the computation until all $j$ values are exhausted. After calculating the R/S values for a large range of different time ranges $j$, we can plot $\log(R/S)_j$ vs. $\log(n)$. We estimate the Hurst exponent $(H)$ by conducting a least squares linear regression with $\log(R/S)$ as the dependent variable and $\log(n)$ as the independent variable and $H$ is the slope of the regression (Maragos and Potamianos, 1999; Hurst, 1951; Hurst *et al.*, 1965; Marwala, 2013). It is possible to relate the fractal dimension and the Hurst exponent as follows (Lunga, 2007; Marwala, 2013):

$$D_f = 2 - H. \tag{1.18}$$

Techniques that estimate the fractal dimensions include using the Box counting dimension (Falconer, 1952; Nelwamondo *et al.*, 2006b: Marwala, 2012, 2013), the Hausdorff dimension (Falconer, 1952) and Minkowski–Bouligand dimension (Schroeder, 1991).

In fractal theory, when $H \in (0.5; 1]$, then the time series is persistent and has a long memory effect on all time scales (Gammel, 1998; Marwala, 2013). We articulate the influence of the present on the future as a correlation function $G$ as follows (Lunga, 2007; Marwala, 2013):

$$G = 2^{2H-1} - 1. \tag{1.19}$$

When $H = 0.5$, then $G = 0$ and the time series is uncorrelated. When $H = 1$, then $G = 1$, and this represents an ideal positive correlation. Alternatively, when $H \in [0; 0.5)$ then the time series signal is anti-persistent. This means that every time a time series has been up in the last period, it is possibly going to be down in the next period.

Marwala (2013) used the Hurst factor to analyse the data in Figures 1.1 and 1.2 to obtain Figures 1.9 and 1.10. Figure 1.9 shows that the data during this period is persistent. This indicates that the signal has long memory effects. Figure 1.10 shows that this data was anti-persistent. This meant that every time the GDP change had been up in the previous period it is most likely going to be down in the next period.

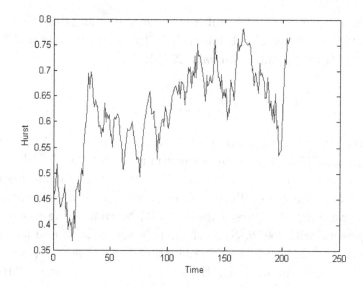

**Figure 1.9**    Hurst of the GDP of the United States from 1947 to 2012.

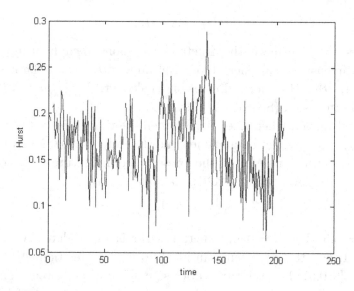

**Figure 1.10**    Hurst of the percentage change of the GDP of the United States from 1947 to 2012.

## 1.6  Stationarity

A stationary process has a joint probability distribution that does not vary with space or time, therefore, certain estimated parameters (e.g. the mean) do not change over space or time (Priestley, 1988; Marwala, 2013).

A non-stationary process has joint probability distribution that varies with space or time. Many techniques were proposed to determine the stationarity of a process. For example, Kiremire and Marwala (2008) proposed the stationarity index based on the quantification of similarities of the auto correlation integral of a subdivision of a time series and the cross-correlation of that subdivision with others of the same time series. Zhou and Kutan (2011) used a nonlinear unit root tests and recursive analysis to study the relationship between the stationarity of real exchange rates and different currencies, different sample periods, and different countries. Caporale and Paxton (2013) investigated inflation stationarity in Latin America. Other applications of stationarity include in inflation rates (Zhou, 2013; Caporale and Paxton, 2011), in consumption–income ratios (Fallahi, 2011), energy consumption (Hasanov and Telatar, 2011), interest rate (Zhou, 2011), commodity prices (Yang *et al.*, 2012), purchasing power parity (Amara, 2011) and flood estimation (Qi, 2017).

For a stochastic process represented by $\{Y_t\}$ with $F_Y(y_{t_1+\varsigma}, \ldots, y_{t_n+\varsigma})$, a cumulative distribution function of the joint distribution, $\{Y_t\}$, at times $\{t_1 + \varsigma, \ldots, t_n + \varsigma\}$, then $\{Y_t\}$ is stationary if for all values of $n$, $\varsigma$ and $\{t_1, \ldots, t_n\}$, $F_Y(y_{t_1+\varsigma}, \ldots, y_{t_n+\varsigma}) = F_Y(y_{t_1}, \ldots, y_{t_n})$. Techniques that quantify stationarity include Kwiatkowski–Phillips–Schmidt–Shin test and Variance Ratio test (Granger and Newbold, 1974; Perron, 1988; Kwiatkowski *et al.*, 1992; Schwert, 1989; Marwala, 2013). The Variance Ratio test is defined as follows (Lo and MacKinlay, 1989; Marwala, 2013):

$$F = \frac{V_e}{V_u}. \tag{1.20}$$

Here, $V_e$ is the explained variance and $V_u$ is the unexplained variance and

$$V_e = \frac{\sum_i n_i (\overline{X}_i - \overline{X})^2}{K - 1}, \tag{1.21}$$

and

$$V_u = \frac{\sum_{ij} (X_{ij} - \overline{X}_i)^2}{N - K}. \tag{1.22}$$

Here, $\overline{X}_i$ is the sample mean of the $i$th group, $n_i$ is the number of observations in the $i$th group, $\overline{X}$ is the complete mean of the data, $X_{ij}$ is the $j$th observation in the $i$th, out of $K$ groups and $N$ is the overall sample size. If the variability ratio is 1, then the data is behaving as a random walk, if it is larger than 1, then it is trending and, therefore, non-stationary and if it is less than one, then it shows a mean reversal. Mean reversal means that changes in one direction lead to probable changes in the opposite direction. Marwala (2013) used the variance ratio to transform Figure 1.1 into Figure 1.11 and Figure 1.2 into Figure 1.12.

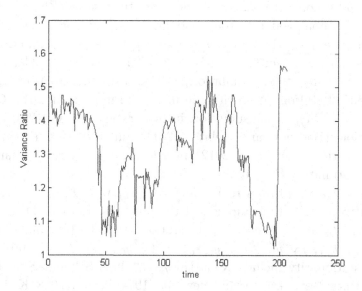

**Figure 1.11**   Variance ratio of the GDP of the United States from 1947 to 2012.

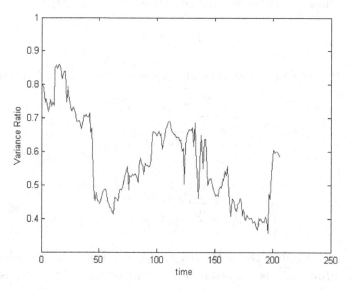

**Figure 1.12**   Variance ratio of the percentage change of the GDP of the United States from 1947 to 2012.

These results indicate that the raw values of the GDP in Figure 1.1 are non-stationary while the percentage change of GDP in Figure 1.2 are stationary.

## 1.7 Common Mistakes on Handling Data

There are common mistakes in artificial intelligence modelling which Hurwitz and Marwala (2012) identified. These are insufficient datasets, inappropriate scaling, time series tracking and inappropriate measure of performance.

Hurwitz and Marwala (2012) observed that prediction strategies are difficult systems, usually involving a cycle of prediction, evaluation, feedback, and recalibration when designed. The cycle comprises a feedback element but not necessarily the predictive procedure. This cycle includes the designer predicting an outcome then evaluating what happens in reality. The goal for recalibration feedback for both prediction and evaluation instruments is that in many more complex systems, what happens in reality is updated, as well as the predictions themselves. Because of this cycle, it is necessary to use unseen set of data to evaluate the performance of the predictive system. Normally, predictive systems use training and verification dataset (de Oliveira *et al.*, 2011; Lam, 2004; Kim, 2002; Bao and Yang, 2008; Marwala, 2013). This is not satisfactory, as neither the predictive system nor the evaluation system ever see the second set of data during the optimization phase. This is nevertheless inadequate, as the calibration of the training system is done with the results of the verification set considered. This necessitates an unseen validation set to be used to validate if the system is truly generalizing. Overlooking this critical phase can give a system result that has merely been tweaked by the designer to fit the specific data, without being able to function correctly in a general setting. The results appear satisfactory as the system has been calibrated precisely to fit the data being used even while the designer has not planned this to be the case. In the case that the predictive system is revisited after the validation set has been used, a new set of unseen validation data must be achieved.

Hurwitz and Marwala (2012) observed that inappropriate scaling error is characterized by expressing the normally large target values of the predicted variable as its actual value, instead of scaling the data to some appropriate level within (or near) the range of the training data (Kaastra and Boyd, 2006; Marwala, 2013). The justification is to offer a precise understanding of the actual target values. The actual data and the predicted data appear to be close in the initial prediction, but experience difficulty to reach the higher values in the range for the later values. The actual error in this initial prediction is obviously very low. It is underestimated by the scale of the data, despite clearly being unusable for any undertaking that necessitates the prediction. Actually, the errors characteristic of the system are frequently hidden by using unsuitable measures of accuracy or performance. It is actually far riskier to commit this error if the target data is reasonably bounded, as the evident lack of fit is not obvious. What is in effect an unusable prediction can certainly be confused for a performing predictive system and leads to all the dangers of prediction-based poor information. The reason for this discrepancy is the high quantitative value of the predictive results, which offer a low registered error for what is really a large trading error. Considering a prediction for a given input–output set with the correct value being 1025 and the system's predicted value being 1010, the actual error in root mean squares (RMS) terms is small, while the effect on predictions is actually quite high especially if this was a price of stock. This explains why an error that appears so small is actually significant enough to render a predictive system unusable. The clear recommendation is to first pre-process the data and as part of that process to scale the data. Depending on the nature of the problem, a scaling factor of anything from the maximum historical value recorded to a fractional amount larger than the maximum historical value can be applied. It is recommended, even though not necessarily relevant to this particular error that one also scales the input data for ease of training and convergence.

Hurwitz and Marwala (2012) observed that time-series tracking error occurs in time series modelling when the predictive system predicts the previous time period's value as the current value. This satisfies the error minimization function's requirement. This error emanates when an attempt is made to do an exact value prediction based upon the time-series data of historical values of the self-same series. Unfortunately, any system based on this assumption is completely unusable as it cannot ever predict an accurate value movement unless by some coincidence every single day's new value is the same as that of the day before. To avoid this error, it is then necessary for the user to reconsider the input–output pairs for the system to learn from and consider the change in value as an output rather than the value itself.

The problem of inappropriate measures of performance is important to deal appropriately with the accuracy of the predictive system to be designed. The problem here lies not with the measurements themselves, but rather on the reliance on them for validating the success of a trading system.

These methods often obscure problems in the system design by looking like successful computational intelligence systems by the standard computational measures (Hurwitz and Marwala, 2012; Marwala, 2013). This includes graphs of receiver operating characteristics curve and other typical computational measures of performance. If any of the preceding errors had been made, they would not be detected by the usual performance measures since they only measure the performance of the system based on the given input and output values. This is a dangerous error to commit, as the system is still concealing any mistakes made, but the user is satisfied to carry on, secure in the success of the system, verified by an inappropriate measure of performance.

## 1.8 Outline of the Book

Chapter 2 describes the MLP neural network, its architecture, how it is trained and applied for both regression and classification problems. The MLP is used to classify mechanical faults, steam generator and interstate conflict and for regression in the modelling of interest rate.

Chapter 3 describes the theory and application of the RBF. It describes two methods used to train the RBF and these are the combination of the $K$-means clustering algorithm and the pseudo-inverse techniques as well as the Expectation Maximization (EM) algorithm. The RBF is applied for modelling the inflation, the steam generator, interstate conflict and caller behaviour classification

Chapter 4 introduces the ARD, which is a method of ranking input variables in the order of their importance on predicting the output. The formulation of the ARD is grounded on the theory of regularization, where one assigns each input its own coefficient. The ARD is applied to rank inputs in interstate conflict model and an inflation model.

Chapter 5 studies Bayesian approach to neural networks, which leads to the concept of the posterior probability function. It describes various methods for estimating the posterior probability function using Hybrid Monte Carlo, Shadow Hybrid Monte Carlo and Separable Shadow Hybrid Monte Carlo. It then applies Bayesian network to classification of interstate conflict.

Chapter 6 studies SVM and how it is implemented for both classification and regression problems. The SVM was applied to classify interstate conflict and to model a steam generator.

Chapter 7 studies the theories and applications of fuzzy logic and neuro-fuzzy systems. It studies transparency in the Takagi–Sugeno neuro-fuzzy model. Fuzzy logic and Takagi–Sugeno neuro-fuzzy model are applied to model a steam generator and prediction of interstate conflict.

Chapter 8 studies rough set theory. It studies the concept of rough sets discretization and introduces neuro-rough sets (NRS). The NRS is based on rough sets and the MLP. The NRS is applied to model HIV and interstate conflict.

Chapter 9 examines hybrid of machines for both classification and regression. The hybrid approach is proven that it is more accurate than the individual methods if the individual methods are not correlated. The hybrid method is applied for fault classification in mechanical systems and caller behaviour classification.

Chapter 10 introduces the auto-associative network to predict missing data. It used two approaches for the missing data system based on auto-associative network. These are the combination of the MLP and the PCA as well as the auto-associative network trained using the MLP and RBF. All these approaches were trained using genetic algorithm. These methods were tested on modelling HIV as well as modelling a beer taster.

Chapter 11 studies the idea of evolving biological systems of Charles Darwin on building evolving intelligent systems in artificial intelligence. Intelligent networks take on new information and evolve them without fully retraining them and this is called incremental learning. This chapter describes and compares Learn++ and Incremental Learning Using Genetic Algorithm (ILUGA) on the Optical Character Recognition (OCR), wine recognition, financial analysis and condition monitoring data.

Chapter 12 studies causality, the Neyman–Rubin, Pearl and Granger causality models. It describes the Neyman–Rubin causal model within the context of missing data estimation framework and directed acyclic graphs. It describes the Granger causality within the context of the identification of the causal relations.

Chapter 13 studies the Gaussian mixture models and applies these to problems in condition monitoring.

Chapter 14 studies Hidden Markov Models and applies them in the problems of condition monitoring and speech recognition.

Chapter 15 studies reinforcement learning. It applies reinforcement learning on the game of Lerpa.

Chapter 16 draws conclusions and future and emerging areas in artificial intelligence are identified and emerging opportunities are drawn.

## 1.9 Conclusions

This chapter described ways and means of handling data. The representations of data in the time, frequency and time–frequency domains are described. Furthermore, the representation of data in the fractal domain is also described. The issue of stationarity which is important to determine whether the AI machine should evolve or remain static is also described. Common mistakes on handling data such as scaling, performance measures, data validation and time series tracking are also described. Thereafter, we describe the outline of the book.

## References

Amara, J. (2011). Testing for stationarity using covariates: An application to purchasing power parity. *Applied Economic Letters*, 18:1295–1301.

Angelini, F., Nicolosi, M. (2010). On the effect of skewness and kurtosis misspecification on the hedging error. *Economic Notes*, 39:203–226.

Bao, D., Yang, Z. (2008). Intelligent stock trading system by turning point confirming and probabilistic reasoning. *Expert Systems with Applications*, 34:620–627.

Caporale, T., Paxton, J. (2011). From debt crisis to tequila crisis: Inflation stationarity through Mexico's turbulent decades. *Applied Economic Letters*, 18:1609–1612.

Caporale, T., Paxton, J. (2013). Inflation stationarity during Latin American inflation: Insights from unit root and structural break analysis. *Applied Economics*, 45:2001–2010.

Caraiani, P. (2012). Stylized facts of business cycles in a transition economy in time and frequency. *Economic Modelling*, 29:2163–2173.

Chang, C.-L., Jimenez-Martin, J.-A., McAleer, M., Amaral, T.P. (2013). The rise and fall of S&P500 variance futures. *North American Journal of Economics and Finance*, 25:151–167.

Chiarella, C., He, X.-Z., Pellizzari, P. (2012). A dynamic analysis of the microstructure of moving average rules in a double auction market. *Macroeconomic Dynamics*, 16:556–575.

Chui, C.K. (1992). *An Introduction to Wavelets*. San Diego: Academic Press.

Clatworthy, M.A., Pong, C.K.M., Wong, W.K. (2012). Auditor quality effects on the relationship between accruals, cash flows and equity returns: A variance decomposition analysis. *Accounting and Business Research*, 42:419–439.

Cohen, L. (1995). *Time–Frequency Analysis*. New York: Prentice-Hall.

Dajcman, S., Festic, M., Kavkler, A. (2012). European stock market comovement dynamics during some major financial market turmoils in the period 1997 to 2010 — A comparative DCC-GARCH and wavelet correlation analysis. *Applied Economic Letters*, 19:1249–1256.

Dark, J.G. (2010). Estimation of time varying skewness and kurtosis with an application to value at risk. *Studies in Nonlinear Dynamics and Economics*, 14:art. no. 3.

de Oliveira F.A., Zarate, L.E., de Azevedo Reis, M., Nobre, C.N. (2011). The use of artificial neural networks in the analysis and prediction of stock prices. In: *Proceedings of the IEEE International Conference on Systems, Man and Cybernetics*, 2151–2155.

Delprat, N., Escudié, B., Guillemain, P., Kronland-Martinet, R., Tchamitchian, P., Torrésani, B. (1992). Asymptotic wavelet and gabor analysis: Extraction of instantaneous frequencies. *IEEE Transactions on Information Theory*, 38:644–664.

di Pierro, M., Mosevichz, J. (2011). Effects of skewness and kurtosis on portfolio rankings. *Quantitative Finance*, 11:1449–1453.

Diavatopoulos, D., Doran, J.S., Fodor, A., Peterson, D.R. (2012). The information content of implied skewness and kurtosis changes prior to earnings announcements for stock and option returns. *Journal of Banking and Finance*, 36:786–802.

Falconer, K. (1952). *Fractal Geometry: Mathematical Foundations and Application.* New York: John Wiley.

Fallahi, F. (2011). Causal relationship between energy consumption (EC) and GDP: A Markov-switching (MS) causality. *Energy*, 36:4165–4170.

Flandrin, P. (1999). Time–frequency/Time–scale analysis. *Wavelet Analysis and its Applications*, 10. Amsterdam: Elsevier.

Gammel, B. (1998). Hurst's rescaled range statistical analysis for pseudorandom number generators used in physical simulations. *The American Physical Society*, 58:2586–2597.

Goupillaud, P., Grossman, A., Morlet, J. (1984). Cycle-octave and related transforms in seismic signal analysis. *Geoexploration*, 23:85–102.

Gradojevic, N. (2012). Frequency domain analysis of foreign exchange order flows. *Economic Letters*, 115:73–76.

Granger, C.W.J., Newbold, P. (1974). Spurious regressions in econometrics. *Journal of Economics*, 2:111–120.

Grossmann, A., Orlov, A.G. (2012). Exchange rate misalignments in frequency domain. *International Review of Economics and Finance*, 24:185–199.

Hacker, S.R., Karlsson, H.K., Månsson, K. (2012). The relationship between exchange rates and interest rate differentials: A wavelet approach. *World Economics*, 35:1162–1185.

Hand, D.J. (2008). *Statistics: A Very Short Introduction.* Oxford: Oxford University Press.

Hasanov, M., Telatar, E. (2011). A re-examination of stationarity of energy consumption: Evidence from new unit root tests. *Energy Policy*, 39:7726–7738.

Haven, E., Liu, X., Shen, L. (2012). De-noising option prices with the wavelet method. *European Journal of Operational Research*, 222:104–112.

Hurst, H.E. (1951). Long term storage capacity of reservoirs. *Transactions of the American Society of Civil Engineers*, 116:770–799.

Hurst, H.E., Black, R.P., Simaika, Y.M. (1965). *Long-term Storage: An Experimental Study.* London: Constable.

Hurwitz, E., Marwala, T. (2012). Common mistakes when applying computational intelligence and machine learning to stock market modelling. arXiv:1208.4429.

Kaastra, L., Boyd, M. (1996). Designing a neural network for forecasting financial and economic time series. *Neurocomputing*, 10:215–236.

Kim, K. (2002). Financial time series forecasting using support vector machines. *Neurocomputing*, 55:307–319.

Kingsbury, N.G. (2001). Complex wavelets for shift invariant analysis and filtering of signals. *Journal of Application and Computational Harmonic Analysis*, 10:234–253.

Kiremire, B.B.E., Marwala, T. (2008). Non-stationarity detection: A stationarity index approach. In: *Proceedings of the IEEE International Congress on Image and Signal Processing*, 373–378.

Kristoufek, L. (2012). Fractal markets hypothesis and the global financial crisis: Scaling, investment horizons and liquidity. *Advances in Complex Systems*, 15:art. no. 1250065.

Krištoufek, L., Vošvrda, M. (2012). Capital markets efficiency: Fractal dimension, hurst exponent and entropy. *Politicka Ekonomie*, 60:208–221.

Kwiatkowski, D., Phillips, P.C.B., Schmidt, P., Shin, Y. (1992). Testing the null hypothesis of stationarity against the alternative of a unit root. *Journal of Econometrics*, 54:159–178.

Lam, M. (2004). Neural network techniques for financial performance prediction: Integrating fundamental and technical analysis. *Decision Support Systems*, 37:567–581.

Liu, S., Hou, S., He, K., Yang, W. (2018). L-Kurtosis and its application for fault detection of rolling element bearings. *Measurement*, 116:523–525.

Lo, A.W., MacKinlay, A.C. (1989). The size and power of the variance ratio test. *Journal of Econometrics*, 40:203–238.

Lunga, D. (2007). Time Series Analysis Using Fractal Theory and Ensemble Classifiers with Application to Stock Portfolio Optimization. Masters Dissertation, University of the Witwatersrand.

Lunga, D., Marwala, T. (2006a). Time series analysis using fractal theory and online ensemble classifiers. *Lecture Notes in Artificial Intelligence*, 4304:312–321.

Lunga, D., Marwala, T. (2006b). Online forecasting of stock market movement direction using the improved incremental algorithm. *Lecture Notes in Computer Science*, 4234:440–449.

Maragos, P., Potamianos, A. (1999). Fractal dimensions of speech sounds: Computation and application to automatic speech recognition. *Journal of the Acoustical Society of America*, 1925–1932.

Marwala, T. (2007). *Computational Intelligence for Modelling Complex Systems*. Delhi: Research India Publications.

Marwala, T. (2012). *Condition Monitoring Using Computational Intelligence Methods*. London: Springer-Verlag.

Marwala, T. (2013). *Economic Modeling Using Artificial Intelligence Methods*. Heidelberg: Springer.

Moon, T.K., Stirling, W.C. (1999). *Mathematical Methods and Algorithms for Signal Processing*. New York: Prentice Hall.

Nelwamondo, F.V., Marwala, T., Mahola, U. (2006a). Early classifications of bearing faults using hidden markov models, Gaussian mixture models, mel-frequency cepstral coefficients and fractals. *International Journal of Innovative Computing, Information and Control*, 2:1281–1299.

Nelwamondo, F.V., Mahola, U., Marwala, T. (2006b). Improving speaker identification rate using fractals. In: *Proceedings of the IEEE International Joint Conference on Neural Networks*, 5870–5875.

Ni, Y.-S., Lee, J.-T., Liao, Y.-C. (2013). Do variable length moving average trading rules matter during a financial crisis period? *Applied Economic Letters*, 20: 135–141.

Papandreou-Suppappola, A. (2002). *Applications in Time–Frequency Signal Processing*. Boca Raton: CRC Press.

Pavlov, V., Hurn, S. (2012). Testing the profitability of moving-average rules as a portfolio selection strategy. *Pacific Basin Finance Journal*, 20:825–842.

Perron, P. (1988). Trends and random walks in macroeconomic time series: Further evidence from a new approach. *Journal of Economic Dynamics and Control*, 12:297–332.

Pradhan, S., George, N.V., Albu, F., Nordholm, S. (2018). Two microphone acoustic feedback cancellation in digital hearing aids: A step size-controlled frequency domain approach. *Applied Acoustics*, 132:142–151.

Priestley, M.B. (1988). *Non-linear and Non-stationary Time Series Analysis*. Waltham: Academic Press.

Prokopczuk, M., Symeonidis, L., Simen, C.W. (2017). Variance risk in commodity markets. *Journal of Banking & Finance*, 81:136–149.

Qi, W. (2017). A non-stationary cost-benefit analysis approach for extreme flood estimation to explore the nexus of 'Risk, Cost and Non-stationarity'. *Journal of Hydrology*, 554:128–136.

Schroeder, M. (1991). *Fractals, Chaos, Power Laws: Minutes from an Infinite Paradise*. New York: W.H. Freeman.

Schwert, W. (1989). Tests for unit roots: A Monte Carlo investigation. *Journal of Business and Economic Statistics*, 7:147–159.

Skjeltorp, J. (2000). Scaling in the Norwergian stock market. *Physica A*, 283:486–528.

Shahbaz, M., Tiwari, A.K., Tahir, M.I. (2012). Does CPI granger-cause WPI? new extensions from frequency domain approach in Pakistan. *Economic Modelling*, 29:1592–1597.

Svensson, M., Krüger, N.A. (2012). Mortality and economic fluctuations: Evidence from wavelet analysis for Sweden 1800–2000. *Journal of Population Economics*, 25:1215–1235.

Tang, Z., Wu, X., Fu, B., Chen, W., Feng, H. (2018). Fast face recognition based on fractal theory. *Applied Mathematics and Computation*, 321(15):721–730.

Tiwari, A.K. (2012). An empirical investigation of causality between producers' price and consumers' price indices in Australia in frequency domain. *Economic Modelling*, 29:1571–1578.

Uematsu, H., Mishra, A.K., Powell, R.R. (2012). An alternative method to estimate income variance in cross-sectional data. *Applied Economic Letters*, 19:1431–1436.

Xu, M., Shang, P. (2018). Analysis of financial time series using multiscale entropy based on skewness and kurtosis. *Physica A*, 490(15):1543–1550.

Yang, C.-H., Lin, C.-T., Kao, Y.-S. (2012). Exploring stationarity and structural breaks in commodity prices by the panel data model. *Applied Economic Letters*, 19:353–361.

Zheng, Z., Washington, S. (2012). On selecting an optimal wavelet for detecting singularities in traffic and vehicular data. *Transportation Research Part C: Emerging Technologies*, 25:18–33.

Zhou, S. (2011). Nonlinear stationarity of real interest rates in the EMU Countries. *Journal of Economic Studies*, 38:691–702.

Zhou, S. (2013). Nonlinearity and stationarity of inflation rates: Evidence from the Eurozone countries. *Applied Economics*, 45:849–856.

Zhou, S., Kutan, A.M. (2011). Is the evidence for PPP reliable? A sustainability examination of the stationarity of real exchange rates. *Journal of Banking and Finance*, 35:2479–2490.

# Chapter 2

# Multi-layer Perceptron

**Abstract.** This chapter describes the multi-layer perceptron (MLP) neural network. It describes the architecture of the MLP, how it is trained and applied for both regression and classification problems. Then in this chapter, the MLP is used to classify mechanical faults and steam generator and for regression in the modelling of interest rate and interstate conflict.

## 2.1 Introduction

In this chapter we introduce the multi-layer perceptron (MLP) neural network. The MLP can be defined as a feed-forward neural network model that approximates a relationship between sets of input data and a set of appropriate output. Its foundation is the standard linear perceptron, and it makes use of three or more layers of neurons (nodes) with nonlinear activation functions and is more powerful than the perceptron. This is because it can distinguish data that is not linearly separable, or separable by a hyperplane. The MLP has been used to model many complex systems in areas such as mechanical and electrical engineering (Marwala, 2012), and interstate conflict (Marwala and Lagazio, 2011) (Marwala, 2009–2015, Marwala *et al.*, 2017; Xing and Marwala, 2018; Marwala and Hurwitz, 2017).

Patel and Marwala (2009) successfully used the MLP for caller interaction classification, whereas Dhlamini and Marwala (2004a) successfully applied the MLP to monitor transformer bushing in an electricity grid. Furthermore, Dhlamini and Marwala compared the MLP to support vector machines and radial basis function in the monitoring of transformer bushings and observed that it is robust and gave good results. Abdella and Marwala (2005b) used the MLP and genetic algorithm to successfully approximate missing data in the HIV database. Mohamed *et al.* (2005) successfully used the MLP to detect epileptiform activity in human EEG signals, whereas Habtemariam *et al.* (2005) successfully used the MLP to predict interstate conflict. Abdella and Marwala (2005a) successfully used the MLP to estimate missing data which are missing-at-random and missing-not-at-random whereas Leke and Marwala (2005) successfully used the MLP to predict the stock price. Dhlamini and Marwala (2005) successfully used an ensemble of MLP networks for transformer bushing. Marwala *et al.* (2005) successfully used the MLP neural networks for fault identification in cylinders whereas Hurwitz and Marwala (2005) used the MLP with the reinforcement learning settings to play a game of Lerpa. Vilakazi and Marwala (2006) successfully used extension neural networks for transformer bushing fault detection and diagnosis whereas Leke *et al.* (2006) successfully used the MLP to predict HIV Status from demographic data. Patel and Marwala (2006) successfully used the MLP to forecast closing stock price indices whereas Msiza *et al.* (2007a) successfully used the MLP for water demand forecasting. Msiza *et al.* (2007b) successfully used and compared the MLP and support vector machines for water demand time whereas Mpanza and Marwala (2011) used the MLP rough set for high-voltage transformer bushings condition monitoring. Hasan *et al.* (2014) successfully used the MLP to monitor and predict gold mine underground dam levels. Bagheri *et al.* (2015) successfully used the MLP to model a sequencing batch reactor to treat municipal wastewater whereas Uysal *et al.* (2016) used the MLP to improve daily streamflow forecasts in mountainous Upper Euphrates. Bastani *et al.* (2013) applied the MLP to predict $CO_2$ loading capacity of chemical absorbents whereas Fan *et al.* (2016) used the MLP to predict chaotic coal prices. Singh *et al.* (2017) used the MLP to model the spatial dynamics of deforestation and fragmentation whereas Deo *et al.* (2018) used the MLP to predict wind speed of target site with limited neighbouring reference station data.

## 2.2  Multi-layer Perceptron

The MLP neural network consists of multiple layers of computational units, usually interconnected in a feed-forward way (Haykin, 1998). These interconnections were inspired by biological neurons. Each neuron in one layer is directly connected to the neurons of the following layer. A fully connected two-layered MLP architecture is used in this chapter. A two-layered MLP architecture shown in Figure 2.1, depending on the complexity of the network can be expanded to multiple layers (Marwala, 2009). This MLP neural

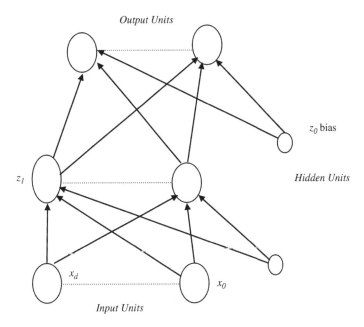

**Figure 2.1**   Feed-forward MLP network having two layers of adaptive weights.

network can be described as follows (Bishop, 1995; Marwala, 2009):

$$y_k = f_{\text{outer}} \left( \sum_{j=1}^{M} w_{kj}^{(2)} f_{\text{inner}} \left( \sum_{i=1}^{d} w_{ji}^{(1)} x_i + w_{j0}^{(1)} \right) + w_{k0}^{(2)} \right). \qquad (2.1)$$

In Equation (2.1) $w_{ji}^{(1)}$ and $w_{ji}^{(2)}$ indicate weights in the first and second layer, respectively, going from input $i$ to hidden unit $j$, $M$ is the number of hidden units, $d$ is the number of output units while $w_{j0}^{(1)}$ and $w_{k0}^{(2)}$ are the free parameters that indicate the biases for the hidden unit $j$ and the output unit $k$. These free parameters can be viewed as a mechanism that makes the model understand the data. In this chapter, the parameter $f_{\text{outer}}(\cdot)$ is the logistic activation function while $f_{\text{inner}}$ is the hyperbolic tangent activation function. The choice of these parameters allows the model to be able to model linear and nonlinear data of any order. The logistic activation function is defined as follows:

$$f_{\text{outer}}(\nu) = \frac{1}{1 + e^{-\nu}}. \qquad (2.2)$$

The logistic activation function maps the interval $(-\infty, \infty)$ onto a $(0, 1)$ interval and can be approximated by a linear activation function provided the magnitude of $\nu$ is small. The hyperbolic tangent activation function is

$$f_{\text{inner}}(\nu) = \tanh(\nu). \tag{2.3}$$

Equation (2.1) is what defines the MLP. The principle followed to estimate the free parameters is the same as that followed in linear regression and is the subject of the next section.

## 2.3  Training the Multi-layered Perceptron

When we talk about the MLP neural network training we mean a process used to identify the weights in Equation (2.1) using the observed data. An objective function that represents some distance between the model prediction and the observed target data with the free parameters as unknown variables must be chosen for optimization. Minimizing this objective function, therefore, identifies the free parameters known as weights in Equation (2.1) given the training data. The paradigm of minimizing the objective function is called the maximum-likelihood approach. An objective function is a mathematical representation of the overall objective of the problem. If the training set $D = \{x_k, y_k\}_{k=1}^{N}$ is used and assuming that the targets $y$ are sampled independently given the inputs $x_k$ and the weight parameters, $w_{kj}$, the objective function, $E$, may, therefore, be written as follows using the sum-of-squares of errors objective function (Bishop, 1995; Marwala, 2009):

$$E = \sum_{n=1}^{N} \sum_{k=1}^{K} \{t_{nk} - y_{nk}\}^2$$

$$= \sum_{n=1}^{N} \sum_{k=1}^{K} \{t_{nk} - y_{nk}(\{x\}, \{w\})\}^2. \tag{2.4}$$

In Equation (2.4), $n$ is the index for the training example, $k$ is the index for the output units, $\{x\}$ is the input vector and $\{w\}$ is the weight vector. The objective function in Equation (2.4) is ideally suited for regression problems and a different objective function will be described later in this chapter to deal with classification problems.

Prior to neural network training, the network architecture needs to be constructed by selecting the number of hidden units, $M$. If $M$ is too small, the neural network will be insufficiently flexible and will give poor generalization of the data because of high bias. However, if $M$ is too large, the neural network will be too complex and, therefore, unnecessarily flexible and will consequently provide poor generalization due to a phenomenon known as over-fitting caused by high variance. The choice of an appropriate $M$ is known as model selection. There are various ways in which this choice is made, and these include through the process of trial and error as well as making this choice part of the optimization problem. However, if this choice is made to be part of the optimization process, then it is difficult to use gradient-based optimization procedures and the only other option that can be used are heuristic optimization methods such as genetic algorithm.

In order to train the MLP network using the maximum-likelihood method, as is done in this chapter, a procedure called back-propagation, which is the subject of the next section, needs to be implemented (Werbos, 1974; Marwala, 2009). Back-propagation is basically a method for finding the derivatives of the error in Equation (2.4) with respect to the network weights. This would then permit us to use the standard gradient-based optimization method to identify the optimal free parameters that are able to best describe the observed training data.

## 2.4  Back-propagation Method

In order to identify the network weights given the training data, an optimization method can be implemented, within the maximum-likelihood approach. In general, the weights can be identified using the following iterative method (Marwala, 2009; Bishop, 1995; Werbos, 1974):

$$\{w\}_{i+1} = \{w\}_i - \eta \frac{\partial E}{\partial \{w\}}(\{w\}_i). \tag{2.5}$$

In Equation (2.5) the parameter $\eta$ is the learning rate while $\{\}$ represents a vector. The minimization of the objective function $E$ is achieved by calculating the derivative of the errors in Equation (2.4) with respect to the network weight. Equation (2.5) is also called the gradient descent equation (Robbins and Monro, 1951). The workings of this equation can be illustrated by Figure 2.2. If the gradient is positive, and the learning rate is always positive the algorithm moves in the negative direction of $\{w\}$ towards a minimum point. If the gradient is negative, the algorithm moves in the positive direction of $\{w\}$, thereby, towards the minimum point. The choice of the learning rate is crucial. If the learning rate is too small, then the algorithm moves slowly towards the minimum point. If the learning rate is too large, the algorithm oscillates around the minimum point with the gradient switching between being negative and positive without

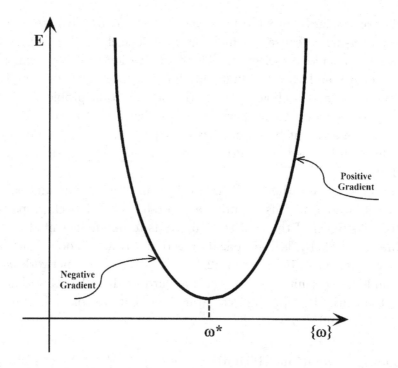

**Figure 2.2** An illustration of an objective function where $E$ is dependent on $\{w\}$.

converging towards a minimum point. The gradient descent equation works if only a gradient can be calculated, and this necessarily means that the objective function must be continuous. In the absence of the closed form of the derivative, a numerical estimation of the gradient may be used. The disadvantage of the gradient descent method is that it is computationally expensive when compared to other techniques such as the conjugate gradient method which will be described below.

$$\frac{\partial E}{\partial w_{kj}} = \frac{\partial E}{\partial a_k}\frac{\partial a_k}{\partial w_{kj}}$$

$$= \frac{\partial E}{\partial y_k}\frac{\partial y_k}{\partial a_k}\frac{\partial a_k}{\partial w_{kj}}$$

$$= \sum_n f'_{\text{outer}}(a_k)\frac{\partial E}{\partial y_{nk}}z_j. \tag{2.6}$$

In Equation (2.6), $z_j = f_{\text{inner}}(a_j)$ and $a_k = \sum_{j=0}^{M} w_{kj}^{(2)} y_j$. The derivative of the error with respect to weight, which connects the hidden to the output layer, is written using the chain rule as follows (Werbos, 1974; Bishop, 1995;

Marwala, 2009):

$$\frac{\partial E}{\partial w_{kj}} = \frac{\partial E}{\partial a_k} \frac{\partial a_k}{\partial w_{kj}}$$

$$= \sum_n f'_{\text{inner}}(a_j) \sum_k w_{kj} f'_{\text{outer}}(a_k) \frac{\partial E}{\partial y_{nk}}. \tag{2.7}$$

In Equation (2.7), $a_j = \sum_{i=1}^{d} w_{ji}^{(1)} x_i$. The derivative of the sum of square cost function in Equation (2.4) may be written as (Werbos, 1974; Bishop, 1995; Marwala, 2009):

$$\frac{\partial E}{\partial y_{nk}} = t_{nk} - y_{nk}, \tag{2.8}$$

while that of the hyperbolic tangent activation function is (Werbos, 1974; Bishop, 1995; Marwala, 2009):

$$f'_{\text{inner}}(a_j) = \text{sech}^2(a_j). \tag{2.9}$$

We have shown how to calculate the gradient of the error with respect to the network weights using the back-propagation algorithm, and the next step is to use Equation (2.5) to update the network weights. This is achieved using an optimization process until some pre-defined stopping condition is achieved. As stated before, if the learning rate in Equation (2.5) is fixed then this is known as the steepest descent optimization method. On the other hand, steepest descent method is not computationally efficient and, therefore, an improved method can be used, and, in this chapter, the scaled conjugate method is chosen (Møller, 1993).

## 2.5 Scaled Conjugate Method

The mechanism in which the free parameters (network weights) are estimated from the data can be achieved using a nonlinear optimization method (Mordecai, 2003). Zhao *et al.* (2018) successfully used the conjugate gradient method for unimodular sequence design whereas Wang *et al.* (2018) used the conjugate gradient method to efficiently train feedforward neural networks. Klein *et al.* (2017) successfully used nonlinear conjugate gradients to efficiently invert geostatistical transient groundwater flow whereas Antoine *et al.* (2017) successfully used the conjugate gradient method for efficient spectral computation of the stationary states of rotating Bose–Einstein condensates. Li *et al.* (2017) successfully used the conjugate gradient method to factorize non-negative matrices.

This chapter uses the scaled conjugate method which is a version of the conjugate gradient method (Marwala, 2009). The scaled conjugate method is an extension of the conjugate gradient method. The weight vector, which offers the minimum error, is attained by taking successive steps through the weight space as shown in the gradient descent equation in Equation (2.5) until convergence which is obtained through some stopping criterion being achieved. Different algorithms choose this learning rate differently. In this section, gradient descent method is discussed, followed by how it is extended to the conjugate gradient method (Hestenes and Stiefel, 1952). For the gradient descent method, the step size is defined as $-\eta \partial E / \partial w$, where the parameter $\eta$ is the learning rate and the gradient of the error is calculated using the back-propagation technique described in the previous section.

If the learning rate is sufficiently small, the value of error decreases at each successive step until a minimum value for the error between the model prediction and training target data is obtained. For the conjugate gradient method, the quadratic function of error is minimized, at each iteration, over a progressively expanding linear vector space that includes the global minimum of the error (Luenberger, 1984; Fletcher, 1987; Bertsekas, 1995). For the conjugate gradient procedure, the following steps are followed (Haykin, 1998) as described by Marwala (2009):

1. Choose the initial weight vector $\{w\}_0$.
2. Calculate the gradient vector $\frac{\partial E}{\partial \{w\}}(\{w\}_0)$.
3. At each step, $n$, use the line search to find $\eta(n)$ that minimizes $E(\eta)$ representing the cost function expressed in terms of $\eta$ for fixed values of $w$ and $-\frac{\partial E}{\partial \{w\}}(\{w_n\})$.
4. Check that the Euclidean norm of the vector $-\frac{\partial E}{\partial w}(\{w_n\})$ is sufficiently less than that of $-\frac{\partial E}{\partial w}(\{w_0\})$.
5. Update the weight vector using Equation (2.5).
6. For $w_{n+1}$ compute the updated gradient: $\frac{\partial E}{\partial \{w\}}(\{w\}_{n+1})$.
7. Use Polak–Ribiére method to calculate:

$$\beta(n+1) = \frac{\nabla E(\{w\}_{n+1})^T (\nabla E(\{w\}_{n+1}) - \nabla E(\{w\}_n)))}{\nabla E(\{w\}_n)^T \nabla E(\{w\}_n)}.$$

8. Update the direction vector:

$$\frac{\partial E}{\partial \{w\}}(\{w\}_{n+2}) = \frac{\partial E}{\partial \{w\}}(\{w\}_{n+1}) - \beta(n+1)\frac{\partial E}{\partial \{w\}}(\{w\}_n).$$

9. Set $n = n + 1$ and go back to step 3.

10. Stop when the following condition is satisfied: $\frac{\partial E}{\partial\{w\}}(\{w\}_{n+2}) = \varepsilon\frac{\partial E}{\partial\{w\}}(\{w\}_{n+1})$ where $\varepsilon$ is a small number.

The scaled conjugate gradient method differs from conjugate gradient method in that it does not involve the line search described in step 3. The step-size (see step 3) is calculated directly by using the following formula (Møller, 1993):

$$\eta(n) = 2\left(\eta(n) - \left(\frac{\partial E(n)}{\partial\{w\}}(n)\right)^T H(n)\left(\frac{\partial E(n)}{\partial\{w\}}(n)\right)\right.$$

$$\left. + \eta(n)\left\|\left(\frac{\partial E(n)}{\partial\{w\}}(n)\right)\right\|^2 \right/ \left\|\left(\frac{\partial E(n)}{\partial\{w\}}(n)\right)\right\|\right)^2, \quad (2.10)$$

where $H$ is the Hessian of the gradient. The scaled conjugate gradient method is used because it has been found to solve the optimization problems encountered when training an MLP network more computationally efficient than the gradient descent and conjugate gradient methods (Bishop, 1995). The convergence of the conjugate gradient method when compared to the steepest descent method is illustrated in Figure 2.3.

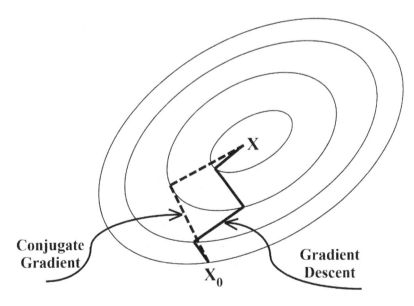

**Figure 2.3** Comparison between the conjugate gradient method and the steepest descent method.

## 2.6 Multi-layer Perceptron Classifier

The previous section dealt with the regression problem. This section deals with the classification problem. In a two-class classification problem, the fitness function is the difference between the neural network's estimated output and the target output, $t$, given in Equation (2.10) for all training patterns. $E$ is the *cross-entropy error function* given by (Bishop, 1995; Marwala, 2009):

$$E = - \sum_{p=1}^{P} \{t_p \ln(y_p) + (1 - t_p) \ln(1 - y_p)\}. \tag{2.11}$$

Therefore, in the MLP context the difference between the regression and classification problems is that in the regression problem we use the sum of squares of error objective function whereas in the classification problem we use the cross-entropy function. Furthermore, for regression problems we use the linear activation function in the outer layer whereas for classification problems we use the logistic activation function in the outer layer. There are many advantages of the cross-entropy function. One of these includes the fact that it permits the interpretation of the output probabilistically without the necessity of invoking a Bayesian formulation.

*Generalization* is the capability of a trained neural network model to classify input patterns that we did not observe during the training of the neural network. Essentially, on pursuing a network that generalizes, one identifies the balance between the capabilities of a network to remember the training data with the capability of the network to estimate data not seen. The generalization of performance is a true reflection of the capacity of a neural network to classify faults. We can prove that by separating the data into training and testing datasets.

Bishop (1995) demonstrated that a minimization of the cross-entropy fitness function in the neural network training with the activation function of a neural network results in the output of a neural network approximating the posterior probability of membership to a specific class, given the input $\{x\}$. If we represent one class by $C_1$ and the other class by $C_2$, then we can write the relations for the posterior probability of class membership as (Bishop, 1995; Marwala and Lagazio, 2011):

$$P(C_1|\{x\}) = y, \tag{2.12}$$

$$P(C_2|\{x\}) = 1 - y. \tag{2.13}$$

Equations (2.12) and (2.13) offer a probabilistic interpretation to the neural network output. On the account of these relationships, it is obvious that the input vector has a high probability of being an element of class $C_1$ when $y$ is close to one and $C_2$ when $y$ is close to zero. If $y$ is close to 0.5, then there is uncertainty in the class membership of the input vector. An elementary method to increase the efficacy of the classifier is to devise an upper and lower rejection threshold to the neural network output (Bishop, 1995; Mohamed, 2003). We express this classification decision rule as follows (Mohamed, 2003; Marwala and Lagazio, 2011):

$$\text{Choose } C_1 \text{ if } y > \gamma,$$

$$\text{Choose } C_2 \text{ if } y < (1 - \gamma), \tag{2.14}$$

$$\text{Otherwise do not classify } \{x\}.$$

The parameter $\gamma$ sets the level of the rejection threshold and permits the engineer to choose the level at which a decision can be made.

## 2.7 Applications to Economic Modelling

Marwala (2013) used the MLP to estimate the consumer price index (CPI). The CPI is a measure of inflation in an economy. The problem of estimating the CPI is a regression problem. It measures the changes in prices of a fixed pre-selected basket of goods. We use a basket of goods, to calculate the CPI, which in South Africa is as follows (Marwala, 2013):

1. Food and non-alcoholic beverages: bread and cereals, meat, fish, milk, cheese, eggs, oils, fats, fruit, vegetables, sugar, sweets, desserts and other foods
2. Alcoholic beverages and tobacco
3. Clothing and footwear
4. Housing and utilities: rents, maintenance, water, electricity and others
5. Household contents, equipment, and maintenance
6. Health: medical equipment, outpatient, and medical service
7. Transport
8. Communication
9. Recreation and culture
10. Education
11. Restaurants and hotels
12. Miscellaneous goods and services: personal care, insurance and financial services.

**Table 2.1**    The variables used to construct the MLP model.

| Variable |
| --- |
| Agriculture, fish, forestry |
| Mining |
| Manufacturing |
| Electricity, gas, water |
| Construction |
| Retail and trade |
| Transport, storage and communication |
| Financial intermediation, insurance, real estate and business services |
| Community, social and personal services |
| Government services |
| Gross value added at basic prices |
| Taxes less subsidies on products |
| Affordability |
| Economic growth |
| Rand/USD exchange |
| Prime interest |
| Repo rate |
| Gross domestic product |
| Household consumption |
| Investment |
| Government consumption |
| Exports |
| Imports |

We weigh this basket and track the variation of prices of these goods from month to month and this is a basis for calculating inflation. In this chapter, we use the CPI data from 1992 to 2011 to model the relationship between economic variables and the CPI. These economic variables are listed in Table 2.1 (Marwala, 2013). They represent the performance of various aspects of the economy represented by 23 variables in agriculture, manufacturing, mining, energy, construction, etc. We constructed a MLP neural network with 23 input variables, 12 hidden nodes and 1 output representing the CPI with the hyperbolic tangent activation function in the hidden layer and a linear activation function in the output layer. To train the MLP network, we use the sum-of-squares of errors objective function.

The MLP with the linear activation function in the output layer and hyperbolic tangent activation function in the hidden nodes and its attributes are in Table 2.2. The sample results obtained can be viewed in Figure 2.4.

The results indicate that for the data under consideration, the MLP is able to predict and model the relationship between the input data as described in Table 2.1 and the CPI.

**Table 2.2** Characteristics of the MLP network and the results.

| Attributes | Number |
|---|---|
| Input nodes | 23 |
| Hidden nodes | 12 |
| Output nodes | 1 |
| Training time (s) | 3.45 |
| Accuracy (%) | 84.6 |

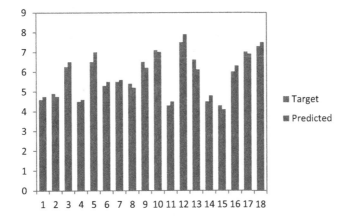

**Figure 2.4** Sample results achieved using the MLP network.

## 2.8 Application to a Steam Generator

Wright and Marwala (2006) modelled the cause–effect relationship of data obtained from a Steam Generator at Abbott Power Plant in the USA. The dataset had 9,600 samples. The cause–effect model contained four causes and one effect. The causes were the input fuel, air, reference level and disturbance defined by the load level. The effect was the steam flow rate. They took the approach that was to train a network with a fixed number of hidden nodes, periodically stopping the training process to determine the error on the validation dataset. Therefore, they observed the training and validation errors during the training process and determined an indication of the generalization ability of the network. They did this for a varying number of hidden nodes, from 4 to 20, for the MLP. They compared the different solutions for the set number of hidden nodes and selected the best network.

Using the procedure discussed above, they found that for the MLP, the most appropriate number of hidden nodes was 8. The results obtained are in

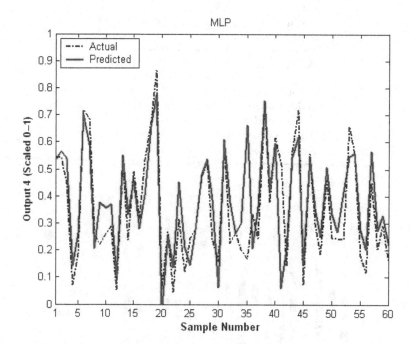

**Figure 2.5** Showing the predicted vs. actual values for the first 60 points for the test dataset applied to the MLP.

**Table 2.3** Performance characteristics for individual MLP.

|  | **MLP** |
|---|---|
| Time to train (s) | 6.98 |
| Time to execute (s) | 0.016 |
| MSE of test dataset | 0.075708 |
| No. of hidden nodes | 8 |
| No. of training cycles | 240 |

Figure 2.5 and Table 2.3 and these results indicate that the MLP modelled the steam generator input–output relationship well.

## 2.9  Application to Cylindrical Shells

Marwala (2012) applied the MLP network to predict the presence and the location of faults in cylinders. The training dataset, had 168 fault cases, with an equal number of fault cases showing that the probabilities of incidence for the eight fault cases were equal. We used the remaining 96 fault cases to

**Table 2.4** Confusion matrix from the classification of fault cases in the test data using.

|  |  | Predicted | | | | | | | |
| --- | --- | --- | --- | --- | --- | --- | --- | --- | --- |
|  |  | [000] | [100] | [010] | [001] | [110] | [101] | [011] | [111] |
| **Actual** | [000] | 36 | 0 | 2 | 1 | 0 | 0 | 0 | 0 |
|  | [100] | 0 | 3 | 0 | 0 | 0 | 0 | 0 | 0 |
|  | [010] | 0 | 0 | 3 | 0 | 0 | 0 | 0 | 0 |
|  | [001] | 0 | 0 | 0 | 3 | 0 | 0 | 0 | 0 |
|  | [110] | 0 | 0 | 0 | 0 | 3 | 0 | 0 | 0 |
|  | [101] | 0 | 0 | 0 | 0 | 0 | 3 | 0 | 0 |
|  | [011] | 0 | 0 | 0 | 0 | 0 | 0 | 3 | 0 |
|  | [111] | 0 | 0 | 1 | 0 | 4 | 3 | 6 | 25 |

test the MLP networks. The MLP neural network had hyperbolic tangent activation function in the hidden layer and logistic activation function in the output layer. We subdivided the training dataset with 168 fault cases into 21 subsets. Each partition had 8 different fault cases. We balanced the training set in terms of the proportion of fault cases present. We trained the MLP networks with 160 fault cases (from Partitions 2 to 21) and validated the networks on the remaining 8 fault cases (from Partition 1). We used the network weights identified as initial weights for training case 2. We trained this case using all partitions apart from Partition 2 and used Partition 2 to validate the trained networks. We conducted the complete training and validation of the networks 21 times until we had used all the validation partitions. The MLP had 10 inputs and 8 hidden nodes and we used the cross-entropy objective function to train the MLP network.

We rounded off fault cases given by a network to the nearest whole number, i.e. 0 and 1. We used the confusion matrix, to assess the predictive capabilities of the trained set of networks and we show this in Table 2.4. We display in this table the predicted fault cases vertically and the actual fault cases horizontally. A row of this matrix indicates all fault cases present in the test data for that particular fault case. In Table 2.4, we observe classification accuracies of 92.3% for [000] cases; all the one- and two-fault cases; and 64.1% for [111] cases.

## 2.10 Application to Interstate Conflict

Marwala and Lagazio (2011) used the MLP network to classify the militarized interstate dispute (MID). They used four variables associated with realist analysis and three 'Kantian' variables. The first variable was *Allies*, a binary measure coded 1 if the members of a dyad are linked by any form of military alliance, and 0 in the absence of military alliance. *Contingency* is also binary, coded 1 if both states share a common boundary and 0 if they do not, and *Distance* is the logarithm, to the base 10, of the distance in kilometres between the two states' capitals. *Major Power* is a binary variable, coded 1 if either or both states in the dyad is a major power and 0 if neither are super powers. *Capability* is the logarithm, to the base 10, of the ratio of the total population plus the number of people in urban areas plus industrial energy consumption plus iron and steel production plus the number of military personnel in active duty plus military expenditure in dollars in the last 5 years measured on stronger country to weak country. The variable *Democracy* is measured on a scale where the value of 10 is an extreme democracy and a value of $-10$ is an extreme autocracy and taking the lowest value of the two countries. The variable *Dependency* is measured as the sum of the countries import and export with its partner divided by the Gross Domestic Product of the stronger country. It is a continuous variable measuring the level of economic interdependence (dyadic trade as a portion of a state's gross domestic product) of the less economically dependent state in the dyad. Marwala and Lagazio (2011) derived these measures from conceptualizations and measurements conducted by the Correlates of War (COW) project (Marwala and Lagazio, 2011). The test set contained 392 dyads, which were conflict dyads and 392 which were non-conflict dyads.

They constructed the MLP network with 7 input units, 10 hidden units, 1 output unit, hyperbolic tangent activation function in the inner layer and logistic activation function in the output layer. They trained the MLP network using the cross-entropy objective function. Table 2.5 gives the confusion matrix for the results. The MLP gave 75% and 76% accuracies, respectively for conflict and peace with the overall average accuracy results of 75.5%.

Table 2.5    Classification results.

| Method | True Conflicts (TC) | False Peaces (FP) | True Peaces (TP) | False Conflicts (FC) |
|---|---|---|---|---|
| MLP | 295 | 97 | 299 | 93 |

## 2.11 Conclusions

We described in this chapter the MLP architecture for both classification and regression. We described the theoretical basis of the MLP for both classification and regression problems. We applied the MLP networks to model the CPI and steam generator in a regression fashion. We applied the MLP network to model faults in cylinders as well as interstate conflict. The results obtained demonstrated that the MLP gave good results when tested.

## References

Abdella, M., Marwala, T. (2005a). Treatment of missing data using neural networks. In: *Proceedings of the IEEE International Joint Conference on Neural Networks*, Montreal, Canada, 598–603.

Abdella, M., Marwala, T. (2005b). The use of genetic algorithms and neural networks to approximate missing data in database. In: *Proceedings of the IEEE 3rd International Conference on Computational Cybernetics*, Mauritius, 207–212.

Antoine, X., Levitt, A., Tang, Q. (2017). Efficient spectral computation of the stationary states of rotating Bose–Einstein condensates by preconditioned nonlinear conjugate gradient methods. *Journal of Computational Physics*, 343:92–109.

Bagheri, M., Mirbagheri, S.A., Ehteshami, M., Bagheri, Z. (2015). Modeling of a sequencing batch reactor treating municipal wastewater using multi-layer perceptron and radial basis function artificial neural networks. *Process Safety and Environmental Protection*, 93:111–123.

Bastani, D., Hamzehie, M.E., Davardoost, F., Mazinani, S., Poorbashiri, A. (2013). Prediction of $CO_2$ loading capacity of chemical absorbents using a multi-layer perceptron neural network. *Fluid Phase Equilibria*, 354:6–11.

Bertsekas, D.P. (1995). *Nonlinear Programming*. Massachusetts, Belmont: Athenas Scientific.

Bishop, C.M. (1995). *Neural Networks for Pattern Recognition*. Oxford: Oxford University Press.

Deo, R.C., Ghorbani, M.A., Samadianfard, S., Maraseni, T., Biazar, M. (2018). Multi-layer perceptron hybrid model integrated with the firefly optimizer algorithm for windspeed prediction of target site using a limited set of neighboring reference station data. *Renewable Energy*, 116, Part A: 309–323.

Dhlamini, S.M., Marwala, T. (2004a). Bushing monitoring using MLP and RBF. In: *Proceedings of the IEEE Africon*, Botswana, Gaborone, 613–617.

Dhlamini, S.M., Marwala, T. (2004b). An application of SVM, RBM and MLP with ARD on bushings. In: *Proceedings of the IEEE Conference on Cybernetics and Intelligent Systems (CIS)*, Singapore, 1254–1259.

Dhlamini, S.M., Marwala, T. (2005). Bushing diagnostics using an ensemble of parallel neural networks. In: *Proceedings of the IEEJ-IEEE Symposium on Electrical Insulating Materials (ISEIM05)*, Fukuoka (Japan), 5–9 June, 289–292.

Fan, X., Wang, L., Li, S. (2016). Predicting chaotic coal prices using a multi-layer perceptron network model. *Resources Policy*, 50:86–92.

Fletcher, R. (1987). *Practical Methods of Optimization*, 2nd edition. New York: Wiley.

Habtemariam. E., Marwala, T., Lagazio, M. (2005). Artificial intelligence for conflict management. In: *Proceedings of the IEEE International Joint Conference on Neural Networks*, Montreal, Canada, 2583–2588.

Hasan, A.N., Twala, B., Marwala, T. (2014). Moving towards accurate monitoring and prediction of gold mine underground dam levels. In: *Proceedings of the 2014 International Joint Conference on Neural Networks (IJCNN)*, 2844–2849.

Haykin, S. (1998). *Neural Networks: A Comprehensive Foundation*. NJ: Prentice Hall.

Hestenes, M.R., Stiefel, E. (1952). Methods of conjugate gradients for solving linear systems. *Journal of Research of the National Bureau of Standards*, 6:409–436.

Hurwitz, E., Marwala, T. (2005). Optimising reinforcement learning for neural networks. In: *Proceedings of the 6th Annual European on Intelligent Games and Simulation*, Leicester, UK, 13–18.

Klein, O., Cirpka, O.A., Bastian, P., Ippisch, O. (2017). Efficient geostatistical inversion of transient groundwater flow using preconditioned nonlinear conjugate gradients. *Advances in Water Resources*, 102:161–177.

Leke, B., Marwala, T. (2005). Optimization of the stock market input time-window using Bayesian neural networks. In: *Proceedings of the IEEE International Conference on Service Operations, Logistics and Informatics*, Beijing, China, 883–894.

Leke, B.B., Marwala, T., Tim, T., Lagazio, M. (2006). Prediction of HIV status from demographic data using neural networks. In: *Proceedings of the IEEE International Conference on Systems, Man and Cybernetics*, Taiwan, 2339–2344.

Li, X., Zhang, W., Don, X. (2017). A class of modified FR conjugate gradient method and applications to non-negative matrix factorization. *Computers & Mathematics with Applications*, 73(2):270–276.

Luenberger, D.G. (1984). *Linear and Nonlinear Programming*, 2nd Edition. Reading, MA: Addison-Wesley.

Marwala T. (2009). *Computational Intelligence for Missing Data Imputation, Estimation, and Management: Knowledge Optimization Techniques*. Information Science Reference Imprint. New York: IGI Global Publications.

Marwala, T. (2010). *Finite Element Model Updating Using Computational Intelligence Techniques*. London: Springer-Verlag.

Marwala, T. (2012). *Condition Monitoring Using Computational Intelligence Methods*. Heidelberg: Springer.

Marwala, T. (2013). *Economic Modeling Using Artificial Intelligence Methods*. Heidelberg: Springer.

Marwala, T. (2014). *Artificial Intelligence Techniques for Rational Decision Making*. Heidelberg: Springer.

Marwala, T. (2015). *Causality, Correlation, and Artificial Intelligence for Rational Decision Making*. Singapore: World Scientific.

Marwala, T., Hurwitz, E. (2017). *Artificial Intelligence and Economic Theory: Skynet in the Market*. Springer.

Marwala, T., Lagazio, M. (2011). *Militarized Conflict Modeling Using Computational Intelligence*. Heidelberg: Springer.

Marwala, T., Boulkaibet, I., Adhikari S. (2017). *Probabilistic Finite Element Model Updating Using Bayesian Statistics: Applications to Aeronautical and Mechanical Engineering*. John Wiley and Sons.

Marwala, T., Chakraverty, S., Mahola, U. (2005). Neural networks and support vector machines for fault identification in cylinders. In: *Proceedings of International Symposium on Neural Networks and Soft Computing in Structural Engineering*, Krakow, Poland.

Mohamed, N. (2003). Detection of Epileptic Activity in the EEG Using Artificial Neural Networks. Master Thesis, University of the Witwatersrand.

Mohamed, M., Rubin, D.M., Marwala, T. (2005). Detection of epileptiform activity in human EEG signals using Bayesian neural networks. In: *Proceedings of the IEEE 3rd International Conference on Computational Cybernetics*, Mauritius, 231–237.

Møller, A.F. (1993). A scaled conjugate gradient algorithm for fast supervised learning. *Neural Networks*, 6:525–533.

Mordecai, A. (2003). *Nonlinear Programming: Analysis and Methods*. Dover Publishing.

Mpanza, L.J., Marwala, T. (2011). Artificial neural network and rough set for HV bushings condition monitoring. *15th IEEE International Conference on Intelligent Engineering Systems*, doi: 10.1109/INES.2011.5954729, 109–113.

Msiza, L.S., Nelwamondo, F.V., Marwala, T. (2007a). Water demand forecasting using multi-layer perceptron and radial basis functions. In: *Proceedings of the IEEE International Joint Conference on Neural Networks*, 13–18.

Msiza. I., Nelwamondo, F.V., Marwala, T. (2007b). Artificial neural networks and support vector machines for water demand time series forecasting. In: *Proceedings of the IEEE International Conference on Systems, Man and Cybernetics*, Montreal, Canada, 638–643,

Patel, P., Marwala, T. (2009). Caller interaction classification: A comparison of real and binary coded GA-MLP techniques. *Advances in Neuro Information Processing, Book Series Lecture Notes in Computer Science*, 5507, 728–735. Berlin/Heidelberg: Springer.

Patel, P.B., Marwala, T. (2006). Forecasting closing price indices using neural networks. In: *Proceedings of the IEEE International Conference on Systems, Man and Cybernetics*, Taiwan, 2351–2356.

Robbins, H., Monro, S. (1951). A stochastic approximation method. *Annals of Mathematical Statistics*, 22:400–407.

Singh, S., Reddy, C.S., Pasha, S.V., Dutta, K., Satish, K.V. (2017). Modeling the spatial dynamics of deforestation and fragmentation using Multi-Layer Perceptron neural network and landscape fragmentation tool. *Ecological Engineering*, 99: 543–551.

Uysal, G., Şensoy, A., Şorman, A.A. (2016). Improving daily streamflow forecasts in mountainous Upper Euphrates basin by multi-layer perceptron model with satellite snow products. *Journal of Hydrology*, 543, Part B: 630–650.

Vilakazi, C.B, Marwala, T. (2006). Bushing fault detection and diagnosis using extension neural network. In: *Proceedings of the 10th IEEE International Conference on Intelligent Engineering Systems*, 170–174.

Wang, J., Zhang, B., Sun, Z., Hao, W., Sun, Q. (2018). A novel conjugate gradient method with generalized Armijo search for efficient training of feedforward neural networks. *Neurocomputing*, 275:308–316.

Werbos, P.J. (1974). Beyond Regression: New Tool for Prediction and Analysis in the Behavioral Sciences. PhD. Thesis, Harvard University.

Wright, S., Marwala, T. (2006). Artificial intelligence techniques for steam generator modelling, arXiv:0811.1711.

Xing, B., Marwala, T. (2018). *Smart Maintenance for Human–Robot Interaction: An Intelligent Search Algorithmic Perspective.* London: Springer.

Zhao, D., Wei, Y., Liu, Y. (2018). Spectrum optimization via FFT-based conjugate gradient method for unimodular sequence design. *Signal Processing*, 142:354–365.

Chapter 3

# Radial Basis Function

**Abstract.** This chapter describes the theory and application of the radial basis function (RBF). It also describes two methods that we use to train the RBF and these are the combination of the $K$-means clustering algorithm and the pseudo-inverse techniques as well as the Expectation Maximization (EM) algorithm. We apply the RBF to regression and classification problems. The regression problems are modelling the CPI as well as modelling the steam generator. The classification problems are modelling interstate conflict and caller behaviour classification. The results obtained indicate that the RBF gave good results, but these results were not as good as the results obtained from the multi-layer perceptron.

## 3.1 Introduction

This chapter introduces the radial basis function (RBF) and its use for regression and classification problems (Marwala, 2009, 2010, 2011, 2012, 2013, 2014, 2015; Marwala *et al.*, 2017; Xing and Marwala, 2018; Marwala and Hurwitz, 2017). The RBF neural network is a feed-forward network trained using a supervised training algorithm (Haykin, 1999; Buhmann and Ablowitz, 2003). The RBF usually has one hidden layer of units whose activation function is chosen from a class of functions called basis functions. A nonlinear function of the distance between the input vector and a prototype vector defines the activation of the hidden units in an RBF neural network (Bishop, 1995).

Arliansyah and Hartono (2015) successfully used the RBF to model trip attraction. The variables used were population size, number of schools, number of students, number of teachers, areas of school buildings, number of offices and number of houses. When they compared this model to the standard regression model, the RBF performed better. Yao *et al.* (2016) used the RBF to successfully simulate slow-release permanganate

Table 3.1    A comparison between the MLP and the RBF paradigms.

| Attribute | MLP | RBF |
|---|---|---|
| Structure | Activation functions, biases, weights in all layers | Activation functions, centres, weights only in the second layer |
| Architecture | Cross-coupled connections on the first and second layers | Cross-coupled connections on the second layer only |
| Data processing | Requires normalization | Does not require normalization |
| Training | Weights and biases are identified simultaneously | Two stages: identifying the centres followed by identifying weights (this is a linear programming exercise) |
| Computational efficiency | Computationally expensive | Computationally cheap |

for groundwater remediation. Milovanović and von Sydo (2017) successfully used the RBF for option pricing problems and observed that the RBF is more computationally efficient than the Black–Scholes approach, yet giving good results. Chandhini *et al.* (2018) successfully applied a RBF method for fractional Darboux problems whereas Majdisova and Skala (2017) applied the RBF to approximate scattered data.

Dhlamini and Marwala (2004) used the RBF successfully to monitor transformer bushing whereas Msiza *et al.* (2007) successfully used the RBF for water demand forecasting. Gidudu *et al.* (2008) used RBF to build support vector machines that performed multiclassifier classification of land cover mapping. Other applications of the RBF include interactive voice response classification in call centres (Patel and Marwala, 2008a, 2008b, 2009a, 2009b, 2010).

Comparing the RBF network to the multi-layer perceptron (MLP) network, which was described in the previous chapter gives the results in Table 3.1.

## 3.2  Radial Basis Function

RBF is a type of neural network falling within the same class as the MLP. RBF network has several advantages though it is similar to a MLP network. The RBF usually trains faster than the MLP networks and is less prone to problems with non-stationary inputs due to the behaviour of the RBF (Bishop, 1995). We can thus describe the RBF network using Figure 3.1, and

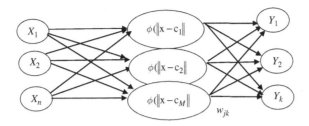

**Figure 3.1**   RBF network having two layers of adaptive weights.

we describe it mathematically as follows (Buhmann and Ablowitz, 2003):

$$y_k(\mathbf{x}) = \sum_{j=1}^{M} w_{jk}\phi_j(\|\mathbf{x} - \mathbf{c}_j\|). \tag{3.1}$$

In Equation (3.1), $w_{jk}$ are the output weights, each corresponding to the connection between a hidden unit and an output unit, M represents the number of hidden units, $\mathbf{c}$ is the $j$th centre, $\phi_j(\mathbf{x})$ is the $j$th nonlinear activation function, $\mathbf{x}$ the input vector, and $k = 1, 2, 3, \ldots, M$ (Bishop, 1995). The selection of the number of hidden nodes, M, is part of the model selection process.

We set the activation in the hidden layers to be a Gaussian distribution $\phi(\|\mathbf{x} - \mathbf{c}\|) = \exp(-\beta(\mathbf{x} - \mathbf{c})^2)$ where $\beta$ is constant. The difference between the RBF and the MLP is that the RBF has weights in the outer layer only while the hidden nodes have what are called the centres. Training the RBF network entails identifying two sets of parameters and these are the centres and the output weights, and both can be viewed as free parameters in a regression framework. There are several ways of estimating the network centres and network weights. In this chapter, we describe two methods, and these are: a two-stage training process used to identify the centres and weights, as well as the expectation maximization (EM) algorithm. The two-stage process involves firstly using self-organizing maps to determine the centres and, in this chapter, the $k$-means clustering method is used with pseudo-inverse technique to identify the weights (Hartigan, 1975). The EM algorithm treats the centres as latent variables and weights as free parameters.

For self-organizing maps, we use the $k$-means algorithm to cluster objects based on attributes into $k$ partitions and here, $k$ represents centres. Borgwardt *et al.* (2017) successfully used the $k$-means algorithm to balance weighted point sets whereas Kakushadze and Yu (2017) used the $k$-means to cluster and model cancer signatures. Bai *et al.* (2017) successfully applied the $k$-means for fast density clustering whereas Khanmohammadi *et al.* (2017)

applied the $k$-means for medical applications. Kant *et al.* (2017) successfully applied the $k$-means for collaborative filtering.

Its objective is to discover the centres of natural clusters in the data and assumes that the object attributes form a vector space. It achieves this by minimizing the total intra-cluster variance, or, the squared error function (Hartigan and Wong, 1979; Marwala, 2009):

$$E = \sum_{i=1}^{C} \sum_{x_j \in S_i} (\mathbf{x}_j - \mathbf{c}_i)^2. \tag{3.2}$$

In Equation (3.2), $C$ is the number of clusters $S_i$, $i = 1, 2, \ldots, M$ and $\mathbf{c}_i$ is the centre of all the points $x_j \in S_i$. In this chapter, we use the Lloyd algorithm to identify the cluster centres (Lloyd, 1982). We initialize the Lloyd's algorithm by dividing the input space into $k$ initial sets randomly or using heuristic data. Then we calculate the mean point for each set and then construct a new partition by associating each point with the closest centre. We then recalculate the centroids for the new clusters and repeat the process by changing these two steps until convergence. We achieve convergence when the centroids no longer change, or the points no longer switch clusters.

After identifying the centres, the next step is to calculate the network weights in Equation (3.1) given the training data. To achieve this, we use the Moore–Penrose pseudo inverse (Moore, 1920; Penrose, 1955; Golub and Van Loan, 1996). The Moore–Penrose pseudo-inverse was successfully used to solve linear systems (Mihailović *et al.*, 2017), in portfolio optimization (Lee and Kim, 2017) as well as sparse signal approximation (Plonka *et al.*, 2016). We should note that once we have identified the centres, then the estimation of the network weights becomes a linear process (Golub and Van Loan, 1996). With the training data and the centres identified, then we can rewrite Equation (3.1) as follows:

$$\mathbf{y} = \boldsymbol{\varphi}\mathbf{w}. \tag{3.3}$$

Here, $\mathbf{y}$ is the output matrix, parameter $\boldsymbol{\varphi}$ is the activation function matrix while $\mathbf{w}$ is the weight matrix. From Equation (3.3), we can observe that to solve for the weight matrix $\mathbf{w}$ we need to invert the activation function matrix $\boldsymbol{\varphi}$. However, this matrix is not square and, therefore, we cannot invert it using standard tools. We can invert this matrix using the Moore–Penrose pseudo-inverse which we can write as follows (Bishop, 1995; Marwala, 2009):

$$\boldsymbol{\varphi}^* = (\boldsymbol{\varphi}\boldsymbol{\varphi}^{\mathbf{T}})^{-1}\boldsymbol{\varphi}^{\mathbf{T}}. \tag{3.4}$$

This, therefore, implies that we can estimate the weight matrix as follows (Bishop, 1995; Marwala, 2009):

$$\mathbf{w} = \boldsymbol{\varphi}^* \mathbf{y}. \tag{3.5}$$

An alternative way of estimating the centres and the network weights of the RBF is the use of the EM algorithm (Little and Rubin, 1987). EM algorithm is used to successfully model the Gaussian process and Maaziz and Kharfouchi (2018) successfully used the EM algorithm to estimate parameters of Markov switching bilinear model. This algorithm was also used in linear composite quantile regression and Lee *et al.* (2017) successfully used the EM algorithm for spatio-temporal disease mapping. Dou *et al.* (2016) successfully used EM algorithm to estimate the Bernstein copula. In the EM algorithm, we iteratively estimate the network weights and centres by repeating the following steps as outlined by Little and Rubin (1987):

1. **The expectation E-step:** In the presence of a set of parameter estimates, for example a mean vector and covariance matrix for a multivariate normal distribution, the E-step estimates the conditional expectation of the complete-data log-likelihood given the observed data and the parameter estimates.
2. **The maximization M-step:** The M-step identifies the parameter estimates that maximize the complete-data log-likelihood from the E-step given a complete-data log-likelihood.

These steps are iterated until convergence. In EM algorithm, if $\mathbf{w}$ indicates unknown parameters and $\mathbf{c}$ indicates the missing data (latent variable), and $\mathbf{X}$ represents the observed data, then we can write the marginal likelihood of the observed data as (Dempster *et al.*, 1977; Snyman, 2005; Little and Rubin, 1987; Nelwamondo *et al.*, 2007; Nelwamondo, 2008):

$$L(\mathbf{w}; \mathbf{X}) = p(\mathbf{X}|\mathbf{w}) = \int p(\mathbf{X}, \mathbf{c}|\mathbf{w}) d\mathbf{c}. \tag{3.6}$$

1. **The expectation E-step:** The conditional expectation of the complete-data log-likelihood given the observed data and the parameter estimates can be calculated as (Dempster *et al.*, 1977; Little and Rubin, 1987; Nelwamondo *et al.*, 2007; Nelwamondo, 2008):

$$Q(\mathbf{w}|\mathbf{w}^{(t)}) = E_{\mathbf{c}|\mathbf{X}, \mathbf{w}^{(t)}} [\log L(\mathbf{w}; \mathbf{X}, \mathbf{c})] \tag{3.7}$$

2. **The maximization M-step:** We calculate the parameter estimates
   that maximize the complete-data log-likelihood from the E-step given a
   complete-data log-likelihood as (Dempster *et al.*, 1977; Little and Rubin,
   1987; Nelwamondo *et al.*, 2007; Nelwamondo, 2008):

$$\mathbf{w}^{(t+1)} = \arg\max_{\mathbf{w}} Q(\mathbf{w}|\mathbf{w}^{(t)}). \qquad (3.8)$$

We can thus estimate $\mathbf{w}^{(t+1)}$ and we repeat this process until we reach
convergence. The EM algorithm can be summarized as follows:

1. Initialize the model parameter $\mathbf{w}$ to some random values,
2. Calculate the probability of each value missing variable $\mathbf{c}$ given $\mathbf{w}$,
3. Then use the computed values of $\mathbf{c}$ to re-estimate a better value of $\mathbf{w}$.

## 3.3  Model Selection

We obtain an appropriate model, given by the size of the hidden nodes,
from the segment of the validation dataset. We achieve this by identifying the
weights and centres through training (using the $k$-means clustering algorithm
and pseudo inverse or EM algorithm or both) the RBF model with a segment
of the data labelled 'training dataset' and choosing the appropriate model
using the validation set. We call the process of selecting an appropriate
model, model selection (Burnham and Anderson, 2002). The process of
deriving a model from data is a non-unique problem. This is because many
models can fit the training data and, therefore, it becomes impossible to
identify the most appropriate model.

   We base the approach of selecting a model on two principles and these
are the goodness of fit and the model's complexity. Essentially, goodness of
fit implies that a good model should predict the validation data, which it
has not seen during the training stage. We base the model selection on the
complexity of the model on the Occam's principle, which states that the best
model is the simplest one.

   In selecting the best model, the two questions that need to be considered
are:

- What is the best balance between the goodness of fit and the complexity
  of the model?
- How do we implement these attributes?

In this chapter, we measure the goodness of fit by the error between the
model's prediction and the validation set, while we measure the complexity

of the model by the number of free parameters in the data. As stated before, we define the free parameters in the RBF model as the network centres and weights. In this chapter, we view model selection as the mechanism for selecting a model that has a good probability of estimating the validation dataset, that it has not seen during the training stage, and the bias and variance are measures of the ability of this model to operate in an acceptable way.

## 3.4 Application to Interstate Conflict

As explained by Marwala and Lagazio (2011), they used the RBF network to classify the militarized interstate dispute (MID). The focus was to look at the percentage of correct MID prediction of the test dataset by each technique. They used 1,000 cases to form a training set, 500 from each group. The test set contained 392 dyads, which were conflict dyads and 392 which were non-conflict dyads.

The RBF neural network requires one to choose the best architecture to give good classification results. They identified the best combination of the number of hidden units, activation function, training algorithm and training cycles that result in a network best able to generalize the test data. They chose 10 hidden units with Gaussian activation function for the RBF network.

Table 3.2 gives the confusion matrix for the results and these are compared to the MLP results from Chapter 2. Although the MLP network performed slightly better than the RBF network in predicting True Conflicts (true positives), they achieve this at the expense of reducing the number of False Peace (true negatives) predicted. Also, MLP picked up on the True Peace (true positives) better than the RBF without reducing the number of False Conflicts (false negatives). Overall, the RBF network predicted conflict and peace with accuracies of 71% and 73%, respectively. The corresponding results for the MLP were better at 75% and 76%, respectively for conflict and peace. The averaged results for correct predictions are 72% for the RBF and 75.5% for the MLP.

Table 3.2 Classification results.

| Method | True Conflicts (TC) | False Peaces (FP) | True Peaces (TP) | False Conflicts (FC) |
|---|---|---|---|---|
| RBF | 278 | 114 | 288 | 104 |
| MLP | 295 | 97 | 299 | 93 |

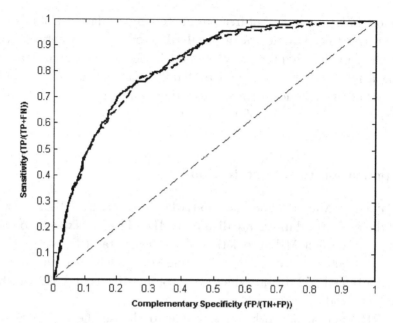

**Figure 3.2**   A graph showing the relevance of each liberal variable with regard to MIDs classification (solid curve is MLP while dashed curve is the RBF).

We evaluate the performance of the classifiers using the Receiver Operating Characteristics (ROC) curve. The ROC curve is a graphical depiction of the sensitivity of the classifier, also called the true positive rate, against the fall-out also called the false positive rate. The fall-out was calculated as the difference between 1 and the specificity.

The ROC graphs for the MLP and the RBF appear in Figure 3.2 (Marwala and Lagazio, 2011). The MLP is clearly better in predicting the conflicts without affecting the prediction of peace.

## 3.5  Call Behaviour Classification

Patel and Marwala (2010) and Patel (2010) examined the caller behaviour classification system illustrated in Figure 3.3. They used this system to identify trends of caller behaviour within the interactive voice recognition (IVR) VXML applications. The RBF and MLP field classifiers were trained based on data extracted from IVR log event files. These files were generated by the IVR platform as specific events occurred during a call to the system. These events included call begin, form enter, form select, automatic speech recognition events, transfer events and call end events which are written to the logs.

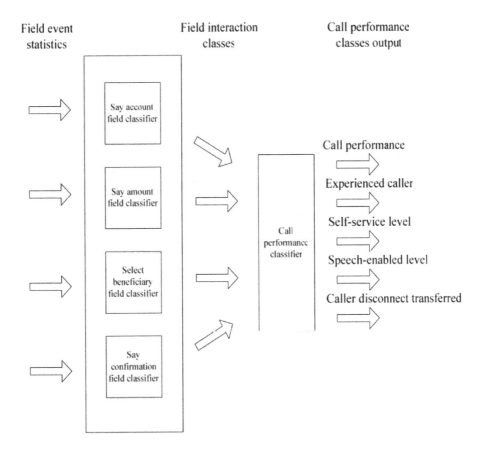

**Figure 3.3** The caller behaviour classification system.

Table 3.3 shows the inputs and outputs of the field classification component. These specific inputs were selected to characterize the caller experience at a field. The outputs of the classifiers summarize the caller field behaviour through the use of interaction classes. The confidence input illustrates the IVR speech recognition probability. The larger the percentage, the greater the probability the system interpreted the caller successfully.

A caller may answer a question the VXML application prompts with a response the application does not accommodate. These events are represented by the no match inputs. In general, most VXML applications accommodate 3 no match events per field. On a third no match event, the call is transferred to a DTMF field. If the caller fails to complete the DTMF field successfully on attempt 1, the call is transferred to a CSA. The same process is used for the third no input and maximum speech timeout events. The no match field classifier inputs assist in identifying callers that misunderstood

**Table 3.3**    The inputs and outputs of the field classifier.

| Inputs | Outputs | Output Interaction Class |
|--------|---------|--------------------------|
| Confidence | Field performance | Good, acceptable, investigate, bad |
| No matches | Field transfer reason | Unknown, difficulty |
| No inputs | Field hang-up reason | Unknown, difficulty |
| Max speech timeouts | Field difficulty attempt | Attempt 1, attempt 2, attempt 3 |
| Barge-ins | Field duration | High, medium, low |
| Hang-up | Field recognition level | High, medium, low |
| Transfer to service agent DTMF transfer duration system error confirmation of transaction | Experienced caller | True, false |

**Table 3.4**    The performance of the RBF and the MLP.

| Type | Classifier | Accuracy | Sensitivity | Specificity |
|------|-----------|----------|-------------|-------------|
| Field 'Say account' classifier | MLP | 0.9513 | 0.9269 | 0.9763 |
| Field 'Say account' classifier | RBF | 0.9376 | 0.9049 | 0.9715 |
| Field 'Say amount' classifier | MLP | 0.9796 | 0.9711 | 0.9883 |
| Field 'Say amount' classifier | RBF | 0.9603 | 0.9404 | 0.9805 |
| Field 'Select beneficiary' classifier | MLP | 0.9722 | 0.9566 | 0.9880 |
| Field 'Select beneficiary' classifier | RBF | 0.9573 | 0.9361 | 0.9789 |
| Field 'Say confirmation' classifier | MLP | 0.9021 | 0.8454 | 0.9625 |
| Field 'Say confirmation' classifier | RBF | 0.9048 | 0.8559 | 0.9565 |
| Call performance classifier | MLP | 0.9918 | 0.9877 | 0.9960 |
| Call performance classifier | RBF | 0.9019 | 0.9677 | 0.8406 |

the VXML prompt as well as unique responses that the VXML application can use to improve field recognition coverage.

Patel and Marwala (2010) used the RBF and MLP methods and generated solutions that achieved accuracy values larger than 90% on unseen validation as well as test data. The MLP field classifier produced the most accurate solutions, outperforming the RBF on both validation and test datasets. This is true for the 'Say account', 'Say amount' and 'Select beneficiary' fields. However, the call performance MLP ANN approach performed the best on validation data. The results on the validation set are shown in Table 3.4. This table uses the accuracy which is the proportion of all classes classified correctly, sensitivity which is a ratio of true positive to the sum of true positives and false negatives as well as specificity which is a ratio of true negative to the sum of true negatives and false positives.

These results show that the RBF performs well but not as good as the MLP network.

## 3.6 Modelling the CPI

Marwala (2013) used the RBF to estimate the consumer price index (CPI). The CPI is a measure of inflation in an economy. The problem of estimating the CPI is a regression problem. It measures the changes in prices of a fixed pre-selected basket of goods. We use a basket of goods, to calculate the CPI, in South Africa as follows (Marwala, 2013):

1. Food and non-alcoholic beverages: bread and cereals, meat, fish, milk, cheese, eggs, oils, fats, fruit, vegetables, sugar, sweets, desserts and other foods
2. Alcoholic beverages and tobacco
3. Clothing and footwear
4. Housing and utilities: rents, maintenance, water, electricity and others
5. Household contents, equipment and maintenance
6. Health: medical equipment, outpatient and medical service
7. Transport
8. Communication
9. Recreation and culture
10. Education
11. Restaurants and hotels
12. Miscellaneous goods and services: personal care, insurance and financial services.

We weigh this basket and track the variation of prices of these goods from month to month and this is a basis for calculating inflation. In this chapter, we use the CPI data from 1992 to 2011 to model the relationship between economic variables and the CPI. These economic variables are listed in Table 3.5 (Marwala, 2013). They represent the performance of various aspect of the economy represented by 23 variables in the agriculture, manufacturing, mining, energy, construction, etc. We constructed a multi-layered perceptron neural network with 12 input variables, 8 hidden nodes, and 1 output representing the CPI. To train the RBF network we use the EM algorithm.

The results and attributes of the RBF and MLP are shown in Table 3.6.

**Table 3.5**   The variables used to construct the RBF.

| Variable |
|---|
| Agriculture, fish and forestry |
| Mining |
| Manufacturing |
| Electricity, gas and water |
| Construction |
| Retail and trade |
| Transport, storage and communication |
| Financial intermediation, insurance, real estate and business services |
| Community, social and personal services |
| Government services |
| Gross value added at basic prices |
| Taxes less subsidies on products |
| Affordability |
| Economic growth |
| Rand/USD exchange |
| Prime interest |
| Repo rate |
| Gross domestic product |
| Household consumption |
| Investment |
| Government consumption |
| Exports |
| Imports |

**Table 3.6**   Characteristics of the RBF network and the results.

| Attributes | MLP | RBF |
|---|---|---|
| Input nodes | 12 | 12 |
| Hidden nodes | 8 | 8 |
| Output nodes | 1 | 1 |
| Training time (s) | 3.45 | 0.36 |
| Accuracy (%) | 84.6 | 82.7 |

The results indicate that the MLP performed better than the RBF.

## 3.7  Modelling Steam Generator

Wright and Marwala (2006) modelled the cause–effect relationship of data obtained from a Steam Generator at Abbott Power Plant in the USA. The dataset had 9600 samples. The cause–effect model contained four causes and one effect. The causes were the input fuel, air, reference level and

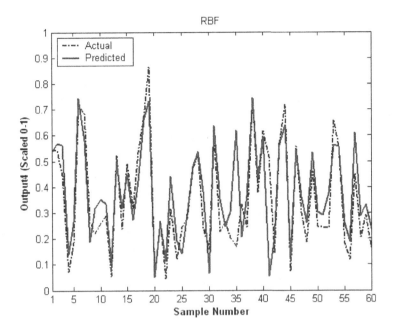

**Figure 3.4**  Showing the predicted vs. actual values for the first 60 points of output 4 for the test dataset applied to the RBF.

**Table 3.7**  Performance characteristics for individual MLP and RBF.

|                          | **MLP**   | **RBF**   |
| ------------------------ | --------- | --------- |
| Time to train (s)        | 6.98      | 13        |
| Time to execute (s)      | 0.016     | 0.031     |
| MSE of test dataset      | 0.075708  | 0.076360  |
| No. of hidden nodes      | 8         | 30        |
| No. of training cycles   | 240       | 150       |

disturbance defined by the load level. The effect is the steam flow rate. They took the approach that was to train a network with a fixed number of hidden nodes, periodically stopping the training process to determine the error on the validation dataset. Therefore, they observed the training and validation errors during the training process and determined an indication of the generalization ability of the network. They did this for a varying number of hidden nodes, from 4 to 20, for the RBF. They compared the different solutions for the set number of hidden nodes and selected the best network. Using the procedure discussed above, they found that for the RBF the most appropriate number of hidden nodes was 8 and the MLP used attributes identified in Chapter 2. The results obtained are in Figure 3.4 and Table 3.7

and these results indicate that the RBF modelled the steam generator input–output relationship well but not as good as MLP.

## 3.8  Conclusions

This chapter studied the RBF and compared it to the MLP network. The theory of the RBF was described and two methods for training the RBF were also described, and these were, the $k$-means clustering method and Moore–Penrose pseudo-inverse, as well as, the EM algorithm. The RBF was implemented for classification and regression problems. The classification problems were the interstate conflict and caller behaviour classification. The regression problems were the steam generator and CPI prediction. It was observed that the RBF gives good results, but they were consistently worse than those from the MLP.

## References

Arliansyah, J., Hartono, Y. (2015). Trip attraction model using radial basis function neural networks. *Procedia Engineering*, 125:445–451.

Bai, L., Cheng, X., Liang, J., Shen, H. (2017). Fast density clustering strategies based on the $k$-means algorithm. *Pattern Recognition*, 71:375–386.

Bishop, C.M. (1995). *Neural Networks for Pattern Recognition*. Oxford: Oxford University Press.

Borgwardt, S., Brieden, A., Gritzmann, P. (2017). An LP-based $k$-means algorithm for balancing weighted point sets. *European Journal of Operational Research*, 263(2):349–355.

Burnham, K.P., Anderson, D.R. (2002). *Model Selection and Multimodel Inference: A Practical-Theoretic Approach*. Berlin: Springer-Verlag.

Buhmann, M.D., Ablowitz, M.J. (2003). *Radial Basis Functions: Theory and Implementations*. Cambridge: Cambridge University Press.

Chandhini, G., Prashanthi, K.S., Antony, V., Vijesh, A. (2018). Radial basis function method for fractional Darboux problems. *Engineering Analysis with Boundary Elements*, 86:1–18.

Dempster, A.P., Laird, N.M., Rubin, D.B. (1977). Maximum likelihood for incomplete data via the EM algorithm. *Journal of the Royal Statistical Society*, B39:1–38.

Dhlamini, S.M., Marwala, T. (2004). Bushing monitoring using MLP and RBF. In: *Proceedings of the IEEE Africon*, Gaborone, Botswana, 613–617.

Dou, X., Kuriki, S., Lin, G.D., Richards, D. (2016). EM algorithms for estimating the Bernstein copula. *Computational Statistics & Data Analysis*, 93:228–245.

Gidudu, G.H., Marwala, T. (2008). An SVM multiclassifier approach to land cover mapping. *ASPRS 2008 Annual Conference*, Portland, Oregon.

Golub, G.H., van Loan, C.F. (1996). *Matrix Computation*. Maryland: Johns Hopkins University Press.

Hartigan, J.A. (1975). *Clustering Algorithms*. New Jersey: Wiley.

Hartigan, J.A., Wong, M.A. (1979). A *K*-means clustering algorithm. *Applied Statistics*, (28):100–108.

Haykin, S. (1999). *Neural Networks*. New Jersey: Prentice-Hall.

Kakushadze, Z., Yu, W. (2017). *K*-means and cluster models for cancer signatures. *Biomolecular Detection and Quantification*, 13:7–31.

Kant, S., Mahara, T., Jain, V.K., Jain, D.K., Sangaiah, A.K. (2017). Leader Rank based *k*-means clustering initialization method for collaborative filtering. *Computers & Electrical Engineering*, in press, corrected proof, Available online 19 December 2017.

Khanmohammadi, S., Adibeig, N., Shanehbandy, S. (2017). An improved overlapping *k*-means clustering method for medical applications. *Expert Systems with Applications*, 67:12–18.

Lee, M., Kim, D. (2017). On the use of the Moore–Penrose generalized inverse in the portfolio optimization problem. *Finance Research Letters*, 22:259–267.

Lee, J.S.W., Nguyen, P., Brown, P.E., Stafford, J., Saint-Jacques, N. (2017). A local-EM algorithm for spatio-temporal disease mapping with aggregated data. *Spatial Statistics*, 21, Part A:75–95.

Little, R.J.A., Rubin, D.D. (1987). *Statistical Analysis with Missing Data*. New York: John Wiley.

Lloyd, S.O. (1982). Least squares quantization in PCM. *IEEE Transactions on Information Theory*, (28):129–137.

Maaziz, M., Kharfouchi, S. (2018). Parameter estimation of Markov switching bilinear model using the (EM) algorithm. *Journal of Statistical Planning and Inference*, 192:35–44.

Majdisova, Z., Skala, V. (2017). Radial basis function approximations: Comparison and applications. *Applied Mathematical Modelling*, 51:728–743.

Marwala, T. (2009). *Computational Intelligence for Missing Data Imputation, Estimation, and Management: Knowledge Optimization Techniques*, Information Science Reference Imprint. New York: IGI Global Publications.

Marwala, T. (2010). *Finite Element Model Updating Using Computational Intelligence Techniques*. London: Springer-Verlag.

Marwala, T. (2012). *Condition Monitoring Using Computational Intelligence Methods*. Heidelberg: Springer.

Marwala, T. (2013). *Economic Modeling Using Artificial Intelligence Methods*. Heidelberg: Springer.

Marwala, T. (2014). *Artificial Intelligence Techniques for Rational Decision Making*. Heidelberg: Springer.

Marwala, T. (2015). *Causality, Correlation, and Artificial Intelligence for Rational Decision Making*. Singapore: World Scientific.

Marwala, T., Hurwitz, E. (2017). *Artificial Intelligence and Economic Theory: Skynet in the Market*. Berlin, Heidelberg: Springer.

Marwala, T., Lagazio, M. (2011). *Militarized Conflict Modeling Using Computational Intelligence*. Heidelberg: Springer. Translated into Chinese by the National Defence Industry Press.

Marwala, T., Boulkaibet, I., Adhikari, S. (2017). *Probabilistic Finite Element Model Updating Using Bayesian Statistics: Applications to Aeronautical and Mechanical Engineering*. Berlin, Heidelberg: John Wiley and Sons.

Mihailović, B., Jerković, V.M., Malešević, B. (2017). Solving fuzzy linear systems using a block representation of generalized inverses: The Moore–Penrose inverse. *Fuzzy Sets and Systems*, in press, corrected proof, Available online 10 November 2017.

Milovanović, S., von Sydo, L. (2017). Radial basis function generated finite differences for option pricing problems. *Computers & Mathematics with Applications*, in press, corrected proof, Available online 1 December 2017.

Moore, E.H. (1920). On the reciprocal of the general algebraic matrix. *Bulletin of the American Mathematical Society*, (26):394–395.

Msiza, I.S., Nelwamondo, F.V., Marwala, T. (2007). Water demand forecasting using multi-layer perceptron and radial basis functions. In: *Proceedings of the IEEE International Joint Conference on Neural Networks*, 13–18.

Nelwamondo, F.V. (2008). Computational Intelligence Techniques for Missing Data Imputation. PhD Thesis, University of the Witwatersrand.

Nelwamondo, F.V., Mohamed, S., Marwala, T. (2007). Missing data: A comparison of neural network and expectation maximization techniques. *Current Science*, 93(11): 1514–1521.

Patel, P.B. (2010). An IVR Call Performance Classification System Using Computational Intelligence Techniques. PhD Thesis, University of the Witwatersrand.

Patel, P.B., Marwala, T. (2008a). Interactive voice response field classifiers. In: *Proceedings of the IEEE International Conference on Man, Systems and Cybernetics*, 3425–3430.

Patel, P.B., Marwala, T. (2008b). Interactive voice response field classifiers. In: *Proceedings of the IEEE International Conference on Man, Systems and Cybernetics*, 3425–3430.

Patel, P.B., Marwala, T. (2009a). Genetic algorithms, neural networks, fuzzy inference system, support vector machines for call performance classification. *IEEE International Conference on Machine Learning Application*, 415–420.

Patel, P.B., Marwala, T. (2009b). Caller behaviour classification a comparison of SVM and FIS techniques. *Lecture Notes in Computer Science*, Springer, 199–208.

Patel, P.B., Marwala, T. (2010). Caller behaviour classification using computational intelligencer methods. *International Journal of Neural Systems*, doi: 10.1142/S0129065710002255, 87–93.

Penrose, R. (1955). A generalized inverse for matrices. In: *Proceedings of the Cambridge Philosophical Society*, 406–413.

Plonka, G., Hoffmann, S., Weickert, J. (2016). Pseudo-inverses of difference matrices and their application to sparse signal approximation. *Linear Algebra and its Applications*, 503:26–47.

Wright, S., Marwala, T. (2006). Artificial Intelligence techniques for steam generator modelling. arXiv:0811.1711.

Xing, B., Marwala, T. (2018). *Smart Maintenance for Human–Robot Interaction: An Intelligent Search Algorithmic Perspective*. London: Springer.

Yao, G., Bliss, K.M., Crimi, M., Fowler, K.R., Evans, P.J. (2016). Radial basis function simulation of slow-release permanganate for groundwater remediation via oxidation. *Journal of Computational and Applied Mathematics*, 307:235–247.

Chapter 4

# Automatic Relevance Determination

**Abstract.** This chapter introduces the automatic relevance determination (ARD), which is a method of ranking input variables in the order of their importance on predicting the output. In the formulation of the ARD, we ground it in the theory of regularization, where we assign each input its own coefficient. We apply the ARD to rank inputs in a model that relates certain variables to interstate conflict as well as inputs in a model that predicts inflation.

## 4.1 Introduction

Advances in artificial intelligence have allowed us to model complex input–output relationships. For example, Lunga and Marwala (2006) used neural networks to create input–output relationships between observed financial data and the future trajectory. Marwala (2000, 2003) used the multi-layer perceptron neural network to build a model of vibration data and the damaged state of structures. Applications of neural networks to model complex relationships include, for missing data estimation (Marwala, 2009), in robotics (Xing and Marwala, 2018), in understanding economics (Marwala and Hurwitz, 2017; Marwala, 2013), in decision-making (Marwala, 2014, 2015) and in finite element models (Marwala and Sibisi, 2005). Further applications of neural networks include damage detection (Marwala and Hunt HEM, 1999; Marwala, 2009, 2012), interstate conflict (Marwala and Lagazio, 2004, 2011) and in the detection of epileptic activity (Mohamed *et al.*, 2006). The use of neural networks to model complex relationships is often classified as a black-box modelling. This is because it is difficult to understand what is going on in these models. The question on how to make these models transparent is an ongoing research question. Often, when these models are used, we pre-process the data, and often this involves mixing them and thereby making the task of untangling them difficult.

For example, one way of pre-processing the data is to use the principal component analysis which effectively combines all the variables, thus making the task of untangling them difficult. One method of understanding the data is to use the automatic relevance determination (ARD) method.

We use the ARD in order to study the complex relationships that exist in the data and estimate the relevance of each variable. We base the ARD method in this chapter on the Bayesian framework (Neal, 1998; MacKay, 1991, 1992). Sandhu *et al.* (2017) successfully used the ARD for Bayesian model and applied it successfully to nonlinear dynamical systems. Renkens and Van hamme (2017) used the ARD for non-negative dictionary learning in the Gamma–Poisson model whereas Wang and Lu (2006) successfully used the ARD to estimate interval of urban ozone level and select relevant factors. Nummenmaa *et al.* (2007) successfully used the ARD in neuroimaging application. Ulusoy and Bishop (2006) successfully used the ARD to identify relevant features for object recognition of 2D images. Other successful applications of the ARD include in ischaemic episodes (Smyrnakis and Evans, 2007), to identify regions of the thalamus involving schizophrenia (Browne, 2006), in EEG signals (Wu *et al.*, 2010) and to estimate relevant variables in classifying ovarian tumours (Van Calster *et al.*, 2006).

At the core of the ARD method are the following mathematical techniques, which we describe in detail in this chapter: neural networks, Bayesian framework, evidence framework and optimization methods. We apply the ARD to understand interstate conflict as well as to model inflation.

## 4.2 Mathematical Basis of the Automatic Relevance Determination

In this section, we define the ARD method as an efficient technique to determine the relevance of each input variable in its ability to predict the output in an input–output model. It achieves this by optimizing the hyperparameters, to maximize the evidence in the Bayesian formulation of training a neural network. One component of the ARD is a multi-layer perceptron (MLP) neural network, which we describe in the next section.

### 4.2.1 Neural networks

A neural network is an information processing method that is inspired by the way biological nervous systems, like the human brain, process information. It is a computational machine emulating the way the brain processes information (Haykin, 1999). It is a remarkably powerful mechanism that has found successful applications in mechanical engineering (Vilakazi and Marwala, 2007, finance (Patel and Marwala, 2006), statistics (Marwala, 2009), political science (Lagazio and Marwala, 2005), to detect faults in induction motors (Ghate *et al.*, 2010) and to study gene association to diseases (Zhang *et al.*, 2008). Furthermore, the MLP was successful in detecting premature ventricular contractions (Ebrahimzadeh and Khazaee, 2010) as well as to design robots (Chiddarwar *et al.*, 2010). Neural networks are generalized regression and classification models that can model any data, linear or nonlinear. A multi-layer perceptron neural network consists of four main components (Bishop, 1995; Haykin, 1999):

- the processing units $u_j$, where each $u_j$ has a certain activation level $a_j(t)$ at any point in time;
- weighted inter-connections between various processing units. These inter-connections determine how the activation of one unit leads to the input for another unit;
- an activation rule, which acts on the set of input signals at a unit to produce a new output signal; and
- a learning rule that specifies how to adjust the weights for a given input/output pair.

Because of their capacity to derive meaning from complex data, we use multi-layer perceptron neural networks to extract patterns and detect trends that we find too complex to observe using many other computational methods. A trained neural network is an expert in the class of information we use to train it and can then be used to provide predictions given new situations (Lunga and Marwala, 2006; Leke *et al.*, 2007). The structure of neural processing units and their inter-connections have a huge impact on the processing abilities of neural networks and there are different connections that define how data flows between the input, hidden and output layers. We show a diagram of the MLP in Figure 4.1 (Marwala, 2009).

This network architecture contains hidden units and output units and has one hidden layer. We show the bias parameters in the first layer as mapping weights from an extra input having a fixed value of $x_0 = 1$. We show the bias parameters in the second layer as weights from an extra hidden unit, with the activation fixed at $z_0 = 1$. The model in Figure 4.1 can consider the intrinsic dimensionality of the data. These models approximate any continuous function to arbitrary accuracy if the number of hidden units, $M$, is sufficiently large. We write the relationship between the output, $y$,

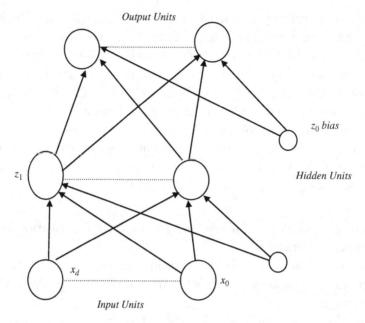

**Figure 4.1**   Feed-forward MLP network having two layers of adaptive weights (Marwala, 2009).

and input, $x$, as follows (Bishop, 1995):

$$y_k = f_{\text{outer}} \left( \sum_{j=1}^{M} w_{kj}^{(2)} f_{\text{inner}} \left( \sum_{i=1}^{d} w_{ji}^{(1)} x_i + w_{j0}^{(1)} \right) + w_{k0}^{(2)} \right). \qquad (4.1)$$

Here, $w_{ji}^{(1)}$ and $w_{ji}^{(2)}$ indicate neural network weights in the first and second layers, respectively, going from input $i$ to hidden unit $j$, $M$ is the number of hidden units, $d$ is the number of output units while $w_{j0}^{(1)}$ indicates the bias for the hidden unit $j$. The function $f_{\text{inner}}(\cdot)$ is the activation function in the inner layer whereas $f_{\text{outer}}(\cdot)$ is the activation in the outer layer. The training of conventional neural networks identifies the network weights, while the training of probabilistic neural networks identifies the distributions of the network weights. We choose an objective function to identify the weights in Equation (4.1) given the observed data. An *objective function* is a mathematical representation of the overall objective of the problem.

If we use the training set $D = \{x_k, y_k\}_{k=1}^{N}$, where superscript $N$ is the number of training examples, and assuming that the targets $y$ are sampled independently given the $k$th inputs $x_k$ and the weight parameters $w_{kj}$, then the objective function, $E$, may be written using the cross-entropy cost function (Bishop, 1995):

$$E_D = -\beta \sum_{n=1}^{N} \sum_{k=1}^{K} \{t_{nk} \ln(y_{nk}) + (1 - t_{nk}) \ln(1 - y_{nk})\}. \quad (4.2)$$

Here, $t_{nk}$ is the target vector for the $n$th output and $k$th training example, $N$ is the number of training examples, $K$ is the number of network output units, $n$ is the index for the training pattern, $\beta$ is the data contribution to the error, and $k$ is the index for the output unit. The cross-entropy objective function is suitable for classification problems whereas the sum-of-squares objective function is suitable for regression problems. We discussed the details on this in Chapter 2.

The cross-entropy cost function is based on the idea that the value of the output represents the probability $P(C1|x)$ for class C1. We can regularize Equation (4.2) by introducing extra information to the objective function with a penalty function to solve an ill-posed problem or to prevent over-fitting by ensuring smoothness of the solution, to balance complexity and accuracy, using (Bishop, 1995):

$$E_W = -\frac{\alpha}{2} \sum_{j=1}^{W} w_j^2. \quad (4.3)$$

Here, $\alpha$ is the prior contribution to the regularization error, and $W$ is the number of network weights. This regularization parameter penalizes weights of large magnitudes (Bishop, 1995). By combining Equations (4.2) and (4.3), we can write the overall fitness function as follows (Bishop, 1995):

$$E = \beta E_D + \alpha E_W$$

$$= -\beta \sum_{n=1}^{N} \sum_{k=1}^{K} \{t_{nk} \ln(y_{nk}) + (1 - t_{nk}) \ln(1 - y_{nk})\} - \frac{\alpha}{2} \sum_{j=1}^{W} w_j^2. \quad (4.4)$$

## 4.2.2 Bayesian framework

We deem the multi-layered neural networks as parameterized classification models that make probabilistic assumptions about the data. We facilitate the probabilistic outlook of these models by using the Bayesian framework. We view learning algorithms as methods for finding parameter values that look probable in the light of the data. We implement the learning process by dividing the data into training, validation and testing sets. We do this to select an unbiased model. Another way of achieving this is by using the regularization framework, which comes naturally from the Bayesian formulation.

Thomas Bayes (1702–1761) proved a case of the Bayes' theorem and Pierre–Simon Laplace (1749–1827) generalized the theorem and applied it to problems such as celestial mechanics, medical statistics and reliability (Stigler, 1986; Fienberg, 2006; Bernardo, 2005). The Bayesian method traditionally used uniform priors and later complemented with a technique the maximum-likelihood or frequentist approach. The maximum-likelihood approach identifies the most likely solution without regard to the probability distribution of that solution. The maximum-likelihood approach is a special case of Bayesian results representing the most probable solution in the distribution of the posterior probability function. The Bayesian techniques are comprised of the following ideas (Bishop, 1995):

- The usage of hierarchical models and the marginalization over the values of irrelevant parameters using methods such as the Markov chain Monte Carlo techniques.
- In the progressive application of the Bayes' theorem, we obtain data points after estimating a posterior distribution and the posterior equals the following prior.
- In the frequentist approach, a hypothesis is a proposition, which we must prove right or wrong. In the Bayesian approach, a hypothesis has a probability.

Bayesian technique was successfully applied to many problems including probabilistic risk assessment (Kelly and Smith, 2009), modelling integrated river basin management (Barton *et al.*, 2008), to model mobile robot's behaviour (Lazkano *et al.*, 2007), to diagnose airplane engines (Sahin *et al.*, 2007) and for environmental modelling (Uusitalo, 2007). Recent applications of Bayesian approach include in agriculture (Drury *et al.*, 2017), to quantify the uncertainty rock strength (Contreras *et al.*, 2017), in tourism study (Assaf *et al.*, 2018), in clinical trials (Thorlund *et al.*, 2017) and to study flows in heterogeneous random media (Yang *et al.*, 2017). The problem of identifying the weights ($w_i$) and biases (with subscripts 0 in Figure 4.1) in the hidden layers may be posed in the Bayesian form as (Bishop, 1995):

$$P(\mathbf{w}|\mathbf{D}) = \frac{P(\mathbf{D}|\mathbf{w})P(\mathbf{w})}{P(\mathbf{D})}, \tag{4.5}$$

where $P(\mathbf{w})$ is the probability distribution function of the weight-space in the absence of any data, also known as the prior distribution and $\mathbf{D} \equiv (y_1, \ldots, y_N)$ is a matrix containing the identity of damage data. The quantity

$P(\mathbf{w}|\mathbf{D})$ is the posterior probability distribution after the data have been seen and $P(\mathbf{D}|\mathbf{w})$ is the likelihood function.

(A) *Likelihood function*

The likelihood function is a probability of the data given the assumed model. We can write the likelihood function mathematically as follows by using the cross-entropy error (Edwards, 1972; Bishop, 1995):

$$P([D]|\{w\}) = \frac{1}{Z_D} \exp(-\beta E_D)$$

$$= \frac{1}{Z_D} \exp\left(\beta \sum_n^N \sum_k^K \{t_{nk} \ln(y_{nk}) + (1 - t_{nk}) \ln(1 - y_{nk})\}\right).$$

$$(4.6)$$

In Equation (4.6), $E_D$ is the objective (e.g. cross-entropy) function, $\beta$ represents the hyperparameters, and $Z_D$ is a normalization constant, which we can estimate as follows:

$$Z_D - \int_{-\infty}^{\infty} \exp\left(\beta \sum_n^N \sum_k^K \{t_{nk} \ln(y_{nk}) + (1 - t_{nk}) \ln(1 - y_{nk})\}\right) d\{w\}.$$

$$(4.7)$$

(B) *Prior function*

The prior probability distribution is the probability of the free parameters and is a subjective estimation by a knowledgeable expert (Jaynes, 1968; Bernardo, 1979). There are different kinds of priors and these include informative and uninformative priors. An *informative prior* reveals precise information about a variable while an *uninformative prior* shows ambiguous information about a variable. We write a prior distribution that assumes that model parameters are of the same order of magnitude as follows (Bishop, 1995):

$$P(\{w\}) = \frac{1}{Z_w} \exp(-E_W)$$

$$= \frac{1}{Z_w} \exp\left(-\frac{\alpha}{2} \sum_j^W w_j^2\right).$$

$$(4.8)$$

Parameter $\alpha$ represents the hyperparameters, and $Z_w$ is the normalization constant, which we can estimate as follows:

$$Z_w = \int_{-\infty}^{\infty} \exp\left(-\frac{\alpha}{2} \sum_j^W w_j^2\right) d\{w\}.$$

$$(4.9)$$

The prior distribution of a Bayesian approach is the regularization parameter. As indicated before, regularization introduces an extra information
to the objective function, through a penalty function, to solve ill-posed
problems or to prevent overfitting. This ensures the smoothness of the
solution to balance complexity with accuracy.

(C) *Posterior function*

The posterior probability is the probability of the network weights given the
observed data. It is a conditional probability allocated after we observe the
evidence, i.e. data (Lee, 2004). We estimate it by multiplying the likelihood
function by the prior function and dividing by a normalization function (i.e.
the evidence). By combining Equations (4.6) and (4.8), we can write the
posterior distribution as (Bishop, 1995):

$$P(w|D) = \frac{1}{Z_s} \exp\left(\beta \sum_{n}^{N}\sum_{k}^{K}\{t_{nk}\ln(y_{nk}) + (1 - t_{nk})\ln(1 - y_{nk})\} - \frac{\alpha}{2}\sum_{j}^{W} w_j^2\right),$$

(4.10)

where

$$Z_E(\alpha, \beta) = \int \exp(-\beta E_D - \alpha E_W) dw$$

$$= \left(\frac{2\pi}{\beta}\right)^{N/2} + \left(\frac{2\pi}{\alpha}\right)^{W/2}.$$

(4.11)

The distribution in Equation (4.10) is a canonical distribution. Training the
network using a Bayesian approach gives the probability distribution of the
weights in Equation (4.1). The Bayesian approach automatically penalizes
highly complex models. This means selecting automatically an optimal model
without applying independent methods such as cross-validation (Bishop,
1995).

## 4.2.3  Automatic relevance determination

We construct the ARD by associating the hyperparameters of the prior with
each input variable. This, therefore, requires us to generalize Equation (4.10)
as (MacKay, 1991; 1992):

$$E_W = \frac{1}{2}\sum_{k} \alpha_k \mathbf{w}^T \mathbf{I}_k \mathbf{w}.$$

(4.12)

Here, superscript $T$ is the transpose, $k$ is the weight group and $\mathbf{I}$ is the identity matrix. By using the generalized prior, the posterior probability becomes (Bishop, 1995):

$$P(\mathbf{w}|\mathbf{D}, H_i)$$

$$= \frac{1}{Z_s} \exp\left( \beta \sum_n \{t_n \ln y(\mathbf{x}_n) + (1 - t_n) \ln(1 - y(\mathbf{x}_n))\} - \frac{1}{2} \sum_k \alpha_k \mathbf{w}^T \mathbf{I}_k \mathbf{w} \right),$$

$$= \frac{1}{Z_E} \exp(-E(\mathbf{w})), \tag{4.13}$$

where

$$Z_E(\alpha, \beta) = \left(\frac{2\pi}{\beta}\right)^{N/2} + \prod_k \left(\frac{2\pi}{\alpha_k}\right)^{W_k/2}. \tag{4.14}$$

Here, $W_k$ is the number of weights in group $k$.

Using the Taylor expansion, the error in Equation (4.4) becomes

$$E^*(\mathbf{w})$$

$$= -\sum_n \beta\{t_n \ln(y(\mathbf{x}_n)) + (1 - t_n) \ln(1 - y(\mathbf{x}_n))\} + \frac{1}{2} \sum_k \alpha_k \mathbf{w}^T \mathbf{I}_k \mathbf{w}$$

$$\approx E(\mathbf{w}_{\text{MP}}) + \frac{1}{2}(\mathbf{w} - \mathbf{w}_{\text{MP}})^T \mathbf{A}(\mathbf{w} - \mathbf{w}_{\text{MP}}), \tag{4.15}$$

where

$$[A] = \beta \nabla \nabla E_D + \sum_k \alpha_k \mathbf{I}_k. \tag{4.16}$$

Here, the subscript MP indicates the Most Probable weights, superscript $T$ stands for the transpose and $\mathbf{A}$ stands for the Hessian matrix. We write the evidence as follows (Bishop, 1995):

$$p(\mathbf{D}|\alpha, \beta) = \frac{1}{Z_D Z_W} \int \exp(-E(\mathbf{w}))d\mathbf{w}$$

$$= \frac{Z_E}{Z_D Z_W}$$

$$= \frac{\left(\frac{2\pi}{\beta}\right)^{N/2} + \prod_k \left(\frac{2\pi}{\alpha_k}\right)^{W_k/2}}{\left(\frac{2\pi}{\beta}\right)^{N/2} \prod_k \left(\frac{2\pi}{\alpha_k}\right)^{W_k/2}}. \tag{4.17}$$

Maximizing the log evidence gives the following estimations for the hyper-parameters:

$$\beta^{\text{MP}} = \frac{N - \gamma}{2E_D(\{w\}^{\text{MP}})}, \tag{4.18}$$

$$\alpha_k^{\text{MP}} = \frac{\gamma_k}{2E_{W_k}(\{w\}^{\text{MP}})}, \tag{4.19}$$

where $\gamma = \sum_k \gamma_k$, $2E_{W_k} = \mathbf{w}^T \mathbf{I}_k \mathbf{w}$ and:

$$\gamma_k = \sum_j \left( \frac{\pi_j - \alpha_k}{\eta_j} \left( \mathbf{V}^T \mathbf{I}_k \mathbf{V} \right)_{jj} \right), \tag{4.20}$$

and $\eta_j$ are the eigenvalues of $\mathbf{A}$, and $\mathbf{V}$ are the eigenvalues such that $\mathbf{V}^T \mathbf{V} = \mathbf{I}$.

To determine the relevance of each input variable, the $\alpha_k^{\text{MP}}$, $\beta^{\text{MP}}$, and the Most Probable weight, $\{w\}^{\text{MP}}$, are determined using the evidence framework (MacKay, 1991):

1. Choose randomly the initial values for the hyperparameters.
2. Train the neural network using the scaled conjugate gradient algorithm to obtain $\mathbf{w}^{\text{MP}}$.
3. Estimate the hyperparameters using Equations (4.18) and (4.19).
4. Repeat steps 2 and 3 until convergence.

## 4.3  Application to Interstate Conflict

Marwala and Lagazio (2011) implemented the ARD to understand the influence of the input parameters on the militarized interstate dispute (MID). They used four variables associated with realist analysis and three 'Kantian' variables. The first variable is *Allies*, a binary measure coded 1 if the members of a dyad are linked by any form of military alliance, and 0 in the absence of military alliance. *Contingency* is also binary, coded 1 if both states share a common boundary and 0 if they do not, and *Distance* is the logarithm, to the base 10, of the distance in kilometres between the two states' capitals. *Major Power* is a binary variable, coded 1 if either or both states in the dyad is a major power and 0 if neither are super powers. *Capability* is the logarithm, to the base 10, of the ratio of the total population plus the number of people in urban areas plus industrial energy consumption plus iron and steel production plus the number of military personnel in active duty plus military expenditure in dollars in the last 5 years measured on stronger country to weak country. The variable *Democracy* is measured on a scale where the value of 10 is an extreme democracy and a value of $-10$ is an extreme autocracy and taking the lowest value of the two countries. The variable *Dependency* is defined as the sum of the countries import and export with its partner divided by the Gross Domestic Product of the stronger country. It is a continuous variable measuring the level of economic interdependence (dyadic trade as a portion of a state's gross domestic product) of the less economically dependent state in the dyad. Marwala and Lagazio (2011) derived these measures from conceptualizations and measurements conducted by the Correlates of War (COW) project.

They chose the politically relevant population (all dyads containing a major power) because it sets a hard test for prediction. Omitting all distant dyads composed of weak states means that much of the influence of the variables that are not very amenable to policy intervention (distance and national power) are eliminated. By that omission, they made our job harder by reducing the predictive power of such variables, but it also makes it more interesting. By applying the training and validation sampling technique they showed that a strong performance is achieved even when the analysis is restricted to the politically relevant group. By focusing only on dyads that either involve major powers or are contiguous, they tested the discriminative power of the neural network on a difficult set of cases.

Marwala and Lagazio (2011) used the COW data to generate the training and testing sets. The training dataset consists of 500 conflicts and 500 non-conflict cases, and the test data consists of 392 conflict cases and 392 peace cases. They used a balanced training set, with a randomly selected equal number of conflicts and non-conflicts cases, to produce robust classifications and stronger insights on the reasons for conflicts. The data are normalized to fall between 0 and 1. The MLP architecture was chosen using $M = 10$, a logistic function in the output layer and a hyperbolic function in the hidden layer as the optimal architecture.

Following the work of Marwala and Lagazio (2011), they used the ARD to rank liberal variables and their influence on the MID. They implemented the ARD, then calculated the hyperparameters, and then calculated the inverse of the hyperparameters. They obtained the results in Figure 4.2 (Marwala and Lagazio, 2011) and these indicated that the *Dependency* variable had the highest influence, followed by *Capability*, followed by *Democracy* and then *Allies*. The remaining three variables, that is, *Contingency*, *Distance* and *Major Power*, have similar impact although it is much smaller in comparison

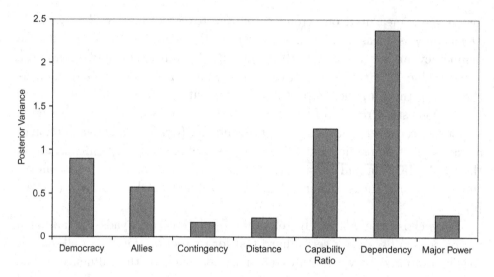

**Figure 4.2**  Relevance of each liberal variable with regards to the classification of MIDs.

with the other two liberal variables, democracy and economic interdependence and the two realist variables, allies and difference in capabilities.

The results show that all the liberal variables used influence the conflict and peace outcome. However, alliance, and power ratio play a part in providing opportunities and incentives for interstate action and therefore they affect peace or conflict between states. The three remaining realist variables, *Distance, Contingency* and *Major Power* cannot be ignored.

## 4.4  Applications of ARD in Inflation Modelling

Marwala (2013) applied the ARD to identify variables that drive inflation. Inflation is measured using a concept called Consumer Price Index (CPI). The CPI is a measure of inflation in an economy. It measures the changes in prices of a fixed pre-selected basket of goods. A basket of goods, which Marwala (2013) used to calculate the CPI was as follows (Marwala, 2013):

1. Food and non-alcoholic beverages: bread and cereals, meat, fish, milk, cheese, eggs, oils, fats, fruit, vegetables, sugar, sweets, desserts and other foods
2. Alcoholic beverages and tobacco
3. Clothing and footwear
4. Housing and utilities: rents, maintenance, water, electricity and others
5. Household contents, equipment and maintenance

6. Health: medical equipment, outpatient and medical service
7. Transport
8. Communication
9. Recreation and culture
10. Education
11. Restaurants and hotels
12. Miscellaneous goods and services: personal care, insurance and financial services.

We weigh this basket and track the variation of prices of these goods from month to month and this is a basis for calculating inflation. We must note that there is normally a debate as to whether this basket of goods is appropriate. We use the CPI data from 1992 to 2011 to model the relationship between economic variables and the CPI. These economic variables are listed in Table 4.1. They represent the performance of various

Table 4.1   Automatic relevance with multi-layer perceptron.

| Variable | Alpha | Inverse Alpha | Relative Weights |
|---|---|---|---|
| Agriculture fish forestry | 14.4832 | 0.0690 | 1.79 |
| Mining | 5.7440 | 0.1741 | 4.51 |
| Manufacturing | 24.2071 | 0.0413 | 1.07 |
| Electricity gas water | 6.8551 | 0.1459 | 3.78 |
| Construction | 7.3717 | 0.1357 | 3.51 |
| Retail and trade | 15.0679 | 0.0664 | 1.72 |
| Transport, storage and communication | 2.3174 | 0.4315 | 11.18 |
| Financial intermediation, insurance, real estate and business services | 0.9391 | 1.0648 | 27.59 |
| Community, social and personal services | 0.4626 | 2.1616 | 56.00 |
| Government services | 7.2632 | 0.1377 | 3.57 |
| Gross value added at basic prices | 4.7935 | 0.2086 | 5.40 |
| Taxes less subsidies on products | 0.6467 | 1.5462 | 40.06 |
| Affordability | 1.0664 | 0.9377 | 24.29 |
| Economic growth | 4.0215 | 0.2487 | 6.44 |
| Rand/USD exchange | 25.8858 | 0.0386 | 1.00 |
| Prime interest | 5.5639 | 0.1797 | 4.66 |
| Repo rate | 5.5639 | 0.1797 | 4.66 |
| Gross domestic product | 0.2545 | 3.9287 | 101.78 |
| Household consumption | 0.4407 | 2.2692 | 58.79 |
| Investment | 0.5909 | 1.6924 | 43.84 |
| Government consumption | 7.5703 | 0.1321 | 3.42 |
| Exports | 20.8664 | 0.0479 | 1.24 |
| Imports | 5.9678 | 0.0386 | 1.00 |

aspect of the economy represented by 23 variables in the agriculture, manufacturing, mining, energy, construction, etc. sectors. A multi-layered perceptron neural network with 23 input variables, 12 hidden nodes and 1 output representing the CPI is constructed. The ARD-based MLP network was trained using the scaled conjugate gradient method and the results indicating the relevance of each variable are in Table 4.1 (Marwala, 2013).

From Table 4.1, the following variables are essential for modelling the CPI and these are mining, transport, storage and communication, financial intermediation, insurance, real estate and business services, community, social and personal services, gross value added at basic prices, taxes less subsidies on products, affordability, economic growth, repo rate, gross domestic product, household consumption, and investment. These results are based on the dataset being analysed and the methodology used which is the ARD based on the MLP and may change depending on the changes on any of these methods and data.

## 4.5  Conclusions

This chapter described the MLP architecture and how its training is formulated using the Bayesian approach. Then we discussed the development of the ARD. We then implemented the ARD to assess the relevance of variables on inflation modelling as well as modelling interstate conflict.

## References

Assaf, A.G., Tsionas, M., Oh, H. (2018). The time has come: Toward Bayesian SEM estimation in tourism research. *Tourism Management*, 64:98–109.

Barton, D.N., Saloranta, T., Moe, S.J., Eggestad, H.O., Kuikka, S. (2008). Bayesian belief networks as a meta-modelling tool in integrated river basin management — pros and cons in evaluating nutrient abatement decisions under uncertainty in a Norwegian river basin. *Ecology Economics*, 66:91–104.

Bernardo, J.M. (1979). Reference posterior distributions for Bayesian inference. *Journal of the Royal Statistical Society*, 41:113–147.

Bernardo, J.M. (2005). *Reference Analysis*, Handbook of Statistic, 25:17–90.

Bishop, C.M. (1995). *Neural Networks for Pattern Recognition*. Oxford: Oxford University Press.

Browne, A. (2006). Using neural networks with automatic relevance determination to identify regions of the thalamus implicated in schizophrenia. In: *Proceedings of the IEEE International Joint Conference on Neural Networks*, 97–101.

Chiddarwar, S.S., Babu, N.R. (2010). Comparison of RBF and MLP neural networks to solve inverse kinematic problems for 6R serial robots by a fusion approach. *Engineering Application of Artificial Intelligence*, 23:1083–1092.

Contreras, L.F., Brown, E.T., Ruest, M. (2017). Bayesian data analysis to quantify the uncertainty of intact rock strength. *Journal of Rock Mechanics and Geotechnical Engineering*, in press, accepted manuscript, Available online 30 December.

Drury, B., Valverde-Rebaza, J., Moura, M-F., de Andrade Lopes, A. (2017). A survey of the applications of Bayesian networks in agriculture. *Engineering Applications of Artificial Intelligence*, 65:29–42.

Ebrahimzadeh, A., Khazaee, A. (2010). Detection of premature ventricular contractions using MLP neural networks: A comparative study. *Measurement*, 43:103–112.

Edwards, A.W.F. (1972). *Likelihood.* Cambridge: Cambridge University Press.

Fienberg, S.E. (2006). When did Bayesian inference become "Bayesian"? *Bayesian Analysis*, 1:1–40.

Ghate, V.N., Dudul, S.V. (2010). Optimal MLP neural network classifier for fault detection of three phase induction motor. *Expert System with Applications*, 37:3468–3481.

Haykin, S. (1999). *Neural Networks.* New Jersey: Prentice-Hall.

Jaynes, E.T. (1968). Prior probabilities. *IEEE Transactions on System, Man and Cybernetics*, 4:227–241.

Kelly, D.L., Smith, C.L. (2009). Bayesian inference in probabilistic risk assessment — the current state of the art. *Reliability Engineering & System Safety*, 94:628–643.

Lagazio, M., Marwala, T. (2005). Assessing different Bayesian neural network models for militarized interstate dispute. *Social Science Computer Review*, 24:1–12.

Lazkano, E., Sierra, B., Astigarraga, A., Martínez-Otzeta, J.M. (2007). On the use of Bayesian networks to develop behaviours for mobile robots. *Robotics and Autonomous Systems*, 55:253–265.

Lee, P.M. (2004). *Bayesian Statistics, An Introduction.* New Jersey: Wiley & Sons.

Leke, B., Marwala, T., Tettey, T. (2007). Using inverse neural network for HIV adaptive control. *International Journal of Computer Intelligence Research*, 3:11–15.

Lunga, D., Marwala, T. (2006). On-line forecasting of stock market movement direction using the improved incremental algorithm. *Lecture Notes in Computer Science*, 4234:440–449.

MacKay, D.J.C. (1991). Bayesian Methods for Adaptive Models. PhD Thesis, California Institute of Technology.

MacKay, D.J.C. (1992). A practical Bayesian framework for back propagation networks. *Neural Computation*, 4:448–472.

Marwala, T. (2000). On damage identification using a committee of neural networks. *Journal of Engineering Mechanics*, 126:43–50.

Marwala, T. (2003). Fault classification using pseudo modal energies and neural networks. *American Institute of Aeronaut and Astronaut*, 41:82–89.

Marwala, T. (2009). *Computational Intelligence for Missing Data Imputation, Estimation and Management: Knowledge Optimization Techniques.* New York: IGI Global Publications.

Marwala, T. (2012). *Condition Monitoring Using Computational Intelligence Methods.* Heidelberg: Springer.

Marwala, T. (2013). *Economic Modeling Using Artificial Intelligence Methods.* Heidelberg: Springer.

Marwala, T. (2014). *Artificial Intelligence Techniques for Rational Decision Making.* Heidelberg: Springer.

Marwala, T. (2015). *Causality, Correlation, and Artificial Intelligence for Rational Decision Making.* Singapore: World Scientific.

Marwala, T., Hurwitz, E. (2017). *Artificial Intelligence and Economic Theory: Skynet in the Market.* Springer.

Marwala, T., Hunt, H.E.M. (1999). Fault identification using finite element models and neural networks. *Mechanical System and Signal Processing*, 13:475–490.

Marwala, T., Lagazio, M. (2004). Modelling and controlling interstate conflict. In: *Proceedings of the IEEE International Joint Conference on Neural Networks*, 1233–1238.

Marwala, T., Lagazio, M. (2011). *Militarized Conflict Modeling Using Computational Intelligence*. Heidelberg: Springer.

Marwala, T., Sibisi, S. (2005). Finite element model updating using Bayesian framework and modal properties. *Journal of Aircraft*, 42:275–278.

Mohamed, N., Rubin, D., Marwala, T. (2006). Detection of epileptiform activity in human EEG signals using Bayesian neural networks. *Neural Information Processing*, 10:1–10.

Nummenmaa, A., Auranen, T., Hämäläinen, M.S., Jääskeläinen, I.P. and Lampinen, J. (2007). Automatic relevance determination based hierarchical Bayesian MEG inversion in practice. *NeuroImage*, 37(3):876–889.

Patel, P., Marwala, T. (2006). Neural networks, fuzzy inference systems and adaptive-neuro fuzzy inference systems for financial decision making. *Lecture Notes in Computer Science*, 4234:430–439.

Renkens, V., Van hamme, H. (2017). Automatic relevance determination for nonnegative dictionary learning in the Gamma-Poisson model. *Signal Processing*, 132: 121–133.

Sahin, F., Yavuz, M.Ç., Arnavut, Z., Uluyol, Ö. (2007). Fault diagnosis for airplane engines using Bayesian networks and distributed particle swarm optimization. *Parallel Computing*, 33:124–143.

Sandhu, R., Pettit, C., Khalil, M., Poirel, D., Sarkar, A. (2017). Bayesian model selection using automatic relevance determination for nonlinear dynamical systems. *Computer Methods in Applied Mechanics and Engineering*, 320:237–260.

Smyrnakis, M.G., Evans, D.J. (2007). Classifying ischemic events using a Bayesian inference multilayer perceptron and input variable evaluation using automatic relevance determination. *Computers in Cardiology*, 305–308.

Stigler, S.M. (1986). *The History of Statistics*. Massachusetts: Harvard University Press.

Thorlund, K., Golchi, S. Mills, E. (2017). Bayesian adaptive clinical trials of combination treatments. *Contemporary Clinical Trials Communications*, 8:227–233.

Ulusoy, I., Bishop, C.M. (2006). Automatic relevance determination for the estimation of relevant features for object recognition. In: *Proceedings of the 2010 IEEE 14th Signal Processing and Communications Applications*, 1–4.

Uusitalo, L. (2007). Advantages and challenges of Bayesian networks in environmental modelling. *Ecological Modelling*, 203:312–318.

Van Calster, B., Timmerman, D., Nabney, I.T., Valentin, L., Van Holsbeke, C., Van Huffel, S. (2006). Classifying ovarian tumors using Bayesian multi-layer perceptrons and automatic relevance determination: A multi-center study. In: *Proceedings of the Engineering in Medicine and Biology Society*, 5342–5345.

Vilakazi, B.C., Marwala, T. (2007). Condition monitoring using computational intelligence. In: Laha, D., Mandal, P. (ed.), *Handbook on Computational Intelligence in Manufacturing and Production Management*, illustrated edn., New York: IGI Publishers.

Wang, D., Lu, W.-Z. (2006). Interval estimation of urban ozone level and selection of influential factors by employing automatic relevance determination model. *Chemosphere*, 62(10):1600–1611.

Wu, W., Chen, Z., Gao, S., Brown, E.N. (2010). Hierarchical Bayesian modeling of inter-trial variability and variational Bayesian learning of common spatial patterns from multichannel EEG. In: *Proceedings of the 2010 IEEE International Conference on Acoustics Speech and Signal Processing*, 501–504.

Xing, B., Marwala, T. (2018). *Smart Maintenance for Human–Robot Interaction: An Intelligent Search Algorithmic Perspective*. London: Springer.

Yang, K., Guha, N., Efendiev, Y., Mallick, B.K. (2017). Bayesian and variational Bayesian approaches for flows in heterogeneous random media. *Journal of Computational Physics*, 345:275–293.

Zhang, J., Liu, S., Wang, Y. (2008). Gene association study with SVM, MLP, and cross-validation for the diagnosis of diseases. *Progress in Natural Science*, 18:741–750.

# Chapter 5

# Bayesian Networks

**Abstract.** This chapter describes Bayesian approaches to neural networks. Firstly, it describes how we formulate the training of neural networks using Bayesian approach. The outcome of the Bayesian approach to neural network is the posterior probability function. Then we describe various methods for estimating the posterior probability function using Hybrid Monte Carlo (HMC), Shadow Hybrid Monte Carlo (SHMC) and Separable Shadow Hybrid Monte Carlo (S2HMC). We then applied Bayesian network to classification of interstate conflict. When these techniques were applied to interstate conflict, the S2HMC performed the best followed by the SHMC followed by the Hybrid Monte Carlo.

## 5.1 Introduction

In the previous chapters, we described how to train a neural network using the maximum-likelihood approach and scaled conjugate method. The problem with the maximum-likelihood approach is that it only offers an optimal network without regard to the probability distribution of such a network. The Bayesian approach offers such a probability network. The outcome of the Bayesian formulation to neural network training is the posterior probability function. Much of the work on Bayesian network is how we can estimate this probability. Several methods can estimate the posterior probability function (Marwala, 2001; Marwala, 2012; Marwala, 2013; Marwala and Lagazio, 2011).

One method proposed for Bayesian training of neural networks is to approximate the posterior probability function with a Gaussian approximation using a Taylor expansion (MacKay, 1992, 1991). With this assumption, we calculate the posterior probability function by maximizing the evidence, by calculating the values of the hyperparameters that are most probable and then integrating them over the weight space by applying an approximation around the most likely weights. In this regard, we maximize the evidence by using standard optimization methods that are used in the maximum-likelihood approach. This Gaussian approach to estimating the posterior probability is a bad approximation and a better approximation is the one based on the Monte Carlo, which has been used extensively in statistical mechanics (Neal, 1993). In statistical mechanics, we derive the macroscopic thermodynamic properties from the state space, i.e. the position and momentum of miniscule objects such as molecules. The number of degrees of freedom that these objects have is enormous, so the only way to solve this problem is to formulate it in a probabilistic framework.

Monte Carlo methods are a type of numerical technique that depend on repetitive random sampling to estimate the results. We use Monte Carlo methods to simulate complex systems where close form or deterministic solutions are inaccessible. This is because of their dependence on repeated computation of random or simulated random numbers (Kandela *et al.*, 2010). Simulated annealing is one of the Monte Carlo methods that has been successful.

Simulated annealing is a Monte Carlo technique that is inspired by the process of annealing where metals recrystallize, or liquids freeze, and is used to sample a probability (Torabzadeh and Zandieh, 2010; Ozgan and Saruhan, 2010; Paydar *et al.*, 2010; Naderi *et al.*, 2009). In the annealing process, we heat a metal until it is molten and then we decrease its temperature slowly in such a way that the metal is virtually in thermodynamic equilibrium. As the temperature drops, the system becomes more ordered, approaching a *frozen* state. If we direct the cooling technique inefficiently or the initial temperature of the object is not adequately high, the system quenches, forming defects or freezing out in meta-stable states, indicating that the system is trapped in a local minimum energy state.

Metropolis *et al.* (1953) proposed the procedure that we follow to simulate the annealing procedure, and it encompasses selecting an initial state and temperature, and maintaining the temperature the same, disturbing the initial formation and calculating the probability of the new state. If the new probability is higher than the previous probability, then we accept the new state, otherwise if the opposite is the case, then we accept the state with a low probability. Simulated annealing replaces a current solution with a 'nearby' random solution using a probability that depends on the difference between the differences in probability. The temperature reduces throughout the process, so as temperature approaches zero, there are less random changes in the solution. Simulated annealing keeps moving towards the best solution, except that it has the advantage of reversal in the optimum solution, but it can move to a solution with worse solution than it has currently achieved. However, the advantage of this is that it ensures that the solution is not local, but global. This is an advantage of simulated annealing over other sampling techniques, but its disadvantage is high computational cost.

Another way of sampling the posterior probability is to use a genetic Markov Chain Monte Carlo (MCMC) (Marwala, 2007a). Genetic programming efficiently samples through the parameter space, and thereby increases the likelihood of attaining a global posterior distribution rather than a local one. The reason for its success is that sampling in binary space has high probability of sampling the most probable parameters. The inspiration behind genetic programming is Darwin's theory of natural evolution (Marwala, 2010) where we use the principles of the survival of the fittest and natural selection to explain the evolution of species. Genetic programming technique applies a population of binary-string chromosomes. Each of these strings is the discretized representation of a point in the search. On generating a new population, three operators are used, and these are crossover, mutation and reproduction. We use these operators to implement genetic MCMC sampling. MCMC method is a random walk Monte Carlo method where we create a Markov chain to identify an equilibrium distribution. The MCMC consists of a Markov process and a Monte Carlo simulation (Liesenfeld and Richard, 2008). After many random walk steps, the retained states will converge to a desired posterior distribution. In principle, as the number of steps approaches infinity, the accuracy of the estimated probability distribution becomes ideal.

The crossover operator mixes genetic information in the population by cutting pairs of chromosomes at random points along their length and exchanging the cut sections. This joins successful operators together. The mutation operator picks a binary digit of the chromosomes at random and inverts it. This has a potential of introducing new information to the population. Reproduction takes successful chromosomes and reproduces them in accordance with their fitness functions. The genetic MCMC is different from the standard MCMC in that we replace the random walk in the classical MCMC with a procedure inspired by Darwin's theory of evolution and it operates in floating-point space.

Gibbs sampling is a procedure to create a sequence of samples from the joint probability distribution of at least two random variables to estimate a joint distribution, the marginal distribution of one of the variables and the expected value of a variable. Gibbs sampling is a type of MCMC technique and is a mechanism for statistical inference. It is a random procedure, which substitutes deterministic techniques. Gibbs sampling is appropriate in cases where the joint distribution is unknown or is complex to sample directly, but we know the conditional distribution of each variable and it is easy to sample. The Gibbs sampling procedure produces an example from the distribution of each variable, conditional on the present values of the other variables. The series of samples creates a Markov chain, and the stationary distribution of the Markov chain is the joint distribution (Gelman *et al.*, 1995).

## 5.2  Neural Networks

We now express the multi-layer perceptron (MLP) neural network model in the Bayesian context. A MLP is applied to map the input variables ($x$) and output ($y$) and we write the relationship between the $k$th, $y_k$ output and the input vector, $x$, as follows (Bishop, 1995; Marwala, 2009):

$$
y_k = f_{\text{outer}} \left( \sum_{j=1}^{M} w_{kj}^{(2)} f_{\text{inner}} \left( \sum_{i=1}^{d} w_{ji}^{(1)} x_i + w_{j0}^{(1)} \right) + w_{k0}^{(2)} \right). \tag{5.1}
$$

Here, $w_{ji}^{(1)}$ and $w_{ji}^{(2)}$ indicate the weights in the first and second layers, respectively, going from input $i$ to hidden unit $j$, $M$ is the number of hidden units, $d$ is the number of output units, while $w_{j0}^{(1)}$ indicates the bias for the hidden unit $j$ and $w_{k0}^{(2)}$ indicates the bias for the output unit $k$.

Selecting a suitable network architecture is a vital aspect of model building. Furthermore, in selecting the suitable MLP model, another significant decision lies in the choice of the right number of hidden units ($M$), and the category of functional transformations that they achieve. This is because a large value of $M$ yields very flexible networks, which may learn not only the data structure but also the fundamental noise in the data. As an alternative, a small value of $M$ creates networks that are incapable of modelling complex relationships. We pose the problem of identifying the weights and biases in neural networks in the Bayesian framework as (Bishop, 1995; Marwala, 2011, 2014, 2015):

$$
P(\mathbf{w}|\mathbf{D}) = \frac{P(\mathbf{D}|\mathbf{w})P(\mathbf{w})}{P(\mathbf{D})}, \tag{5.2}
$$

where $P(\mathbf{w})$ is the probability distribution function of the weight-space in the absence of any data, also known as the prior distribution function and **D** is a matrix containing the data. The expression $P(\mathbf{w}|\mathbf{D})$ is the posterior probability distribution function after the data have been observed, $P(\mathbf{D}|\mathbf{w}])$ is the likelihood function and $P(\mathbf{D})$ is the normalization function, also known as the 'evidence'. For the MLP, we expand Equation (5.2) by applying the cross-entropy error function to give (Bishop, 1995; Marwala, 2009):

$$
P(\mathbf{w}|\mathbf{D}) = \frac{1}{Z_s} \exp \left( \beta \sum_n^N \sum_k^K \{t_{nk} \ln(y_{nk}) \right.
$$

$$
\left. + (1 - t_{nk}) \ln(1 - y_{nk})\} - \sum_j^W \frac{\alpha_j}{2} w_j^2 \right), \tag{5.3}
$$

where

$$
Z_S(\alpha, \beta) = \left( \frac{2\pi}{\beta} \right)^{N/2} + \left( \frac{2\pi}{\alpha} \right)^{W/2}. \tag{5.4}
$$

The cross-entropy function is applied for classification problems otherwise we apply sum-of-squares-of-error function for regression problems. The advantage of the weight-decay prior distribution is that it penalizes the weights with large magnitudes. In Equation (5.3), $n$ is the index for the training pattern, hyperparameter $\beta$ is the data contribution to the error, $k$ is the index for the output unit, $t_{nk}$ is the target output corresponding to the $n$th training pattern and $k$th output unit and $y_{nk}$ is the corresponding predicted output. The parameter $\alpha_j$ is another hyperparameter, which determines the relative contribution of the regularization term on the training error. The hyperparameters may be set for groups of weights. We solve Equation (5.3) by numerically sampling posterior probability, applying methods such as Monte Carlo method, simulated annealing, genetic Monte Carlo method or the hybrid Monte Carlo (HMC) (Marwala *et al.*, 2017). The next sections describe some of these sampling methods.

## 5.3 Hybrid Monte Carlo

This chapter applies the HMC technique to identify the posterior probability of the weight vectors given the training data (Zhang *et al.*, 2010; Bogaerts, 2009; Suzuki *et al.*, 2010; Qian *et al.*, 2011). Kulak (2009) applied a HMC method to simulate fluorescence anisotropy. This Monte Carlo technique applies the gradient of the error that is calculated by applying the back-propagation method (Ghoufi and Maurin, 2010; Aleksandrov *et al.*, 2010;

Rei *et al.*, 2010). The use of the gradient method ensures that the simulation samples throughout the regions of higher probabilities and thus increases the time it takes to converge on a stationary probability distribution function. We view this technique as a type of a Markov chain with transition between states achieved by alternating the 'stochastic' and 'dynamic moves'. The 'stochastic' moves allow the procedure to explore states with different total energy while we attain the 'dynamic' moves by applying the Hamiltonian dynamics and permitting the procedure to explore states with the total energy approximately constant. We view the HMC method as a combination of Monte Carlo sampling procedure, which we guide by the gradient of the probability distribution function at each state.

Using the HMC method, we analyse a dynamic system by introducing an auxiliary variable, known as the momentum, $p \in R^d$. We treat the weight vector, $\mathbf{w}$, as displacement with the Hamiltonian dynamics context. Thus, Duane *et al.* (1987) defined the total energy (or Hamiltonian function) of the dynamic system as (Marwala *et al.*, 2017):

$$H(\mathbf{w}, \mathbf{p}) = V(\mathbf{w}) + W(\mathbf{p}), \tag{5.5}$$

where $V(\mathbf{w})$ represents the potential energy, which can be defined by $V(\mathbf{w}|\mathbf{D}) = -\ln(p(\mathbf{w}|\mathbf{D}))$, where $p(\mathbf{w}|\mathbf{D})$ is the posterior probability density (or distribution) function, while $W(\mathbf{p})$ is the kinetic energy and is given by $W(\mathbf{p}) = \mathbf{p}^{\mathsf{T}} \mathbf{M}^{-1} \mathbf{p}/2$ which depends only on $\mathbf{p}$ and a selected positive definite matrix $\mathbf{M} \in R^{d \times d}$. The partial derivative of the Hamiltonian function, which determines the variation of the pair $(\mathbf{w}, \mathbf{p})$ over time is given by (Duane *et al.* (1987) and Boulkaibet *et al.* (2017)):

$$\frac{d\mathbf{w}}{dt} = \frac{\partial H}{\partial \mathbf{p}} = \mathbf{M}^{-1}\mathbf{p}(t), \tag{5.6}$$

$$\frac{d\mathbf{p}}{dt} = \frac{\partial H}{\partial \mathbf{w}} = -\nabla V(\mathbf{w}(t)). \tag{5.7}$$

The HMC has several properties that need to be satisfied to construct the Markov Chain and these are (Duane *et al.*, 1987; Neal, 1993; Boulkaibet *et al.*, 2014):

1. Time reversibility: It is invariant under $\mathbf{w}' = \mathbf{w}$, $\mathbf{p}' = \mathbf{p}$ and $t' = t$. This shows that the Hamiltonian dynamics is invariant to the direction of time.
2. Conservation of energy: The $H(\mathbf{w}, \mathbf{p})$ is the same at all times.
3. Conservation of state space volumes due to Liouville's theorem (Rossberg, 1983; Goldstein, 1980; Arnold, 1989).

In this chapter, we implement the Molecular Dynamic (MD) simulations under the conditions of the canonical ensemble. The density function $P(\mathbf{w}|\mathbf{D})$ of the canonical ensemble follows a Boltzmann distribution (Boulkaibet *et al.*, 2014). This is a good illustration of the distribution of the Hamiltonian system, where a positive feature of this ensemble is that the position $\mathbf{w}$ and momentum $\mathbf{p}$ are independent for separable Hamiltonian functions (Skeel and Tupper, 2005). We write the joint distribution function derived from the Hamiltonian function as (Boulkaibet, 2015):

$$P(\mathbf{w}, \mathbf{p}) \propto \exp(-\beta_B H(\mathbf{w}, \mathbf{p})), \tag{5.8}$$

where $\beta_B = \frac{1}{K_B T}$, $K_B$ is the Boltzmann constant, and $T$ is a constant temperature. Sampling $\mathbf{w}$ from the posterior distribution can also be obtained by sampling the pair $(\mathbf{x}, \mathbf{p})$ from the joint distribution $P(\mathbf{w}|\mathbf{D})$, where $\mathbf{w}$ and $\mathbf{p}$ are independent using $H(\mathbf{w}, \mathbf{p})$, which is a separable Hamiltonian function. The evolution of $(\mathbf{w}, \mathbf{p})$ through time $t$ can be achieved, numerically, by using the leapfrog scheme (Cheung and Beck, 2009; Boulkaibet *et al.*, 2014):

$$\mathbf{p}\left(t + \frac{\delta t}{2}\right) = \mathbf{p}(\tau) - \frac{\delta t}{2}\nabla V(\mathbf{x}(t)), \tag{5.9}$$

$$\mathbf{w}(t + \delta t) = \mathbf{w}(t) + \delta t \mathbf{M}^{-1}\mathbf{p}\left(t + \frac{\delta t}{2}\right), \tag{5.10}$$

$$\mathbf{p}(t + \delta t) = \mathbf{p}\left(t + \frac{\delta t}{2}\right) - \frac{\delta t}{2}\nabla V(\mathbf{w}(t + \delta t)), \tag{5.11}$$

where $\delta t$ is the time step and the gradient $\nabla V$ is achieved numerically using the finite difference approach (Boulkaibet, 2015). Here, $\Delta = [\Delta_1, \Delta_2, \ldots, \Delta_N]$ is the perturbation vector. Practically, the leapfrog algorithm does not preserve the property of Equations (5.6) and (5.7), where the probability density function is proportional to $\exp(-\beta_B H(\mathbf{w}, \mathbf{p}))$. To satisfy the property of Equations (5.6) and (5.7), we add the Monte Carlo accept-reject step. In such a case, after each iteration of Equations (5.9)–(5.11), the resulting candidate state is accepted or rejected according to the Metropolis criterion based on the value of the Hamiltonian $H(\mathbf{w}, \mathbf{p})$ (Metropolis *et al.*, 1953). Thus, if the pair $(\mathbf{w}, \mathbf{p})$ is the initial state and $(\mathbf{w}^*, \mathbf{p}^*)$ is the state after Equations (5.9) to (5.11) have been updated, then the new candidate $(\mathbf{w}^*, \mathbf{p}^*)$ is accepted with probability of $\min(1, \exp(-\beta_B \Delta H))$, where $\Delta H = H(\mathbf{w}^*, \mathbf{p}^*) - H(\mathbf{w}, \mathbf{p})$. The vector $\mathbf{w}^*$ obtained is then used for the next iteration. The number of $\mathbf{w}$ samples $(N_S)$ is the criterion to stop this algorithm. The summary of the HMC algorithm is as follows (Boulkaibet, 2015):

1. Initialize the algorithm by specifying $\mathbf{w}_0$.
2. Initialize $\mathbf{p}_0$ in such a way that $\mathbf{p}_0 \sim N(0, \mathbf{M})$.
3. Initialize the leapfrog algorithm with $(\mathbf{w}, \mathbf{p})$ and run the algorithm for $L$ time steps to obtain $(\mathbf{w}^*, \mathbf{p}^*)$.
4. Update the model and then compute $H(\mathbf{w}^*, \mathbf{p}^*)$.
5. Accept $(\mathbf{w}^*, \mathbf{p}^*)$ with probability $\min(1, \exp(-\beta_B \Delta H))$.
6. Repeat steps (3–5) for $N_S$ samples.

## 5.4 Shadow Hybrid Monte Carlo (SHMC) Method

The SHMC technique is a generalization of the HMC where the central notion is to apply a modified Hamiltonian estimate $\widetilde{H}(\mathbf{w}, \mathbf{p})$ to sample from the extended phase-space of the shadow Hamiltonian rather than sampling from the configuration space alone (Boulkaibet, 2015; Escribano *et al.*, 2014). Fernández-Pendás *et al.* (2014) successfully applied a generalized shadow hybrid Monte Carlo (SHMC) for simulation of MDs. A generalized SHMC method was to simulate complex biological processes. Clark *et al.* (2011) proposed a HMC method, which had integrators that conserve some Hamiltonian whereas Sweet *et al.* (2009) proposed a separable shadow Hamiltonian hybrid Monte Carlo method that efficiently generates momenta. The SHMC method solves the problem of the decrease of the acceptance rate of the HMC technique when the system size $d$ and/or time step $\delta t$ is relatively large. This is because the SHMC technique expands the HMC time step. The formulation of the SHMC method requires the introduction of a constant parameter $c$ as well as the function $\widetilde{P}(\mathbf{w}, \mathbf{p})$, which is a target density function for the SHMC, where the following relationship can be written as follows (Boulkaibet, 2015; Boulkaibet *et al.*, 2017):

$$\widetilde{P}(\mathbf{w}, \mathbf{p}) \propto \exp(-\beta_B \widetilde{H}(\mathbf{w}, \mathbf{p})). \tag{5.12}$$

Here,

$$\widetilde{H}(\mathbf{w}, \mathbf{p}) = \max(H(\mathbf{w}, \mathbf{p}), \mathbf{H}_{[2k]}(\mathbf{w}, \mathbf{p}) - \mathbf{c}). \tag{5.13}$$

$\widetilde{H}(\mathbf{w}, \mathbf{p})$ is an accurate estimate of the shadow Hamiltonian and the constant $\mathbf{c}$ permits $H_{[2k]}(\mathbf{w}, \mathbf{p})$ to differ from $H(\mathbf{w}, \mathbf{p})$ because $H_{[2k]}(\mathbf{w}, \mathbf{p})$ can have a significant separation from the original Hamiltonian $H(\mathbf{w}, \mathbf{p})$.

On implementing the SHMC algorithm, we generate a new set of momentum $\mathbf{p}$ from a Gaussian $N(0, \mathbf{M})$ probability distribution function. Nevertheless, we accept or reject this momentum vector using the Metropolis algorithm, which is a non-separable Hamiltonian function. We solve the complexity of drawing new momenta from the non-separable Hamiltonian function by using the von Neumann technique (von Neumann, 1951; Fishman, 2000). We implement this technique by allowing for a complicated target distribution $f(z)$ from where the samples are sampled. The Metropolis algorithm generates a random number with a probability distribution function $f(z)$ and then we divide the probability distribution function as follows: $f(z) = Cg(z)h(z)$, where $h(z)$ is a simple probability distribution function, $C$ is a constant and $0 \leq g(z) \leq 1$. Thereafter, we generate a random variable $Z$ with a probability distribution function of $h(z)$ and then generate a uniform random number $U$ from $(0, 1)$. As a final point, if $U \leq g(z)$, then $Z$ has the probability distribution function of $f(z)$ or else we repeat the process and in the case of $f(z) = \widetilde{P}(\mathbf{w}, \mathbf{p})$ then (Boulkaibet, 2015; Boulkaibet *et al.*, 2017):

$$\widetilde{P}(\mathbf{w}, \mathbf{p}) = \exp(-\beta_B \max(H(\mathbf{w}, \mathbf{p}), H_{[2k]}(\mathbf{w}, \mathbf{p}) - c))$$
$$= \exp(-\beta_B H(\mathbf{w}, \mathbf{p})) \min(1, \exp\{-\beta_B (H_{[2k]}(\mathbf{w}, \mathbf{p}) - c - H(\mathbf{w}, \mathbf{p}))\}).$$
$$(5.14)$$

We can rewrite Equation (5.14) as follows (Boulkaibet, 2015; Boulkaibet *et al.*, 2017):

$$\widetilde{P}(\mathbf{w}, \mathbf{p}) = \exp(-\beta_B V(\mathbf{w})) \exp(-\beta_B W(\mathbf{p}))$$
$$\times \min\left(1, \exp\left\{-\beta_B \left(\frac{H_{[2k]}(\mathbf{w}, \mathbf{p}) \cdots}{-c - H(\mathbf{w}, \mathbf{p})}\right)\right\}\right). \quad (5.15)$$

For the case where $C = \exp(-\beta_B V(\mathbf{w}))$, $h(\mathbf{p}) = \exp(-\beta_B W(\mathbf{p}))$ and $g(\mathbf{p}) = \min(1, \exp\{-\beta_B (H_{[2k]}(\mathbf{w}, \mathbf{p}) - c - H(\mathbf{w}, \mathbf{p}))\})$, then we generate the vector $\mathbf{p}$ from the Gaussian distribution $h(\mathbf{p})$ and then we accept or reject the sample using the following criterion:

$$\min(1, \exp\{-\beta_B (H_{[2k]}(\mathbf{w}, \mathbf{p}) - c - H(\mathbf{w}, \mathbf{p}))\}). \quad (5.16)$$

We repeat the acceptance criterion until we accept a new momentum vector. Selecting the correct parameter $c$ can improve the efficiency of this technique by decreasing the number of efforts essential to produce the new momentum vector. We then assemble the system using a MD procedure. We summarize the SHMC algorithm as follows (Boulkaibet *et al.*, 2014; Izaguirre and Hampton, 2004):

1. Set initial value $\mathbf{w_0}$.
2. Repeat for $N_S$ samples.

Monte Carlo (MC) step (Li *et al.*, 2015; Nakano, 2015; Zhang and You, 2015):

(a) Produce $\mathbf{p}$ such that $\mathbf{p} \sim N(0, \boldsymbol{M})$,
(b) Accept with probability $\min(1, \exp\{-\beta_B(H_{[2k]}(\mathbf{w}, \mathbf{p}) - c - H(\mathbf{w}, \mathbf{p}))\})$,
(c) Repeat until a new $\mathbf{p}$ is accepted.

MD step (Xie *et al.*, 2015; Li *et al.*, 2015; Abe and Tasaki, 2015):

(a) Initialize the extended leapfrog algorithm with $(\mathbf{w}, \mathbf{p})$ and run the algorithm for $L$ time steps to obtain $(\mathbf{w}^*, \mathbf{p}^*)$.
(b) Compute $\widetilde{H}(\mathbf{w}^*, \mathbf{p}^*)$.
(c) Accept $(\mathbf{w}^*, \mathbf{p}^*)$ with probability $\min(1, \exp\{-\beta_B \Delta \widetilde{H}\})$.

The MC and MD steps depend on the parameter $c$ and this parameter has a significant effect on the simulation. When $c$ is positively large, the SHMC algorithm is equivalent to the HMC algorithm with different momentum. This decreases the MD step acceptance rate in the case where $\delta t$ and/or system size are large or else, the MC step acceptance rate increases. A large negative $c$ value increases the acceptance rate of the MD step and decreases the acceptance rate of the MC step for the case where $\delta t$ and/or system size are large. We can modify the algorithm so that we choose the value of $c$ to be proportional to the average difference between the Hamiltonian and the shadow Hamiltonian. We perform this as follows (Boulkaibet, 2015; Boulkaibet *et al.*, 2017):

1. Implement the SHMC between 50 and 100 iterations and save $\Delta H = H_{[2k]}(\mathbf{w}^*, \mathbf{p}^*) - H(\mathbf{w}, \mathbf{p})$ in a vector for all iterations.
2. Calculate the expected value $\overline{\Delta H}$ and standard deviation $\sigma_{\Delta H}$ for the obtained vector.
3. Select $c$ using the following formula: $c = \overline{\Delta H} - 1.2 \times \sigma_{\Delta H}^2$.

Lastly, in order to compute the balanced values of the mean, we reweigh the results using the formula $P(\mathbf{w}, \mathbf{p})/\widetilde{P}(\mathbf{w}, \mathbf{p})$ before estimating the averages. We obtain the average of an observable, $B$, by (Boulkaibet, 2015;

Boulkaibet *et al.*, 2017):

$$\langle B \rangle = \frac{\sum_{i=1}^{Ns} B \cdot a_i}{\sum_{i=1}^{Ns} a_i}, \quad \text{where } a_i = \frac{\exp(-\beta_B H(\mathbf{w}, \mathbf{p}))}{\exp(-\beta_B \widetilde{H}(\mathbf{w}, \mathbf{p}))}. \tag{5.17}$$

The weighted vector parameter $\widetilde{\boldsymbol{w}}$ is explained by the mean value of the estimated parameter which is given by (Boulkaibet, 2015; Boulkaibet *et al.*, 2017):

$$\widehat{\widetilde{\boldsymbol{w}}} = E(\widetilde{\boldsymbol{w}}) \cong \frac{1}{N_s} \sum_{i=1}^{N_s} \widetilde{\boldsymbol{w}}^i, \tag{5.18}$$

where $\widetilde{\boldsymbol{w}} = \frac{\boldsymbol{w} \cdot a_i}{\sum_{i=1}^{Ns} a_i}$ and the mean value can be calculated as follows (Boulkaibet, 2015; Boulkaibet *et al.*, 2017):

$$\widehat{\widetilde{\boldsymbol{w}}} \cong \frac{1}{N_s} \sum_{i=1}^{N_s} \frac{a_i}{\sum_{j=1}^{Ns} a_j} \widetilde{\boldsymbol{w}}^i = \frac{1}{\sum_{j=1}^{Ns} a_j} \frac{1}{N_s} \sum_{i=1}^{N_s} a_i \boldsymbol{w}^i = \frac{1}{\sum_{j=1}^{Ns} a_j} E(\boldsymbol{w} \cdot \boldsymbol{a}^T). \tag{5.19}$$

By tracing the same thinking, the variance of the weighted estimated parameter is (Boulkaibet, 2015; Boulkaibet *et al.*, 2017):

$$V(\widetilde{\boldsymbol{w}}) = E((\widetilde{\boldsymbol{w}} - \widehat{\widetilde{\boldsymbol{w}}})^2) \cong V(\boldsymbol{w}) \frac{\sum_{i=1}^{Ns} a_i^2}{(\sum_{j=1}^{Ns} a_j^2)}, \tag{5.20}$$

where $V(\boldsymbol{w})$ is the un-weighted variance and the standard deviation (the error) is given by $\sigma_{\widetilde{\boldsymbol{w}}} = \sqrt{V(\widetilde{\boldsymbol{w}})}$.

On studying the Hamiltonian systems, the consequence of the discretization error can be understood by investigating the 'modified equations' of this system (Skeel and Hardy, 2001; Engle *et al.*, 2005; Boulkaibet *et al.*, 2017). These equations are exactly reproducible by using the approximate discrete solution and we represent them by an asymptotic expansion in powers of the discretization parameter (Creutz, 1988; Kennedy and Pendleton, 1991; Hairer *et al.*, 2006). The modified integrator is Hamiltonian if and only if $\partial_y \boldsymbol{\varphi}(\boldsymbol{y})^T J \partial_y \boldsymbol{\varphi}(\boldsymbol{y}) \equiv J$, where $\boldsymbol{y} = \boldsymbol{\varphi}(\boldsymbol{y})$ is a numerical integrator, $J = \begin{bmatrix} 0 & I \\ -I & 0 \end{bmatrix}$, and $I$ is an identity matrix (Skeel and Hardy, 2001), and this property is known as symplectic. The numerical solution of a symplectic integrator remains approximately equal to the solution of a modified Hamiltonian for an extended amount of time (Skeel and Hardy, 2001). The leapfrog integrator is symplectic and, therefore, we express its modified differential equation as Hamiltonian, and the modified Hamiltonian of this integrator is as follows (Skeel and Hardy, 2001; Boulkaibet, 2015; Boulkaibet *et al.*, 2017):

$$H^{\delta t} = H + \delta t^2 \left( \frac{1}{12}\{W, \{W, V\}\} - \frac{1}{24}\{V, \{V, W\}\} \right)$$

$$+ \delta t^4 \Big( \frac{7}{5760}\{V, \{V, \{V, \{V, W\}\}\}\} - \frac{1}{720}\{W, \{W, \{W, \{W, V\}\}\}\}$$

$$+ \frac{1}{360}\{V, \{W, \{W, \{W, V\}\}\}\} + \frac{1}{360}\{W, \{V, \{V, \{V, W\}\}\}\}$$

$$- \frac{1}{480}\{V, \{V, \{W, \{W, V\}\}\}\} + \frac{1}{120}\{W, \{W, \{V, \{V, W\}\}\}\} \Big) + \cdots .$$

$$(5.21)$$

Here, the expression $\{A, B\} = \nabla_\theta A \nabla_p B - \nabla_p A \nabla_\theta B$ indicates the Poisson bracket of two functions and depends on $\mathbf{w}$ and $\mathbf{p}$. We achieve this formula from the symmetric Baker–Campbell–Hausdorff formula and demonstrate how to calculate a modified Hamiltonian using a splitting technique with the objective being to calculate (Hausdorff, 1906; Hairer *et al.*, 2006; Skeel and Hardy, 2001; Boulkaibet, 2015; Boulkaibet *et al.*, 2017):

$$H_{[2k]} = H^{\delta t}(\mathbf{w}, \mathbf{p}) + \mathrm{o}(\delta \mathbf{t^{2k}}). \qquad (5.22)$$

Here, $H_{[2k]}(\mathbf{w}, \mathbf{p})$ is a shadow Hamiltonian of the order $2k$ and this structure augments a new position variable and a conjugate momentum variable $\beta(t)$ to attain a modified Hamiltonian $\overline{H}(\boldsymbol{y}) = \frac{1}{2}\dot{\boldsymbol{y}}^T \boldsymbol{J} \boldsymbol{y}^T$, and here, $y = [\mathbf{w}^T, \alpha, \mathbf{p}^T, \beta]^T$ and $\alpha = 1$. This modified Hamiltonian is homogeneous of order 2, and, $\boldsymbol{y}$ using a numerical solution of the modified Hamiltonian system and the resulting solution satisfies Equation (5.22) (Skeel and Hardy, 2001). The expression for the 4th and 8th shadow Hamiltonians, $k = 2$ and $k = 4$, respectively, are given as (Boulkaibet, 2015; Boulkaibet *et al.*, 2017):

$$H_{[4]}(\mathbf{w}, \mathbf{p}) = \mathbf{A_{10}} - \frac{1}{6}\mathbf{A_{12}}, \qquad (5.23)$$

$$H_{[8]}(\mathbf{w}, \mathbf{p}) = \mathbf{A_{10}} - \frac{2}{7}\mathbf{A_{12}} - \frac{19}{210}\mathbf{A_{14}} + \frac{5}{42}\mathbf{A_{32}} - \frac{1}{140}\mathbf{A_{34}}. \qquad (5.24)$$

Here, the $\mathbf{A_{ij}}$ are defined as (Boulkaibet, 2015; Boulkaibet *et al.*, 2017):

$$\mathbf{A_{ij}} = \{\mu\delta^i \mathbf{w}\delta^j \mathbf{p} - \delta^j \mathbf{w}\delta^i \mathbf{p} - \mu\delta^i \beta : \quad j = 0$$

$$\mathbf{A_{ij}} = \{\mu\delta^i \mathbf{w}\delta^j \mathbf{p} - \delta^j \mathbf{w}\mu\delta^i \mathbf{p} : \quad j \neq 0.$$

$$(5.25)$$

In Equation (5.25), $\delta\mathbf{w}$ indicates the central difference of vector $\mathbf{w}$ described by $\mathbf{w} = \mathbf{w}^{\frac{1}{2}} - \mathbf{w}^{-\frac{1}{2}}$, and the averaging operator $\mu\mathbf{w}$ is likewise described by $\mu\mathbf{w} = \frac{1}{2}\left(\mathbf{w}^{\frac{1}{2}} + \mathbf{w}^{-\frac{1}{2}}\right)$, and it should be noted that $\mathbf{w}^{\frac{1}{2}} = w\left(t + \frac{\delta t}{2}\right)$ and $\mathbf{w}^{-\frac{1}{2}} = w\left(t - \frac{\delta t}{2}\right)$. To assess the leapfrog algorithm, we implement Equations (5.18)–(5.20), and compute the term $\beta(t+1)$ from $\beta(t)$ as follows (Boulkaibet, 2015; Boulkaibet *et al.*, 2017):

$$\beta(t + 1) = \beta(t) + \delta t \cdot (\mathbf{w}(t) \cdot \nabla V(\mathbf{w}(t)) - 2V(\mathbf{w}(t)). \tag{5.26}$$

## 5.5 Separable Shadow Hybrid Monte Carlo

The Separable Shadow Hybrid Monte Carlo (S2HMC) algorithm is a modified form of the HMC and SHMC algorithms where a separable shadow Hamiltonian function is used to create samples (Sweet *et al.*, 2009; Boulkaibet *et al.*, 2014; Boulkaibet, 2015; Marwala *et al.*, 2017). A shadow Hamiltonian function signifies an accurate estimate of the Hamiltonian function, which can be more conserved than the original Hamiltonian function when large time steps are used for evolving a leapfrog integrator. Nonetheless, the use of the shadow Hamiltonian function might obfuscate the sampling process of the momentum vector. The S2HMC improves the sampling efficiency by sampling from a Separable Shadow Hamiltonian function by altering the configuration space. These transformations eradicate the utilization of additional parameters such as the constant $c$, in the SHMC algorithm and circumvent the difficulty of using an augmented integrator. Additionally, the process of sampling a new momentum vector is the same as in the HMC algorithm and these enhancements speed up the convergence of averages calculated and the transformations used advance the acceptance rate with a relatively insignificant further computational cost (Sweet *et al.*, 2009; Boulkaibet *et al.*, 2014, 2015, 2017; Boulkaibet, 2015).

The S2HMC algorithm uses the leapfrog integrator to increase the order of accuracy of the sampling technique and this is achieved by altering the configuration space by introducing the *pre-processing* and *post-processing* steps (Sweet *et al.*, 2009; Boulkaibet *et al.*, 2014, 2015, 2017; Boulkaibet, 2015). The modified Hamiltonian function applied in this procedure is conserved to $O(\delta t^4)$ by the treated technique, instead of merely $O(\delta t^2)$ by the untreated technique. Analogous to the SHMC procedure, the S2HMC procedure also necessitates a reweighting step to deal with the alteration of the potential energy. The shadow Hamiltonian function applied in the S2HMC is separable and is in the fourth order (Sweet *et al.*, 2009; Boulkaibet *et al.*, 2014, 2015, 2017; Boulkaibet, 2015):

$$\tilde{H}(\mathbf{w}, \mathbf{p}) = \frac{1}{2}\mathbf{p}^{\mathbf{T}}\mathbf{M}^{-1}\mathbf{p} + V(\mathbf{w}) + \frac{\delta t^2}{24}V_{\mathbf{w}}^{T}\mathbf{M}^{-1}V_{\mathbf{w}} + O(\delta t^4), \qquad (5.27)$$

where $V_{\mathbf{w}}$ is the derivative of the potential energy $V$ with respect to $\mathbf{w}$. The joint distribution derived from the separable Shadow Hamiltonian function can be expressed as $\tilde{P}(\mathbf{w}, \mathbf{p}) \propto \exp(-\beta_B \tilde{H}(\#, \mathbf{p}))$, while the separable shadow Hamiltonian function is derived by using the backward error analysis to the numerical integrator (Blanes *et al.*, 2004). The pre-processing step is expressed as follows (Sweet *et al.*, 2009; Boulkaibet *et al.*, 2014, 2015, 2017; Boulkaibet, 2015):

$$\hat{\mathbf{p}} = \mathbf{p} - \frac{\delta t}{24}(V_{\mathbf{w}}(\mathbf{w} + \delta t\mathbf{M}^{-1}\hat{\mathbf{p}}) - V_{\mathbf{w}}(\mathbf{w} - \delta t\mathbf{M}^{-1}\hat{\mathbf{p}})), \qquad (5.28)$$

$$\hat{\mathbf{w}} = \mathbf{w} + \frac{\delta t^2}{24}\mathbf{M}^{-1}(V_{\mathbf{w}}(\mathbf{w} + \delta t\mathbf{M}^{-1}\hat{\mathbf{p}}) + V_{\mathbf{w}}(\mathbf{w} - \delta t\mathbf{M}^{-1}\hat{\mathbf{p}})). \qquad (5.29)$$

Equations (5.28) and (5.29) necessitate an iterative solution for $\hat{\mathbf{p}}$ and a direct calculation for $\hat{\mathbf{w}}$. We write the post-processing step as follows (Sweet *et al.*, 2009; Boulkaibet *et al.*, 2014, 2015, 2017; Boulkaibet, 2015):

$$\mathbf{w} = \hat{\mathbf{w}} - \frac{\delta t^2}{24}\mathbf{M}^{-1}(V_{\mathbf{w}}(\mathbf{w} + \delta t\mathbf{M}^{-1}\hat{\mathbf{p}}) + V_{\mathbf{w}}(\mathbf{w} - \delta t\mathbf{M}^{-1}\hat{\mathbf{p}})), \qquad (5.30)$$

$$\mathbf{p} = \hat{\mathbf{p}} + \frac{\delta t}{24}(V_{\mathbf{w}}(\mathbf{w} + \delta t\mathbf{M}^{-1}\hat{\mathbf{p}}) - V_{\mathbf{w}}(\mathbf{w} - \delta t\mathbf{M}^{-1}\hat{\mathbf{p}})). \qquad (5.31)$$

Equations (5.30) and (5.31) necessitate an iterative solution for $\mathbf{w}$ and direct calculation for $\mathbf{p}$. To compute balanced values of the mean, the results require to be reweighted and the average of an observable $A$ is written as follows (Sweet *et al.*, 2009; Boulkaibet *et al.*, 2014, 2015, 2017; Boulkaibet, 2015):

$$\langle A \rangle = \frac{\sum_{i=1}^{Ns} B \cdot a_i}{\sum_{i=1}^{Ns} a_i}, \quad \text{where } a_i = \frac{\exp(-\beta_B H(\mathbf{w}, \mathbf{p}))}{\exp(-\beta_B \tilde{H}(\mathbf{w}, \mathbf{p}))}. \qquad (5.32)$$

We can summarize the S2HMC procedure as follows (Sweet *et al.*, 2009; Boulkaibet *et al.*, 2014, 2015, 2017; Boulkaibet, 2015):

1. Initiate $\mathbf{w}_0$.
2. Initiate $\mathbf{p}_0$ so that $\mathbf{p}_0 \sim N(0, \mathbf{M})$.
3. Calculate the initial shadow energy $\tilde{H}(\mathbf{w}, \mathbf{p})$ using Equation (5.27).
4. Pre-processing step: Beginning with $(\mathbf{w}, \mathbf{p})$, calculate iteratively $\hat{\mathbf{p}}$ and directly estimate $\hat{\mathbf{w}}$ using Equations (5.28) and (5.29).

5. Start the leapfrog algorithm with $(\widehat{\mathbf{w}}, \widehat{\mathbf{p}})$ and run for $L$ time steps to attain $(\widehat{\mathbf{w}}^*, \widehat{\mathbf{p}}^*)$.

6. Post-processing step: Beginning with $(\widehat{\mathbf{w}}^*, \widehat{\mathbf{p}}^*)$, calculate iteratively $\mathbf{w}^*$ and directly estimate $\mathbf{p}^*$ using Equations (5.28) and (5.29).

7. Update the model and then compute $H(\mathbf{w}^*, \mathbf{p}^*)$.

8. Accept $(\mathbf{w}^*, \mathbf{p}^*)$ with probability $\min(1, \exp\{-\beta_B \Delta\widetilde{H}\})$.

9. Repeat steps (3)–(8) to obtain $N_s$ samples.

10. Calculate the weight by using Equation (5.32) to calculate the averages of the quantity $\mathbf{A}(\mathbf{w})$.

The idea of the constructed processed integrator is to alter the phase space i.e. pre-processing of the pair $(\mathbf{w}, \mathbf{p})$ where the propagation is conducted in a different space and by using another integrator which has a non-separable shadow Hamiltonian. The inverse of the pre-processing step, which is also called the post-processor step, is evaluated when the output is required and thus the momentum sampling way, compared to the SHMC method, is simplified and an accurate and faster simulation is assured (Blanes *et al.*, 2004; Sweet *et al.*, 2009; Boulkaibet *et al.*, 2015; Boulkaibet, 2015) Changes can be made to improve the S2HMC technique such as sampling the momentum vector by avoiding the dependency between their components when the momentum is drawn. The best approach to handle the dependencies between components, which are unavoidable, is by applying an ordered over-relaxation technique to minimize the random walk in the momentum sampling process. The finite difference estimation is employed to calculate the gradient $V_{\mathbf{w}}$ and this gradient is based on forward and backward Taylor series expansion of the function. Nevertheless, in the situation where the dimension of the uncertain parameters is high, the forward/backward difference estimation could be more practical since it necessitates $d$ which is the dimension of the uncertain parameters evaluation of $V(\mathbf{w})$ to calculate the gradient, while the central difference approximation necessitates $2d$, and the forward difference approximation gradient, which is given by $\frac{\partial V}{\partial E_i} = \frac{V(\mathbf{w}+\Delta h)-V(\mathbf{w})}{h\Delta_i}$. As a final point, in order to compute balanced values of the mean, the results must be reweighted, and this is achieved using $P(\mathbf{w}, \mathbf{p})/\widetilde{P}(\mathbf{w}, \mathbf{p})$ before evaluating the averages.

## 5.6 Comparison of Sampling Methods

The comparison between the HMC, SHMC and S2HMC are shown in Table 5.1.

**Table 5.1**    The Momentum, MD and re-weighting steps for HMC, SHMC and S2HMC algorithms.

| Methods | Sampling New Momentums (MC) Step | The MD Step | Re-weighting Step |
|---|---|---|---|
| HMC | Given **w**, generate $\boldsymbol{p}$ such that $\boldsymbol{p} \sim N(0, \boldsymbol{M})$ | Accept $(\mathbf{w}^*, \mathbf{p}^*)$ with probability $\min(1, \exp\{-\beta_B \Delta H\})$ | — |
| SHMC | Given **w**, generate $\boldsymbol{p}$ such that $\boldsymbol{p} \sim N(0, \boldsymbol{M})$ Accept with probability: $(1, \exp\{-\beta_B(H_{[2k]}(\mathbf{w}, \mathbf{p}) - c - H(\mathbf{w}, \mathbf{p}))\}),$ | Accept $(\mathbf{w}'', \mathbf{p}'')$ with probability $\min(1, \exp\{-\beta_B \Delta \widetilde{H}\})$ where $\widetilde{H} = H_{[2k]}(\mathbf{w}, \boldsymbol{p}) - c$ | The observable $B$ is giving by: $\langle B \rangle = \dfrac{\sum_{i=1}^{Ns} B \cdot a_i}{\sum_{i=1}^{Ns} a_i},$ where $a_i = \dfrac{\exp(-\beta_B H(\mathbf{w}, \mathbf{p}))}{\exp(-\beta_B \widetilde{H}(\mathbf{w}, \mathbf{p}))}$ |
| S2HMC | Given **w**, generate $\boldsymbol{p}$ such that $\boldsymbol{p} \sim N(0, \boldsymbol{M})$ Then solve: $\widehat{\mathbf{p}} = \mathbf{p} - \dfrac{\delta t}{24} \times (V_\mathbf{w}(\mathbf{w} + \delta t \mathbf{M}^{-1} \widehat{\mathbf{p}}) - V_\theta(\mathbf{w} - \delta t \mathbf{M}^{-1} \widehat{\mathbf{p}}))$ | Accept $(\mathbf{w}^*, \mathbf{p}^*)$ with probability $\min(1, \exp\{-\beta_B \Delta \widetilde{H}\})$ | The observable $B$ is giving by: $\langle B \rangle = \dfrac{\sum_{i=1}^{Ns} B \cdot a_i}{\sum_{i=1}^{Ns} a_i},$ where $a_i = \dfrac{\exp(-\beta_B H(\mathbf{w}, \mathbf{p}))}{\exp(-\beta_B \widetilde{H}(\mathbf{w}, \mathbf{p}))}$ |

## 5.7   Interstate Conflict

We implemented the HMC, SHMC and S2HMC to classify interstate conflict as Marwala and Lagazio (2011) did, and the results are in Table 5.2. The selection of the data to be used for training and the variables used were described in Chapter 2. We applied the confusion matrix to analyse the classification results of the three Bayesian methods. The confusion matrix contains information about actual and predicted classifications given by a classification system. These results demonstrate that the S2HMC gave the best results, followed by the SHMC and then the HMC. The sensitivity of the results, which is the proportion of the positive results classified correctly, also called the hit rate is 73.0% when we used the HMC, 73.4% when we used the SHMC and 74.4% when we used the S2HMC. The specificity or the true negative rate was 74.0% for all three sampling methods.

**Table 5.2**   Classification results.

| Method | True Conflicts (TC) | False Peace (FP) | True Peace (TP) | False Conflicts (FC) |
|---|---|---|---|---|
| HMC | 286 | 106 | 290 | 102 |
| SHMC | 288 | 104 | 290 | 102 |
| S2HMC | 292 | 100 | 290 | 102 |

## 5.8 Conclusions

This chapter described the Bayesian approach to neural networks. Then we described various methods for estimating the posterior probability function using IIMC, SHMC and S2HMC. We then applied the Bayesian network to classification of interstate conflict. The S2HMC performed the best followed by the SHMC, then followed by the HMC.

## References

Abe, Y., Tasaki, S. (2015). Molecular dynamics analysis of incoherent neutron scattering from light water via the Van Hove Space–time self-correlation function with a new quantum correction. *Annals of Nuclear Energy*, 83:302–310.

Aleksandrov, T., Desgranges, C., Delhommelle, J. (2010). Vapor-liquid equilibria of copper using hybrid monte carlo wang-landau simulations. *Fluid Phase Equilibria*, 287:79–83.

Arnold, V.I. (1989). *Mathematical Methods of Classical Mechanics*, 2nd Edition. London: Springer.

Bishop, C.M. (1995). *Neural Networks for Pattern Recognition*. London: Oxford.

Blanes, S., Casas, S., Murua, A. (2004). On the numerical integration of ordinary differential equations by processed methods. *SIAM Journal of Numerical Analysis*, 42:531–552.

Bogaerts, A. (2009). Effects of oxygen addition to argon glow discharges: A hybrid monte carlo-fluid modeling investigation. *Spectrochimira Acta Part B: Atomic Spectroscopy*, 64:1266–79.

Boulkaibet, I. (2015). Finite Element Model Updating using Markov Chain Monte Carlo Techniques. PhD Thesis, University of Johannesburg.

Boulkaibet, I., Mthembu, L., Marwala, T., Friswell, M.I., Adhikari, S. (2014). Finite element model updating using the separable shadow hybrid Monte Carlo technique. In: *Topics in Modal Analysis II*, 8:267–275. Cham: Springer.

Boulkaibet, I., Mthembu, L., Marwala, T., Friswell, M.I., Adhikari, S. (2015). Finite element model updating using the shadow hybrid Monte Carlo technique. *Mechanical Systems and Signal Processing*, 52:115–132.

Boulkaibet, I., Mthembu, L., Marwala, T., Friswell, M.I., Adhikari, S. (2017). Finite element model updating using Hamiltonian Monte Carlo techniques. *Inverse Problems in Science and Engineering*, 25(7):1042–1070.

Cheung, S.H., Beck, J.L. (2009). Bayesian model updating using hybrid Monte Carlo simulation with application to structural dynamic models with many uncertain parameters. *Journal of Engineering Mechanics*, 135:243–255.

Clark, M.A., Joó, B., Kennedy, A.D., Silva, P.J. (2011). Improving dynamical lattice QCD simulations through integrator tuning using Poisson brackets and a force-gradient integrator. *Physical Review D*, 84: art. no. 071502.

Creutz, M. (1988). Global Monte Carlo algorithms for many-fermion systems. *Physics Review D*, 38:1228–1238.

Duane, S., Kennedy, A.D., Pendleton, B.J., Roweth, D. (1987). Hybrid Monte Carlo. *Physics Letters B*, 195:216–222.

Engle, R.D., Skeel, R.D., Drees, M. (2005). Monitoring energy drift with shadow hamiltonians. *Journal of Computational Physics*, 206:432–452.

Escribano, B., Akhmatskaya, E., Reich, S., Azpiroz, J.M. (2014). Multiple-time-stepping generalized hybrid Monte Carlo methods. *Journal of Computational Physics*, 280:1–20.

Fernández-Pendás, M., Escribano, B., Radivojević, T., Akhmatskaya, E. (2014). Constant pressure hybrid Monte Carlo simulations in GROMACS. *Journal of Molecular Modeling*, 20, doi: 10.1007/s00894-014-2487-y.

Fishman, G.S. (2000). *Monte Carlo: Concepts, Algorithms, and Applications*. Springer Series in Operations Research, New York: Springer-Verlag.

Gelman, A., Carlin, J.B., Stern, H.S., Rubin, D.B. (1995). *Bayesian Data Analysis*. London: Chapman and Hall

Ghoufi, A., Maurin, G. (2010). Hybrid Monte Carlo simulations combined with a phase mixture model to predict the structural transitions of a porous metal-organic framework material upon adsorption of guest molecules. *Journal of Physical Chemistry C*, 114:6496–6502.

Goldstein, H. (1980). *Classical Mechanics*. Reading: Addison Wesley.

Hairer, E., Lubich, C., Wanner, G. (2006). *Geometric Numerical Integration, Structure-Preserving Algorithms for Ordinary Differential Equations*. Berlin: Springer-Verlag.

Hausdorff, F. (1906). Die Symbolische Exponential formel in der Gruppentheorie. *Ber Verh Saechs Akad Wiss Leipzig*, 58:19–48.

Izaguirre, J.A., Hampton, S.S. (2004). Shadow hybrid Monte Carlo: An efficient propagator in phase space of macromolecules. *Journal of Computational Physics*, 200: 581–604.

Kandela, B., Sheorey, U., Banerjee, A., Bellare, J. (2010). Study of tablet-coating parameters for a pan coater through video imaging and Monte Carlo simulation. *Powder Technology*, 204:103–112.

Kennedy, A.D., Pendleton, B. (1991). Acceptances and autocorrelations in hybrid Monte Carlo. *Nuclear Physics B Proceedings Supplements*, 20:118–121.

Kulak, L. (2009). Hybrid Monte-Carlo simulations of fluorescence anisotropy decay in three-component donor-mediator-acceptor systems in the presence of energy transfer. *Chemical Physics Letters*, 467:435–438.

Li, H.-J., Yi, H.-B., Xu, J.-J. (2015). High-order Cu(II) Chloro-complexes in LiCl Brines: Insights from density function theory and molecular dynamics. *Geochimica et Cosmochimica Acta*, 165:1–13.

Liesenfeld, R., Richard, J. (2008). Improving MCMC, using efficient importance sampling. *Computational Statistics and Data Analysis*, 53:272–288.

MacKay, D.J.C. (1991). Bayesian Methods for Adaptive Models. PhD Thesis, California Institute of Technology.

MacKay, D.J.C. (1992). A practical Bayesian framework for back propagation networks. *Neural Computation*, 4:448–472.

Marwala, T. (2001). Fault Identification Using Neural Networks and Vibration Data. PhD Thesis, University of Cambridge.

Marwala, T. (2007a). Bayesian training of neural network using genetic programming. *Pattern Recognition Letters*, doi: org/10.1016/j.patrec.2007.034.

Marwala, T. (2007b). *Computational Intelligence for Modelling Complex Systems*. Delhi: Research India Publications.

Marwala, T. (2009). *Computational Intelligence for Missing Data Imputation, Estimation and Management: Knowledge Optimization Techniques*. New York: IGI Global Publications.

Marwala, T. (2010). *Finite Element Model Updating Using Computational Intelligence Techniques*. London, UK: Springer.

Marwala, T. (2012). *Condition Monitoring Using Computational Intelligence Methods*. Heidelberg: Springer.

Marwala, T. (2013). *Economic Modeling Using Artificial Intelligence Methods*. Heidelberg: Springer.

Marwala, T. (2014). *Artificial Intelligence Techniques for Rational Decision Making*. Heidelberg: Springer.

Marwala, T. (2015). *Causality, Correlation, and Artificial Intelligence for Rational Decision Making*. Singapore: World Scientific.

Marwala, T., Hurwitz, E. (2017). *Artificial Intelligence and Economic Theory: Skynet in the Market*. Springer.

Marwala, T., Lagazio, M. (2011). *Militarized Conflict Modeling Using Computational Intelligence*. Heidelberg: Springer. Translated into Chinese by the National Defence Industry Press.

Marwala, T., Boulkaibet, I., Adhikari, S. (2017). *Probabilistic Finite Element Model Updating Using Bayesian Statistics: Applications to Aeronautical and Mechanical Engineering*. John Wiley & Sons.

Metropolis, N., Rosenbluth, A., Rosenbluth, M., Teller, A., Teller, E. (1953). Equation of state calculations by fast computing machines. *The Journal of Chemical Physics*, 21:1087–1092.

Naderi, B., Zandieh, M., Khaleghi, A., Balagh, G., Roshanaei, V. (2009). An improved simulated annealing for hybrid flowshops with sequence-dependent setup and transportation times to minimize total completion time and total tardiness. *Expert Systems with Applications*, 36:9625–9633.

Nakano, Y. (2015). Quasi-Monte Carlo methods for Choquet integrals. *Journal of Computational & Applied Mathematics*, 287: art. no. 10081.

Neal, R.M. (1993). *Probabilistic Inference Using Markov Chain Monte Carlo Methods*. Toronto, Canada: University of Toronto Technical Report CRG-TR-93-1.

Ozgan, E., Saruhan, H. (2010). Modeling of asphalt concrete via simulated annealing. *Advances in Engineering Software*, 41:680–683.

Paydar, M.M., Mahdavi, I., Sharafuddin, I., Solimanpur, M. (2010). Applying simulated annealing for designing cellular manufacturing systems using MDmTSP. *Computers and Industrial Engineering*, 59:929–936.

Qian, G., Li, N., Huggins, R. (2011). Using capture-recapture data and hybrid Monte Carlo sampling to estimate an animal population affected by an environmental catastrophe. *Computational Statistics and Data Analysis*, 55:655–666.

Rei, W., Gendreau, M., Soriano, P. (2010). A hybrid Monte Carlo local branching algorithm for the single vehicle routing problem with stochastic demands. *Transport Science*, 44:136–146.

Rossberg, K. (1983). *A First Course in Analytical Mechanics*. New York: Wiley.

Skeel, R.D., Hardy, D.J. (2001). Practical construction of modified Hamiltonians. *SIAM Journal on Scientific Computing*, 23(4):1172–1188.

Skeel, R.D., Tupper, P.F. (2005). *Mathematical Issues in Molecular Dynamics*. Banff International Research Station Reports.

Sweet, C.R., Hampton, S.S., Skeel, R.D., Izaguirre, J.A. (2009). A separable shadow Hamiltonian hybrid Monte Carlo method. *Journal of Chemical Physics*, 131: art. no. 174106.

Suzuki, K., Tachikawa, M., Shiga, M. (2010). Efficient *ab initio* path integral hybrid Monte Carlo based on the fourth-order trotter expansion: Application to fluoride ion-water cluster. *Journal of Chemical Physics*, 132: art. no. 144108.

Torabzadeh, E., Zandieh, M. (2010). Cloud theory-based simulated annealing approach for scheduling in the two-stage assembly flowshop. *Advances in Engineering Software*, 41:1238–1243.

Von Neumann, J. (1951). Various techniques used in connection with random digits. *Applied Mathematics Series*, 12:96–98.

Xie, Z.-C., Gao, T.-H., Guo, X.-T., Xie, Q. (2015). Molecular dynamics simulation of nanocrystal formation and deformation behavior of Ti3Al alloy. *Computational Materials Science*, 98:245–251.

Zhang, L., Bartel, T., Lusk, M.T. (2010). Parallelized hybrid Monte Carlo simulation of stress-induced texture evolution. *Computational Materials Science*, 48:419–425.

Zhang, W., You, C. (2015). Numerical approach to predict particle breakage in dense flows by coupling multiphase particle-in-cell and Monte Carlo methods. *Powder Technology*, 283:128–136.

Chapter 6

# Support Vector Machines

**Abstract.** This chapter describes support vector machines (SVMs). In particular, it describes the SVMs for both classification and regression problems. We applied the support vector machine to classify interstate conflict and to model a steam generator. The results obtained demonstrated that SVMs are a good machine-learning tool.

## 6.1 Introduction

This chapter is on support vector machines (SVMs). SVMs are based on the statistical learning theory and were first proposed by Vapnik (1995b). SVMs work by establishing the linear hyperplane between different classes of data. If the data cannot be linearly separated, SVMs project the data into high dimensions until the data can be linearly separated (Gunn, 1997; Chang et al., 2007; Chuang, 2008; Üstün et al., 2005, 2007; Shen et al., 2017).

Shen et al. (2005) successfully used the SVMs in data visualization, and Marwala et al. (2006) used SVMs to classify mechanical faults. Msiza et al. (2007) successfully used the SVMs to forecast water demand, whereas Chen et al. (2011) used the SVMs to estimate monthly solar radiation and found them to perform better than neural networks on predicting solar radiation. Yeh et al. (2011) Applied SVMs for recognition of counterfeit banknotes, whereas Burgos-Artizzu et al. (2009) used SVMs and images for weed identification. Lin et al. (2011) used the SVMs to predict business failure based on previous financial data, whereas Li-Xia, et al. (2011) used the SVMs and particle swarm optimization for tax forecasting. Pires and Marwala (2004) applied SVMs for option pricing, while Gidudu et al. (2007) applied SVMs in image classification. Zhang et al. (2006) used SVMs for the online health monitoring of large-scale structures, whereas Thissen et al. (2004) used SVMs for spectral regression. Xi et al. (2007) used SVMs for predictive control of a plant. To improve the computational efficiency of the SVMs, Guo and Zhang (2007) developed methods for accelerating SVMs.

Furthermore, applications of SVMs include predicting jet penetration depth (Wang *et al.*, 2010), identifying tool wear (Tao and Tao, 2010), predicting ozone concentration (Ortiz-García *et al.*, 2010) and recognizing people (Palanivel and Yegnanarayana, 2008). Other applications include chemical compound analysis (Zhou *et al.*, 2006) and modelling response (Kim *et al.*, 2008). Recent applications include estimating reliability of dams (Amin Hariri-Ardebili and Pourkamali-Anaraki, 2018), classification of cast iron (Gajalakshmi *et al.*, 2018), predicting Chinese bank notes efficiency (Chen *et al.*, 2018) and detection of myocardial infarction (Dohare *et al.*, 2018).

## 6.2  Support Vector Machines for Classification

SVMs are supervised learning methods used mainly for classification and regression. Vapnik (1995a, 1998) first introduced the statistical learning theory-based SVMs. On formulating SVMs, we conceptualize a data point as a $p$-dimensional vector. The objective of SVMs is to separate such points with a $(p - 1)$-dimensional hyperplane known as a linear classifier. Researchers have developed numerous hyperplanes, and one of these include the one that exhibits the largest separation, also named as *margin*, between the two classes. We can then choose the selected hyperplane to maximize the distance from it to the nearest data point on both sides. We call this the *maximum-margin hyperplane*. We can frame the classification problem as an approximation function $f : R^N \rightarrow \{-1, 1\}$ dependent on input–output training data, which we produce from an independently and identically distributed unknown probability distribution $P(\mathbf{x}, y)$ in such a way that $f$ is able to classify unseen $(\mathbf{x}, y)$ data (Müller *et al.*, 2001; Habtemariam, 2006). The preferred function minimizes the expected error (risk), and we write it as follows (Habtemariam, 2006; Habtemariam *et al.*, 2005; Marwala, 2011, 2014; Marwala *et al.*, 2017):

$$R[f] = \int l(f(\mathbf{x}), y) dP(\mathbf{x}, y), \tag{6.1}$$

where $l$ indicates a loss function (Müller *et al.*, 2001). Because we do not know the fundamental probability distribution $P$, we cannot solve Equation (6.1) implicitly. The best course of action is to identify an upper bound for the risk function, which we write mathematically as follows (Vapnik, 1995a;

Müller *et al.*, 2001; Marwala, 2009, 2012; Marwala and Lagazio, 2011):

$$R[f] = R[f]_{\text{emp}} + \sqrt{\frac{h\left(\ln\frac{2n}{h} + 1\right) - \ln\left(\frac{\delta}{4}\right)}{n}}, \qquad (6.2)$$

where $h \in \mathbb{N}^+$ is the Vapnik–Chervonenkis (VC) dimension of $f \in F$ and $\delta > 0$. We define the VC dimension of a function class $F$ as the biggest number of $h$ coordinates that are divisible in all possible ways by means of functions of that class (Vapnik, 1995b). The empirical error $R[f]_{\text{emp}}$ is a training error given by (Habtemariam, 2006; Marwala and Lagazio, 2011):

$$R[f]_{\text{emp}} = \frac{1}{n} \sum_{i+1}^{n} l(f(\mathbf{x}_i), y_i). \qquad (6.3)$$

Assuming that the training sample is linearly separable by a hyperplane of the form (Habtemariam, 2006; Marwala and Lagazio, 2011):

$$f(x) = \langle \mathbf{w}, \mathbf{x} \rangle + b \quad \text{with } \mathbf{w} \in \chi, \ \mathbf{b} \in \Re, \qquad (6.4)$$

where $\langle \cdot, \cdot \rangle$ denotes the dot product, $\mathbf{w}$ is an adjustable weight vector and $b$ is an offset. We show this classification problem in Figure 6.1 (Müller *et al.*, 2001; Marwala, 2009). According to Vapnik and Lerner (1963), the objective of the learning process is to discover the hyperplane with maximum margin of separation from the class of dividing hyperplanes. We cannot always divide data linearly because of complexity and nonlinearities. SVMs discover a linear separating hyperplane by initially mapping the input space into a higher-dimensional feature space $\mathscr{F}$. This suggests that each training example $x_i$ be substituted by $\Phi(x_i)$ to give (Habtemariam, 2006;

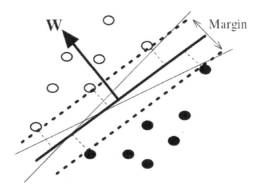

**Figure 6.1**   A linear SVM classifier.

Marwala, 2009):

$$Y_i((\mathbf{w}.\Phi(\mathbf{x}_i) + b), \quad i = 1, 2, \ldots, n. \tag{6.5}$$

The VC dimension, $h$, in the feature space $\mathscr{F}$ is constrained subject to $h \leq \|W\|^2 R^2 + 1$, where $R$ is the radius of the smallest sphere around the training data (Müller *et al.*, 2001; Habtemariam, 2006; Marwala, 2009). Therefore, we can frame minimizing the expected risk as an optimization problem as follows (Burges, 1998; Müller *et al.*, 2001; Schölkopf and Smola, 2003; Marwala, 2015):

$$\text{Minimize}(\mathbf{w}, \mathbf{b}) \frac{1}{2} \|\mathbf{w}\|^2, \tag{6.6}$$

subject to

$$c_i(\{\boldsymbol{w}\}, \{\boldsymbol{x}\}_i - b) \geq 1, \quad i = 1, \ldots, n. \tag{6.7}$$

We call Equations (6.6) and (6.7) the *quadratic programming problem* because it is the problem of optimizing a quadratic function of several variables subject to linear constraints on these variables (Schölkopf and Smola, 2003). From the expressions

$$\|\mathbf{w}\|^2 = \mathbf{w} \cdot \mathbf{w}, \tag{6.8}$$

and

$$\mathbf{w} = \sum_{i=0}^{n} \alpha_i c_i \mathbf{x}_i. \tag{6.9}$$

We can demonstrate that it will be possible to write the duality of the SVMs, by maximizing $\alpha_i$, in the Lagrangian form as follows (Schölkopf and Smola, 2003; Marwala, 2009):

$$L(\alpha) = \sum_{i=1}^{n} \alpha_i - \frac{1}{2} \sum_{i,j} \alpha_i \alpha_j c_i c_j \mathbf{x}_i^T \mathbf{x}_j$$

$$= \sum_{i=1}^{n} \alpha_i - \frac{1}{2} \sum_{i,j} \alpha_i \alpha_j c_i c_j k(\mathbf{x}_i, \mathbf{x}_j), \quad i = 1, \ldots, n, \tag{6.10}$$

subject to

$$\alpha_i \geq 0, \quad i = 1, \ldots, n, \tag{6.11}$$

and to the constraint from the minimization of $\mathbf{b}$:

$$\alpha_i \geq 0, \quad i = 1, \ldots, n, \tag{6.12}$$

and subject to the following constraint:

$$\sum_{i=1}^{n} \alpha_i c_i = 0. \tag{6.13}$$

Here, the kernel is (Müller *et al.*, 2001):

$$k(\mathbf{x}_i, \mathbf{x}_j) = \mathbf{x}_i \cdot \mathbf{x}_j. \tag{6.14}$$

(A) *Soft margin*

Cortes and Vapnik (1995) proposed an improved maximum margin notion that accounts for mislabelled data points. If there is no hyperplane that can exactly divide the 'yes' and 'no' data points, the *Soft margin* technique selects a hyperplane that divides the data points as efficiently as possible but still maximizing the distance to the nearest neatly divided data points. The technique proposes slack variables, $\gamma_i$ which quantify the degree of misclassification of the data point as follows (Cortes and Vapnik, 1995; Marwala, 2009; Parikh and Shah, 2016; Dias and Neto, 2017):

$$c_i(\{\mathbf{w}\} \cdot \{\mathbf{x}\}_i - b) \geq 1 - \gamma_i, \quad 1 \leq i \leq n. \tag{6.15}$$

A function, which penalizes non-zero $\gamma_i$ augments the objective and, therefore, the optimization exhibits a compromise between a large margin and a small error penalty. If a linear penalty function is assumed, then we can write the optimization problem by minimizing $\mathbf{w}$ and $\gamma_i$ through the following function (Cortes and Vapnik, 1995; Marwala, 2009):

$$\frac{1}{2}\|\mathbf{w}\|^2 + C\sum_{i=1}^{n} \gamma_i, \tag{6.16}$$

subject to

$$c_i(\mathbf{w} \cdot \mathbf{x}_i - b) \geq 1 - \gamma_i, \gamma_i \geq 0, \quad i = 1, \ldots, n. \tag{6.17}$$

In Equation (6.16), $C$ is the capacity. We can write Equations (6.16) and (6.17) in the Lagrangian form by optimizing the following equation in terms of $\mathbf{w}$, $\gamma$, $b$, $\alpha$ and $\beta$ as follows (Cortes and Vapnik, 1995; Marwala, 2009):

$$\min_{\mathbf{w},\gamma,b} \max_{\alpha,\beta}$$
$$\left\{ \frac{1}{2}\|\mathbf{w}\|^2 + C\sum_{i=1}^{n} \gamma_i - \sum_{i=1}^{n} \alpha_i[c_i(\mathbf{w} \cdot \mathbf{x}_i - b) - 1 + \gamma_i] - \sum_{i=1}^{n} \beta_i \gamma_i \right\}, \tag{6.18}$$

where $\alpha_i, \beta_i \geq 0$. The main benefit of a linear penalty function is that we automatically remove the slack variables from the dual problem. Therefore,

$C$ only appears as a supplementary constraint on the Lagrange multipliers. The use of nonlinear penalty functions to lessen the impact of outliers makes the optimization problem non-convex and difficult to identify a global solution.

## (B) *Nonlinear classification*

To use the linear SVM procedure to produce nonlinear classifiers, we use the kernel trick to the maximum-margin hyperplanes (Aizerman *et al.*, 1964; Boser *et al.*, 1992; Marwala and Lagazio, 2011). In this technique, the dot product is replaced by a nonlinear kernel function to fit the maximum-margin hyperplane in a transformed feature space. While this dot product transformation may be nonlinear, the transformed space may be in high dimensions. For example, when a Gaussian radial basis function kernel is used, the resultant feature space is a Hilbert space of infinite dimension. Some useful kernel functions include (Vapnik, 1995a; Müller *et al.*, 2001; Zhang and Lin, 2018; Ma and Liu, 2018):

1. The Radial Basis Function:

$$k(\mathbf{x}_i, \mathbf{x}_j) = \exp(-\gamma \|\mathbf{x}_i - \mathbf{x}_j\|^2), \quad \gamma > 0. \tag{6.19}$$

2. The Polynomial (Homogeneous):

$$k(\mathbf{x}_i, \mathbf{x}_j) = (\mathbf{x}_i \cdot \mathbf{x}_j)^d. \tag{6.20}$$

3. The Polynomial (Inhomogeneous):

$$k(\mathbf{x}_i, \mathbf{x}_j) = (\mathbf{x}_i \cdot \mathbf{x}_j + 1)^d. \tag{6.21}$$

4. The Hyperbolic Tangent:

$$k(\mathbf{x}_i, \mathbf{x}_j) = \tan h(\varepsilon \mathbf{x}_i \cdot \mathbf{x}_j + b), \quad \varepsilon > 0; \ b < 0. \tag{6.22}$$

We identify the variables of the maximum-margin hyperplane by optimizing the objective equation. We do this by using an interior point method that identifies a solution for the Karush–Kuhn–Tucker (KKT) conditions of the primal and dual problems (Kuhn and Tucker, 1951; Karush, 1939). To circumvent solving a linear system, including the large kernel matrix, we apply a low rank estimate to the matrix to implement the kernel trick. The KKT conditions are necessary for optimizing a nonlinear programming problem, for the satisfaction of a particular regularity condition (Kuhn and

Tucker, 1951; Karush, 1939; Marwala, 2012; Lee and Yen, 2014; Clempner, 2016; Cortez and Pinto, 2017):

$$\text{Minimize: } f(x), \tag{6.23}$$

subject to

$$g_i(\mathbf{x}) \leq 0; \quad h_j(\mathbf{x}) = 0. \tag{6.24}$$

Here, $g_i$ is the $i$th inequality constraint and $h_i$ is the $i$th equality constraint. The KKT technique permits the inequality constraints by generalizing the technique of Lagrange multipliers, which permits only equality constraints. The necessary conditions for the KKT are (Marwala, 2012; Lee and Yen, 2014; Clempner, 2016; Cortez and Pinto, 2017):

Stationary:

$$\nabla f(\mathbf{x}^*) + \sum_{i=1}^{m} \mu_i \nabla g_i(\{\mathbf{x}^*\}) + \sum_{j=1}^{l} \lambda_j \nabla h_j(\{\mathbf{x}^*\}) = 0,$$

$$i = 1, \ldots, m; \quad j = 1, \ldots, l. \tag{6.25}$$

Primal and dual feasibility as well as complementary slackness:

$$\begin{aligned}
g_i(\mathbf{x}^*) &\leq 0, & i &= 1, \ldots, m, \\
h_j(\mathbf{x}^*) &= 0, & j &= 1, \ldots, l, \\
\mu_i &\geq 0, & i &= 1, \ldots, m, \\
\mu_i g_i(\mathbf{x}^*) &= 0, & i &= 1, \ldots, m.
\end{aligned} \tag{6.26}$$

Researchers view the KKT technique as a generalized version of the Lagrangian approach by setting $m = 0$. In certain circumstances, the necessary conditions are also sufficient for optimization. However, in many situations, the necessary conditions are not sufficient for optimization and further information, such as the second derivative, is necessary. The necessary conditions are sufficient for optimization if the objective function $f$ and the inequality constraints $g_j$ are continuously differentiable convex functions, and the equality constraints $g_j$ have constant gradients.

## 6.3 Support Vector Regression

SVMs have been extended to regression, thus resulting in the term support vector regression (SVR) (Gunn, 1997: Melki *et al.*, 2017; Tsirikoglou *et al.*, 2017; Li *et al.*, 2018). SVR has been successfully used as an analytical model (Soares and Anzanello, 2017) and for global sensitivity analysis (Cheng *et al.*, 2017). The basic idea behind SVR is to map the input space to an output space. Suppose we have the training dataset with one input and one output being considered $\{(x_1, y_1), \ldots, (x_i, y_i)\} \subset \chi \times \Re$, where $\chi$ is the space of the input parameters and $\Re$ denotes the real number set. We desire to find a function $f(x)$ that will map the training inputs to the training outputs. In SVR we intend to find this function that has at most $\varepsilon$ deviation from the actual training targets $y_l$. We can fit several kinds of functions $f(x)$ to map training inputs to training outputs. We call these functions kernel functions. These cannot just be any function because kernel functions must adhere to some criteria (Joachims, 1999). We include slack variables $\xi_i$, $\xi_i^*$ in the optimization problem so that certain infeasible constraints in the minimization of the Euclidean norm can be used and the minimization problem then becomes (Xie *et al.*, 2007; Marwala, 2009):

$$\min \frac{1}{2} \|\mathbf{w}\|^2 + C \sum_{i=1}^{l} (\xi_i + \xi_i^*), \qquad (6.27)$$

subject to

$$\begin{cases} y_i - \langle \mathbf{w}, \mathbf{x}_i \rangle - b \leq \varepsilon + \xi_i, \\ \langle \mathbf{w}, \mathbf{x}_i \rangle + b - y_i \leq \varepsilon + \xi_i^*, \\ \xi_i, \xi_i^* \geq 0, \end{cases} \qquad (6.28)$$

where $l$ is the number of training points used. The constraints above deal with an $\varepsilon$-insensitive loss function used to penalize certain training points that are outside of the bound given by $\varepsilon$, which is a value chosen by the user. There are various other loss functions such as the Huber loss function, which we use, but the most common one is the $\varepsilon$-insensitive loss function, which we write as (Gunn, 2008):

$$|\xi|_\varepsilon = \begin{cases} 0 & \text{if } |\xi| \leq \varepsilon \\ |\xi| - \varepsilon & \text{otherwise.} \end{cases} \qquad (6.29)$$

The value for $C$ is the degree to which deviations from $\varepsilon$ are tolerated (Trafalis and Ince, 2000). We can view this as a measure of over-fitting a function too well to its training points. If the value of $C$ is set too high, then the function found ($f(x)$) will be too well fitted to the training data and will not predict very well on data that is not seen by the training of the function. It means we do not adequately penalize the points lying outside of the bounds given by $\varepsilon$, and this results in the too well fitted function to the training data (Trafalis and Ince, 2000). We can view the illustration fitting of a linear function to the training data in Figure 6.2.

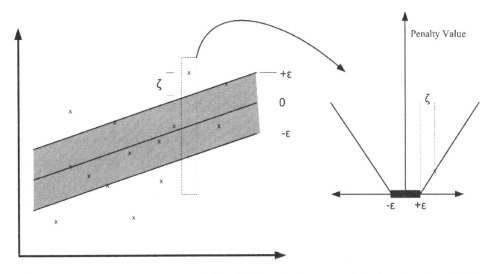

**Figure 6.2** Linear SVR for a set of data (left) and the $\varepsilon$-insensitive loss function (right) (Gunn, 1998).

The optimization problem of Equation (6.27) is then set up to be a quadratic programming problem by first finding the Lagrangian multiplier and applying the KKT conditions (Joachims, 1999). Then, we estimate the values for $\mathbf{w}$ and $b$. In the same way, we can apply a nonlinear model to model the data and using a nonlinear Kernel mapping function to map the data into a high-dimensional feature space where we perform the linear regression. The kernel deals with the issue of the curse of dimensionality and for nonlinear problems we can write the $\varepsilon$-insensitive loss function to give (Gunn, 1998).

$$\max_{\alpha,\alpha^*} W(\alpha, \alpha^*) = \max_{\alpha,\alpha^*} \sum_{i=1}^{l} \alpha^*(y_i - \varepsilon) - \alpha_i(y_i + \varepsilon)$$

$$-\frac{1}{2} \sum_{i=1}^{l} \sum_{j=1}^{l} (\alpha_i^* - \alpha_i)(\alpha_j^* - \alpha_j) K(\mathbf{x}_i, \mathbf{x}_j), \quad (6.30)$$

subject to

$$0 \leq \alpha_i, \alpha_i^* \leq C, \quad i = 1, \ldots, l$$

$$\sum_{i=1}^{l} (\alpha_i - \alpha_i^*) = 0. \quad (6.31)$$

Here, $K$ is the kernel function while $\alpha$ and $\alpha^*$ are Lagrangian multipliers.

Solving Equations (6.30) and (6.31) gives the Lagrangian multipliers, and we write the resulting regression equation as follows (Gunn, 1998; Gaudioso

**Table 6.1**   Comparison of methods.

| Attributes | SVMs | Neural Networks |
|---|---|---|
| General philosophy | • Structural risk minimization<br><br>• Computational complexity does not depend on the size of the input variables<br><br>• Practice derived from theory | • Empirical risk minimization<br><br>• Computational complexity depends on the size of the input variables<br><br>• Theory derived from practice |
| Optimization | Global optimum | Local optimization |
| Generalization | The margin is important for generalization purposes | Weight decay regularization is important to ensure network generalization |
| Model selection | Automatically select the model size by selecting the support vectors | Model is usually selected by using methods such as genetic algorithm or Bayesian formulation |

*et al.*, 2017):

$$f(x) = \sum_{\text{SVs}} (\bar{\alpha}_i - \bar{\alpha}_i^*) K(\mathbf{x}_i, \mathbf{x}) + \bar{b}, \tag{6.32}$$

$$b = -\frac{1}{2} \sum_{i=1}^{l} (\alpha_i - \alpha_i^*)(K(\mathbf{x}_i, \mathbf{x}_r) + K(\mathbf{x}_i, \mathbf{x}_s)). \tag{6.33}$$

We make a comparison between SVMs and neural networks, and this is presented in Table 6.1.

## 6.4 Conflict Modelling

Marwala and Lagazio (2011) modelled international disputes using seven dyadic variables as inputs and conflict status as output. They used the SVM to map the input into a feature space of higher dimensionality by identifying a linear separating hyperplane with a maximum margin of separation between the two classes, which were peace and conflict. There are numerous mapping functions which are called *kernel functions*, and these include linear, polynomial, radial basis functions and sigmoid function. The type of problem at hand determines the selection of a kernel function. As an example, the radial basis function deals better with nonlinear data than the linear kernel functions. Furthermore, the polynomial kernel has several

**Table 6.2** Classification results.

| Method | True Conflicts (TC) | False Peace (FP) | True Peace (TP) | False Conflicts (FC) |
|--------|---------------------|------------------|-----------------|----------------------|
| SVMs | 297 | 95 | 290 | 102 |

hyperparameters, which impact on the complexity of the model and, at times, its values may approach infinity or zero as the point becomes large. The radial basis function is a popular technique to implement as a kernel function for the application of SVMs. We chose the radial basis function kernel because it offered the best results for the classification of interstate conflict. To implement the radial basis function as a kernel function, two parameters are tuned to provide the best result. These parameters were the *penalty parameter* of the error term $C$ and the $\gamma$ *parameter* of the RBF kernel function. Cross-validation and grid-search are two methods that were used to identify an optimal model. The parameters $C = 1$ and $\gamma = 16.75$ gave the best results (Habtemariam, 2006).

Table 6.2 depicts the confusion matrix (i.e. true positives, true negatives, false positives and false negatives) for the results. SVMs predicted true conflict cases (true positives) with a detection rate of 76%. SVM was able to correctly predict peace (true negatives) with a detection rate of 74%. Overall, the SVMs could predict peace and conflict with the prediction rates of 75%.

## 6.5 Steam Generator

Wright and Marwala (2006) applied the SVM regression technique to the steam generator problem. The dataset had 9,600 samples. The cause–effect model contains four causes and one effect. The causes are the input fuel, air, reference level and disturbance defined by the load level. The effect is the steam flow rate. The implementation of the SVM required the selection of two free parameters since a radial basis function was used for the kernel function. Therefore, the optimum values of the two free parameters needed to be determined, and these were the width or bandwidth of the basis function $(\sigma^2)$ and the regularization or penalty parameter $(C)$. An empirical approach was taken to determine the two free parameters. The optimum parameters for the SVM were $\sigma^2$ of 0.1 and C of 10. Figure 6.3 indicates that the SVM

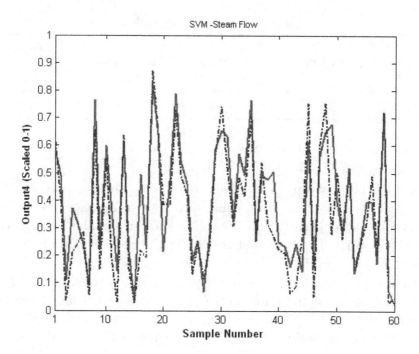

**Figure 6.3**  Showing the predicted vs. actual values for the first 60 points for the test dataset applied to the SVM.

modelled the steam generator input–output relationship well but not as good as MLP.

## 6.6  Conclusions

This chapter described SVMs. It describes the theory of SVMs for both classification and regression problems. We applied the SVM to classify interstate conflicts and to model a steam generator. The results obtained demonstrated that SVMs are a good machine-learning tool.

## References

Aizerman, M., Braverman, E., Rozonoer, L. (1964). Theoretical foundations of the potential function method in pattern recognition learning. *Automation and Remote Control*, 25:821–837.

Amin Hariri-Ardebili, M., Pourkamali-Anaraki, F. (2018). Support vector machine based reliability analysis of concrete dams. *Soil Dynamics and Earthquake Engineering*, 104:276–295.

Boser, B.E., Guyon, I.M., Vapnik, V.N. (1992). A training algorithm for optimal margin classifiers. In: Haussler, D. (ed.), *5th Annual ACM Workshop on COLT*. Pittsburgh: ACM Press.

Burges, C. (1998). A Tutorial on support vector machines for pattern recognition. *Data Mining and Knowledge Discovery*, 2:121–167.

Burgos-Artizzu, X.P., Ribeiro, A., Tellaeche, A., Pajares, G., Fernández-Quintanilla, C. (2009). Improving weed pressure assessment using digital images from an experience-based reasoning approach. *Computers and Electronics in Agriculture*, 65(2):176–185.

Chang, B.R., Tsai, H.F., Young, C.P. (2008). Diversity of quantum optimizations for training adaptive support vector regression and its prediction applications. *Expert Systems with Applications*, 34(4):2612–2621.

Chen, Z., Matousek, R., Wanke, P. (2018). Chinese bank efficiency during the global financial crisis: A combined approach using satisficing DEA and support vector machines. *The North American Journal of Economics and Finance*, 43:71–86.

Chen, J.-L., Liu, H.-B., Wu, W., Xie, D.-T. (2011). Estimation of monthly solar radiation from measured temperatures using support vector machines — A case study. *Renewable Energy*, 36:413–420. 10.1016/j.renene.2010.06.024.

Cheng, K., Lu, Z., Wei, Y., Shi, Y., Zhou, Y. (2017). Mixed kernel function support vector regression for global sensitivity analysis. *Mechanical Systems and Signal Processing*, 96:201–214.

Chuang, C.-C. (2008). Extended support vector interval regression networks for interval input–output data, *Information Sciences*, 178(3):871–891.

Clempner, J.B. (2016). Necessary and sufficient Karush–Kuhn–Tucker conditions for multiobjective Markov chains optimality. *Automatica*, 71.135–142.

Cortes, C., Vapnik, V. (1995). Support-vector networks. *Machine Learning*, 20:273–297.

Cortez, C.A.C., Pinto, J.C. (2017). Improvement of Karush–Kuhn–Tucker conditions under uncertainties using robust decision making indexes. *Applied Mathematical Modelling*, 43:630–646.

Dias, M.L.D., Neto, A.R.R. (2017). Training soft margin support vector machines by simulated annealing: A dual approach. *Expert Systems with Applications*, 87:157–169.

Dohare, A.K., Kumar, V., Kumar, R. (2018). Detection of myocardial infarction in 12 lead ECG using support vector machine. *Applied Soft Computing*, 64:138–147.

Gajalakshmi, K., Palanivel, S., Nalini, N.J., Saravanan, S. (2018). Automatic classification of cast iron grades using support vector machine. *Optik*, 157:724–732.

Gaudioso, M., Gorgone, E., Labbé, M., Rodríguez-Chía, A.M. (2017). Lagrangian relaxation for SVM feature selection. *Computers & Operations Research*, 87:137–145.

Gidudu, A., Hulley, G., Marwala, T. (2007). Image classification using SVMs: One-against-one vs. one-against-all. arXiv:0711.2914.

Gunn, S.R. (1997). Support vector machines for classification and regression. *Technical Report*, Image Speech and Intelligent Systems Research Group, University of Southampton.

Gunn, S.R. (1998). Support vector machines for classification and regression. *ISIS Technical Report*, 14(1):5–16.

Guo, G., Zhang, J.S. (2007). Reducing examples to accelerate support vector regression. *Pattern Recognition Letters*, 28(16):2173–2183.

Habtemariam, E. (2006). Artificial Intelligence for Conflict Management. Master Thesis, University of the Witwatersrand, Johannesburg.

Habtemariam, E., Marwala, T., Lagazio, M. (2005). Artificial intelligence for conflict management. In: *Proceedings of the IEEE International Conference on Neural Networks*, 2583–2588.

Joachims, J. (1999). Making large-scale SVM learning practical, In: B. Scholkopf, C.J.C., Burges and Smola, A.J. (eds.), *Advances in Kernel Methods-Support Vector Learning*. Cambridge, MA, MIT Press, 169–184.

Karush, W. (1939). Minima of Functions of Several Variables with Inequalities as Side Constraints. Master Thesis, University of Chicago.

Kim, D., Lee, H., Cho, S. (2008). Response modeling with support vector regression. *Expert Systems with Applications*, 34:1102–1108.

Kuhn, H.W., Tucker, A.W. (1951). Nonlinear Programming. In: *Proceedings of 2nd Berkeley Symposium*, 481–492.

Lee, G.M., Yen, N.D. (2014). Coderivatives of a Karush–Kuhn–Tucker point set map and applications. *Nonlinear Analysis: Theory, Methods & Applications*, 95:191–201.

Li, S., Fang, H., Liu, X. (2018). Parameter optimization of support vector regression based on sine cosine algorithm. *Expert Systems with Applications*, 91:63–77.

Li-Xia, L., Yi-Qi, Z., Liu, X.Y. (2011). Tax forecasting theory and model based on SVM optimized by PSO. *Expert Systems with Applications*, 38(1):116–120.

Lin, F., Yeh, C.C., Lee, M.Y. (2011). The use of hybrid manifold learning and support vector machines in the prediction of business failure. *Knowledge-Based Systems*, 24(1):95–101.

Ma, X., Liu, Z.-B. (2018). The kernel-based nonlinear multivariate grey model. *Applied Mathematical Modelling*, 56:217–238.

Marwala, T. (2009). *Computational Intelligence for Missing Data Imputation, Estimation, and Management: Knowledge Optimization Techniques*, Information Science Reference Imprint. New York: IGI Global Publications.

Marwala, T. (2012). *Condition Monitoring Using Computational Intelligence Methods*. Heidelberg: Springer.

Marwala, T. (2014). *Artificial Intelligence Techniques for Rational Decision Making*. Heidelberg: Springer.

Marwala, T. (2015). *Causality, Correlation, and Artificial Intelligence for Rational Decision Making*. Singapore: World Scientific.

Marwala, T., Lagazio, M. (2011). *Militarized Conflict Modeling Using Computational Intelligence*. Heidelberg: Springer.

Marwala, T., Boulkaibet, I., Adhikari, S. (2017). *Probabilistic Finite Element Model Updating Using Bayesian Statistics: Applications to Aeronautical and Mechanical Engineering*. John Wiley & Sons.

Marwala, T., Chakraverty, S., Mahola, U. (2006). Fault classification using multi-layer perceptrons and support vector machines. *International Journal of Engineering Simulation*, 7(1):29–35.

Msiza, I., Nelwamondo, F.V., Marwala, T. (2007). Artificial neural networks and support vector machines for water demand time series forecasting. In: *IEEE International Conference on Systems, Man and Cybernetics*, Montreal, Canada, 638–643.

Melki, G., Cano, A., Kecman, V., Ventura, S. (2017). Multi-target support vector regression via correlation regressor chains. *Information Sciences*, 415–416:53–69.

Müller, K.R., Mika, S., Ratsch, G., Tsuda, K., Scholkopf, B. (2001). An Introduction to Kernel-Based Learning Algorithms. In: *IEEE Transactions on Neural Networks*, 12: 181–201.

Ortiz-García, E.G., Salcedo-Sanz, S., Pérez-Bellido, Á.M., Portilla-Figueras, J.A., Prieto, L. (2010). Prediction of hourly O3 concentrations using support vector regression algorithms. *Atmospheric Enviornment*, 44:4481–4488.

Palanivel, S., Yegnanarayana, B. (2008). Multimodal person authentication using speech, face and visual speech [modalities]. *Computer Vision and Image Understanding*, 109:44–55.

Parikh, K.S., Shah, T.P. (2016). Support vector machine — A large margin classifier to diagnose skin illnesses. *Procedia Technology*, 23:369–375.

Pires, M.M., Marwala, T. (2004). Option pricing using neural networks and support vector machines, In: *Proceedings of the IEEE International Conference on Systems, Man and Cybernetics*, The Hague, Netherland, 1279–1285.

Schölkopf, B., Smola, A.J. (2003). *A Short Introduction to Learning with Kernels.* Heidelberg: Springer.

Shen, R., Fu, Y., Lu, H. (2005). A novel image watermarking scheme based on support vector regression, *Journal of Systems and Software*, 78(1):1–8.

Shen, X., Niu, L., Qi, Z., Tian, Y. (2017). Support vector machine classifier with truncated pinball loss. *Pattern Recognition*, 68:199–210.

Soares, F., Anzanello, M.J. (2018). Support vector regression coupled with wavelength selection as a robust analytical method. *Chemometrics and Intelligent Laboratory Systems*, 172:167–173.

Tao, X., Tao, W. (2010). Cutting tool wear identification based on wavelet package and SVM. In: *Proceedings of the World Congress on Intelligent Control and Automation*, 5953–5957.

Thissen, U., Pepers, M., Üstün, B., Melssen, W.J., Buydens, L.M.C. (2004). Comparing support vector machines to PLS for spectral regression applications, *Chemometrics and Intelligent Laboratory Systems*, 73(2):169–179.

Trafalis, T.B., Ince, H. (2000). Support vector machine for regression and applications to financial forecasting In: *IEEE INNS ENNS International Joint Conference on Neural Networks*, Como, Italy.

Tsirikoglou, P., Abraham, S., Contino, F., Lacor, C., Ghorbaniasl, G. (2017). A hyper-parameters selection technique for support vector regression models. *Applied Soft Computing*, 61:139–148.

Üstün, B., Melssen, W.J., Buydens, L.M.C. (2007). Visualisation and interpretation of support vector regression models. *Analytica Chimica Acta*, 595(1–2):299–309.

Üstün, B., Melssen, W.J., Oudenhuijzen, M., Buydens, L.M.C. (2005). Determination of optimal support vector regression parameters by genetic algorithms and simplex optimization. *Analytica Chimica Acta*, 544(1–2):292–305.

Vapnik, V. (1995a). *The Nature of Statistical Learning Theory.* Springer.

Vapnik, V. (1995b). Support-vector networks. *Machine Learning*, 20:273–297.

Vapnik, V. (1998). *Statistical Learning Theory.* New York: Wiley-Interscience.

Vapnik, V., Lerner, A. (1963). Pattern recognition using generalized portrait method. *Automatation and Remote Control*, 24:774–780.

Wang, C.-H., Zhong, Z.-P., Li, R.E.J.-Q. (2010). Prediction of jet penetration depth based on least square support vector machine. *Powder Technology*, 203:404–411.

Wright, S., Marwala, T. (2006). Artificial Intelligence Techniques for Steam Generator Modelling. arXiv: 0811.1711.

Xi, X.-C., Poo, A.-N., Chou, S.-K. (2007). Support vector regression model predictive control on a HVAC plant, *Control Engineering Practice*, 15(8):897–908.

Xie, X., Liu, W.T., Tang, B. (2008). Spacebased estimation of moisture transport in marine atmosphere using support vector regression. *Remote Sensing of Environment*, 112(4):1846–1855.

Yeh, C.-Y., Su, W.-P., Lee, S.-J. (2011). Employing multiple-kernel support vector machines for counterfeit banknote recognition. *Applied Soft Computing*, 11(1): 1439–1447.

Zhang, J., Sato, T., Iai, S. (2006). Support vector regression for on-line health monitoring of large-scale structures. *Structural Safety*, 28(4):392–406.

Zhang, L., Lin, J., Karim, R. (2018). Adaptive kernel density-based anomaly detection for nonlinear systems. *Knowledge-Based Systems*, 139:50–63.

Zhou, Y.-P., Jiang, J.-H., Lin, W.-Q., Zou, H.-Y., Wu, H.-L., Shen, G.-L., Yu, R.-Q. (2006). Boosting support vector regression in QSAR studies of bioactivities of chemical compounds, *European Journal of Pharamatical Sciences*, 28:344–353.

# Chapter 7

# Fuzzy Logic

**Abstract.** This chapter studies the theories and applications of fuzzy logic and neuro-fuzzy systems. It studies the level of transparency of the Takagi–Sugeno (TS) neuro-fuzzy model. Furthermore, it applies these techniques for modelling a steam generator and prediction of interstate conflict. We observe that fuzzy logic can model the steam generator well. Furthermore, we observe that neuro-fuzzy system can model interstate conflict. The neuro-fuzzy system is able to offer some rules that describe the relationships in the data.

## 7.1 Introduction

In this chapter, we discuss the theory and applications of fuzzy logic and a neuro-fuzzy network. We apply fuzzy systems to model interstate disputes and steam generator. We use fuzzy logic primarily because fuzzy systems are better able to give rules that define interrelationships that exist in a dataset than other competing methods such as neural networks and support vector machines, and therefore they are transparent.

Demirli and Khoshnejad (2009) successfully used fuzzy system to design an automated parallel parking system whereas Zhou *et al.* (2010) successfully used the fuzzy inference system (FIS) to analyse carbon capturing. Kurtulus and Razack (2010) successfully used the neuro-fuzzy system to model daily discharge responses of a large karstic aquifer whereas Talei *et al.* (2010) successfully used the neuro-fuzzy systems to model rainfall. Petropoulos *et al.* (2017) successfully used fuzzy logic to classify wine quality whereas Sathishkumar and Parthasarathy (2017) successfully used it to control induction motor drive. Hamamoto *et al.* (2018) successfully used fuzzy logic for network anomaly detection whereas Harrag and Messalti (2018) successfully used fuzzy logic to improve fuel cell, and Theodoridou *et al.* (2017) successfully used fuzzy logic for spatial analysis of groundwater levels.

On creating models for complex real-world systems, we pursue two main approaches, and these are the *White Box* and *Black Box* models. White box models refer to the derivation of an expression describing a system using physical laws, e.g. Newton's law of gravitation or finite element models (Jang *et al.*, 1997; Marwala, 2010; Marwala *et al.*, 2017). Black box models that are more common to machine learning and approximate complex models using equations physically unlinked to the system being modelled (Hagiwara and Mita, 2002; Schölkopf and Smola, 2002; Hurtado, 2003; Mitra *et al.*, 2004; Huang and Kecman, 2005; Tripathi *et al.*, 2006; Nelwamondo *et al.*, 2006; Marwala *et al.*, 2006; Lo, 2008; Marwala, 2009; Marwala and Lagazio, 2011).

Researchers have explored the lack of transparency of artificial intelligence methods such as neural networks and support vector machines on modelling systems (Tettey, 2007; Marwala, 2012). In many applications, a neural network requires the use of inputs, from a given process, for it to estimate at a corresponding output (Marwala, 2013). In certain applications, researchers have used an inverse neural network, where they trained the neural network to provide the inputs to a process, given the outputs (Bishop, 1995; Leke *et al.*, 2007; Marwala, 2014). One major disadvantage that the researchers identified is that the neural network can give output results without offering a chance for one to obtain a causal interpretation of the results (Marwala, 2009; Patel and Marwala, 2006; Marwala, 2015). The lack of transparency of the model limits the confidence of applying machine-learning techniques such as neural networks and support vector machines.

We view neuro-fuzzy models as an alternative that bridges the gap between white box and black box modelling (Haykin, 1999; Patel and Marwala, 2010). This is because neuro-fuzzy models combine available knowledge of a process with data obtained from the process. The advantage of these types of neuro-fuzzy models is that they facilitate the integration of expert knowledge into the modelling process and allow knowledge discovery to happen. The Takagi–Sugeno (TS) neuro-fuzzy model is a universal approximator that researchers use in data-driven identification problems, and researchers classify it as a grey box model (Marwala, 2007; Bih, 2006; Takagi and Sugeno, 1985; Tettey and Marwala, 2006a; Tettey and Marwala, 2006b; Beck *et al.*, 2000; Jones *et al.*, 1996; Tettey, 2007; Habtemariam and Marwala, 2005).

We apply the fuzzy logic approach to model interstate conflict as well as steam generator (Thompson and Tucker, 1997; Mansfield and Snyder, 1997; Oneal and Russet, 1997, 1999; Barbieri, 1996; Beck *et al.*, 1998; Lagazio and Russet, 2004; Marwala and Lagazio, 2004).

## 7.2  Fuzzy Logic Theory

Fuzzy logic is a technique of mapping an input space to an output space by means of a list of linguistic rules that consist of the if-then statements (Bih, 2006; Marwala and Lagazio, 2011). Fuzzy logic has four objects, and these are fuzzy sets, membership functions, fuzzy logic operators and fuzzy rules (Cox, 1994; Von Altrock, 1995; Biacino and Gerla, 2002; Marwala, 2013).

In set theory, an object either is an element or is not an element of a specific set (Devlin, 1993; Ferreirós, 1999; Johnson, 1972). It is, therefore, possible to define if an object belongs to a specific set because a set has distinct boundaries, if an object cannot realize partial membership. An alternative approach of discerning this is that an object's belonging to a set is either true or false. A characteristic function for a classical set has a value of one if the object belongs to the set and a value of zero if the object does not belong to the set (Cantor, 1874). For example, if a set $X$ represents all possible heights of people, one could define a 'tall' subset for any person who is above or equal to a specific height $x$, and anyone below $x$ does not belong to the 'tall' subset but to a 'short' subset. This is clearly intransigent as we label a person just below the boundary as being short when they are obviously tall to some degree. Consequently, we do not allow in-between values such as legitimately tall. In addition, these clear-cut defined boundaries can be very subjective in terms of what a person may define as belonging to a specific set.

The key objective of fuzzy logic is to allow a more flexible representation of sets of objects by using a fuzzy set. A fuzzy set does not have as clear-cut boundaries as a classical set. In fuzzy sets, we characterize objects by a degree of membership to a specific set (Hájek, 1995; Halpern, 2003; Wright and Marwala, 2006; Hájek, 1998). Consequently, we can represent intermediate values of objects in a way that is closer to the way the human brain thinks, as opposed to the clear cut-off boundaries in classical sets.

A membership function defines the degree that an object belongs to a certain set or class. The membership function is a curve that maps the input space variable to a number between zero and one, representing the degree that a specific input variable belongs to a specific set (Klir and Folger, 1988; Klir *et al.*, 1997; Klir and Yuan, 1995). A membership function can be a curve of any shape. Using the example above, there would be two subsets, one for tall and one for short that would overlap. In this way, a person can have a partial participation in each of these sets, therefore, determining the degree to which the person is both tall and short.

We define logical operators to generate new fuzzy sets from the existing fuzzy sets. In classical set theory, there are three key operators used to define logical expressions and these are intersection, union and the complement (Kosko, 1993; Kosko and Isaka, 1993). We use these operators in fuzzy logic and adapt them to deal with partial memberships. We give the minimum operation to the intersection (AND operator) of two fuzzy sets and give the maximum operator the union (OR operator) of two fuzzy sets (Novák, 1989; Novák, 2005; Novák *et al.*, 1999). We use these logical operators in the rules and determination of the final output fuzzy set.

Fuzzy rules formulate the conditional statements, which we use to model the input–output relationships of the system, and we express this in natural language. These linguistic rules are in the form of if-then statements, which use the logical operators and membership functions to produce an output. An important property of fuzzy logic is the use of linguistic variables. Linguistic variables are variables that take words or sentences as their values instead of numbers (Zadeh, 1965; Zemankova-Leech, 1983; Zimmermann, 2001). Each linguistic variable takes a linguistic value that corresponds to a fuzzy set, and we call the set of values that it can take the term set. For example, a linguistic variable, *weight*, could have the following term set {*very fat, fat, medium, thin, very thin*}. A single fuzzy rule is of the form (Marwala and Lagazio, 2011):

$$\text{if } x \text{ is } A \text{ then } y \text{ is } B, \tag{7.1}$$

where $A$ and $B$ are fuzzy sets defined for the input and output space respectively. Both $x$ and $y$ are linguistic variables, while $A$ and $B$ are the linguistic values or labels represented by the membership functions. Each rule consists of two parts: the antecedent and the consequent. The antecedent is the component of the rule falling between the if-then and maps the input $x$ to the fuzzy set $A$, using a membership function. The consequent is the component of the rule after the then and maps the output $y$ to a membership function. The input membership values act like weighting factors to determine their influence on the fuzzy output sets. A fuzzy system consists of a list of these if-then rules that we evaluate in parallel. The antecedent can have more than one linguistic variable, these inputs are combined using the AND operator.

We evaluate each of the rules for an input set and its corresponding output. If an input corresponds to two linguistic variable values, then we evaluate the rules associated with both these values. Additionally, we evaluate the rest of the rules, however, they do not influence the results as the linguistic variable have a value of zero. Therefore, if the antecedent is true to some degree, the consequent is also true to some degree (Zadeh, 1965). We compute the degree of each linguistic output value by performing a combined logical sum for each membership function (Zadeh, 1965) after which we aggregate all the combined sums for a specific linguistic variable. These last stages involve the use of an inference method, which map the result onto an output membership function (Zadeh, 1965).

We perform defuzzification process, where we produce a single numeric output. One method of computing the degree of each linguistic output value is to take the maximum of all rules describing this linguistic output value, and we take the output as the centre of gravity of the area under the effected part of the output membership function. There are other inference methods such as averaging, and sum mean square. Figure 7.1 shows the steps involved in creating an input–output mapping using fuzzy logic.

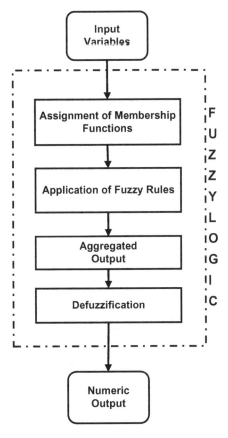

**Figure 7.1**   Showing the steps involved in the application of fuzzy logic to a problem (Wright and Marwala, 2006).

The use of a series of fuzzy rules, and inference methods to produce a defuzzified output constitute a FIS. The final configuration in which the aggregation process takes place and the method of defuzzification can differ depending on the implementation of the chosen FIS. Mamdani (1974) proposed the approach discussed above.

There are several other types of FISs, which vary according to the fuzzy reasoning and the form of the if-then statements applied. One of these methods is the Takagi–Sugeno–Kang neuro-fuzzy method (Takagi and Sugeno, 1985; Araujo, 2008). This technique is like the Mamdani approach described above except that the consequent part is of a different form and, as a result, the defuzzification procedure is different. The if-then statement of a Sugeno fuzzy system expresses the output of each rule as a function of the input variables and has the form (Sugeno and Kang, 1988; Sugeno, 1985):

$$\text{if } x \text{ is } A \text{ and } y \text{ is } B \text{ then } z = \mathrm{f}(x, y). \qquad (7.2)$$

## 7.3 Neuro-fuzzy Models

Neuro-fuzzy denotes the hybridization of neural networks and fuzzy logic (Jang, 1993; Maalej et al., 2017; Ichalal et al., 2018). It creates an intelligent system that combines the human-like reasoning style of fuzzy systems with the learning structure of neural networks. The resulting architecture is a universal approximator with an interpretable if-then rule. The advantage of neuro-fuzzy systems implicates two conflicting characteristics in fuzzy modelling: interpretability vs. accuracy and, in reality, only one of the two characteristics prevails. The neuro-fuzzy in fuzzy modelling research field is divided into two areas. The first is the linguistic fuzzy model which focuses on interpretability and was described in the previous section. For example, the Mamdani model and precise fuzzy modelling focused on accuracy, for example, the TS neuro-fuzzy model and the Takagi–Sugeno–Kang neuro-fuzzy model (Sugeno and Kang, 1988; Sugeno, 1985; Takagi and Sugeno, 1985; Araujo, 2008).

Hsu and Lin (2009) successfully used neuro-fuzzy system with a rein-forcement group cooperation-based symbiotic evolution to solve various control problems whereas Kwong et al. (2009) successfully used a neuro-fuzzy network to model customer satisfaction. Iplikci (2010) suc-cessfully used neuro-fuzzy systems to control nonlinear systems whereas Montazer et al. (2010) successfully used it for Farsi numeral characters recognition. Cetisli (2010) successfully used an adaptive neuro-fuzzy classifier for recognition problems.

Other successful uses of neuro-fuzzy systems include for system identification (Abiyev *et al.*, 2011), for control systems (Cano-Izquierdo *et al.*, 2010), and to predict solubility of gases in polystyrene (Khajeh and Modarress, 2010). Further applications include to predict the performance of impact hammer (Kucuk *et al.*, 2011), to predict tip speed ratio in wind turbines (Ata and Kocyigit, 2010), to model response of sand mixture (Cabalar *et al.*, 2010), to identify flow regimes (El-Sebakhy, 2010), to predict stream flow (Shiri and Kisi, 2010) and to predict capacity of Ferro-cement members (Mashrei *et al.*, 2010). Recent applications of neuro-fuzzy systems include for observer design (Srinivasarengan *et al.*, 2017), to estimate non-measured premises (Maalej *et al.*, 2017), payload estimation and control (Beyhan *et al.*, 2017) and to generalize Lyapunov functions (Gonzalez *et al.*, 2017).

Fuzzy logic is an imprecise model of reasoning, such as common-sense reasoning, for uncertain and complex processes. It resembles human reasoning in its use of approximate information and uncertainty to generate decisions. The FIS maps fuzzy or crisp inputs to the output, which is usually a fuzzy set. This FIS performs a composition of the inputs using fuzzy set theory, fuzzy *if-then* rules and fuzzy reasoning to arrive at the output. More specifically, the fuzzy inference process involves the fuzzification of the input variables, i.e. partitioning of the input data into fuzzy sets, evaluation of rules, aggregation of the rule outputs and, finally, the defuzzification, i.e. extraction of a crisp value which best represents a fuzzy set of the result.

There are two popular fuzzy models, and these are the Mamdani model and the TS neuro-fuzzy model. The TS neuro-fuzzy model is suited for data-driven identification and is a universal approximator (Tettey and Marwala, 2007). The TS neuro-fuzzy model is suited for nonlinear functions arbitrarily given that the number of rules is not limited. We show a diagram of a two-input and single output TS neuro-fuzzy model in Figure 7.2 (Babuska and Verbruggen, 2003).

In the TS neuro-fuzzy model, the antecedent part of the rule is a fuzzy proposition and we show the consequent function as a linear function of the input variables as follows (Takagi and Sugeno, 1985):

$$R_i \colon \text{If } \mathbf{x} \text{ is } A_i \text{ then } y_i = a_i^T \mathbf{x} + b_i, \tag{7.3}$$

where $R_i$ is the $i$th fuzzy rule, $\mathbf{x}$ is the input vector, $A_i$ is a fuzzy set, $a_i$ is the consequence parameter vector, $b_i$ is a scalar offset and $i = 1, 2, \ldots, K$. The parameter $K$ is the number of rules in the fuzzy model. If there are too few

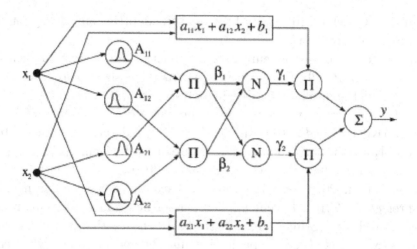

**Figure 7.2**    An example of a two-input first-order TS fuzzy model.

rules in the fuzzy model, it may not be possible to accurately model a process. Too many rules may lead to an overly complex model with redundant fuzzy rules which compromises the integrity of the model (Sentes *et al.*, 1998). We can determine the optimum number of rules using a cross-validation process (Bishop, 1995). We choose the optimum number of rules from the model with the lowest error and standard deviation. The final antecedent values in the model describe the fuzzy regions in the input space in which the consequent functions are valid.

The first step in any inference procedure is the partitioning of the input space to form the antecedents of the fuzzy rules. We choose the shapes of the membership functions of the antecedents to be Gaussian or triangular. We choose the Gaussian membership function of the following form (Zadeh, 1965):

$$\mu^i(x) = \prod_{j=1}^{n} e^{-\frac{(x_j - c_j^i)^2}{(b_j^i)^2}}.$$
$$(7.4)$$

Here, $\mu^i$ is the combined antecedent value for the $i$th rule, $n$ is the number of antecedents belonging to the $i$th rule, $c$ is the centre of the Gaussian function and $b$ describes the variance of the Gaussian membership function.

The consequent function in the TS neuro-fuzzy model can be either constant or linear. We show the linear consequent function as follows

(Babuska and Verbruggen, 2003):

$$y_i = \sum_{j=1}^{n} p_{ij}x_j + p_{i0}, \qquad (7.5)$$

where $p_{ij}$ is the $j$th parameter of the $i$th fuzzy rule. If a constant is used as the consequent function, i.e. $y_i = p_i$, the zero-order TS neuro-fuzzy model becomes a special case of the Mamdani inference system (Mamdani, 1974). We compute the output $y$ of the entire inference system by taking a weighted average of the individual rules' contributions as shown in (Babuska and Verbruggen, 2003):

$$y = \frac{\sum_{i=1}^{K} \beta_i(\mathbf{x})y_i}{\sum_{i=1}^{K} \beta_i(\mathbf{x})}$$

$$= \frac{\sum_{i=1}^{K} \beta_i(\mathbf{x})(a_i^T \mathbf{x} + b_i)}{\sum_{i=1}^{K} \beta_i(\mathbf{x})}, \qquad (7.6)$$

where $\beta_i(\mathbf{x})$ is the activation of the $i$th rule. The $\beta_i(\mathbf{x})$ can be a complex expression but it is equivalent to the degree of fulfilment of the $i$th rule. The parameters $a_i$ are then approximate models of the nonlinear system under consideration (Babuska, 1991).

When setting up a fuzzy rule-based system we are required to optimize parameters such as membership functions and consequent parameters. To optimize these parameters, the fuzzy system relies on training algorithms inherited from artificial neural networks such as gradient descent-based learning. It is for this reason that we refer to these as the neuro-fuzzy models. There are two approaches to training neuro-fuzzy models (Babuska and Verbruggen, 2003):

1. We may extract fuzzy rules from expert knowledge and use these to create an initial model. The parameters of the model can then be fine-tuned using data collected from the operational system being modelled.
2. We determine the number of rules from collected numerical data using a model selection technique. We optimize the parameters of the model using the existing data.

The motivation for using a TS neuro-fuzzy model in this work is that it is suitable for data-driven identification and is considered to be a grey box. Unlike other computational intelligence methods, once optimized, it is possible to extract information which allows one to understand the process being modelled.

## 7.4  Steam Generator

Wright and Marwala (2006) applied the fuzzy systems technique to the steam generator problem. The dataset had 9,600 samples. The cause–effect model contained four causes and one effect. The causes were the input fuel, air, reference level and disturbance defined by the load level. The training process involved modifying the membership function parameters of the FIS to emulate the training dataset to within some error criteria. Wright and Marwala (2006) implemented the Sugeno-type system for the Adaptive Neuro-Fuzzy Inference System (ANFIS). The FIS allows for a training and validation dataset to be used. The idea is that overtraining will be avoided as it is expected that the validation error will decrease as training takes place until a certain point where the validation error begins to increase, indicating overtraining. The learning process is similar to neural networks except that different parameters are being adjusted.

The ANFIS constructs a FIS in which its membership function parameters are adjusted by a training algorithm. In this way, the parameters of the membership functions change through the process of learning. The FIS uses either back-propagation or a hybrid method (least squares and back-propagation) to train.

The FIS had 11 different membership functions available, of which 8 were used with the Adaptive Neuro-Fuzzy System: Triangular function, trapezoidal, 2 different Gaussian functions, bell function, Sigmoidal Difference function (difference of 2 Sigmoidal functions), Sigmoidal product function (product of 2 Sigmoidal functions) and polynomial Pi curves.

In the FIS, the number of input membership functions and the type of membership function used could be modified. The number of membership functions was left at the default of 2 per input, giving 8 input membership functions. Firstly, an FIS structure was initialized which could then be adjusted to model the dataset provided. The generated FIS structure contained 16 fuzzy rules.

The Polynomial Pi membership function produced the most accurate results for modelling. The Gaussian membership function was not appropriate this time as the validation error only increased and did not decrease at all. The results Wright and Marwala (2006) obtained were good and are shown in Table 7.1, and Figure 7.3 shows the Actual vs. Predicted values

**Table 7.1** Showing the results obtained for the simulations done for Output 4 for the ANFIS.

| Output | Polynomial Pi Curve |
|---|---|
| MSE | 0.014330 |
| Training time (s) | 132 |
| Execute time (s) | 0.046 |
| No. of training cycles | 120 |
| No. fuzzy rules | 16 |

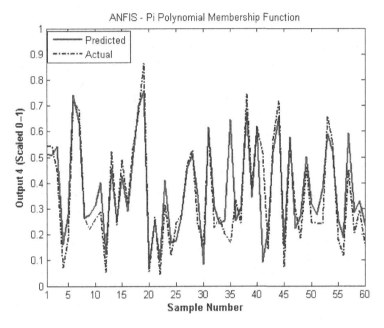

**Figure 7.3** Showing the predicted vs. actual values for the first 60 points for the test dataset applied to the FIS.

for first 60 samples of the test dataset using a Polynomial Pi membership function.

The FIS was easy to implement, and the results obtained show that it can accurately model a system.

## 7.5 Interstate Conflict

Marwala and Lagazio (2011) evaluated the TS neuro-fuzzy on its ability to classify interstate conflict. Marwala and Lagazio (2011) trained the model

Table 7.2   Classification results.

| Method | True Conflicts (TC) | False Peace (FP) | True Peace (TP) | False Conflicts (FC) |
|---|---|---|---|---|
| TS neuro-fuzzy | 303 | 89 | 288 | 104 |

using a balanced training set containing 1,000 instances. This was to ensure that they gave both *conflict* and *peace* outcomes equal importance. Marwala and Lagazio (2011) tested the model on the selected balanced set, which contained 392 peace cases and 392 conflict cases. They showed the confusion matrix for the TS neuro-fuzzy with a cut-off of 0.5 which is in Table 7.2.

The results obtained demonstrate that detection rate of conflict was 77% when using the TS neuro-fuzzy model The detection rate for peace was 73% when using the TS neuro-fuzzy model. Overall, when they implemented this method, the detection rate of a correct outcome was 75%. Furthermore, the area under the receiver operating characteristics curve when they used this method was 0.86.

They found that it was possible to use the TS neuro-fuzzy model for rule extraction. Two fuzzy rules were extracted from the model and these are shown below (Marwala and Lagazio, 2011):

*If $u_1$ is $A_{11}$ and $u_2$ is $A_{12}$ and $u_3$ is $A_{13}$ and $u_4$ is $A_{14}$ and $u_5$ is $A_{15}$ and $u_6$ is $A_{16}$ and $u_7$ is $A_{17}$ then:*

$$y_1 = -1.9 \times 10^{-1}u_1 - 1.3 \times 10^{-1}u_2 + 0.0 \times 10^0 u_3$$
$$- 6.1 \times 10^{-1}u_4 - 1.3 \times 10^{-1}u_5$$
$$- 1.3 \times 10^0 u_6 + 4.7 \times 10^{-1}u_7 + 9.0 \times 10^{-1}.$$

*If $u_1$ is $A_{21}$ and $u_2$ is $A_{22}$ and $u_3$ is $A_{23}$ and $u_4$ is $A_{24}$ and $u_5$ is $A_{25}$ and $u_6$ is $A_{26}$ and $u_7$ is $A_{27}$ then:*

$$y_2 = -2.8 \times 10^{-1}u_1 + 6.3 \times 10^{-2}u_2 + 2.5 \times 10^{-1}u_3$$
$$- 7.6 \times 10^{-1}u_4 - 8.9 \times 10^{-1}u_5$$
$$- 9.0 \times 10^0 u_6 + 0.0 \times 10^0 u_7 + 3.7 \times 10^{-1}.$$

The symbols from $u_1$ to $u_7$ are the input vector which consists of *Democracy, Dependency, Capability, Alliance, Contiguity, Distance,* and *Major Power.*

The rules are quite complex, and there is a need to simplify them in order to interpret them. Marwala and Lagazio (2011) found that when applying automated techniques to obtain fuzzy models, unnecessary complexity is often present (Sentes *et al.*, 1998).

In their case, the TS fuzzy model contains only two fuzzy rules. The removal of a fuzzy set like the universal set leaves only one remaining fuzzy set. The result of this is that when the input is partitioned into only one fuzzy set, it introduces difficulty on expressing the premise in linguistic terms. To simplify the fuzzy rules and avoid the redundant fuzzy sets, the number of inputs were pruned into the TS neuro-fuzzy model to four variables. These variables are *Democracy, Dependency, Alliance* and *Contiguity*. The rules extracted can be simplified to represent them in the commonly used linguistic terms. We still express mathematically the consequent part, together with the firing strength of the rule. Marwala and Lagazio (2011) wrote the translated fuzzy rules, with the firing strengths omitted as follows:

*If* Democracy Level *is* low *and* Alliance *is* strong *and* Contiguity *is* true *then:*

$$y_1 = -3.87 \times 10^{-1}u_1 - 9.19 \times 10^{-1}u_3 - 7.95 \times 10^{-1}u_4 + 3.90 \times 10^{-1}$$

*If* Democracy Level *is* high *and* Alliance *is* weak *and* Contiguity *is* false *then:*

$$y_2 = -1.25 \times 10^{-1}u_1 - 5.62 \times 10^{-1}u_3 - 2.35 \times 10^{-1}u_4 + 4.23 \times 10^{-1}.$$

From observing the above rules, it is evident that the model is not quite as transparent as we would like it to be. This is because the consequent of each of the rules is still a mathematical expression. To validate the model, we still have to apply expert knowledge of the problem domain. For instance, from the combination of the two statements, we can extrapolate that if the level of *Democracy* of two countries is *low*, they have a *strong* alliance and they *share a border*, there is a reasonable chance that the countries can find themselves in a conflict situation. This seems to indicate that the opportunities, provided by geographical proximity, must be in place for an interstate interaction to degenerate into conflict when democracy is lacking. Also, it appears to indicate that when this dangerous combination is in place (lack of democracy and proximity), economic interdependence or share alliances cannot alone prevent a dispute between two countries to occur, regardless of the level of economic ties or alliances that may exist between them. This result appears to strongly support democratic peace theory, and democracy as a key and necessary factor for peace. If we find values of *Democracy, Alliance* and *Contiguity* which have a membership value of one, which means very low democracy, shared membership in alliances as well as geographical proximity, we can then use these as inputs to the model to see if it confirms our extracted knowledge. It is found that by using these values and an arbitrary *Dependency* value, the model gives an output decision value $y = 0.6743$, which means it predicts a conflict will occur. By validating the model with similar statements, we can get insight for how much confidence we can put in the system. The model can further be used to test hypothetical scenarios in a similar way to which it is validated. The neuro-fuzzy model, therefore, offers a method of forecasting international conflict while also catering for the cases where causal interpretations are required.

## 7.6　Conclusions

In this chapter, we studied the theories of fuzzy logic and neuro-fuzzy systems. Furthermore, we applied these techniques for modelling a steam generator and prediction of interstate conflict. We observed that fuzzy logic was able to model the steam generator well. Furthermore, we observed that neuro-fuzzy system was able to model interstate conflict. In particular, the neuro-fuzzy system was able to offer some rules that describe the relationships in the data.

## References

Abiyev, R.H., Kaynak, O., Alshanableh, T., Mamedov, F. (2011). A type-2 neuro-fuzzy system based on clustering and gradient techniques applied to system identification and channel equalization. *Applied Soft Computing*, 11:1396–1406.

Araujo, E. (2008). Improved Takagi-Sugeno fuzzy approach. In: *Proceedings of the IEEE International Conference on Fuzzy Systems*, 1154–1158.

Ata, R., Kocyigit, Y. (2010). An adaptive neuro-fuzzy inference system approach for prediction of tip speed ratio in wind turbines. *Expert Systems with Applications*, 37:5454–5460.

Babuska, R. (1991). Fuzzy Modeling and Identification. PhD Thesis, Technical University of Delft.

Babuska, R., Verbruggen, H. (2003). Neuro-fuzzy methods for nonlinear system identification. *Annual Review in Control*, 27:73–85.

Barbieri, K. (1996). Economic interdependence — A path to peace or a source of interstate. *Journal of Peace Research*, 33:29–49.

Beck, N., Katz, J., Tucker, R. (1998). Taking time seriously: Time-series cross-section analysis with a binary dependent variable. *American Journal of Political Science*, 42:1260–1288.

Beck, N., King, G., Zeng, L. (2000). Improving quantitative studies of international conflict: A conjecture. *American Political Science Review*, 94:21–35.

Beyhan, S., Sarabi, F.E., Lendek, Z., Babuška, R. (2017). Takagi–Sugeno fuzzy payload estimation and adaptive control. *IFAC-PapersOnLine*, 50(1):844–849.

Biacino, L., Gerla, G. (2002). Fuzzy logic, continuity and effectiveness. *Archive for Mathematical Logic*, 41:643–667.

Bih, J. (2006). Paradigm shift — An introduction to fuzzy logic. *IEEE Potentials*, 6–21.

Bishop, C. (1995). *Neural Networks for Pattern Recognition*. Oxford: Oxford University Press.

Cabalar, A.F., Cevik, A., Gokceoglu, C., Baykal, G. (2010). Neuro-fuzzy based constitutive modeling of undrained response of Leighton Buzzard sand mixtures. *Expert System with Applications*, 37:842–851.

Cano-Izquierdo, J., Almonacid, M., Ibarrola, J.J. (2010). Applying neuro-fuzzy model dFasArt in control systems. *Engineering Applications of Artificial Intelligence*, 23:1053–1063.

Cantor, G. (1874). Über eine Eigenschaft des Inbegriffes aller reellen algebraischen Zahlen. *Crelles J f. Math*, 77:258–262.

Cetisli, B. (2010). Development of an adaptive neuro-fuzzy classifier using linguistic hedges: Part 1. *Expert Systems with Applications*, 37:6093–6101.

Cox, E. (1994). *The Fuzzy Systems Handbook: A Practitioner's Guide to Building, Using, Maintaining Fuzzy Systems*. Boston: AP Professional.

Demirli, K., Khoshnejad, M. (2009). Autonomous parallel parking of a car-like mobile robot by a neuro-fuzzy sensor-based controller. *Fuzzy Sets and Systems*, 160:2876–2891.

Devlin, K. (1993). *The Joy of Sets*. Berlin: Springer Verlag.

El-Sebakhy, E.A. (2010). Flow regimes identification and liquid-holdup prediction in horizontal multiphase flow based on neuro-fuzzy inference systems. *Mathematics and Computers in Simulation*, 80:1854–1866.

Ferreirós, J. (1999). *Labyrinth of Thought: A History of Set Theory and its Role in Modern Mathematics*. Basel: Birkhäuser.

Gonzalez, T., Sala, A., Bernal, M., Robles, R. (2017). A generalisation of line-integral Lyapunov function for Takagi-Sugeno systems. *IFAC-PapersOnLine*, 50(1):2983–2988.

Habtemariam, E.A., Marwala, T. (2005). Artificial intelligence for conflict management. In: *Proceedings of the IEEE International Joint Conference on Neural Networks*, 2583–2588.

Hagiwara, H., Mita, A. (2002). Structural health monitoring system using support vector machine. *Advanced Building Technologies*, 28:481–488.

Hájek, P. (1995). Fuzzy logic and arithmetical hierarchy. *Fuzzy Sets and Systems*, 3:359–363.

Hájek, P. (1998). *Metamathematics of Fuzzy Logic*. Dordrecht: Kluwer.

Halpern, J.Y. (2003). *Reasoning about Uncertainty*. Cambridge, MA: MIT Press.

Hamamoto, A.H., Carvalho, L.F., Sampaio, L.D.H., Abrão, T., Proença, M.L. (2018). Network Anomaly Detection System using Genetic Algorithm and Fuzzy Logic. *Expert Systems with Applications*, 92:390–402.

Harrag, A., Messalti, S. (2018). How fuzzy logic can improve PEM fuel cell MPPT performances? *International Journal of Hydrogen Energy*, 43(1):537–550.

Haykin, S. (1999). *Neural Networks: A Comprehensive Foundation*. New Jersey: Prentice Hall.

Hsu, Y.-C., Lin, S.-F. (2009). Reinforcement group cooperation-based symbiotic evolution for recurrent wavelet-based neuro-fuzzy systems. *Journal of Neurocomputing*, 72:2418–2432.

Huang, T.M., Kecman, V. (2005). Gene extraction for cancer diagnosis by support vector machines — An improvement. *Artificial Intelligence in Medicine*, 35:185–194.

Hurtado, J.E. (2003). Relevance of support vector machines for stochastic mechanics. *Computational Fluid and Solid Mechanics*, 20:2298–2301.

Ichalal, D., Marx, B., Mammar, S., Maquin, D., Ragot, J. (2018). How to cope with unmeasurable premise variables in Takagi–Sugeno observer design: Dynamic extension approach. *Engineering Applications of Artificial Intelligence*, 67:430–435.

Iplikci, S. (2010) Support vector machines based neuro-fuzzy control of nonlinear systems. *Journal of Neurocomputing*, 73:2097–2107.

Jang, J.-S.R. (1993). ANFIS: Adaptive-network-based fuzzy inference system. *IEEE Transactions on Systems, Man and Cybernetics*, 23:665–685.

Jang, J.S.R., Sun, C.T., Mizutani, E. (1997). *Neuro-Fuzzy and Soft Computing: A Computational Approach to Learning and Machine Intelligence*. Toronto: Prentice Hall.

Johnson, P. (1972). *A History of Set Theory*. Prindle: Weber & Schmidt.

Jones, D., Bremer, S., Singer, J. (1996). Militarized interstate disputes, 1816–1992 rationale, coding rules and empirical patterns. *Conflict Management and Peace Science*, 15:585–615.

Khajeh, A., Modarress, H. (2010). Prediction of solubility of gases in polystyrene by adaptive neuro-fuzzy inference system and radial basis function neural network. *Expert Systems with Applications*, 37:3070–3074.

Klir, G.J., Folger, T.A. (1988). *Fuzzy Sets, Uncertainty, and Information*. New Jersey: Prentice Hall.

Klir, G.J., Yuan, B. (1995). *Fuzzy Sets and Fuzzy Logic: Theory and Applications*. New Jersey: Prentice Hall.

Klir, G.J., St Clair, U.H., Yuan, B. (1997). *Fuzzy Set Theory: Foundations and Applications*. New Jersey: Prentice Hall.

Kosko, B. (1993). *Fuzzy Thinking: The New Science of Fuzzy Logic*. New York: Hyperion.

Kosko, B., Isaka, S. (1993). Fuzzy logic. *Scientific American*, 269:76–81.

Kucuk, K., Aksoy, C.O., Basarir, H., Onargan, T., Genis, M., Ozacar, V. (2011). Prediction of the performance of impact hammer by adaptive neuro-fuzzy inference system modelling. *Tunnelling and Underground Space Technology*, 26:38–45.

Kurtulus, B., Razack, M. (2010). Modeling daily discharge responses of a large karstic aquifer using soft computing methods: Artificial neural network and neuro-fuzzy. *Journal of Hydrology*, 381:10–111.

Kwong, C.K., Wong, T.C., Chan, K.Y. (2009). A methodology of generating customer satisfaction models for new product development using a neuro-fuzzy approach. *Expert Systems with Applications*, 36:11262–11270.

Lagazio, M., Russett, B. (2004). A neural network analysis of MIDs, 1885–1992: Are the patterns stable? *In the Scourge of War: New Extensions on an Old Problem, ch. Towards a Scientific Understanding of War: Studies in Honor of J. David Singer.* Ann Arbor: University of Michigan Press.

Leke, B., Marwala, T., Tettey, T. (2007). Using inverse neural network for HIV adaptive control. *International Journal of Computing Intelligence Research*, 3:11–15.

Lo, S. (2008). Web service quality control based on text mining using support vector machine. *Expert Systems with Applications*, 34:603–610.

Maalej, S., Kruszewski, A., Belkoura, L. (2017). Stabilization of Takagi–Sugeno models with non-measured premises: Input-to-state stability approach. *Fuzzy Sets and Systems*, 329(15):108–126.

Mamdani, E.H. (1974). Application of fuzzy algorithms for the control of a dynamic plant. In: *Proceedings of IEE*, 121:1585–1588.

Mansfield, E.D., Snyder, J. (1997). A tale of two democratic peace critiques: A reply to Thompson and Tucker. *Journal of Conflicts Resolution*, 41:457–461.

Marwala, T. (2007). *Computational Intelligence for Modelling Complex Systems*. Delhi: Research India Publications.

Marwala, T. (2009). *Computational Intelligence for Missing Data Imputation, Estimation and Management: Knowledge Optimization Techniques*. New York: IGI Global Publications.

Marwala, T. (2010). *Finite Element Model Updating Using Computational Intelligence Techniques*. London: Springer-Verlag.

Marwala, T. (2012). *Condition Monitoring Using Computational Intelligence Methods*. Heidelberg: Springer.

Marwala, T. (2013). *Economic Modeling Using Artificial Intelligence Methods*. Heidelberg: Springer.

Marwala, T. (2014). *Artificial Intelligence Techniques for Rational Decision Making*. Heidelberg: Springer.

Marwala, T. (2015). *Causality, Correlation, and Artificial Intelligence for Rational Decision Making*. Singapore: World Scientific.

Marwala T., Lagazio, M. (2004). Modelling and controlling interstate conflict. In: *Proceedings of the IEEE International Joint Conference on Neural Networks*, 1233–1238.

Marwala, T., Lagazio, M. (2011). *Militarized Conflict Modeling Using Computational Intelligence*. Heidelberg: Springer. Translated into Chinese by the National Defence Industry Press.

Marwala, T., Boulkaibet, I., Adhikari, S. (2017). *Probabilistic Finite Element Model Updating Using Bayesian Statistics: Applications to Aeronautical and Mechanical Engineering*. John Wiley & Sons.

Marwala, T., Chakraverty, S., Mahola, U. (2006). Fault classification using multi-layerperceptrons and support vector machines. *International Journal of Engineering Simulation*, 7:29–35.

Mashrei, M.A, Abdulrazzaq, N., Abdalla, T.Y., Rahman, M.S. (2010). Neural networks model and adaptive neuro-fuzzy inference system for predicting the moment capacity of ferrocement members. *Engineering Structure*, 32:1723–1734.

Mitra, P., Shankar, B.U., Pal, S.K. (2004) Segmentation of multispectral remote sensing images using active support vector machines. *Pattern Recognition Letters*, 25:1067–1074.

Montazer, G.A., Saremi, H.Q., Khatibi, V. (2010). A neuro-fuzzy inference engine for farsi numeral characters recognition. *Expert Systems with Applications*, 37:6327–6337.

Nelwamondo, F.V., Marwala, T., Mahola, U. (2006). Early classifications of bearing faults using hidden markov models, Gaussian mixture models, Mel-frequency cepstral coefficients and fractals. *International Journal of Innovative Computing Information and Control*, 2:1281–1299.

Novák, V. (1989). *Fuzzy Sets and their Applications*. Bristol: Adam Hilger.

Novák, V. (2005). On Fuzzy Type Theory. *Fuzzy Sets and Systems*, 149:235–273.

Novák, V., Perfilieva, I., Močkoř, J. (1999). *Mathematical Principles of Fuzzy Logic*. Dordrecht: Kluwer Academic.

Oneal, J., Russet, B. (1997). The classical liberals were right: Democracy, interdependence and conflict, 1950–1985. *International Studies Quarterly*, 41:267–294.

Oneal J., Russet, B. (1999). Prediction and classification with neural network models. *Sociological Methods and Research*, 4:499–524.

Patel, P.B., Marwala, T. (2006). Forecasting closing price indices using neural networks. In: *Proceedings of the IEEE International Conference on Systems, Man and Cybernetics*, 2351–2356.

Patel, P.B., Marwala, T. (2010). Caller behaviour classification using computational intelligence methods. *International Journal of Neural Systems*, 20:87–93.

Petropoulos, S., Spyridon Karavas, C., Balafoutis, A.T., Paraskevopoulos, I., Kotseridis, Y. (2017). Fuzzy logic tool for wine quality classification. *Computers and Electronics in Agriculture*, 142, Part B:552–562.

Sathishkumar, H., Parthasarathy, S.S. (2017). A novel fuzzy logic controller for vector controlled induction motor drive. *Energy Procedia*, 138:686–691.

Schölkopf, B., Smola, A.J. (2002). *Learning with Kernels*. Cambridge: MIT Press.

Sentes, M., Babuska, R., Kaymak, U., van Nauta Lemke, H. (1998). Similarity Measures in Fuzzy Rule Base Simplification. *IEEE Transactions on Systems, Man and Cybernetics*, 28:376–386.

Shiri, J., Kisi, O. (2010). Short-term and long-term streamflow forecasting using a wavelet and neuro-fuzzy conjunction model. *Journal of Hydrology*, 394:486–493.

Srinivasarengan, K., Ragot, J., Maquin, D., Aubrun, C. (2017). An adaptive observer design for Takagi–Sugeno type nonlinear system. *IFAC-PapersOnLine*, 50(1):826–831.

Sugeno, M. (1985). *Industrial Applications of Fuzzy Control*. Amsterdam: Elsevier Science Publication Company.

Sugeno, M., Kang, G. (1988). Structure identification of fuzzy model. *Fuzzy Sets and Systems*, 28:15–33.

Takagi, T., Sugeno, M. (1985). Fuzzy identification of systems and its applications to modeling and control. *IEEE Transactions on Systems, Man, and Cybernetics*, 15:116–132.

Talei, A., Hock, L., Chua, C., Quek, C. (2010). A novel application of a neuro-fuzzy computational technique in event-based rainfall-runoff modeling. *Expert Systems with Applications*, 37:7456–7468.

Tettey, T. (2007). A Computational Intelligence Approach to Modelling Interstate Conflict: Conflict and Causal Interpretations. Master Thesis, University of the Witwatersrand, Johannesburg.

Tettey, T., Marwala, T. (2006a). Controlling interstate conflict using neuro-fuzzy modeling and genetic algorithms. In: *Proceedings of the 10th International Conference on Intelligent Engineering Systems*, 30–34.

Tettey, T., Marwala, T. (2006b). Neuro-fuzzy modeling and fuzzy rule extraction applied to conflict management. *Lecture Notes in Computer Science*, 4234:1087–1094.

Tettey, T., Marwala, T. (2007). Conflict modelling and knowledge extraction using computational intelligence methods. In: *Proceedings of the 11th IEEE International Conference on Intelligent Engineering Systems*, 161–166.

Theodoridou, P.G., Varouchakis, E.A., Karatzas, G.P. (2017). Spatial analysis of groundwater levels using Fuzzy Logic and geostatistical tools. *Journal of Hydrology*, 555:242–252.

Thompson, W., Tucker, R. (1997). A tale of two democratic peace critiques. *Journal of Conflicts Resolution*, 41:428–454.

Tripathi, S., Srinivas, V.V., Nanjundiah, R.S. (2006). Downscaling of precipitation for climate change scenarios: A support vector machine approach. *Journal of Hydrology*, 330:621–640.

Von Altrock, C. (1995). *Fuzzy Logic and Neurofuzzy Applications Explained*. New Jersey: Prentice Hall.

Wright, S., Marwala, T. (2006). *Artificial Intelligence Techniques for Steam Generator Modelling*. arXiv:0811.1711.

Zadeh, L.A. (1965). Fuzzy sets. *Informations and Control*, 8:338–353.

Zemankova-Leech, M. (1983). Fuzzy Relational Data Bases. PhD Dissertation, Florida State University.

Zhou, Q., Chan, C.W., Tontiwachwuthikul, P. (2010). An application of neuro-fuzzy technology for analysis of the $CO_2$ capture process. *Fuzzy Sets and Systems*, 161:2597–2611.

Zimmermann, H. (2001). *Fuzzy Set Theory and its Applications*. Boston: Kluwer Academic Publishers.

# Chapter 8

# Rough Sets

**Abstract.** This chapter describes rough set theory. Then it studies the concept of rough sets discretization. It introduces neuro-rough sets, which is based on rough sets and the multi-layered perceptron. It then studies application of neuro-rough sets on modelling HIV. It subsequently studies the use of different discretization methods and rough sets to model the stock market. Thereafter, it studies the use of rough sets to model interstate conflict.

## 8.1 Introduction

Rough set theory, introduced by Pawlak (1991), is a mathematical tool that deals with vagueness and uncertainty. It approximates sets that are difficult to describe with available information and is part of artificial intelligence. The advantage of rough sets is that it does not require rigid *a priori* assumptions about the mathematical nature of such complex relationships, as commonly used multivariate statistical techniques do (Machowski and Marwala, 2005; Crossingham *et al.*, 2008). Rough set theory assumes that the information of interest is associated with some information of its universe of discourse (Crossingham and Marwala, 2008b). Details on rough sets can be found in Tettey *et al.* (2007), Marwala and Crossingham (2008, 2009), Crossingham *et al.* (2009), Crossingham and Marwala (2008a), Ohrn (1999), Pe-a *et al.* (1999), Tay and Shen (2003), Golan and Ziarko (1995) and Rowland *et al.* (1998).

Rough sets theory was successfully applied in remote sensing (Xie *et al.*, 2011), in protein interaction prediction (Chen *et al.*, 2011), reasoning classification (Salamó and López-Sánchez, 2011), controlling reagents (Zhang *et al.*, 2010), credit scoring (Wang *et al.*, 2010), medical diagnostics (Chen *et al.*, 2010) and prediction of customer churn (Lin *et al.*, 2011). Other successful applications include: assessing personnel efficiency by Azadeh *et al.* (2011), distributor selection (Zou *et al.*, 2011), resource allocation (Huang *et al.*, 2011), rare-earth extraction (Gong *et al.*, 2010), predicting soil mixture (Yan *et al.*, 2010) and modelling brand trust (Liao *et al.*, 2010). For knowledge acquisition from data with numerical attributes, special techniques are applied. One important aspect of rough set implementation is the *discretization* step which we take before using rule induction or decision tree generation (Crossingham and Marwala, 2007). Some methods to perform the task of discretization are Boolean Reasoning (BR), equal-width-bin (EWB) partitioning and equal-frequency-bin (EFB) partitioning (Jaafar *et al.*, 2006; Fayyad and Irani, 1993).

This chapter studies various aspects of rough sets including discretization, optimization and neuro-rough models. We apply the rough sets theory to model HIV and interstate conflict.

## 8.2  Rough Sets

The main goal of rough sets is to synthesize approximations of concepts from the acquired data (Crossingham, 2007; Pawlak and Munakata, 1996). Rough set theory deals with the approximation of sets that are difficult to describe with the available information (Ohrn and Rowland, 2000). It also deals with the classification of imprecise, uncertain or incomplete information. We form two approximations, namely the upper and lower approximations to deal with inconsistent information. We represent the data using an information table.

Rough set theory uses a set of rules, which we express in terms of linguistic variables. Rough sets are important to artificial intelligence and cognitive science. They are highly applicable to the tasks of machine learning and decision analysis with uncertainties. Because they are rule-based, rough sets are transparent, but they are not as accurate. Certainly, they are not good as universal approximators, as other machine-learning tools such as neural networks are in their predictions. In machine learning, there is always a trade-off between prediction accuracy and transparency.

Crossingham and Marwala (2007) presented an approach to optimize the rough set partition sizes using various optimization techniques. Rough set theory provides a technique of reasoning from vague and imprecise data (Goh and Law, 2003). The basis of rough sets technique is the assumption that some observed information is somehow associated with some information in the universe of the discourse (Komorowski *et al.*, 1999; Yang and John, 2006; Kondo, 2006; Marwala, 2015). Objects with the same information are indiscernible in the view of the available information. An elementary set consisting of indiscernible objects forms a basic granule of knowledge. We refer to a union of an elementary set as a *crisp set*; otherwise, the set is *rough*.

### 8.2.1 Information system

An information system ($\Lambda$), is defined as a pair $(U, A)$ where $U$ is a finite set of objects called the universe and $A$ is a non-empty finite set of attributes as shown in Equation (8.1) below (Crossingham, 2007; Yang and John, 2006; Nelwamondo, 2008; Marwala, 2009; Marwala and Lagazio, 2011):

$$\Lambda = (U, A). \tag{8.1}$$

Every attribute $a \in A$ has a value, which must be a member of a value set $V_a$ of the attribute $a$ (Dubois, 1990; Crossingham, 2007; Marwala, 2012):

$$a : U \rightarrow V_a. \tag{8.2}$$

We define a rough set with a set of attributes and the indiscernibility relation between them. We discuss the indiscernibility in the next sub-section.

### 8.2.2 The indiscernibility relation

The indiscernibility relation is one of the fundamental ideas of rough set theory (Grzymala-Busse and Siddhaye, 2004; Zhao *et al.*, 2007; Pawlak and Skowron, 2007; Marwala, 2013). *Indiscernibility* simply implies similarity (Goh and Law, 2003) and, therefore, these sets of objects are indistinguishable. Given an information system $\Lambda$ and subset $B \subseteq A$, $B$ the indiscernibility determines a binary relation $I(B)$ on $U$ such that (Pawlak *et al.*, 1988; Ohrn, 1999; Wu *et al.*, 2003; Ohrn and Rowland, 2000; Marwala, 2013):

$$(x, y) \in I(B)$$
$$if \text{ and } only \text{ } if, \tag{8.3}$$
$$a(x) = a(y)$$

for all $a \in A$ where $a(x)$ denotes the value of attribute $a$ for element $x$. Equation (8.3) implies that any two elements that belong to $I(B)$ should be identical from the point of view of $a$. Suppose $U$ has a finite set of $N$ objects $\{x_1, x_2, \ldots, x_N\}$. Let $Q$ be a finite set of $n$ attributes $\{q_1, q_2, , q_n\}$ in the same information system $\Lambda$, then (Inuiguchi and Miyajima, 2007;

Crossingham, 2007; Marwala, 2014):

$$\Lambda = \langle U, Q, V, f \rangle, \tag{8.4}$$

where $f$ is the total decision function, called the *information function*. From the definition of the indiscernibility relation that we give in this section, any two objects have a similarity relation to attribute $a$ if they have the same attribute values everywhere.

### 8.2.3  Information table and data representation

We use an information table in rough sets theory to represent the data. We arrange data in the information table based on their condition attributes and decision attribute $(D)$. *Condition attributes* and *decision attributes* are analogous to the independent variables and dependent variable (Goh and Law, 2003). We divide these attributes into $C \cup D = Q$ and $C \cup D = 0$.

We can classify an information table into *complete* and *incomplete classes*. All objects in a complete class have known attribute values $B$, whereas we consider an information table incomplete if at least one attribute variable has a missing value. We give an example of an incomplete information table in Table 8.1. We represent data in the table where each row represents an instance, sometimes referred to as an object. Every column represents an attribute, which is a measured variable. We refer to this kind of table as an *Information System* (Komorowski *et al.*, 1999; Leung *et al.*, 2006; Marwala, 2009).

### 8.2.4  Decision rules induction

Rough sets also involve generating decision rules for a given information table. We base these rules on condition attributes values (Bi *et al.*, 2003;

**Table 8.1**  An example of an information table with missing values.

|   | $B_1$ | $B_2$ | $B_3$ | D |
|---|---|---|---|---|
| 1 | 1 | 1 | 0.2 | ? |
| 2 | 1 | 2 | 0.3 | A |
| 3 | 0 | 1 | 0.3 | P |
| 4 | ? | 3 | 0.3 | ? |
| 5 | 0 | 3 | 0.4 | A |
| 6 | 0 | 2 | 0.2 | P |
| 7 | 1 | 4 | 4 | ? |

Slezak and Ziarko, 2005). The rules are presented in an '*if CONDITION(S)-then DECISION*' format. Stefanowski (1998) successfully used a rough set approach for inference in decision rules whereas Wang *et al.* (2006) used rough set theory in brain glioma based on Magnetic Resonance Imaging (MRI).

### 8.2.5 The lower and upper approximation of sets

We define the lower and upper approximations of sets based on the indiscernibility relation. The *lower approximation* is the collection of cases whose equivalent classes are contained in the cases to be approximated. The *upper approximation* is the collection of classes that are partially contained in the set to be approximated (Rowland *et al.*, 1998; Degang *et al.*, 2006; Witlox and Tindemans, 2004). Let us define the concept $X$ as a set of all cases defined by a specific value of the decision. We call any finite union of elementary set associated with $B$, a *B-definable set* (Grzymala-Busse and Siddhaye, 2004). We approximate the set $X$ by two $B$-definable sets, referred to as the $B$-lower approximation denoted by $\underline{B}X$ and $B$-upper approximation $\overline{B}X$. The $B$-lower approximation is defined as (Bazan *et al.*, 2004; Crossingham, 2007; Marwala, 2009):

$$\underline{B}X = \{x \in U \,|\, [x]_B \subseteq X\}, \tag{8.5}$$

and we define the $B$-upper approximation as (Crossingham, 2007; Marwala, 2009):

$$\overline{B}X = \{x \in U \,|\, [x]_B \cap X \neq 0\}. \tag{8.6}$$

Researchers have used other methods to define the lower and upper approximations for a completely specified decision table. Some of the common ones include approximating the lower and upper approximations of $X$ using Equations (8.7) and (8.8), as follows (Grzymala-Busse, 2004; Crossingham, 2007; Marwala, 2009):

$$\cup \{[x]_B \,|\, x \in U, [x]_B \subseteq X\}, \tag{8.7}$$

$$\cup \{[x]_B \,|\, x \in U, [x]_B \cap X \neq 0\}. \tag{8.8}$$

We can modify the definition of definability in cases of incompletely specified tables. In this case, we call any finite union of characteristic sets of $B$'s, a *B-definable set*. We discuss three different definitions of approximations from Grzymala-Busse and Siddhaye (2004). Again, letting $B$ be a subset of $A$ of all attributes and $R(B)$ be the characteristic relation of the incomplete decision table with characteristic sets $K(x)$, where $x \in U$, we define the following (Grzymala-Busse, 2004; Crossingham, 2007):

$$\underline{B}X = \{x \in U \mid K_B(x) \subseteq X\}, \tag{8.9}$$

and

$$\overline{B}X = \{x \in U \mid K_B(x) \cap X \neq 0\}. \tag{8.10}$$

We refer to Equations (8.9) and (8.10) as *singletons*. We define the lower and upper approximations of incompletely specified datasets as:

$$\cup \{K_B(x) \mid x \in U, K_B(x) \subseteq X\}, \tag{8.11}$$

and

$$\cup \{K_B(x) \mid x \in U, K_B(x) \cap X = 0\}. \tag{8.12}$$

We can find more information on these methods in Grzymala-Busse and Hu (2001), Grzymala-Busse and Siddhaye (2004) and Crossingham (2007). It follows from these properties that we can only define a crisp set if $\underline{B}(X) = \overline{B}(X)$. We define roughness as the difference between the upper and the lower approximation.

### 8.2.6 Set approximation

Pawlak (1991) presented various properties of rough sets. One property of rough set theory is the definability of a rough set (Quafafou, 2000). We discussed this above for the case when the lower and upper approximations are equal. Otherwise, if this is not the case, then the target set is un-definable. Some of the special cases of definability are (Pawlak *et al.*, 1988; Crossingham, 2007; Nelwamondo, 2008; Marwala, 2009):

1. *Internally definable* set: Here, $\underline{B}X \neq 0$ and $\overline{B}X = U$. The attribute set $B$ has objects that certainly are elements of the target set $X$, even though there are no objects that we can definitively exclude from the set $X$.
2. *Externally definable* set: Here, $\underline{B}X = 0$ and $\overline{B}X \neq U$. The attribute set $B$ has no objects that certainly are elements of the target set $X$, even though there are objects that we can definitively exclude from the set $X$.
3. *Totally un-definable* set: Here, $\underline{B}X = 0$ and $\overline{B}X = U$. The attribute set $B$ has no objects that certainly are elements of the target set $X$, even though there are no objects that we can definitively exclude from the set $X$.

### 8.2.7 The reduct

Another property of rough sets is the reduct. An interesting analysis is whether there are attributes $B$ in the information system that are more important to the knowledge represented in the equivalence class structure than other attributes. It is essential to find out if there is a subset of attributes, which, by itself, could completely describe the knowledge in the database. We call this attribute set as the *reduct*.

Beynon (2001) observed that the elementary feature of the variable precision rough set model entailed an exploration for subsets of condition attributes, which give identical information for classification functions as the complete set of given attributes. Beynon labelled these subsets *approximate reducts* and described these for an identified classification error represented by $\beta$. Furthermore, he then identified specific anomalies and fascinating implications for identifying $\beta$-reducts, which guaranteed a general knowledge like that obtained from the full set of attributes.

Terlecki and Walczak (2007) described the relations between rough set reducts and emerging patterns. From this study, they established a practical application for these observations to the minimal reduct problem using these to test the differentiating factor of an attribute set. Shan and Ziarko (1995) formally defined a *reduct* as a subset of attributes $RED \subseteq B$ such that:

1. $[x]_{RED} = [x]_B$. That is, the equivalence classes that are induced by reducing the attribute set $RED$ are identical to the similar class structure that was induced by the full attribute set $B$.
2. Attribute set $RED$ is minimal because $[x]_{(RED-A)} \neq [x]_B$ for any attribute $A \in RED$. In simple form, there is no attribute that can be taken away from the set $RED$ without altering the equivalence classes $[x]_B$.

We can visualize a reduct as an adequate set of features that can sufficiently well express the category's structure. One characteristic of a reduct in an information system is that it is not unique because there may be other subsets of attributes, which may still preserve the equivalence class structure conveyed in the information system. We call the set of characteristics that are common in all reducts a *core*.

### 8.2.8 Boundary region

The boundary region, which we can write as the difference $\overline{B}X - \underline{B}X$, is a region which is composed of objects that cannot be included nor excluded as members of the target set $X$. In simple terms, the lower approximation of a target set is an approximation, which consists only of those objects, which we can positively identify as members of the set. The upper approximation is a loose approximation and includes objects that may be members of the target set. The boundary region is the region in between the upper approximation and the lower approximation.

### 8.2.9 Rough membership functions

Rough membership function is a function $\mu_A^x : U \rightarrow [0,1]$ that, when applied to object $x$, quantifies the degree of overlap between set $X$ and the indiscernibility set to which $x$ belongs. We use the rough membership function to calculate the plausibility and we define this as (Pawlak, 1991; Crossingham, 2007):

$$\mu_A^x(X) = \frac{|[x]_B \cap X|}{|[x]_B|}. \tag{8.13}$$

We can view the rough membership function as a fuzzification with rough approximation. It ensures the translation from rough approximation into membership function. We derive the outstanding feature of a rough membership function from data (Hoa and Son, 2008; Crossingham, 2007).

## 8.3 Discretization Methods

The methods that allow continuous data to be processed involve discretization. There are several methods available to perform discretization, but the two popular ones are EWB partitioning and EFB partitioning (Crossingham, 2007).

### 8.3.1 Equal-width-bin (EWB) partitioning

EWB partitioning divides the range of observed values of an attribute into $k$ equal sized bins (Crossingham, 2007). One notable problem of this method is that it is vulnerable to outliers that may drastically skew the data range. We eliminate this problem through the pre-processing step of cleaning the data. The way data can be discretized using EWB follows (Crossingham, 2007; Marwala, 2009):

1. Evaluate the Smallest and Largest value for each attribute and label these values $S$ and $L$.
2. Write the width of each interval, $W$, as $W = \frac{L-S}{4}$.

3. Determine the interval boundaries through $S + W$, $S + 2W$, $S + 3W$. We can determine these boundaries for any number of intervals $k$, up to the term $S + (k - 1)W$.

### 8.3.2 Equal-frequency-bin (EFB) partitioning

EFB partitioning sorts the values of each attribute in ascending order and divides them into $k$ bins where (given $m$ instances) each bin contains $m/k$ adjacent values. In most instances, there probably exist duplicated values. We implement the EFB partitioning as follows (Crossingham, 2007; Marwala, 2009):

1. Arrange the values of each attribute $(v_1^a, v_2^a, v_3^a, \ldots, v_m^a)$ into intervals whereby $m$ is the number of instances.
2. Each interval therefore is made of the following sequential values $\lambda = \frac{m}{4}$.
3. The cut-off points may be computed using the following equation which is valid for $i = 1, 2, 3$ where $k$ intervals can be calculated for $i = 1, \ldots, k - 1$:

$$c_i = \frac{v_{i\lambda} + v_{i\lambda+1}}{2}$$

### 8.4 Rough Set Formulation

We classify rough sets modelling into these five stages (Crossingham, 2007):

1. Select the data.
2. Pre-process the data to ensure that it is ready for analysis by discretizing the data and removing unnecessary data (cleaning the data).
3. If reducts are considered, use the cleaned data to generate reducts.
4. Extract rules.
5. Test the newly created rules on a test set.

The procedure for computing rough sets and extracting rules are in Algorithm 1 (Crossingham, 2007). At the fifth stage involving testing the newly created rules on a test set, we estimate the prediction error of the rough set model. We write the equation representing the mapping between the inputs $x$ to the output $\gamma$ using rough set as:

$$\gamma = f(G_x, N_r, R), \tag{8.14}$$

where $\gamma$ is the output, $G_x$ is the granulization of the input space into high, low, medium etc, $N_r$ is the number of rules and $R$ depicts the rules. For

---

**Algorithm 1:** Procedure to generate a rough set model (Crossingham, 2007)

---

| | |
|---|---|
| Input: | Condition and Decision Attributes |
| Output: | Certain and Possible Rules |

1     Obtain the dataset to be used;
2     **Repeat**
3          **for** *conditional_attribute* ← 1 to *size_of_training_data* **do**
4                Pre-process data to ensure that it is ready for analysis;
5                Discretize the data according to the optimization technique;
6                Compute the lower approximation, as defined in Equation (8.9);
7                Compute the upper approximation, as defined in Equation (8.10);
8                From the general rules, calculate plausibility measures for an object $x$ belonging to set $X$, as defined by Equation (8.13);
9                Extract the *certain* rules from the lower approximation generated for each subset;
10               Similarly, extract the *possible* rules from the upper approximation of each subset;
11               Remove the generated rules for the purposes of testing on unseen data;
12               Compute the classifier performance;
13          **End**
14     **until** Optimization technique termination condition;

---

a given nature of granulization, the rough set model can give the optimal number and nature of rules and the accuracy of prediction.

## 8.5   Rough Sets vs. Fuzzy Sets

Fuzzy sets are sets that have elements with degrees of membership. Zadeh (1965) introduced fuzzy sets as an expansion of the classical concept of sets. In classical set theory, the membership of elements in a set is evaluated in binary terms, that is, it is, either, a member of that set or it is not a member of that particular set. Fuzzy set theory allows the steady evaluation of the membership of elements in a set. Thus, a fuzzy set is a generalized version of a classical set and conversely a classical set is a special case of the membership function of a fuzzy set, which only permits the values 0 or 1. Thus far, fuzzy set theory has not generated any results that differ from the results from a probability or classical set theory.

Table 8.2 shows the difference between rough and fuzzy sets (Chanas and Kuchta, 1992).

The next sections introduce the neuro-rough system that combines both rough sets and neural networks. The advantage of this is that it brings to

**Table 8.2**    Comparison of fuzzy and rough.

| Attributes | Rough Sets | Fuzzy Sets |
|---|---|---|
| General philosophy | Designed to deal with vagueness of data. Lower and upper approximation Discretization of the input variables | Fuzzy sets have fuzzification of the input variables |
| Optimization | Optimization through the discretization | Optimization through the selection of membership functions |
| Generalization | Reducts are used to generalize | 'If-then' rules are used to generalize |

the fore the transparency advantages of rough sets and accuracy advantages of neural networks (Marwala and Crossingham, 2008).

## 8.6 Multi-layer Perceptron Model

One component of the neuro-rough model is the multi-layered network. This network architecture contains hidden units and output units and normally has one hidden layer. The bias parameters in the first layer are weights from an extra input having a fixed value of $x_0 = 1$. The bias parameters in the second layer are weights from an extra hidden unit, with the activation fixed at $z_0 = 1$. The model is able to take into account the intrinsic dimensionality of the data. The output of the $j$th hidden unit is obtained by calculating the weighted linear combination of the $d$ input (Bishop, 2006; Marwala, 2001). We can relate the input $x$ to the output $y$ by a two-layered nonlinear mathematical expression as follows (Bishop, 1995):

$$y_k = f_{\text{outer}} \left( \sum_{j=1}^{M} w_{kj}^{(2)} f_{\text{inner}} \left( \sum_{i=1}^{d} w_{ji}^{(1)} x_i + w_{j0}^{(1)} \right) + w_{k0}^{(2)} \right). \tag{8.15}$$

Here, $w_{ji}^{(1)}$ indicates the weight in the first layer, going from input $i$ to hidden unit $j$ while $w_{j0}^{(1)}$ indicates the bias for the hidden unit $j$. Furthermore, $w_{kj}^{(2)}$ indicates the weight in the second layer, going from input $j$ to hidden unit $k$ while $w_{k0}^{(2)}$ indicates the bias for the outer unit $k$. The $f_{\text{inner}}$ function represents the activation function of the inner layer and the $f_{\text{outer}}$ function represents the activation function of the outer layer (Bishop, 1995; Marwala, 2007a). Models of this form can approximate any continuous function to arbitrary accuracy if the number of hidden units, $M$, is sufficiently large.

## 8.7  Neuro-rough Model

If we combine Equations (8.14) and (8.16), it is possible to relate the input $x$ to the output $y$ by a two-layered nonlinear mathematical expression as follows (Marwala and Crossingham, 2008):

$$y_k = f_{\text{outer}}\left(\sum_{j-1}^{M}\gamma_{kj}(G_x, R, N_r)f_{\text{inner}}\left(\sum_{i=1}^{d}w_{ji}^{(1)}x_i + w_{j0}^{(1)}\right) + w_{k0}^{(2)}\right). \quad (8.16)$$

The biases in Equation (8.16) may be absorbed into the weights by including extra input variables set permanently to 1, making $x_0 = 1$ and $z_0 = 1$, to give:

$$y_k = f_{\text{outer}}\left(\sum_{j=0}^{M}\gamma_{kj}(G_x, R, N_r)f_{\text{inner}}\left(\sum_{i=0}^{d}w_{ji}^{(1)}x_i\right)\right). \quad (8.17)$$

We represent this equation schematically by Figure 8.1. To train this model, we use the Bayesian framework (Bishop, 1995; Marwala and Crossingham, 2008).

### 8.7.1  Bayesian training on rough sets

The Bayesian framework can be written as (Marwala, 2007a, 2007b; Bishop, 2006):

$$P(\mathbf{M}\,|\,\mathbf{D}) = \frac{P(\mathbf{D}\,|\,\mathbf{M})P(\mathbf{M})}{P(\mathbf{D})}, \quad (8.18)$$

where

$$\mathbf{M} = \left\{\begin{array}{c}\mathbf{w}\\G_x\\N_r\\R\end{array}\right\}.$$

The parameter $P(\mathbf{M}\,|\,\mathbf{D})$ is the probability of the rough set model given the observed data, $P(\mathbf{D}\,|\,\mathbf{M})$ is the probability of the data given the assumed rough set model, also called the likelihood function. $P(\mathbf{M})$ is the prior probability of the rough set model. $P(\mathbf{D})$ is the probability of the data and is also called the evidence. We treat the evidence as the normalization constant. We estimate the likelihood function and the resulting error as

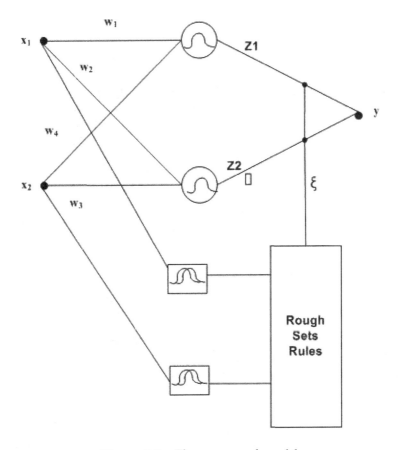

**Figure 8.1**  The neuro-rough model.

follows (Bishop, 1995):

$$P(\mathbf{D}\,|\,\mathbf{M}) = \frac{1}{z_1}\exp\left(\sum_{l}^{L}\sum_{k}^{K}\left(t_{lk} - f_{\text{outer}}\left(\sum_{j=0}^{M}\gamma_{kj}(G_x, R, N_r)\right.\right.\right.$$

$$\left.\left.\left.\times f_{\text{inner}}\left(\sum_{i=0}^{d}w_{ji}^{(1)}x_i\right)\right)\right)^2_{lk}\right). \tag{8.19}$$

Here, $z_1$ is the normalization constant, $L$ is the number of outputs while $K$ is the number of training examples. The prior probability in this problem is linked to the concept of reducts, which was explained earlier, and it is the prior knowledge that the best rough set model is the one with the minimum number of rules ($N_r$), and that the best network is the one whose weights are of the same order of magnitude. We write it as follows (Marwala and

Crossingham, 2008):

$$P(\mathbf{M}) = \frac{1}{z_2} \exp\left(-\alpha N_r - \beta \sum w^2\right), \tag{8.20}$$

where $z_2$ is the normalization constant and $\beta$ is the hyperparameter of the network weights. The posterior probability of the model given the observed data is thus:

$$P(\mathbf{M} \mid \mathbf{D}) = \frac{1}{z_1} \exp\left(\sum_l^L \sum_k^K \left(t_{lk} - f_{\text{outer}}\left(\sum_{j=0}^M \gamma_{kj}(G_x, R, N_r)\right.\right.\right.$$

$$\left.\left.\left. \times f_{\text{inner}}\left(\sum_{i=0}^d w_{ji}^{(1)} x_i\right)\right)\right)^2_{lk} - \alpha N_r - \beta \sum w^2\right), \tag{8.21}$$

where $z$ is the normalization constant and $\alpha$ is the hyperparameter of the number of rules. Since the number and the rules given the data depends on the nature of granulization, we shall sample in the granule space as well as the network weights using a procedure called Markov Chain Monte Carlo (MCMC) simulation (Marwala, 2007a; Bishop, 2006).

## 8.7.2  Markov Chain Monte Carlo (MCMC)

The way in which we randomly sample the probability distribution in Equation (8.20) to generate a succession of granule-weight vectors and accepting or rejecting them is based on how probable they are, using Metropolis *et al.* (1953) algorithm (Marwala and Crossingham, 2008). This process requires a generation of large samples of granules for the input space and the network weights. This in many cases is not computationally efficient. The MCMC creates a chain of granules and network weights and accepts or rejects them using Metropolis algorithm. The application of Bayesian approach and MCMC neuro-rough sets, results in the probability distribution function of the granules and network weights. This in turn leads to the distribution of the neuro-rough model outputs. From these distribution functions, we calculate the average prediction of the neuro-rough set model and the variance of that prediction. We represent the probability distributions of a neuro-rough set model by granules and network weights.

We implement the MCMC method by sampling a stochastic process consisting of random variables ({$\mathbf{gw}$} representing granules and weight vectors) $\{\mathbf{gw_1}, \mathbf{gw_2}, \cdot, \mathbf{gw_n}\}$ by introducing random changes to granule-weight vector $\{\mathbf{gw}\}$ and either accepting or rejecting the state according to Metropolis algorithm given the differences in posterior probabilities between two states that are in transition (Metropolis *et al.*, 1953). We represent this procedure that ensures that states with high probability form the majority of the Markov chain mathematically as:

if $P(\mathbf{M}\,|\,\mathbf{D})_{\text{new}} > P(\mathbf{M}\,|\,\mathbf{D})_{\text{old}}$ accept state $(\mathbf{M}_{\text{new}})$

else

accept $(P(\mathbf{M}\,|\,\mathbf{D})_{\text{new}})$ with probability $\hspace{3cm}$ (8.22)

$$\frac{P(\mathbf{M}\,|\,\mathbf{D})_{\text{new}}}{P(\mathbf{M}\,|\,\mathbf{D})_{\text{old}}} > \zeta.$$

Here, $\zeta$ is uniformly generated to fall between 0 and 1, else reject and randomly generate another model $P(\mathbf{M}\,|\,\mathbf{D})_{\text{new}}$.

The steps described above may be summarized as follows:

**Step 1**: Randomly generate the granule weight vector $\{\mathbf{gw}\}_n$

**Step 2**: Estimate the posterior probability $P_n$ and vector $\{\mathbf{gw}\}_n$

**Step 3**: Introduce random changes to vector $\{\mathbf{gw}\}_n$ to form vector $\{\mathbf{gw}\}_{n+1}$

**Step 4**: Estimate the posterior probability $P_{n+1}$ using the vector $\{\mathbf{gw}\}_{n+1}$

**Step 5**: Accept or reject vector $\{\mathbf{gw}\}_{n+1}$ using Metropolis algorithm

**Step 6**: Go to step 3 and repeat the process until enough samples of distribution have been achieved

## 8.8 Modelling of HIV

Marwala and Crossingham (2008) applied rough sets to create a model that used demographic characteristics to estimate the risk of HIV. HIV is the cause of AIDS and ravaged many communities (Lasry *et al.*, 2007; Poundstone *et al.*, 2004). Leke *et al.* (2006b) used the individual characteristics as well as social and demographic factors to determine the risk of HIV using neuro-rough models formulated using Bayesian approach, and trained using Markov Chain Monte Carlo method. Although Leke *et al.* (2007) achieved good accuracy when using the neural networks method, neural networks method is disadvantageous due to its 'black box' nature, which is that it is not transparent. To improve transparency, Marwala and Crossingham (2007) used the Bayesian rough set theory (RST) to forecast and interpret the causal effects of HIV and obtain good accuracy and relevant rules that govern the relationships between demographic characteristics and HIV.

Marwala and Crossingham (2007) obtained the dataset used from the South African antenatal sero-prevalence survey of 2001 (Department of Health, 2001). The Department of Health obtained the data through questionnaires completed by pregnant women attending selected public clinics across all nine provinces in South Africa. The six demographic variables considered were race, age of mother, education, gravidity, parity and, age of father, with the outcome or decision being either HIV positive or negative. The HIV status was the decision represented in binary form as either a 0 or 1, with a 0 representing HIV negative and a 1 representing HIV positive. Marwala and Crossingham (2007) discretized the input data into four partitions because it gave a good balance between computational efficiency and accuracy. The parents' ages were an integer, education was an integer, where 13 is the highest level of education, indicating tertiary education. Gravidity defined as the number of times a woman has fallen pregnant, whereas parity is the number of times that a woman has given birth. They trained the neuro-rough models by sampling in the granule and weight space and accepting or rejecting samples using Metropolis *et al.* algorithm (1953) and, 12945 cases were used to train the model.

The input data was therefore the demographic characteristics explained earlier and the output was the plausibility of HIV with 1 representing 100% plausibility that a person is HIV positive and $-1$ indicating 100% plausibility of HIV negative. The neuro-rough model constructed had seven inputs, five hidden nodes, hyperbolic tangent function in the inner layer ($f_{inner}$) and logistic function in the outer layer ($f_{outer}$). When training the neuro-rough models using Markov Chain Monte Carlo, 500 samples were accepted and retained. This means that there were 500 sets of rules and weights where each set contained 50 up to 550 numbers of rules with an average of 88 rules. The distributions of these rules over the 500 samples are in Figure 8.2. They retained 500 samples because the simulation had converged to a stationary distribution and this is in Figure 8.3.

They interpreted this figure in the light of the fact that on calculating the posterior probability, they used the knowledge that fewer rules and weights of the same order of magnitudes were more desirable. Therefore, the Bayesian neuro-rough model was able to select the number of rules in addition to the partition sizes and weights. The average accuracy achieved was 62%. This accuracy can be compared with the accuracy of Bayesian multi-layered perceptron trained using hybrid Monte Carlo by Tim and Marwala (2006), which gave the accuracy of 62%, and Bayesian rough sets

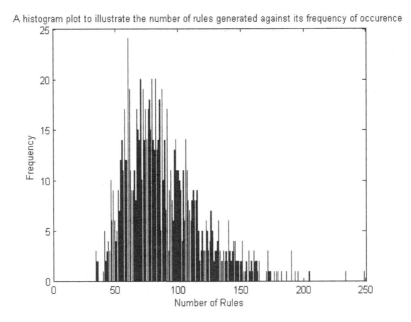

**Figure 8.2**  The distribution of number of rules.

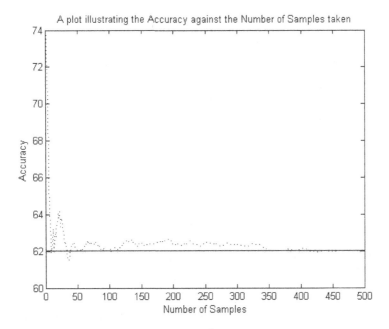

**Figure 8.3**  A figure indicating the convergence as the number of samples increase.

by Marwala and Crossingham (2007), which gave the accuracy of 58%, all on the same database. The results showed that the incorporation of rough sets into the multi-layered perceptron neural network to form neuro-rough model does not compromise on the results obtained from a traditional Bayesian neural network, but it added a dimension of rules. The receiver operator characteristics (ROC) curve showed the area under the curve to be 0.59. This shows that the neuro-rough model proposed is able to estimate the HIV status.

Once we applied the Bayesian neuro-rough model to the HIV data, unique distinguishable cases and indiscernible cases were identified. From the dataset of 12945 cases, the data was only a representative of 452 cases out of the possible 4096 unique combinations. The lower approximation cases are rules that always hold or are definite cases, while we can state the upper approximation with certain plausibility. An example of both cases that was extracted from the approach is: **If** Race = AF **and** Mother's Age = Young **and** Education = Secondary **and** Gravidity = Low **and** Parity = Low **and** Father's Age = Young **then** $\gamma = -0.75$ meaning probably HIV negative. This demonstrates that the Bayesian neuro-rough model allows us to extract rules in linguistic terms.

## 8.9  Application to Modelling the Stock Market

Following on the work of Khoza and Marwala (2011), the Johannesburg Stock Exchange's All Share Index (ALSI) from 2006 to 2011 was modelled. The data was randomly divided into 75% and 25% ratio. 75% of the data was used for training and 25% was used for validation. There was a total of 10 attributes used and these are shown in Table 8.3 (Khoza and Marwala, 2011).

The decision attribute in this chapter can be represented as follows (Khoza and Marwala, 2011):

$$D = \frac{\sum_{i=1}^{i=n}((n+1) - i) \times \|\text{Close}(i) - \text{Close}(i-1)\|}{\sum_{n=1}^{n} i}. \tag{8.23}$$

The decision attribute was normalized to limit its value to fall between $-1$ and $+1$. A value of $+1$ demonstrates that every day for the next $n$ days into the future the price closes higher than today, and, likewise, a value of $-1$ shows that every day for the next $n$ days into the future the price closes lower than it is at present. Essentially, $D$ is an indicator on whether we buy or sell, and it indicates the future direction of the index.

When they applied the rough set to model the stock market, as described above, the dominance of each attribute as measured as an appearance

**Table 8.3**   Table of attributes.

| Attributes | Description |
|---|---|
| Open | The opening price |
| High | The highest registered price on the day |
| Low | The lowest registered price on the day |
| Close | The closing price |
| Adjusted close | The adjusted closing price |
| Moving average | Moving average over five days |
| Momentum | $P_i - P_{i-4}$ |
| Rate of Change (ROC) | $\dfrac{\text{Momentum}}{P_i} \times 100$ |
| Disparity | $\dfrac{P_i}{\text{Moving average}} \times 100$ |
| Decision (D) | Decision attribute |

**Table 8.4**   Attribute used to model the stock market.

| Attribute | Count | Percentage (%) |
|---|---|---|
| Open | 54 | 29.35 |
| High | 73 | 39.67 |
| Low | 81 | 44 |
| Close | 71 | 38.58 |
| Adj Close | 54 | 29.34 |
| MAV | 68 | 36.95 |
| Momentum | 72 | 39.14 |
| ROC | 69 | 37.5 |
| Disparity | 89 | 48.37 |

percentage of the total number of reducts generated is shown in Table 8.4 (Khoza and Marwala, 2011).

To provide comparison, they built rules using the 182 reducts created in the first stage of the previous phase and then a second set of rules was extracted using only the core reduct. With 182 reducts, a total of 1004 rules were created and with the core reduct, above a total of 246 rules were generated.

The decision table was built by having columns as several technical indicators and the rows indicating trading data at each point in time, whereas the window offers a 'snapshot' of the state of the market in that period. The parameters that influenced the accuracy of the model were the data split

**Table 8.5**    Discretization algorithm accuracy comparison.

| Discretization Algorithm | Evaluation Criteria | | |
|---|---|---|---|
| | Reducts | Rules | Accuracy (%) |
| EFB (with four data cuts) | 182 | 1004 | 86.8 |
| BR | 2 | 1510 | 57.7 |
| Entropy | 2 | 484 | 64.5 |
| Naïve algorithm | 32 | 31188 | 43 |

**Table 8.6**    EFB cuts comparison.

| EFB Cuts | Evaluation Criteria | | |
|---|---|---|---|
| | Reducts | Rules | Accuracy (%) |
| 3 | 171 | 943 | 66.0 |
| 4 | 182 | 1004 | 86.8 |
| 5 | 190 | 1856 | 77.3 |
| 6 | 197 | 2450 | 76.1 |

ratio, discretization algorithm and the classifier technique. To build the most robust model, the correct combination of these parameters is necessary.

Because it was observed that the quality of the model, its accuracy, depends heavily on the discretization algorithm (Khoza and Marwala, 2011), used several discretization algorithms so as to assess which gave the best results. These were: EFB, the BR algorithm, Entropy/MDL algorithm and the Naïve algorithm. Table 8.5 shows the results obtained when these algorithms were used.

From the results in Table 8.5, it is observed that the EFB gave the best results. The relationship between the number of data cuts and accuracy when the EFB was implemented is shown in Table 8.6.

As shown in Table 8.6, it was observed that four data cuts offered the best results, from which other tuning of parameters can be based. The difference in accuracy and rules generated from the EFB (4 data cuts) with the normal reducts and the core reducts are shown in Table 8.7.

Table 8.7 demonstrates a trade-off between the number of rules generated and the accuracy of the model. Rough set model's confusion matrix is shown in Table 8.8 for the core reduct based system.

**Table 8.7** Normal and core reduct comparison.

| Reducts | Rules | Accuracy (%) |
|---|---|---|
| Normal | 1,004 | 86.8 |
| Core reduct | 246 | 80.4 |

**Table 8.8** Rough set model confusion matrix.

| | | Predicted | | |
|---|---|---|---|---|
| | | 0 | 1 | |
| Actual | 0 | 147 | 14 | 0.9130 |
| | 1 | 43 | 87 | 0.6692 |
| | | 0.7736 | 0.8613 | **0.8041** |

**Table 8.9** Classification results.

| Method | True Conflicts (TC) | False Peaces (FP) | True Peaces (TP) | False Conflicts (FC) |
|---|---|---|---|---|
| Rough sets: EWB | 272 | 120 | 291 | 99 |
| Rough sets: EFB | 292 | 100 | 268 | 124 |

## 8.10 Interstate Conflict

Crossingham (2007) and Crossingham and Marwala (2007) studied rough sets to model interstate conflict. They used seven variables to predict interstate conflict and these variables were allies, contiguity, major powers, distance, capability, Democracy and Dependency. Details on this can be found in Marwala and Lagazio (2011).

The training process resulted in 125 rules for the EWB rough set model and 90 rules for the EFB rough set model. The detection rate of conflict when they used the EFB rough set model was 74%. The detection rate of conflict when they used the EWB rough set model was 69%. The peace detection rate when they used the EFB rough set model was 68%. The peace detection rate when they used the EWB rough set model was 75%. We show these results in Table 8.9 (Marwala and Lagazio, 2011).

Overall, the detection rate for a correct outcome when the EFB rough set model was used was 71% and when the EWB rough set model was used was 72%. Furthermore, the Area Under the receiver operating characteristics Curves (AUC) were, 0.77 for the EWB rough set model and 0.76 for the EFB rough set model. The rough set rules extracted when they used the EWB was:

If *Allies* = 1 (True) and *Contiguity* = 0 (False) and *Major Powers* = 1 (True) and *Distance* = 8 (High) and *Capability* = 9 (High) and *Democracy* = 10 (High) and *Dependency* = 0.17 (High) Then *Outcome* = Most Probably Peace.

## 8.11  Conclusions

This chapter described rough set theory. Then it studied the concept of rough sets discretization. Subsequently, it introduced neuro-rough sets, which is based on rough sets and the multi-layered perceptron. It then studied application of neuro-rough sets on modelling HIV. Furthermore, it studied the use of different discretization methods and rough sets to model the stock market. Thereafter, we studied the use of rough sets to model interstate conflict.

## References

Azadeh, A., Saberi, M., Moghaddam, R.T., Javanmardi, L. (2011). An integrated data envelopment analysis — Artificial neural network-rough set algorithm for assessment of personnel efficiency. *Expert Systems with Applications*, 38:1364–1373.

Bazan, J., Nguyen, H.S., Szczuka, M. (2004). A view on rough set concept approximations. *Fundamenta Informaticae*, 59:107–118.

Beynon, M. (2001). Reducts within the variable precision rough sets model: A further investigation. *European Journal of Operational Research*, 134:592–605.

Bi, Y., Anderson, T., McClean, S. (2003). A rough set model with ontologies for discovering maximal association rules in document collections. *Knowledge-Based Systems*, 16:243–251.

Bishop, C.M. (1995). *Neural Networks for Pattern Recognition*. New York, USA: Oxford University Press.

Bishop, C.M. (2006). *Pattern Recognition and Machine Intelligence*. Berlin, Germany: Springer.

Chanas, S., Kuchta, D. (1992). Further remarks on the relation between rough and fuzzy sets. *Fuzzy Sets and Systems*, 47:391–394.

Chen, C., Shen, J., Chen, B., Shang, C.-X., Wang, Y.-C. (2010). Building symptoms diagnosis criteria of traditional chinese medical science treatment on the elderly's Pneumonia by the rough set theory. In: *Proceedings of the 29th Chinese Control Conference*, 5268–5271.

Chen, R., Zhang, Z., Wu, D., Zhang, P., Zhang, X., Wang, Y., Shi, Y. (2011). Prediction of protein interaction hot spots using rough set-based multiple criteria linear programming. *Journal of Theoretical Biology*, 269:174–180.

Crossingham, B. (2007). Rough Set Partitioning Using Computational Intelligence Approach. Unpublished Master Thesis, University of the Witwatersrand, Johannesburg.

Crossingham, B., Marwala, T. (2007). Using optimisation techniques to granulise rough set partitions. *Computer Models for Life Science*, 952:248–257.

Crossingham, B., Marwala, T. (2008a). Using genetic algorithms to optimise rough set partition sizes for HIV data analysis. *Studies in Computational Intelligence*, 78:245–250.

Crossingham, B., Marwala, T. (2008b). Using optimisation techniques for discretizing rough set partitions. *International Journal of Hybrid Intelligent Systems*, 5:219–236.

Crossingham, B., Marwala, T., Lagazio, M. (2008). Optimised rough sets for modeling interstate conflict. In: *Proceedings of the IEEE International Conference on Systems, Man, and Cybernetics*, 1198–1204.

Crossingham, B., Marwala, T., Lagazio, M. (2009). Evolutionarily optimized rough set partitions. *ICIC Express Letters*, 3:241–246.

Degang, C., Wenxiu, Z., Yeung, D., Tsang, E.C.C. (2006). Rough approximations on a complete completely distributive lattice with applications to generalized rough sets. *Information Science*, 176:1829–1848.

Department of Health (2001). National HIV and syphilis sero-prevalence survey of women attending public antenatal clinics in South Africa. Available at: https://www.gov.za/sites/default/files/hivsyphilis_0.pdf.

Dubois, D. (1990). Rough fuzzy sets and fuzzy rough sets. *International Journal of General Systems*, 17:191–209.

Fayyad, U., Irani, K. (1993). Multi-interval discretization of continuous valued attributes for classification learning. In: *Proceedings of the 13th International Joint Conference on Artificial Intelligence*, Los Alamos, CA, 1022–1027.

Goh, C., Law, R. (2003). Incorporating the rough sets theory into travel demand analysis. *Tourism Management*, 24:511–517.

Golan, R.H., Ziarko, W. (1995). A methodology for stock market analysis utilizing rough set theory. In: *Proceedings of Computational Intelligence for Financial Engineering*, 32–40.

Gong, J., Yang, H., Zhong. L. (2010). Case-based reasoning based on rough set in rare-earth extraction process. In: *Proceedings of the 29th Chinese Control Conference*, 70–1706.

Grzymala-Busse, J.W. (2004). Three approaches to missing attribute values — A rough set perspective. In: *Proceedings of the IEEE 4th International Conference on Data Mining*, 57–64.

Grzymala-Busse, J.W., Hu, M. (2001). A comparison of several approaches to missing attribute values in data mining. *Lecture Notes in Artificial Intelligence*, 205:378–385.

Grzymala-Busse, J.W., Siddhaye, S. (2004). Rough set approaches to rule induction from incomplete data. In: *Proceedings of the 10th International Conference on Information Process and Management of Uncertainty in Knowledge-Based Systems*, 2:923–930.

Hoa, N.S., Son, N.H. (2008). Rough set approach to approximation of concepts from taxonomy. Available at: http://logic.mimuw.edu.pl/publikacje/SonHoaKDO04.pdf.

Huang, C.-C., Liang, W.-Y., Shian-Hua, L., Tseng, T.-L., Chiang, H.-Y. (2011). A rough set based approach to patent development with the consideration of resource allocation. *Expert Systems with Applications*, 38:1980–1992.

Inuiguchi, M., Miyajima, T. (2007). Rough set based rule induction from two decision tables. *European Journal of Operational Research*, 181:1540–1553.

Jaafar, A.F.B., Jais, J., Hamid, M.H.B.H.A., Rahman, Z.B.A., Benaouda, D. (2006). Using rough set as a tool for knowledge discovery in DSS. In: *Proceedings of the 4th International Conference on Multimedia and Information and Communication Technology in Education*, 1011–1015.

Khoza, M., Marwala, T. (2011). A rough set theory based predictive model for stock prices. In: *IEEE 12th International Symposium on Computational Intelligence and Informatics (CINTI)*, Budapest, 57–62.

Komorowski, J., Pawlak, Z., Polkowski, L., Skowron, A. (1999). A rough set perspective on data and knowledge. In: Klösgen W., Zytkow, J.M., Klosgen, W., Zyt, J. (eds.), *The Handbook of Data Mining and Knowledge Discovery*. New York: Oxford University Press.

Kondo, M. (2006). On the structure of generalized rough sets. *Information Science*, 176:589–600.

Lasry, G., Zaric, S., Carter, M.W. (2007). Multi-level resource allocation for HIV prevention: A model for developing countries. *European Journal of Operational Research*, 180:786–799.

Leke, B.B., Marwala, T., Tettey, T. (2006a). Autoencoder networks for HIV classification. *Current Science*, 91:1467–1473.

Leke, B.B., Marwala, T., Tettey, T. (2007). Using inverse neural network for HIV adaptive control. *International Journal of Computational Intelligence Research*, 3:11–15.

Leke, B.B., Marwala, T., Tim, T., Lagazio, M. (2006b). Prediction of HIV status from demographic data using neural networks. In: *Proceedings of the IEEE International Conference on Systems, Man and Cybernetics*. Taiwan, 2339–2444.

Leung, Y., Wu, W., Zhang, W. (2006). Knowledge acquisition in incomplete information systems: A rough set approach. *European Journal of Operational Research*, 168:164–180.

Liao, S.-H., Chen, Y.-J., Chu, P.-H. (2010). Rough-set-based association rules applied to brand trust evaluation model. *Lecture Notes in Computer Science*, 6443: 634–641.

Lin, C.-S., Tzeng, G.-H., Chin, Y.-C. (2011). Combined rough set theory and flow network graph to predict customer churn in credit card accounts. *Expert Systems with Applications*, 38:8–15.

Machowski, L.A., Marwala, T. (2005). Using object oriented calculation process framework and neural networks for classification of image shapes. *International Journal of Innovative Computing, Information and Control*, 1:609–623.

Marwala, T. (2001). Fault Identification Using Neural Networks and Vibration Data. Doctor of Philosophy Thesis, University of Cambridge.

Marwala, T. (2007a). Bayesian training of neural network using genetic programming. *Pattern Recognition Letters*, 28(12):1452–1458. Available at: http://dx.doi.org/10. 1016/j.patrec.2007.03.004.

Marwala, T. (2007b). *Computational Intelligence for Modelling Complex Systems*, Research India Publishers (in press).

Marwala, T. (2009). *Computational Intelligence for Missing Data Imputation, Estimation, and Management: Knowledge Optimization Techniques*, Information Science Reference Imprint. New York: IGI Global Publications.

Marwala, T. (2012). *Condition Monitoring Using Computational Intelligence Methods*. Heidelberg: Springer.

Marwala, T. (2013). *Economic Modeling Using Artificial Intelligence Methods*. Heidelberg: Springer.

Marwala, T. (2014). *Artificial Intelligence Techniques for Rational Decision Making*. Heidelberg: Springer.

Marwala, T. (2015). *Causality, Correlation, and Artificial Intelligence for Rational Decision Making.* Singapore: World Scientific.

Marwala, T., Crossingham, B. (2007). Bayesian approach to rough set. arXiv 0704.3433.

Marwala, T., Crossingham, B. (2008). Neuro-rough Models for Modelling HIV. In: *Proceedings of the IEEE International Conference on System, Man, and Cybernetics,* 3089–3095.

Marwala T., Crossingham, B. (2009). Bayesian rough sets. *ICIC Express Letters,* 3:115–120.

Marwala, T., Lagazio, M. (2011). *Militarized Conflict Modeling Using Computational Intelligence.* Heidelberg: Springer. Translated into Chinese by the National Defence Industry Press.

Metropolis, N., Rosenbluth, A.W., Rosenbluth, M.N., Teller, A.H., Teller, E. (1953). Equations of state calculations by fast computing machines. *Journal of Chemical Physics,* 21:1087–1092.

Nelwamondo, F.V. (2008). Computational Intelligence Techniques for Missing Data Imputation. PhD Thesis, University of the Witwatersrand, Johannesburg.

Ohrn, A. (1999). Discernibility and Rough Sets in Medicine: Tools and Applications. Unpublished PhD Thesis, Norwegian University of Science and Technology.

Ohrn, A., Rowland, T. (2000). Rough sets: A knowledge discovery technique for multifactorial medical outcomes. *American Journal of Physical Medicine and Rehabilitation,* 79:100–108.

Quafofou, M. (2000). α-RST. A generalization of rough set theory. *Information Science,* 124:301–316.

Pawlak, Z. (1991). *Rough Sets — Theoretical Aspects of Reasoning about Data.* Dordrecht: Kluwer Academic Publishers.

Pawlak, Z., Munakata, T. (1996). Rough control application of rough set theory to control. In: *Proceedings of the 4th European Congress on Intelligent Techniques and Soft Computing,* 209–218.

Pawlak, Z., Skowron, A. (2007). Rough sets and boolean reasoning. *Information Science,* 177:41–73.

Pawlak, Z., Wong, S.K.M., Ziarko, W. (1988). Rough sets: Probabilistic versus deterministic approach. *International Journal of Man–Machine Studies,* 29: 81–95.

Pe-a, J., Ltourneau, S., Famili, A. (1999). Application of rough sets algorithms to prediction of aircraft component failure. In: *Proceedings of the 3rd International Symposium on Intelligent Data Analysis,* Amsterdam.

Poundstone, K.E., Strathdee, S.A., Celentano, D.D. (2004). The social epidemiology of human immunodeficiency virus/acquired immunodeficiency syndrome. *Epidemiological Reviews,* 26:22–35.

Rowland, T., Ohno-Machado, L., Ohrn, A. (1998). Comparison of multiple prediction models for ambulation following spinal cord injury. In: *Proceedings of the AMIA Symposium,* 31:528–532.

Salamó, M., López-Sánchez, M. (2011). Rough set based approaches to feature selection for case-based reasoning classifiers. *Pattern Recognition Letters,* 32:280–292.

Shan, N., Ziarko, W. (1995). Data-based acquisition and incremental modification of classification rules. *Computational Intelligence,* 11:357–370.

Slezak, D., Ziarko, W. (2005). The investigation of the Bayesian rough set model. *International Journal of Approximate Reasoning,* 40:81–91.

Stefanowski, J. (1998). On rough set based approaches to induction of decision rules. In: Polkowski, L., Skowron, A. (ed.), *Rough Sets in Knowledge Discovery 1: Methodology and Applications.* Heidelberg: Physica-Verlag.

Tay, F.E.H., Shen, L. (2003). Fault diagnosis based on rough set theory. *Engineering Applications of Artificial Intelligence*, 16, 39–43.

Terlecki, P., Walczak, K. (2007). On the relation between rough set reducts and jumping emerging patterns. *Information Sciences*, 177:74–83.

Tettey, T., Nelwamondo, F.V., Marwala, T. (2007). HIV data analysis via rule extraction using rough sets. In: *Proceedings of the 11th IEEE International Conference on Intelligent Engineering Systems*, 105–110.

Tim, T.N., Marwala, T. (2006). Computational intelligence methods for risk assessment of HIV. In: Sun I. Kim and Tae Suk Sah (eds.), *Imaging the Future Medicine, Proceedings of the IFMBE*, 14:3581–3585. Berlin Heidelberg, Springer-Verlag.

Wang, J., Guo, K., Wang, S. (2010). Rough set and Tabu search based feature selection for credit scoring. *Procedia Computer Science*, 1:2433–2440.

Wang, W., Yang, J., Jensen, R., Liu, X. (2006). Rough set feature selection and rule induction for prediction of malignancy degree in brain glioma. *Computer Programs and Methods in Bioscience*, 83:147–156.

Witlox, F., Tindemans, H. (2004). The application of rough sets analysis in activity based modelling: Opportunities and constraints. *Expert Systems with Applications*, 27:585–592.

Wu, W., Mi, J., Zhang, W. (2003). Generalized fuzzy rough sets. *Information Science*, 151:263–282.

Xie, F., Lin, Y., Ren, W. (2011). Optimizing model for land use/land cover retrieval from remote sensing imagery based on variable precision rough sets. *Ecological Modelling*, 222:232–240.

Yan, W., Liu, W., Cheng, Z., Kan, J. (2010). The prediction of soil moisture based on rough set-neural network model. In: *Proceedings of the 29th Chinese Control Conference*, 2413–2415.

Yang, Y., John, R. (2006). Roughness bound in set-oriented rough set operations. In: *Proceedings of the IEEE International Conference on Fuzzy Systems*, 1461–1468.

Zadeh, L.A. (1965). Fuzzy sets. *Information and Control*, 8:338–353.

Zhang, Y., Zhu, J., Zhang, Z.-Y. (2010). The research of reagent adding control in anionic reverse flotation process based on rough set theory. In: *Proceedings of the 29th Chinese Control Conference*, 3487–3491.

Zhao, Y., Yao, Y., Luo, F. (2007). Data analysis based on discernibility and indiscernibility. *Information Science*, 177:4959–4976.

Zou, Z., Tseng, T.-L., Sohn, H., Song, G., Gutierrez, R. (2011). A rough set based approach to distributor selection in supply chain management. *Expert Systems with Applications*, 38:106–115.

## Chapter 9

# Hybrid Machines

**Abstract.** In this chapter, a hybrid of machines for both classification and regression are introduced. The hybrid approach is mathematically explained, and it is proven that it is more accurate than the individual methods if the individual methods are not correlated. We applied the hybrid method to two sets of problems, and these were for fault classification in mechanical systems and caller behaviour classification. The results obtained demonstrated that the hybrid method performs better than the individual method.

## 9.1 Introduction

In earlier chapters, we studied various artificial intelligence techniques, and these included the multi-layer perceptron (MLP), radial basis function (RBF), support vector machines (SVMs) and fuzzy logic. These techniques each have their own advantages and disadvantages. For example, the MLP couples input variables together such that it is not straightforward to infer the impact of an input variable on the output. However, the MLP has been found to be an accurate machine-learning methodology. In fact, the MLP is so successful that it is the basis of what we now call deep learning, which is just a large version of the MLP neural network.

The RBF is a close cousin of the MLP network. Its cross-coupling characteristics are not as rich as that of the MLP. The RBF has a distinct advantage in that it is relatively easy to train.

The SVM is another type of technique that is based on the principle of drawing the most optimal linear hyperplane that divides different classes of data. This is an efficient process. To deal with the fact that the linear hyperplane might not necessarily be possible particularly for high dimensional data, SVM introduces the concept of a kernel, which increases the dimension of the data until it can be linearly separated.

Fuzzy logic is another algorithm that has been introduced to handle situations where precision is an issue. Problems where precision is the issue include problems with linguistic variables. Fuzzy logic is called a transparent model because it is easy to extract rules that define interrelationships in the data. The disadvantage of fuzzy logic is that though they are transparent, they are not very accurate. Fuzzy logic has been extended to combine them with neural networks and this is called neuro-fuzzy models. This makes neuro-fuzzy models transparent and accurate.

We also described rough sets, which are intelligent lookup-tables, which are closer to fuzzy logic. Again, rough sets are transparent and even more transparent than fuzzy logic but are not as accurate as neural networks. Also, rough sets have been combined with neural networks to make them both transparent and accurate.

Because each of these methods offer their own advantages as well as disadvantages, it is logical to combine all of them to form one procedure (Jafari *et al.*, 2011; Perrone and Cooper, 1993). This is achieved by hybridizing them to form what is conventionally called a committee of networks. There are many ways to combine these methods, and these include voting classifiers among others.

Successful applications of the hybrid of networks include to predict rock permeability (Bagheripour, 2014), for oil reservoir characterization (Oloso *et al.*, 2017), to estimate pressure (Barbosa *et al.*, 2015) and for residual lifestyle prediction (Sbarufatti *et al.*, 2016). In this chapter, we first mathematically study the hybrid method and the advantages that it offers compared to the individual methods. We then apply the hybrid approach to the faults identification problem in mechanical systems as well as caller behaviour classification.

## 9.2  Hybrid Machine

In this chapter, we describe the hybrid of intelligent networks. Applications of hybrid networks include applying the hybrid of probabilistic RBF neural networks to identify palm prints (Du *et al.*, 2007). Marwala *et al.* (2001) applied a hybrid of agents and genetic programming to evolve a stock market prediction system. Successful studies of hybrid machines also include: Anthony (2007) who studied fixed combinations of intelligent machines and Sheikh-Ahmad *et al.* (2007) who used hybrid neural networks for force prediction models in a milling process. Marwala (2001, 2012) identified faults in structures using a hybrid of neural networks. Abdel-Aal (2005a) proposed a three-member hybrid of MLP networks to improve electric load forecasting whereas Abdel-Aal (2005b) improved diversity of a hybrid machine by training the networks with different data. Karimpouli *et al.* (2010) used a hybrid of neural networks to predict the permeability of petroleum reservoirs Kadkhodaie-Ilkhchi *et al.* (2009) used a hybrid of neural networks to predict normalized oil content from logged oil-well data from South Pars Gas Field in the Persian Gulf. Jafari *et al.* (2011) used a hybrid of neural networks with a fuzzy genetic algorithm in the petroleum industry. van Hinsbergen *et al.* (2009) used a Bayesian hybrid of neural networks to estimate travel times. Successful uses of the hybrid approach further include human face recognition (Zhao *et al.*, 2004), swallow acceleration signal recognition (Das *et al.*, 2001), salient features selection (Bacauskiene and Verikas, 2004), speaker verification (Reddy and Buch, 2003), fire detection (Fernandes *et al.*, 2004), permeability prediction (Chen and Lin, 2006) and missing data estimation (Marwala, 2009).

The hybrid approach is also called ensembles of networks. There are many types of hybrid network ensembles. These include the Bayes Optimal Classifier (BOC), Bayesian model averaging, bagging, boosting and stacking.

### 9.2.1 Bayes optimal classifier

The BOC is an ensemble of all the hypotheses in the hypothesis space organized in such a way that no other ensemble can perform better than it (Bishop, 1995; Marwala, 2012). The vote of each hypothesis depends on the likelihood that we sample the training dataset from a system where that hypothesis is true. To enable training data of finite size, we multiply each hypothesis' vote by the prior probability of that hypothesis. We write the BOC as (Bishop, 1995; Marwala, 2012):

$$y = \arg\max_{c_j \in C} \sum_{h_i \in H} P(c_j|h_i)P(T|h_i)P(h_i). \tag{9.1}$$

Here, $y$ is the approximated class, $C$ is a full set with all classes, $H$ is the hypothesis space, $P$ is the probability and $T$ is the training dataset. The BOC shows a hypothesis that is not necessarily located in $H$. The hypothesis characterized by the BOC is the optimal hypothesis in the ensemble space. Nevertheless, we only apply the BOC to the simplest of problems. There are numbers of explanations why we cannot practically apply the BOC, including the fact that the hypothesis spaces are too large to iterate. Many hypotheses give only a predicted class instead of the probability for each class. Calculating the unbiased estimate of the probability of the training set, given a hypothesis, is difficult and estimating prior probability for each hypothesis is not feasible.

### 9.2.2 Bayesian model averaging

Bayesian model averaging is an ensemble method that aims to estimate the BOC by sampling hypotheses from the hypothesis space and combining these hypotheses using a Baye's framework (Hoeting *et al.*, 1999; Marwala, 2012). As opposed to the BOC, Bayesian model averaging can be practically applied using procedures such as Monte Carlo sampling methods (Marwala, 2009). Researchers have demonstrated that under certain conditions, when we sample and average the hypotheses according to Baye's theorem, this procedure produces an expected error that is at most twice the expected error of the BOC (Haussler *et al.*, 1994). Nevertheless, Bayesian model averaging has the shortcoming of over-fitting and performs worse empirically than simple ensembles do, for instance bagging (Domingos, 2000).

Park and Grandhi (2010) successfully used the Bayesian model averaging to combine the predictions of a system response into a single prediction and applied this to a nonlinear spring-mass system, a laser peening process and a composite material.

Successful applications of Bayesian model averaging are to estimate heat wave mortality risk (Bobb *et al.*, 2011), forecast industrial production (Feldkircher, 2011), assess of environmental stressors (Boone *et al.*, 2011), analyse schizophrenia (Tsai *et al.*, 2011), quantify uncertainty in computer simulation (Park and Grandhi, 2010), study atmospheric dispersion (Potempski *et al.*, 2010) and analyse microarray data survival (Bichindaritz and Annest, 2010).

### 9.2.3 Bagging

Bagging, or Bootstrap averaging combines models fitted to bootstrap samples of a training dataset to reduce the variance of the prediction model (Breiman, 1996; Yu, 2011; Hernandez-Lobato *et al.*, 2011; Hu *et al.*, 2011; Marwala, 2012; Ng *et al.*, 2018). Bagging essentially entails randomly selecting a part of the training data, using this part to train a model and then repeating this process. Thereafter, we combine all trained models with equal weights to form an ensemble. It was applied successfully to simulate classification and regression problems (Pino-Mejias *et al.*, 2008), for speaker recognition (Kyung and Lee, 1999), for credit scoring (Louzada *et al.*, 2011), in spectral clustering (Jia *et al.*, 2011), on gene expression data (Hanczar and Nadif, 2011), in zero-inflated data (Osawa *et al.*, 2011) and energy forecasting (de Oliveira and Oliveira, 2018).

### 9.2.4 Boosting

Boosting incrementally builds an ensemble by training each new model with data that the previously trained model misclassified and the ensemble is a combination of all trained models (Khoshgoftaar *et al.*, 2011; Marwala, 2012; Ahachad *et al.*, 2017). Successful applications of boosting are in sequential Monte Carlo methods (Jasra and Holmes, 2011), estimating single-index models (Leitenstorfer and Tutz, 2011), in cross-product coverage (Baras *et al.*, 2011), for classification (Kajdanowicz and Kazienko, 2011), for noisy unbalanced data (Khoshgoftaar *et al.*, 2011) and for modelling energy consumption (Touzani *et al.*, 2018).

### 9.2.5 Stacking

The critical prior belief in the scientific method is that one can select from a set of models by comparing them on data that was not used to train the models (Marwala, 2012). We can use this prior belief to select among a set of models based on a single dataset by using a technique called cross-validation (Bishop, 1995; Marwala, 2012). We do this by dividing the dataset into a *held-in* dataset, which we use to create the models, and a *held-out* dataset, which we use to test the created models (Sill *et al.*, 2009; Shiraishi and Fukumizu, 2011; Marwala, 2012).

*Stacking* takes advantage of this prior belief using the performance on the held-out data to combine the models instead of selecting from them the best performing model when tested on the held-out data. The ensemble usually performs better than any single one of the trained models (Wolpert, 1992). It has been successfully applied in both supervised learning (regression) and unsupervised learning (density estimation), and to approximate Baggings' error rate (Breiman, 1996; Smyth and Wolpert, 1999; Wolpert and Macready, 1999; Rokach, 2010; Tang *et al.*, 2010). The stacking method performs better than the Bayesian model-averaging technique (Clarke, 2003). Stacking was successfully applied for face recognition (Drygajlo *et al.*, 2011), for object recognition (Larios *et al.*, 2011), for remote sensing (Huang *et al.*, 2011), for credit scoring (Wang *et al.*, 2011), aging face verification (Li *et al.*, 2010) and to map forest change (Healey *et al.*, 2018).

### 9.2.6 Evolutionary machines

Evolutionary hybrid machines are techniques for making the construction of the hybrid adapt in line with the environment. We achieve this by evolving the weighting function that defines the contribution of each individual machine, with respect to the overall outcome of the hybrid (Marwala, 2012). Marwala (2009) introduced a hybrid of networks for missing data estimation. Evolving networks have been the topic of study for some time (Marwala, 2009). Rajan and Mohan (2007) applied an evolutionary programming method based on simulated annealing to solve the unit commitment problem. Basu (2004) applied an evolutionary programming technique to create an interactive fuzzy satisfying scheme and used this for short-term hydrothermal scheduling. Shi and Xu (2001) used a self-adaptive evolutionary programming technique to optimize power systems. Cao *et al.* (2000) used an evolutionary programming technique in a mixed-variable optimization problem.

### 9.3  Theory of Hybrid Networks

We describe a hybrid of networks shown in Figure 9.1 (Marwala, 2012). The hybrid method in this figure consists of three networks and the output is the weighted average of the outputs of these three networks. The ideas presented in this section adapt the work of Perrone and Cooper (1993) and were successfully applied to mechanical engineering (Marwala and Hunt, 1999; Marwala, 2000). The hybrid of networks provides results that are more reliable than when using networks in isolation.

We write the mapping of the three different sets of input data to the outputs ($y_1$, $y_2$, and $y_3$) as the desired function plus an error. For notational accessibility, we assume the mapping functions to have single outputs, $y_1$, $y_2$ and $y_3$, and their respective inputs are $\alpha$, $\chi$ and $\kappa$. We can write these as follows (Perrone and Cooper, 1993; Marwala, 2000, 2010):

$$y_1(\alpha) = h(\alpha) + e_1(\alpha), \tag{9.2}$$

$$y_2(\chi) = h(\chi) + e_2(\chi), \tag{9.3}$$

$$y_3(\kappa) = h(\kappa) + e_3(\kappa). \tag{9.4}$$

Here, $h(\cdot)$ is an approximated mapping function; and $e(\cdot)$ is the error. The mean square errors (MSE) for model $y_1(\alpha)$, $y_2(\chi)$ and $y_3(\kappa)$ may be written

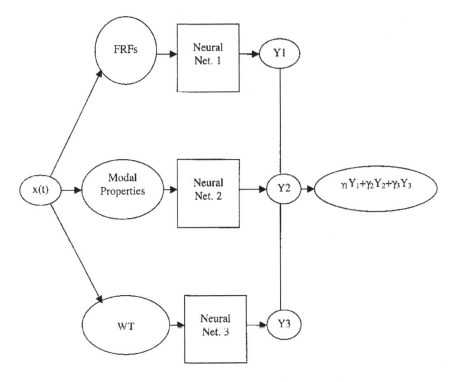

**Figure 9.1**   Illustration of hybrid of networks.

as follows (Perrone and Cooper, 1993; Marwala, 2012):

$$E_1 = \varepsilon[\{y_1(\boldsymbol{\alpha}) - h(\boldsymbol{\alpha})\}^2] = \varepsilon[e_1^2], \tag{9.5}$$

$$E_2 = \varepsilon[\{y_2(\boldsymbol{\chi}) - h(\boldsymbol{\chi})\}^2] = \varepsilon[e_2^2], \tag{9.6}$$

$$E_3 = \varepsilon[\{y_2(\boldsymbol{\kappa}) - h(\boldsymbol{\kappa})\}^2] = \varepsilon[e_3^2]. \tag{9.7}$$

In Equations (9.5)–(9.7), $\varepsilon[\cdot]$ indicates the expected value and corresponds to integration over the input data, and Perrone and Cooper (1993) defined this as follows:

$$\varepsilon[e_1^2] \equiv \int e_1^2(\boldsymbol{\alpha})p(\boldsymbol{\alpha})d\boldsymbol{\alpha}, \tag{9.8}$$

$$\varepsilon[e_2^2] \equiv \int e_2^2(\boldsymbol{\chi})p(\boldsymbol{\chi})d\boldsymbol{\chi}, \tag{9.9}$$

$$\varepsilon[e_3^2] \equiv \int e_3^2(\boldsymbol{\kappa})p(\boldsymbol{\kappa})d\boldsymbol{\kappa}. \tag{9.10}$$

Here, $p[\cdot]$ is the probability density function, and $d[\cdot]$ is a differential operator. Perrone and Cooper (1993) defined the average MSE of the three networks acting individually as follows:

$$E_{AV} = \frac{E_1(\alpha) + E_2(\chi) + E_3(\kappa)}{3}$$

$$= \frac{1}{3}(\varepsilon(e_1^2) + \varepsilon(e_2^2) + \varepsilon(e_3^2)). \tag{9.11}$$

### 9.3.1 Equal weights

The output of the hybrid of networks is the average of the outputs. We can write the hybrid networks prediction in the following form by giving equal weighting functions (Perrone and Cooper, 1993):

$$y_{COM} = \frac{1}{3}(y_1(\alpha) + y_2(\chi) + y_3(\kappa)). \tag{9.12}$$

We can write the MSE of the hybrid as follows:

$$E_{COM} = \varepsilon\left[\left(\frac{1}{3}\{y_1(\alpha) + y_2(\chi) + y_3(\kappa)\} - \frac{1}{3}[h(\alpha) + h(\chi) + h(\kappa)]\right)^2\right]$$

$$= \varepsilon\left[\left(\frac{1}{3}\{[y_1(\alpha) - h(\alpha)] + [y_2(\chi) - h(\chi)] + [y_3(\kappa) - h(\kappa)]\}\right)^2\right]$$

$$= \varepsilon\left[\left(\frac{1}{3}\{e_1 + e_2 + e_3\}\right)^2\right]$$

$$= \frac{1}{9}(\varepsilon[e_1^2] + 2(\varepsilon[e_1 e_2] + \varepsilon[e_1 e_2] + \varepsilon[e_2 e_3] + \varepsilon[e_1 e_3]) + \varepsilon[e_2^2] + \varepsilon[e_3^2]). \tag{9.13}$$

If we assume that, the errors ($e_1$, $e_2$ and $e_3$) are uncorrelated, then:

$$\varepsilon[e_1 e_2] = \varepsilon[e_1 e_2] = \varepsilon[e_2 e_3] = \varepsilon[e_1 e_3] = 0. \tag{9.14}$$

Substituting Equation (9.14) in Equation (9.13), Perrone and Cooper (1993) related the error of the hybrid to the average error of the networks acting individually as follows:

$$E_{COM} = \frac{1}{9}(\varepsilon[e_1^2] + \varepsilon[e_2^2] + \varepsilon[e_3^2])$$

$$= \frac{1}{3}E_{AV}. \tag{9.15}$$

Equation (9.15) demonstrates that the MSE of the hybrid is one-third of the average MSE of the individual technique. From Equation (9.15), we can deduce that the MSE of the hybrid is always equal to or less than the average MSE of the three methods acting individually.

### 9.3.2 Variable weights

The three networks might not essentially have the same predictive capability. To accommodate the strength of each technique, the network should be given suitable weighting functions. We explain later how we evaluate these weighting functions when there is no prior knowledge of the strength of each approach.

We define the output as the combination of the three independent networks with estimated weighting functions as:

$$y_{COM} = \gamma_1 y_1(\alpha) + \gamma_2 y_2(\chi) + \gamma_3 y_3(\kappa). \tag{9.16}$$

Here, $\gamma_1$, $\gamma_2$ and $\gamma_3$ are the weighting functions and $\gamma_1 + \gamma_2 + \gamma_3 = 1$. We can write the MSE due to the weighted hybrid as follows (Marwala, 2000):

$$
\begin{aligned}
E_{COM} &= \varepsilon[(\gamma_1 y_1(\alpha) + \gamma_2 y_2(\chi) + \gamma_3 y_3(\kappa) - [\gamma_1 h(\alpha) + \gamma_2 h(\chi) + \gamma_3 h(\kappa)])^2] \\
&= \varepsilon[(\gamma_1 [y_1(\alpha) - h(\alpha)] + \gamma_2 [y_2(\chi) - h(\chi)] + \gamma_3 [y_3(\kappa) - h(\kappa)])^2] \\
&= \varepsilon[(\gamma_1 e_1 + \gamma_2 e_2 + \gamma_3 e_3)^2].
\end{aligned}
\tag{9.17}
$$

Perrone and Cooper (1993) wrote Equation (9.17) in the Lagrangian form as follows:

$$E_{COM} = \varepsilon[(\gamma_1 e_1 + \gamma_2 e_2 + \gamma_3 e_3)^2] + \lambda(1 - \gamma_1 - \gamma_2 - \gamma_3). \tag{9.18}$$

Here, $\lambda$ is the Lagrangian multiplier. Perrone and Cooper (1993) calculated the derivative of the error in Equation (9.18) with respect to $\gamma_1$, $\gamma_2$, $\gamma_3$ and $\lambda$ then equated this to zero as:

$$\frac{dE_{COM}}{d\gamma_1} = 2e_1 \varepsilon[(\gamma_1 e_1 + \gamma_2 e_2 + \gamma_3 e_3)] - \lambda = 0, \tag{9.19}$$

$$\frac{dE_{COM}}{d\gamma_2} = 2e_2 \varepsilon[(\gamma_1 e_1 + \gamma_2 e_2 + \gamma_3 e_3)] - \lambda = 0, \tag{9.20}$$

$$\frac{dE_{COM}}{d\gamma_3} = 2e_3 \varepsilon[(\gamma_1 e_1 + \gamma_2 e_2 + \gamma_3 e_3)] - \lambda = 0, \tag{9.21}$$

$$\frac{dE_{COM}}{d\lambda} = 1 - \gamma_1 - \gamma_2 - \gamma_3 = 0. \tag{9.22}$$

In solving Equations (9.19)–(9.22), Perrone and Cooper (1993) obtained the minimum error when the weights are:

$$\gamma_1 = \frac{1}{1 + \frac{\varepsilon[e_1^2]}{\varepsilon[e_2^2]} + \frac{\varepsilon[e_1^2]}{\varepsilon[e_3^2]}}, \tag{9.23}$$

$$\gamma_2 = \frac{1}{1 + \frac{\varepsilon[e_2^2]}{\varepsilon[e_1^2]} + \frac{\varepsilon[e_2^2]}{\varepsilon[e_3^2]}}, \tag{9.24}$$

$$\gamma_3 = \frac{1}{1 + \frac{\varepsilon[e_3^2]}{\varepsilon[e_1^2]} + \frac{\varepsilon[e_3^2]}{\varepsilon[e_2^2]}}. \tag{9.25}$$

Perrone and Cooper (1993) generalized Equations (9.23)–(9.25) for a hybrid with $n$-trained networks as follows:

$$\gamma_i = \frac{1}{\sum_{j=1}^{n} \frac{\varepsilon[e_i^2]}{\varepsilon[e_j^2]}}. \tag{9.26}$$

From Equation (9.26), we derived the following conditions (Marwala, 2000):

$$\varepsilon[e_1^2] = \varepsilon[e_2^2] = \varepsilon[e_3^2] \Rightarrow \gamma_1 = \gamma_2 = \gamma_3 = \frac{1}{3}, \tag{9.27}$$

$$\varepsilon[e_3^2] < \varepsilon[e_2^2] < \varepsilon[e_1^2] \Rightarrow \gamma_1 < \gamma_2\langle\gamma_3;\gamma_3\rangle\frac{1}{3}, \tag{9.28}$$

$$\varepsilon[e_1^2] < \varepsilon[e_2^2] < \varepsilon[e_3^2] \Rightarrow \gamma_3 < \gamma_2\langle\gamma_3;\gamma_1\rangle\frac{1}{3}. \tag{9.29}$$

Because we do not know which network is more accurate in each instance, the weighting functions are determined from the data used to train the networks (prior knowledge) and this is *stacking*. The simultaneous use of three independent (uncorrelated) methods results in the increased reliability of the combination.

## 9.4  Condition Monitoring

We apply the hybrid method to fault identification using vibration data (Ewins, 1995). Vibration data can be expressed in many forms but in this chapter, we represent them using the pseudo-modal energies, modal data and wavelet data (Newland, 1993; Maia and Silva, 1997; Marwala, 1999, 2001, 2012).

Marwala (2000) trained the first network using the pseudo-modal energies, which were extracted from the vibration data, to predict faults in structures. There is a relationship between the pseudo-modal energies and the spatial properties of the structure. From the vibration data modal properties, the natural frequencies and modal properties, may be extracted using a process called modal analysis (Ewins, 1995; Maia and Silva, 1997). The modal properties data are related to the spatial properties of the structure. Marwala (2000) trained the second network using the modal properties to predict faults in the data.

The wavelet transform (WT) of a signal is an illustration of a time–frequency decomposition, which highlights the local features of a signal (Daubechie, 1991; Newland, 1993). The relationship between the physical properties of the structure and the WT of the impulse of a unit magnitude may be used to identify faults on structures. Marwala (2000) constructed the third network to map the WT to faults.

Marwala (2000) viewed neural networks as parameterized graphs that make probabilistic assumptions about data. He viewed learning algorithms as methods for finding parameter values that look probable considering the data. The type of neural network he applied was the MLP (Jordan and Bishop, 1996). The MLP can approximate any continuous function to an arbitrary accuracy if the number of hidden units is sufficiently large. For this chapter, the output units represent the identity of faults and the inputs are the pseudo-modal energies, modal properties or WT.

Marwala applied the hybrid procedure to identify faults in a population of cylindrical shells and the details of this experiment may be found in Marwala (1999).

Marwala (2000) divided each cylinder into three sub-structures, and holes of 12 mm diameter were drilled into each sub-structure. For one cylinder, the first type of fault was a zero-fault scenario, and its identity was [000]. The second type of fault was a one-fault scenario, and if it was in sub-structure 1, its identity was [100]. The third type of fault was a two-fault scenario, and if the faults were in sub-structures 1 and 2, the identity of this case was [110]. The final type of fault was a three-fault scenario, and the identity of this case was [111].

Marwala identified and used the measured data, pseudo-modal energies, modal properties, and wavelet data to train three neural networks. The WT network was trained using wavelet data. This network had 18 input parameters, 9 hidden units, and 3 output units. He applied the hybrid using the weighting obtained from the validation data.

When the networks were evaluated using the data not used for training, the results in Tables 9.1–9.4 were obtained. These results indicate that the hybrid approach gave the best results followed by the pseudo-modal

**Table 9.1**   Confusion matrix from the classification of fault cases in the test data using the pseudo-modal-energy network.

|        |        | Predicted |       |       |       |       |       |       |       |
|--------|--------|-----------|-------|-------|-------|-------|-------|-------|-------|
|        |        | [000]     | [100] | [010] | [001] | [110] | [101] | [011] | [111] |
| Actual | [000]  | 37        | 2     | 0     | 0     | 0     | 0     | 0     | 0     |
|        | [100]  | 0         | 3     | 0     | 0     | 0     | 0     | 0     | 0     |
|        | [010]  | 0         | 0     | 3     | 0     | 0     | 0     | 0     | 0     |
|        | [001]  | 0         | 0     | 0     | 3     | 0     | 0     | 0     | 0     |
|        | [110]  | 0         | 0     | 0     | 0     | 3     | 0     | 0     | 0     |
|        | [101]  | 0         | 0     | 0     | 0     | 0     | 3     | 0     | 0     |
|        | [011]  | 0         | 0     | 0     | 0     | 0     | 0     | 3     | 0     |
|        | [111]  | 0         | 0     | 0     | 0     | 5     | 1     | 1     | 32    |

**Table 9.2**   Confusion matrix from the classification of fault cases in the test data using the modal-energy-network.

|        |        | Predicted |       |       |       |       |       |       |       |
|--------|--------|-----------|-------|-------|-------|-------|-------|-------|-------|
|        |        | [000]     | [100] | [010] | [001] | [110] | [101] | [011] | [111] |
| Actual | [000]  | 38        | 0     | 0     | 1     | 0     | 0     | 0     | 0     |
|        | [100]  | 0         | 3     | 0     | 0     | 0     | 0     | 0     | 0     |
|        | [010]  | 0         | 0     | 3     | 0     | 0     | 0     | 0     | 0     |
|        | [001]  | 0         | 0     | 0     | 3     | 0     | 0     | 0     | 0     |
|        | [110]  | 0         | 0     | 0     | 0     | 3     | 0     | 0     | 0     |
|        | [101]  | 0         | 0     | 0     | 0     | 0     | 3     | 0     | 0     |
|        | [011]  | 0         | 0     | 0     | 0     | 0     | 0     | 3     | 0     |
|        | [111]  | 0         | 0     | 0     | 0     | 5     | 2     | 6     | 26    |

**Table 9.3**   Confusion matrix from the classification of fault cases in the test data using the wavelet-network.

|        |        | Predicted |       |       |       |       |       |       |       |
|--------|--------|-----------|-------|-------|-------|-------|-------|-------|-------|
|        |        | [000]     | [100] | [010] | [001] | [110] | [101] | [011] | [111] |
| Actual | [000]  | 35        | 0     | 0     | 1     | 0     | 0     | 0     | 0     |
|        | [100]  | 0         | 1     | 0     | 0     | 0     | 0     | 0     | 0     |
|        | [010]  | 2         | 0     | 3     | 0     | 0     | 0     | 0     | 0     |
|        | [001]  | 0         | 2     | 0     | 2     | 0     | 0     | 0     | 0     |
|        | [110]  | 0         | 0     | 0     | 0     | 3     | 0     | 0     | 1     |
|        | [101]  | 0         | 0     | 0     | 1     | 0     | 3     | 0     | 0     |
|        | [011]  | 0         | 0     | 0     | 0     | 0     | 0     | 3     | 0     |
|        | [111]  | 1         | 0     | 0     | 0     | 5     | 2     | 6     | 25    |

**Table 9.4** Confusion matrix from the classification of fault cases in the test data using the committee-network.

| | | Predicted | | | | | | | |
|---|---|---|---|---|---|---|---|---|---|
| | | [000] | [100] | [010] | [001] | [110] | [101] | [011] | [111] |
| Actual | [000] | 38 | 1 | 0 | 0 | 0 | 0 | 0 | 0 |
| | [100] | 0 | 3 | 0 | 0 | 0 | 0 | 0 | 0 |
| | [010] | 0 | 0 | 3 | 0 | 0 | 0 | 0 | 0 |
| | [001] | 0 | 0 | 0 | 3 | 0 | 0 | 0 | 0 |
| | [110] | 0 | 0 | 0 | 0 | 3 | 0 | 0 | 0 |
| | [101] | 0 | 0 | 0 | 0 | 0 | 3 | 0 | 0 |
| | [011] | 0 | 0 | 0 | 0 | 0 | 0 | 3 | 0 |
| | [111] | 0 | 0 | 1 | 0 | 3 | 0 | 1 | 34 |

energy network, and then the modal-property network. The wavelet-network performed the worst.

## 9.5 Caller Behaviour

Patel and Marwala (2010) examined the caller behaviour classification system to be used to identify trends of caller behaviour. They trained the field classifiers using data extracted from interactive voice recognition (IVR) log event files. These files were generated by the IVR platform as specific events occurred during a call to the system. Events such as call begin, form enter, form select, automatic speech recognition events, transfer events and call end events were written to the logs.

These specific inputs have been selected to characterize the caller experience at a field within a VXML application. The outputs of the classifiers summarize the caller field behaviour using interaction classes. More details on this can be found in Patel and Marwala (2010). The MLP, RBF, fuzzy inference systems (FIS) and SVM architectures were used to build these classifiers (Bishop, 1995). These techniques were described earlier in this book.

The artificial intelligence methods used produced highly accurate field and call performance classifiers. The MLP, RBF and the SVM techniques produced accuracy results that are higher than 90% on unseen test data, whereas, the FIS classifier yielded accuracies less than 85%.

The MLP field classifiers produced the most accurate solutions, out-performing the RBF and SVM field classifiers for the 'Say account', 'Say amount' and 'Select beneficiary' fields. However, for the 'Say confirmation' field, SVM classifier achieved the best results. The call performance SVM classifiers proved to be the most accurate, achieving an accuracy of 99.19% on test data. To improve the accuracy of the field and call performance classifiers, hybrids of networks were considered. Hybrids of field 'Say account', 'Say amount', 'Select beneficiary' and 'Say confirmation' classifiers, consisting of the most accurate MLP, RBF as well as SVM networks, were developed. The call performance hybrid of classifiers consisted of the best MLP, FIS and SVM models.

Therefore, a combination of networks as a classifier was expected to outperform a single network classifier. The outputs of classifiers were fed into a voting system. The voting system determined the final output of the ensemble. If most of the classifiers within the ensemble categorized an output into a certain class, the voting system would classify the output of the ensemble as the class. If all the models within the ensemble classified an output into different classes, the voting system would classify the output of the ensemble as undecided.

As shown in Tables 9.5–9.7, the ensemble of classifiers proved to be an accurate solution. These results show the accuracy, sensitivity and specificity of these classifiers. These metrics confirmed that the ensemble

**Table 9.5**    The performance metrics for the field 'Say amount' classifier.

|        | Accuracy   | Sensitivity | Specificity |
|--------|------------|-------------|-------------|
| MLP    | 0.9603     | 0.9404      | 0.9805      |
| RBF    | 0.9603     | 0.9404      | 0.9805      |
| FIS    | 0.8254     | 0.6847      | 0.9951      |
| SVM    | 0.9263     | 0.8948      | 0.9589      |
| Hybrid | **0.9683** | **0.9575**  | **0.9792**  |

**Table 9.6**    The performance metrics for the field 'Say confirmation' classifier.

|        | Accuracy   | Sensitivity | Specificity |
|--------|------------|-------------|-------------|
| MLP    | 0.9021     | 0.8454      | 0.9625      |
| RBF    | 0.9048     | 0.8559      | 0.9565      |
| FIS    | 0.7947     | 0.6576      | 0.9604      |
| SVM    | 0.9029     | 0.8523      | 0.9564      |
| Hybrid | **0.9068** | **0.8590**  | **0.9573**  |

**Table 9.7** The performance metrics for the 'Call performance' classifier.

|        | Accuracy | Sensitivity | Specificity |
|--------|----------|-------------|-------------|
| MLP    | 0.9918   | 0.9877      | 0.9960      |
| RBF    | 0.9019   | 0.9677      | 0.8406      |
| FIS    | 0.9108   | 0.9333      | 0.8888      |
| SVM    | 0.9919   | 0.9889      | 0.9949      |
| Hybrid | **0.9925** | **0.9908**  | **0.9941**  |

of field 'Say amount' classifiers and the ensemble of field 'Say confirmation' classifiers outperform the MLP, RBF, FIS as well as SVM field performance classification solutions.

However, the MLP classifiers for these fields had a larger specificity value for both the validation and test datasets. This indicates that the MLP classifiers for these fields have a larger negative classification rate on both the datasets. Similarly, the ensemble of call performance classifiers also outperformed the single classifier solutions. As a result, the hybrid of classifiers is the preferred solution for 'Say amount' and 'Say confirmation' field classification. When comparing the call performance classifiers developed, the ensemble of classifiers has the best generalization capabilities. Therefore, the ensemble of classifiers is also the preferred solution for call performance classification.

## 9.6 Conclusions

This chapter introduced a hybrid of machines for both classification and regression. It was mathematically explained that the hybrid techniques were more accurate than the individual methods if these individual methods are not correlated. These techniques were applied to two sets of problems and these were fault classification in mechanical systems and caller behaviour classification. On the fault classification problem, the hybrid method was made of three sets of MLP networks which were trained using three different sets of data being the modal properties, WT and pseudo-modal energies. The hybrid approach was found to perform better than the individual methods. The caller behaviour classifiers were made of the MLP, RBF, SVM and FIS networks. The results obtained showed that the hybrid approach performed better than when these methods were used individually.

# References

Abdel-Aal, R.E. (2005a). Improving electric load forecasts using network committees. *Electric Power Systems Research*, 74:83–94.

Abdel-Aal, R.E. (2005b). Improved classification of medical data using abductive network committees trained on different feature subsets. *Computer Methods and Programs in Biomedicine*, 80:141–153.

Ahachad, A., Álvarez-Pérez, L., Figueiras-Vidal, A.R. (2017). Boosting ensembles with controlled emphasis intensity. *Pattern Recognition Letters*, 88:1–5.

Anthony, M. (2007). On the generalization error of fixed combinations of classifiers. *Journal of Computer and System Sciences*, 73:725–734.

Bacauskiene, M., Verikas, A. (2004). Selecting salient features for classification based on neural network committees. *Pattern Recognition Letters*, 25:1879–1891.

Bagheripour, P. (2014). Committee neural network model for rock permeability prediction. *Journal of Applied Geophysics*, 104:142–148.

Baras, D., Fine, S., Fournier, L., Geiger, D., Ziv, A. (2011). Automatic boosting of cross-product coverage using bayesian networks. *International Journal on Software Tools for Technology Transfer*, 13:247–261.

Barbosa, B.H.G., Gomes, L.P., Teixeira, A.F., Aguirre, L.A. (2015). Downhole pressure estimation using committee machines and neural networks. *IFAC-PapersOnLine*, 48(6):286–291.

Basu, M. (2004). An interactive fuzzy satisfying method based on evolutionary programming technique for multiobjective short-term hydrothermal scheduling. *Electric Power Systems Research*, 69:277–285.

Bichindaritz, I., Annest, A. (2010). Case based reasoning with bayesian model averaging: An improved method for survival analysis on microarray data. *Lecture Notes in Computer Science*, 6176:346–359.

Bishop, C.M. (1995). *Neural Networks for Pattern Recognition*. Oxford: Oxford University Press.

Bobb, J.F., Dominici, F., Peng, R.D. (2011). A Bayesian model averaging approach for estimating the relative risk of mortality associated with heat waves in 105 U.S. cities. *Biometrics* 67(4):1605–1616.

Boone, E.L., Ye, K., Smith, E.P. (2011). Assessing environmental stressors via Bayesian model averaging in the presence of missing data. *Environmetrics*, 22:13–22.

Breiman, L. (1996). Bagging predictors. *Machine Learn*, 24:123–140.

Cao, Y.J., Jiang, L., Wu, Q.H. (2000). An evolutionary programming approach to mixed-variable optimization problems. *Applied Mathematical Modelling*, 24:931–942.

Chen, C.H., Lin, Z.S. (2006). A committee machine with empirical formulas for permeability prediction. *Computers & Geoscience*, 32:485–496.

Clarke, B. (2003). Comparing Bayes model averaging and stacking when model approximation error cannot be ignored. *Journal of Machine Learning Research*, 4:683–712.

Das, A., Reddy, N.P., Narayanan, J. (2001). Hybrid fuzzy logic committee neural networks for recognition of swallow acceleration signals. *Computer Methods and Programs in Biomedicine*, 64:87–99.

Daubechie, I. (1991). The wavelet transform, time-frequency localization and signal processing. *IEEE Transactions on Information Theory*, 36:961–1005.

de Oliveira, E.M., Oliveira, F.L.C. (2018). Forecasting mid-long term electric energy consumption through bagging ARIMA and exponential smoothing methods. *Energy*, 144:776–788.

Domingos, P. (2000). Bayesian averaging of classifiers and the overfitting problem. In: *Proceedings of the 17th International Conference on Machine Learning*, 223–230.

Drygajlo A., Li, W., Qiu, H. (2011). Adult face recognition in score-age-quality classification space. *Lecture Notes in Computer Science*, 6583:205–216.

Du, J., Zhai, C., Wan, Y. (2007). Radial basis probabilistic neural networks committee for palmprint recognition. *Lecture Notes in Computer Science*, 4492:819–824.

Ewins, D.J. (1995). *Modal Testing: Theory and Practice*. Letchworth: Research Studies Press.

Feldkircher, M. (2011). Forecast combination and bayesian model averaging: A Prior sensitivity analysis. *Journal of Forecast*, 31(4):361–376.

Fernandes, A.M., Utkin, A.B., Lavrov, A.V., Vilar, R.M. (2004). Development of neural network committee machines for automatic forest fire detection using lidar. *Pattern Recognition*, 37:2039–2047.

Hanczar, B., Nadif, M. (2011). Using the bagging approach for biclustering of gene expression data. *Neurocomputing*, 74:1595–1605.

Haussler, D., Kearns, M., Schapire, R.E. (1994). Bounds on the sample complexity of Bayesian learning using information theory and the VC dimension. *Machine Learning*, 14:83–113.

Healey, S.P., Cohen, W.B., Yang, Z., Brewer, C.K., Zhu, Z. (2018). Mapping forest change using stacked generalization: An ensemble approach. *Remote Sensing of Environment*, 204:717–728.

Hernandez-Lobato, D., Martinez-Munoz, G., Suarez, A. (2011). Empirical analysis and evaluation of approximate techniques for pruning regression bagging ensembles. *Neurocomputing*, 74:2250–2264.

Hoeting, J.A., Madigan, D., Raftery, A.E., Volinsky, C.T. (1999). Bayesian model averaging: A tutorial. *Statistical Science*, 14:382–401.

Hu, G., Mao, Z., He, D., Yang, F. (2011). Hybrid modeling for the prediction of leaching rate in leaching process based on negative correlation learning bagging ensemble algorithm. *Computers and Chemical Engineering*, 35(12):2611–2617.

Huang, X., Zhang, L., Gong, W. (2011). Information fusion of aerial images and LIDAR data in urban areas: Vector-stacking, re-classification and post-processing approaches. *International Journal of Remote Sensing*, 32:69–84.

Jafari, S.A., Mashohor, S., Jalali Varnamkhasti, M. (2011). Committee neural networks with fuzzy genetic algorithm. *Journal of Petroleum Science and Engineering*, 76: 217–223.

Jasra, A., Holmes, C.C. (2011). Stochastic boosting algorithms. *Statistics and Computing*, 21:335–347.

Jia, J., Xiao, X., Liu, B., Jiao, L. (2011). Bagging-based spectral clustering ensemble selection. *Pattern Recognition Letters*, 32:1456–1467.

Jordan, M.I., Bishop, C.M. (1996). Neural Networks. MIT Tech Rep A.I. Memo No. 1562, Cambridge: Massachusetts Institute of Technology.

Kadkhodaie-Ilkhchi, A., Reza Rezaee, M., Rahimpour-Bonab, H. (2009). A committee neural network for prediction of normalized oil content from well log data: An example from south pars gas field, Persian Gulf. *Journal of Petroleum Science and Engineering*, 65:23–32.

Kajdanowicz, T., Kazienko, P. (2011). Structured output element ordering in boosting-based classification. *Lecture Notes in Computing Science*, 6679: 221–228.

Karimpouli, S., Fathianpour, N., Roohi, J. (2010). A new approach to improve neural networks' algorithm in permeability prediction of petroleum reservoirs using supervised committee machine neural network (SCMNN). *Journal of Petroleum Science and Engineering*, 73:227–232.

Khoshgoftaar, T.M., van Hulse, J., Napolitano, A. (2011). Comparing boosting and bagging techniques with noisy and imbalanced data. *IEEE Transactions on Systems, Man, and Cybernetic Part A: Systems and Humans*, 41:552–568.

Kyung, Y.J., Lee, H.S. (1999). Bootstrap and aggregating VQ classifier for speaker recognition. *Electron Letters*, 35:973–974.

Larios, N., Lin, J., Zhang, M., Lytle, D., Moldenke, A., Shapiro, L., Dietterich, T. (2011). Stacked spatial-pyramid kernel: An object-class recognition method to combine scores from random trees. In: *Proceedings of the IEEE Workshop on Applications of Computer Vision*, 329–335.

Leitenstorfer, F., Tutz, G. (2011). Estimation of single-index models based on boosting techniques. *Statistics Modelling*, 11:203–217.

Li, W., Drygajlo, A., Qiu, H. (2010). Aging face verification in score-age space using single reference image template. In: *Proceedings of the IEEE 4th International Conference on Biometrics: Theory, Applications and Systems*, 1–7.

Louzada, F., Anacleto-Junior, O., Candolo, C., Mazucheli, J. (2011). Poly-bagging predictors for classification modelling for credit scoring. *Expert Systems with Applications*, 38:12717–12720.

Maia, N.M.M., Silva, J.M.M. (1997). *Theoretical and Experimental Modal Analysis*. Letchworth: Research Studies Press.

Marwala, T. (1999). Probabilistic Damage Identification Using Neural Networks and Modal Properties. University of Cambridge Tech Rep CUED/C-MECH/TR-76, Cambridge: University of Cambridge

Marwala, T. (2000). On damage identification using a committee of neural networks. *Journal of Engineering Mechanics*, 126:43–50.

Marwala, T. (2001). Probabilistic fault identification using a committee of neural. *Networks and Vibration Data, Journal of Aircraft*, 38:138–146.

Marwala, T. (2009). *Computational Intelligence for Missing Data Imputation, Estimation, and Management: Knowledge Optimization Techniques*. New York: IGI Global Publications.

Marwala, T. (2010). *Finite Element Model Updating Using Computational Intelligence Techniques*. London, UK: Springer-Verlag.

Marwala, T. (2012). *Condition Monitoring Using Computational Intelligence Methods*. Heidelberg: Springer.

Marwala, T., Hunt, H.E.M. (1999). Fault identification using finite element models and neural networks. *Mechanical Systems and Signal Processing*, 13:475–490.

Marwala, T., de Wilde, P., Correia, L., Mariano, P., Ribeiro, R., Abramov, V., Szirbik, N., Goossenaerts, J. (2001). Scalability and optimisation of a committee of agents using genetic algorithm. In: *Proceedings of the International Symposium on Software Computing and Intelligent Systems for Industries*, 1–6.

Newland, D.E. (1993). *An Introduction to Random Vibration, Spectral and Wavelet Analysis*. Longman, New York: Harlow and John Wiley.

Ng, W.W.Y., Zhou, X., Tian, X., Wang, X., Yeung, D.S. (2018). Bagging–boosting-based semi-supervised multi-hashing with query-adaptive re-ranking. *Neurocomputing*, 275:916–923.

Oloso, M.A., Hassan, M.G., Bader-El-Den, M.B., Buick, J.M. (2017). Hybrid functional networks for oil reservoir PVT characterisation. *Expert Systems with Applications*, 87:363–369.

Osawa, T., Mitsuhashi, H., Uematsu, Y. and Ushimaru, A. (2011). Bagging GLM: Improved generalized linear model for the analysis of zero-inflated data. *Ecological Informatics.* 6:270–275. 10.1016/j.ecoinf.2011.05.003.

Park, I., Grandhi, R.V. (2010). Quantification of multiple types of uncertainty in computer simulation using Bayesian model averaging. In: *Proceedings of the 51st AIAA/ ASME/ASCE/AHS/ASC Structures, Structural Dynamics and Materials Conference,* 1–6.

Patel, P.B. Marwala, T. (2010). Caller behaviour classification using computational intelligencer methods. *International Journal of Neural Systems.* doi: 10.1142/S0129065710002255, 87–93.

Perrone, M.P., Cooper, L.N. (1993). When networks disagree: Ensemble methods for hybrid neural networks. In: Mammone, R.J. (ed.), *Artificial Neural Networks for Speech and Vision.* London: Chapman and Hall.

Pino-Mejias, R., Jimenez-Gamero, M.D., Cubiles-de-la-Vega, M.D., Pascual-Acosta, A. (2008). Reduced bootstrap aggregating of learning algorithms. *Pattern Recognition Letters,* 29:265–271.

Potempski, S., Galmarini, S., Riccio, A., Giunta, G. (2010). Bayesian model averaging for emergency response atmospheric dispersion multimodel ensembles: Is it really better? How many data are needed? Are the weights portable? *Journal of Geophysical Research,* doi:10.1029/2010JD014210.

Rajan, C.C.A., Mohan, M.R. (2007). An evolutionary programming based simulated annealing method for solving the unit commitment problem. *International Journal of Electrical Power & Energy Systems,* 29:540–550.

Reddy, N.P., Buch, O.A. (2003). Speaker verification using committee neural networks. *Computer Methods and Programs in Biomedicine,* 72:109–115.

Rokach, L. (2010). Ensemble-based classifiers. *Artificial Intelligence Review,* 33:1–39.

Sbarufatti, C., Corbetta, M., Manes, A., Giglio, M. (2016). Sequential Monte-Carlo sampling based on a committee of artificial neural networks for posterior state estimation and residual lifetime prediction. *International Journal of Fatigue,* 83, Part 1:10–23.

Sheikh-Ahmad, J., Twomey, J., Kalla, D., Lodhia, P. (2007). Multiple regression and committee neural network force prediction models in milling FRP. *Machining Science and Technology,* 11:391–412.

Shi, L., Xu, G. (2001). Self-adaptive evolutionary programming and its application to multi-objective optimal operation of power systems. *Electric Power Systems Research,* 57:181–187.

Shiraishi, Y., Fukumizu, K. (2011). Statistical approaches to combining binary classifiers for multi-class classification. *Neurocomputing,* 74:680–688.

Sill, J., Takacs, G., Mackey, L., Lin, D. (2009). Feature-weighted linear stacking. arXiv:0911.0460.

Smyth, P., Wolpert, D.H. (1999). Linearly combining density estimators via stacking. *Machine Learning Journal,* 36:59–83.

Tang, B., Chen, Q., Wang, X., Wang, X. (2010). Reranking for stacking ensemble learning. *Lecture Notes in Computer Science,* 6443:575–584.

Touzani, S., Granderson, J., Fernandes S. (2018). Gradient boosting machine for modeling the energy consumption of commercial buildings. *Energy and Buildings,* 158: 1533–1543.

Tsai, M.Y., Hsiao, C.K., Chen. W.J. (2011). Extended Bayesian model averaging in generalized linear mixed models applied to Schizophrenia family data. *Annals of Human Genetics,* 75:62–77.

van Hinsbergen, C.P.I.J., van Lint, J.W.C., van Zuylen, H.J. (2009). Bayesian committee of neural networks to predict travel times with confidence intervals. *Transpertation Research Part C: Emerging Technology*, 17:498–509.

Wang, G., Hao, J., Ma, J., Jiang, H. (2011). A comparative assessment of ensemble learning for credit scoring. *Expert Systems with Applications*, 38:223–230.

Wolpert, D.H. (1992). Stacked Generalization. *Neural Networks*, 5:241–259.

Wolpert, D.H., Macready, W.G. (1999). An efficient method to estimate bagging's generalization error. *Machine Learning Journal*, 35:41–55.

Yu, Q. (2011). Weighted bagging: A modification of adaboost from the perspective of importance sampling. *Journal of Applied Statistics*, 38:451–463.

Zhao, Z.Q., Huang, D.S., Sun, B.Y. (2004). Human face recognition based on multi-features using neural networks committee. *Pattern Recognition Letters*, 25:1351–1358.

**Chapter 10**

# Auto-associative Networks

**Abstract.** This chapter introduces the auto-associative network to predict missing data. Two approaches were used to construct a missing data system based on auto-associative network. These were the combination of multi-layer perceptron neural networks and the principal component analysis (PCA) as well as the auto-associative network trained using the multi-layer perceptron (MLP) and radial basis function (RBF). All these approaches were implemented using genetic algorithm. These methods were tested on modelling HIV as well as modelling beer taster. The results obtained showed that the auto-associative networks are a viable technique for estimating missing data.

## 10.1 Introduction

Memory is an essential part of our universe. It manifests itself in many forms and these include cosmological, geological and even biological memory. For example, with regard to the Big Bang theory, we can use cosmic microwave background to extract the times at which several events happened including the time of the Big Bang (Hubble, 1929; Hawking and Ellis, 1973; Drees, 1990). In the geological world, we can chronologically date geological strata to time using techniques such as carbon dating. In this way, one can extract the Earth's history by timing and relating events (Gradstein *et al.*, 2005). The other form of memory is biological memory. This is enabled by the brain. The brain consists of billions of connections of neurons, and if a person or animal is still alive, it is able to store and process information (White *et al.*, 1986; Heisenberg *et al.*, 1995; Soengas and Aldegunde, 2002).

From the human brain, we are able to synthesize an artificial brain, and this is what is called a neural network. Neural networks fall under a discipline called artificial intelligence. It works by assigning network weights in the neural network such that the neural network is able to accurately

179

describe the data. This means that these network weights are supposed to be able to capture and remember the interrelationships that exist in the data (Schmidhuber, 1992; McCulloch and Pitts, 1943; Kleene, 1956). One particular type of a neural network is called auto-associative network. Auto-associative network is also called memory network because it seeks to view the world and reproduce what it has seen (Kosko, 1988; Hopfield, 1982).

This chapter studies auto-associative networks. To build these networks, we use neural networks i.e. radial basis function (RBF) and multi-layer perceptron (MLP) as well as the principal component analysis (PCA). These auto-associative networks are then used to estimate missing data. This they do by using genetic algorithm (GA). GA is an optimization method which is based on the principles of Darwin's theory of natural selection (Holland, 1975; Goldberg, 2002). This missing data estimation procedure is applied to modelling HIV as well as to construct an artificial beer taster.

## 10.2  Auto-associative Networks

Auto-associative neural networks are neural networks where the input and the output are the same, and therefore the number of inputs is equal to the number of outputs (Sherrington and Wong, 1989; Rios and Kabuka, 1995; Thompson *et al.*, 2002; Marwala, 2009). In auto-associative networks, there are usually fewer hidden nodes than input nodes and this results in a butterfly-like structure. The auto-associative network is preferred in recall applications as it can map linear and nonlinear relationships between all the inputs. The auto-associative structure results in the compression of data into a smaller dimension and then decompressing it into the output layer. Auto-associative networks have been used in several applications including missing data imputation (Abdella and Marwala, 2005; Nelwamondo and Marwala, 2008).

Auto-associative networks have been used successfully for network instability detection (Marais and Marwala, 2004), data visualization (Aldrich, 1998), fault detection (Huang *et al.*, 2002), in memory retrieval and spontaneous activity bumps in small-world networks (Anishchenko and Treves, 2006) and in process monitoring Zhao and Xu (2005) used this for multivariate statistical process monitoring. More details on the auto-associative neural networks are given in Kramer (1992) and Marseguerra and Zoia (2005).

In this chapter, we see how an auto-associative network can be constructed using many proven intelligent machines such as the RBF and the MLP. An example of the auto-associative network constructed using the

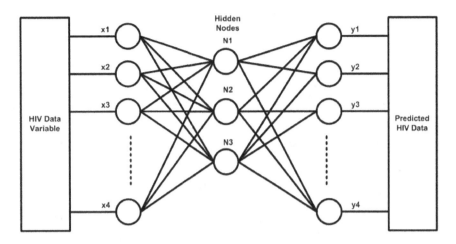

**Figure 10.1**   Auto-associative neural network.

MLP neural network is shown in Figure 10.1. In this figure, the HIV data is fed into the network and the network is trained to recall the inputs.

Another way of constructing the auto-associative network is using the PCA.

## 10.3 Principal Component Analysis

PCA (Shlens, 2005; Xie *et al.*, 2007) is a statistical technique commonly used to find patterns in high dimensional data (Smith, 2002). It operates by what researchers call the eigenvalue analysis. Eigenvalue analysis gives eigenvalues, which correspond to the natural frequencies and eigenvectors, which correspond to the mode shapes. Once the characteristics of the data are expressed as mode shapes and natural frequencies, then these can be used in conjunction with an optimization routine for missing data estimation.

Examples of the use of the PCA include to recognize patient anaesthetic levels (Linkens and Vefghi, 1997), quantify brain function (Yap *et al.*, (1996), damage detection in buildings (Ko *et al.*, 2002), behaviour of aerosol (Mirme *et al.*, 1996), to analyse water quality (Sârbu and Pop, 2005), in environmental science (Johnson *et al.*, 2007), to analyse meteorites (Penttilä *et al.*, 2018), for process monitoring (Fezai *et al.*, 2018), for energy security measurement (Radovanović *et al.*, 2018) and for characterizing of the base of a skull (Schaal *et al.*, 2017).

We implement the PCA as follows:

- From a dataset, the mean of each dimension is subtracted from the data.
- Calculate the covariance matrix of the data.

- Calculate the eigenvalues and eigenvectors of the covariance matrix. The highest eigenvalue corresponds to the eigenvector that is the principal component.

Researchers and practitioners used the PCA for data compression. They do this by choosing certain eigenvectors to reduce the dimension of the data by using only the largest eigenvalues and their corresponding eigenvectors. Thus, the data compression or transformation is (Sârbu and Pop, 2005; Marwala, 2009):

$$[\mathbf{P}] = [\mathbf{D}][\mathbf{PC}], \tag{10.1}$$

where $[\mathbf{D}]$ is the original dataset, $[\mathbf{PC}]$ is the principal component matrix and $[\mathbf{P}]$ is the transformed data. The PCA multiplication results in a dataset that shows the relationships between the data whether smaller or the same dimension. To return to the original data, the following equation is used (Sârbu and Pop, 2005; Marwala, 2009):

$$[\mathbf{D}'] = [\mathbf{P}][\mathbf{PC}]^{-1}. \tag{10.2}$$

Here, $[\mathbf{D}']$ is the re-transformed data. If we use all the principal components from the covariance matrix, then $[\mathbf{D}] \approx [\mathbf{D}']$. We can use the transformed data ($[\mathbf{D}]$) in conjunction with the artificial neural network (ANN) to increase the efficiency of the ANN by reducing its complexity. This results from the property of the PCA of extraction of linear relationships between the data variables, thus the ANN only needs to extract the nonlinear relationships. This then results in less training cycles. Thus, ANNs can be built more efficiently. Figure 10.2 shows this concept.

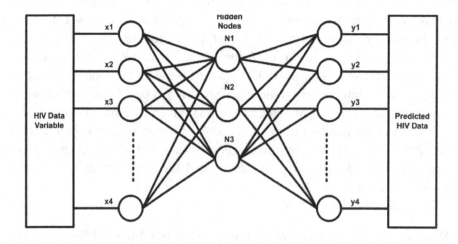

**Figure 10.2**    PCA auto-associative neural network.

## 10.4 Missing Data Estimation

The missing data estimation algorithms studied in this chapter use neural network models. These models are trained to recall themselves (i.e. predict its input vector) and are called the auto-associative neural network. Mathematically, the auto-associative neural network can be written as follows (Marwala, 2009):

$$\mathbf{y} = f(\mathbf{x}, \mathbf{w}). \tag{10.3}$$

In Equation (10.3), $\mathbf{y}$ is the output vector, $\mathbf{x}$ the input vector and $\mathbf{w}$ the vector of network weights. Since the network is trained to predict its own input vector, the input vector $\mathbf{x}$ is approximately equal to output vector $\mathbf{y}$ and therefore $\mathbf{x} \approx \mathbf{y}$.

In reality, the input vector $\mathbf{x}$ and output vector $\mathbf{y}$ will not always be perfectly the same. Therefore, we use an error function expressed as the difference between the input and output vector and this is formulated as (Marwala, 2009):

$$\mathbf{e} = \mathbf{x} - \mathbf{y}. \tag{10.4}$$

Substituting the value of $\mathbf{y}$ from Equation (10.3) into Equation (10.4), the following expression is obtained (Marwala, 2009):

$$\mathbf{e} = \mathbf{x} - f(\mathbf{x}, \mathbf{w}). \tag{10.5}$$

We aim for the error to be minimized and be non-negative and hence, the error function can be rewritten as a square of Equation (10.5) (Marwala, 2009):

$$\mathbf{e} = (\mathbf{x} - f(\mathbf{x}, \mathbf{w}))^2. \tag{10.6}$$

In the case of missing data, some of the values for the input vector $\mathbf{x}$ are not available. Hence, we can categorize the input vector elements into $\mathbf{x}$ known vector represented by $\mathbf{x}_k$ and $\mathbf{x}$ unknown vector represented by $\mathbf{x}_u$. Rewriting Equation (10.6) in terms of $\mathbf{x}_k$ and $\mathbf{x}_u$, we have (Marwala, 2009):

$$\mathbf{e} = \left( \left\{ \begin{matrix} \mathbf{x}_k \\ \mathbf{x}_u \end{matrix} \right\} - f \left( \left\{ \begin{matrix} \mathbf{x}_k \\ \mathbf{x}_u \end{matrix} \right\}, \mathbf{w} \right) \right)^2. \tag{10.7}$$

The error vector in Equation (10.7) can be reduced into a scalar by integrating over the size of the input vector and the number of training examples as follows (Marwala, 2009):

$$E = \left\| \left( \begin{Bmatrix} \mathbf{x}_k \\ \mathbf{x}_u \end{Bmatrix} - f\left( \begin{Bmatrix} \mathbf{x}_k \\ \mathbf{x}_u \end{Bmatrix}, \mathbf{w} \right) \right) \right\|. \tag{10.8}$$

Here, $\| \ \|$ is Euclidean norm. Equation (10.8) is called the missing data estimation equation. To approximate the missing input values, Equation (10.8) is minimized and evolutionary techniques such as GA can be used (Holland, 1975; Koza, 1992; Falkenauer, 1997; Goldberg, 2002; Fogel, 2006).

## 10.5  Genetic Algorithm (GA)

GA used to optimize Equation (10.8) is an algorithm used to identify approximate solutions to difficult problems. It uses the principles of evolutionary biology, to computer science, to identify the optimum solution (Michalewicz, 1996; Mitchell, 1996; Mohammed *et al.*, 2007). This uses biologically derived techniques such as inheritance, mutation, natural selection and recombination to approximate an optimal solution to difficult problems. In GA, learning is a competition among a population of evolving candidate problem solutions. A fitness function evaluates each solution to decide whether it contributes to the next generation of solutions. Through operations analogous to gene transfer in sexual reproduction, the algorithm creates a new population of candidate solutions (Goldberg, 1989; Houck *et al.*, 1995).

The three most important aspects of GAs are definition of the objective function, definition and implementation of the genetic representation and definition as well as implementation of the genetic operators (Michalewicz, 1996; Houck *et al.*, 1995). GA has been proven to be successful in optimization problems such as wire routing, scheduling, adaptive control, game playing, cognitive modelling, transportation problems, travelling salesman problems, optimal control problems and database query optimization (Michalewicz, 1996; Marwala, 2002, 2004; Marwala and Chakraverty, 2006; Crossingham and Marwala, 2007; Hulley and Marwala, 2007; de Oliveira *et al.*, 2018; Arakaki and Usberti, 2018; Guerrero *et al.*, 2017; Tseng *et al.*, 2018; Dao *et al.*, 2017).

To implement GAs, we follow these steps: initialization, selection, reproduction and termination. Initially, a large number of possible individual solutions are randomly generated to form an initial population. This initial population should cover a good representation of the solution space. The size of the population depends on the nature of the problem and is determined by the number of variables. If there are two variables missing, the size of the population must be higher than if there is one variable missing.

For every generation, we select the proportion of the existing population to breed a new population. We conduct this selection using the fitness-based process, where we measure the fitness of the solutions by the error function. Some selection methods rank the fitness of each solution and choose the best solutions while other procedures rank a randomly chosen sample of the population for computational efficiency.

The majority of the selection functions tend to be stochastic in nature and thus are designed in such a way that a selection process is conducted on a small proportion of less fit solutions. This ensures that diversity of the population of possible solutions is maintained at a high level and, therefore, avoiding convergence on poor and incorrect solutions. There are many selection methods, and these include roulette wheel selection, which is used in this chapter.

Roulette-wheel selection is a genetic operator utilized for selecting potentially useful solutions in GA optimization process. Each possible procedure is assigned the fitness function which we use to map the probability of selection with each individual solution. Suppose the fitness, $f_i$, is of individual $i$ in the population, the probability that this individual is selected is (Marwala, 2009):

$$p_i = \frac{f_i}{\sum_{j=1}^{N} f_j}. \tag{10.9}$$

Here, $N$ is the total population size. This process ensures that candidate solutions with a higher fitness have a lower probability that they may be eliminated, than those with lower fitness. Similarly, solutions with low fitness have a low probability of surviving the selection process. The advantage of this is that even though a solution may have low fitness, it may still contain some components which may be useful in the future.

Reproduction generates subsequent population of solutions from those selected through genetic operators which are crossover and mutation. The crossover operator mixes genetic information in the population by cutting pairs of chromosomes at random points along their length and exchanging over the cut sections to join successful operators together. Crossover occurs with a certain probability and the probability of crossover is higher than the probability of mutation. One example of crossover is simple crossover where one crossover point is selected, binary string from beginning of chromosome to the crossover point is copied from one parent, and the rest is copied from the second parent. For example, when **10001**010 undergoes simple crossover with 10011**110** it becomes **10001110.**

The mutation operator selects a binary digit of the chromosomes at random and inverts it. This introduces to the population new information. Mutation has a certain probability and the probability of mutation is low (i.e. less than 1%). One example of mutation is the binary mutation which is used (Goldberg, 1989). When binary mutation is used, a number written in binary form is chosen and its value is inverted. For an example: 01101111 may become 01100111.

The processes described result in the subsequent generation of a population of solutions that are different from the previous generation and that have average fitness that is higher than the previous generation. The process described is repeated until a termination condition has been achieved because either a desired solution is found that satisfies the objective function or a specified number of generations has been reached or the solution's fitness converged or any combinations these. The process described above can be expressed as in Figure 10.3 and written in pseudo-code algorithmic form as (Goldberg, 1989; Marwala, 2009):

1. Choose the initial population
2. Estimate the fitness (from the error function) of each individual in the population
3. Repeat

    a. Choose individuals with higher fitness to reproduce
    b. Generate new population using crossover and mutation to produce offspring

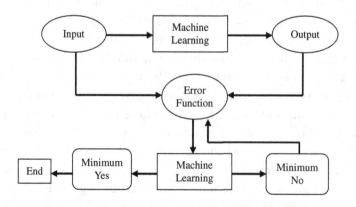

**Figure 10.3**   Missing data procedure.

c. Calculate the fitness of each offspring

d. Replace low fitness section of population with offspring

4. Until termination

## 10.6 Machine Learning

To implement the auto-associative network, we need to use machine-learning techniques and here we briefly discuss the MLP and RBF networks. The MLP and RBF have been used in many complex problems such as modelling HIV (Marwala, 2007b), in finite element models (Marwala, 2010), for interstate conflict (Marwala and Lagazio, 2011), for condition monitoring (Marwala, 2012), for economic modelling (Marwala, 2013), for modelling causality (Marwala, 2014), for rational decision making (2015), for understanding economic theory (Marwala and Hurwitz, 2017) and in robotics (Xing and Marwala, 2018).

The MLP are feed-forward neural networks with an architecture comprising of the input layer and the output layer. Each layer is formed from smaller units known as neurons. Neurons in the input layer receive the input signals and distribute them forward to the network. In the subsequent layers, each neuron receives a signal, which is a weighted sum of the outputs of the nodes in the layer below. Inside each neuron, an activation function is used to control the output thereof. This network determines a nonlinear mapping from an input vector to the output vector, parameterized by a set of network weights, which we refer to as the vector of weights. The first step in approximating the weight parameters of the model is finding the approximate architecture of the MLP. The number of hidden units, the type of activation function, as well as the number of input and output variables define the architecture. The second step estimates the weight parameters using the training set. Training estimates the network weight vector to ensure that the output is as close as possible to the target vector. The problem of identifying the weights in the hidden layers can be solved by maximizing the probability of the weight parameter using Bayes' rule. In the Bayesian approach, the training data, the evidence term that balances between fitting the data well and avoiding overly complex models and the prior probability of the network weights are used to estimate the posterior probability function (Bishop, 1995). The training of the neural network using Bayesian approach can be conducted using different Monte Carlo methods. Some of these methods include the Markov Chain Monte Carlo method, hybrid Monte Carlo and Shadow hybrid Monte Carlo method (Marwala *et al.*, 2017). Bayesian based training of the neural network is advantageous because it can give probability distributions. Successful applications of the MLP include to predict coal prices (Fan *et al.*, 2016), to recognize phoneme (Cardona *et al.*, 2017), for time series prediction (Ravi *et al.*, 2017), for cellular manufacturing scheduling (Delgoshaei and Gomes, 2016) and pipeline leakage detection (Zadkarami *et al.*, 2016).

The RBF neural network is like the MLP and is a feedforward network trained using a supervised training algorithm (Haykin, 1998). It is structured with one hidden layer of units whose activation function is selected from a class of functions called the basis function. The activation of the hidden units in an RBF neural network is given by a nonlinear function of the distance between the input vector and a prototype vector (Bishop, 1995).

Even as though the RBF is related to the MLP, it has several advantages. It is generally faster to train than the MLP and is less prone to problems with non-stationary inputs (Bishop, 1995). It is, however, unstable to train. The RBF differs from the MLP in that it has weights in the outer layer only, while the hidden nodes have what are called the centres. Training the RBF network entails identifying two sets of parameters and these are the centres in the hidden nodes and the output weights.

Successful applications of the RBF include for option pricing (Milovanović and von Sydow, 2017), to model laminar flow and heat transfer (Grabski and Kołodziej, 2017), to predict wax deposition rate (Xie and Xing, 2017), to predict mechatronic process (de Jesús Rubio *et al.*, 2017) and for image segmentation (Li and Li, 2016).

## 10.7  Modelling HIV

Marwala (2009) used the method comprising the PCA, auto-associative neural network (ANN) and genetic algorithm (PCA–ANN–GA) for missing data estimation. The data that was used was the HIV dataset with variables age of female, age gap, educational level of female, gravidity, parity, province of origin, race, Rapid Plasma Reagin (RPR), regional weighting parameter (WTREV) and HIV. The use of computational intelligence to model HIV was conducted by many researchers (Tim and Marwala, 2006; Leke *et al.*, 2006; Crossingham and Marwala, 2008; Marivate *et al.*, 2008; Mistry *et al.*, 2009). These are shown in Table 10.1. The six demographic variables missing were race, age of mother, education, gravidity, parity and, age of father, with the outcome or decision being either HIV positive or negative. The variables that were missing were the HIV status, Age, Age group, Parity and Gravidity. The testing sets were composed of three different datasets made up of 1000 random records each. This offered an unbiased result as

**Table 10.1** Variables used.

| Variable | Type | Range |
|---|---|---|
| HIV status | Binary | [0, 1] |
| Education | Integer | 0–13 |
| Age group | Integer | 14–60 |
| Age gap | Integer | 1–7 |
| Gravidity | Integer | 0–11 |
| Parity | Integer | 0–40 |
| Race | Integer | 1–5 |
| Province | Integer | 1–9 |
| Region | Integer | 1–36 |
| RPR | Integer | 0–2 |
| WTREV | Continuous | 0.638–1.2743 |

**Table 10.2** PCA–ANN–GA results.

| PCA–ANN–GA-11 (%) | Run 1 | Run 2 | Run 3 | Average |
|---|---|---|---|---|
| HIV classification | 65.0 | 61.6 | 62.8 | 63.1 |
| Education level | 27.8 | 27.3 | 28.2 | 27.8 |
| Gravidity | 87.6 | 86.5 | 87.1 | 87.1 |
| Parity | 87.5 | 86.3 | 87.7 | 87.2 |
| Age | 94.9 | 94.8 | 93.5 | 95.7 |
| Age gap | 98.1 | 98.3 | 96.9 | 97.4 |
| **PCA–ANN–GA-10(%)** | **Run 1** | **Run 2** | **Run 3** | **Average** |
| HIV classification | 64.2 | 60.9 | 67.2 | 64.1 |
| Education level | 27.0 | 31.3 | 30.2 | 29.5 |
| Gravidity | 86.4 | 86.3 | 88.2 | 61.0 |
| Parity | 86.2 | 86.2 | 87.6 | 86.7 |
| Age | 8.0 | 8.2 | 12.1 | 9.4 |
| Age gap | 23.9 | 20.0 | 24.1 | 22.7 |

testing with only one test set can have results, which were the best but may be biased due to the data used. Different measures of accuracy were used to evaluate the effectiveness of the imputation methods. These were intended to offer understanding of the results as well as to measure the effectiveness of the proposed method.

The PCA–ANN–GA technique was run with two configurations. The first configuration had no compression (PCA–ANN–GA-11) indicating the transformation from 11 inputs to 11 outputs. The second configuration had a compression of 1 value thus is named PCA–ANN–GA-10, indicating the compression and transformation from 11 inputs to 10 inputs. The results of the test are shown in Table 10.2.

The results obtained by Mistry *et al.* (2008) showed that PCA–ANN–GA-11 indicated good estimation for all the variables except education level. Furthermore, the PCA–ANN–GA-10 performed poorly on Age and Age Gap while giving good results on the other variables. This resulted from the loss of information during the compression stage.

## 10.8  Artificial Beer Taster

Marwala (2009) constructed an artificial beer taster using characteristics such as colour of beer, smell and chemical components. Therefore, the artificial beer taster has the following variables: alcohol, present extract, real extract, PE–LE, which stands for present extract minus limit extract, pH, iron, acetaldehyde, DMS, which stands for dimethyl sulfide, ethyl acetate, iso-amyl acetate, total higher alcohols, colour, bitterness and amount of carbohydrates. These variables capture the colour, smell and chemical components of the beer and are normally used to predict the beer taste score. Conventionally, the taste scores are obtained from a panel of tasters. Marwala (2009) used neural networks to create a system that predicts taste scores, and this is shown in Figure 10.4. These parameters were measured and sometimes one or more of these measurements may not be available due to problems such as instrumentation failure. In such a situation, it is important to estimate these missing values because it would be impossible to predict the taste scores. More information on this artificial taster can be found in Marwala (2005).

These beer characteristic variables were used to train the MLP and RBF neural networks. These neural networks mapped all the 14 variables onto themselves, in an auto-associative manner using the MLP and RBF networks. A total of 1200 data examples were provided and 400 were used for training, further 400 were used for validation and 400 for testing. The sizes of the hidden nodes of these networks that are evaluated vary from 7 to 11 and the performances of these networks are shown in Table 10.3. This table shows that the optimal network architectures contained 14 inputs, 10 hidden neurons and 14 outputs for the MLP network as well as 14 inputs, 9 hidden neurons and 14 outputs for the RBF network. The activation functions for the MLP network were the hyperbolic tangent function in the hidden units and linear activation function in the outer units. For the RBF, the Gaussian activation function was used for the hidden nodes and linear activation function for the output layer.

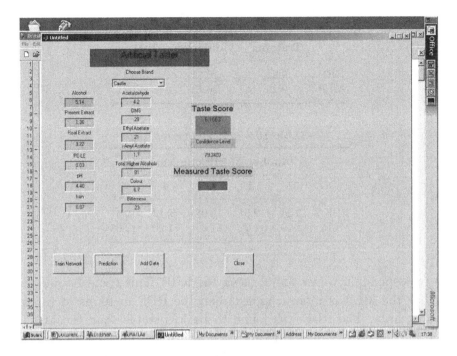

**Figure 10.4**  The artificial taster developed to taste beer.

**Table 10.3**  Standard error.

| Number of Hidden Nodes | 7 | 8 | 9 | 10 | 11 |
|---|---|---|---|---|---|
| RBF | 11.56 | 10.81 | **10.67** | 11.21 | 11.45 |
| MLP | 11.86 | 11.43 | 11.10 | **10.72** | 10.88 |

An additional set of 100 data points were used to test the ability of the proposed procedure to estimate missing values. The GA in the proposed missing data estimation procedure is implemented with 70% probability of reproduction, 3% mutation rate and 60% crossover rate.

Cases of 1, 2, 3, 4 and 5 missing values in a single record were examined to investigate the accuracy of the approximated values as the number of missing cases within a single record increased. The results obtained are given in Tables 10.4 and 10.5.

The results show that the models' approximations of missing data are highly accurate. There is no significant difference among the approximations obtained for different number of missing cases within a single record. Approximations obtained using the MLP in all the missing cases were better

**Table 10.4**   Standard error.

|     | Training | Validation | Testing |
|-----|----------|------------|---------|
| RBF | 9.32     | 10.67      | 11.94   |
| MLP | 9.29     | 10.72      | 11.03   |

**Table 10.5**   Standard error.

| | Number of Missing Variables | | | | |
|-----|-------|-------|-------|-------|-------|
|     | **1** | **2** | **3** | **4** | **5** |
| RBF | 12.26 | 12.67 | 12.08 | 12.13 | 12.41 |
| MLP | 11.99 | 11.72 | 11.71 | 11.90 | 12.05 |

than corresponding values found using the RBF. This could be due to the fact that the MLP is more complex than the RBF in terms of the order of nonlinearity. The RBF was found to be less stable than the MLP due to the calculation of the pseudo-inverse which sometimes results in singular matrices. However, the RBF was found to be more computationally efficient than the MLP.

## 10.9   Conclusions

This chapter introduced the auto-associative network to predict missing data. Two approaches were adopted, and these were the combination of neural networks and the PCA as well as the MLP and RBF. All these approaches were implemented using GA. These methods were tested on modelling HIV as well as modelling beer taster. The results obtained showed that the auto-associative networks are a viable technique for estimating missing data.

## References

Abdella, M., Marwala, T. (2005). Treatment of missing data using neural networks. In: *Proceedings of the IEEE International Joint Conference on Neural Networks*, Montreal, Canada, 598–603.

Aldrich, C. (1998). Visualization of transformed multivariate datasets with autoassociative neural networks, *Pattern Recognition Letters*, 19(8):749–764.

Anishchenko, A., Treves, A. (2006). Autoassociative memory retrieval and spontaneous activity bumps in small-world networks of integrate-and-fire neurons, *Journal of Physiology*, 100(4):225–236.

Arakaki, R.K., Usberti, F.L. (2018). Hybrid genetic algorithm for the open capacitated arc routing problem. *Computers & Operations Research*, 90:221–231.

Bishop, C.M. (1995). *Neural Networks for Pattern Recognition*. Oxford: Oxford University Press.

Cardona, D.A.B., Nedjah, N., Mourelle, L.M. (2017). Online phoneme recognition using multi-layer perceptron networks combined with recurrent non-linear autoregressive neural networks with exogenous inputs. *Neurocomputing*, 265:78–90.

Crossingham, B., Marwala, T. (2007). Using genetic algorithms to optimise rough set partition sizes for HIV data analysis. *Studies in Computational Intelligence*, 78:245–250.

Crossingham, B., Marwala, T. (2008). Using genetic algorithms to optimise rough set partition sizes for HIV data analysis. *Advances in Intelligent and Distributed Computing, Studies in Computational Intelligence*, 78:245–250.

Dao, S.D., Abhary, K., Marian, R. (2017). An innovative framework for designing genetic algorithm structures. *Expert Systems with Applications*, 90:196–208.

de Jesús Rubio, J., Elias, I., Cruz, D.R., Pacheco, J. (2017). Uniform stable radial basis function neural network for the prediction in two mechatronic processes. *Neurocomputing*, 227:122–130.

de Oliveira, L.L., Freitas, A.A., Tinós, R. (2018). Multi-objective genetic algorithms in the study of the genetic code's adaptability. *Information Sciences*, 425:48–61.

Delgoshaei, A., Gomes, C. (2016). A multi-layer perceptron for scheduling cellular manufacturing systems in the presence of unreliable machines and uncertain cost. *Applied Soft Computing*, 49:27–55.

Drees, W.B. (1990). *Beyond the Big Bang: Quantum cosmologies and God*. Chicago, Cambridge: Open Court Publishing.

Falkenauer, E. (1997). *Genetic Algorithms and Grouping Problems*. Chichester, England: John Wiley & Sons.

Fan, X., Wang, L., Li, S. (2016). Predicting chaotic coal prices using a multi-layer perceptron network model. *Resources Policy*, 50:86–92.

Fezai, R., Mansouri, M., Taouali, O., Harkat, M.F., Bouguila, N. (2018). Online reduced kernel principal component analysis for process monitoring. *Journal of Process Control*, 61:1–11.

Fogel, D.B. (2006). *Evolutionary Computation: Toward a New Philosophy of Machine Intelligence*, 3rd Edition. Piscataway, NJ: IEEE Press.

Goldberg, D.E. (1989). *Genetic Algorithms in Search, Optimization, and Machine Learning*. Reading, MA: Addison-Wesley.

Goldberg, D.E. (2002). *The Design of Innovation: Lessons from and for Competent Genetic Algorithms*. Reading, MA: Addison-Wesley.

Grabski, J.K., Kołodziej, J.A. (2017). Laminar fluid flow and heat transfer in an internally corrugated tube by means of the method of fundamental solutions and radial basis functions. *Computers & Mathematics with Applications*, in press, corrected proof, Available online 6 December 2017.

Gradstein, F.M., Ogg, J.G., Smith, Alan G., (eds.), (2005). *A Geologic Time Scale 2004*. Chicago, Cambridge: Cambridge University Press.

Guerrero, M., Montoya, F.G., Baños, R. (2017). A. Alcayde, C. Gil. Adaptive community detection in complex networks using genetic algorithms. *Neurocomputing*, 266:101–113.

Hawking, S.W., Ellis, G.F.R. (1973). *The Large-Scale Structure of Space–Time*. Cambridge University Press.

Haykin, S. (1998). *Neural Networks: A Comprehensive Foundation*. NJ: Prentice Hall.

Heisenberg, M., Heusipp, M., Wanke, C. (1995). Structural plasticity in the *Drosophila* brain. *Journal of Neuroscience*, 15:1951–1960.

Holland, J.H. (1975). *Adaptation in Natural and Artificial Systems*. Ann Arbor: University of Michigan Press.

Hopfield, J.J. (1982). Neural networks and physical systems with emergent collective computational abilities. In: *Proceedings of the National Academy of Sciences of the United States of America*, 79(8):2554–2558.

Houck, C.R., Joines, J.A., Kay, M.G. (1995). A genetic algorithm for function optimisation: A MATLAB implementation, Technical Report NCSU-IE TR 95-09, North Carolina State University.

Huang, J., Shimizu, H., Shioya, S. (2002). Data preprocessing and output evaluation of an autoassociative neural network model for online fault detection in virginiamycin production, *Journal of Bioscience and Bioengineering*, 94(1):70–77.

Hubble, E. (1929). A relation between distance and radial velocity among extra galactic nebulae. In: *Proceedings of the National Academy of Sciences USA*, 15(3):168–73.

Hulley, G., Marwala, T. (2007). Genetic algorithm based incremental learning for optimal weight and classifier selection. Computational models for life sciences. *American Institute of Physics Series*, 952:258–268.

Johnson, G.W., Ehrlich, R., Full, W., Ramos, S. (2007). Principal components analysis and receptor models in environmental forensics, *Introduction to Environmental Forensics*, 2nd Edition, 207–272.

Kleene, S.C. (1956). Representation of events in nerve nets and finite automata. *Annals of Mathematics Studies*, (34):3–41.

Ko, J.M., Zhou, X.T., Ni, Y.Q. (2002). Seismic damage evaluation of a 38-storey building model using measured FrF data reduced via principal component analysis, *Advances in Building Technology*, 953–960.

Kosko, B. (1988). Bidirectional Associative Memories. *IEEE Transactions on Systems, Man, and Cybernetics*, 18(1).

Koza, J. (1992). *Genetic Programming: On the Programming of Computers by Means of Natural Selection*, Cambridge, MA: MIT Press.

Kramer, M.A. (1992). Autoassociative neural networks, *Computers and Chemical Engineering*, 16(4):313–328.

Leke, B., Marwala, T., Tettey, T. (2006). Autoencoder networks for HIV classification. *Current Science*, 9(11):1467–1473.

Li, S., Li, X. (2016). Radial basis functions and level set method for image segmentation using partial differential equation. *Applied Mathematics and Computation*, 286:29–40.

Linkens, D.A., Vefghi, L. (1997). Recognition of patient anaesthetic levels: neural network systems, principal components analysis, and canonical discriminant variates, *Artificial Intelligence in Medicine*, 11(2):155–173.

Marais, E., Marwala, T. (2004). Predicting global Internet instability caused by worms using neural networks. In: *Proceedings of the Annual Symposium of the Pattern Recognition Association of South Africa*. Cape Town, 81–85.

Marivate, V.N., Nelwamondo, V.F., Marwala, T. (2008). Investigation into the use of autoencoder neural networks, principal component analysis and support vector regression in estimating missing HIV data, In: *Proceedings of the 17th World Congress of The International Federation of Automatic Control*, Seoul, Korea, July 6–11, 682–689.

Marseguerra, M., Zoia, A. (2005). The autoassociative neural network in signal analysis: I. The data dimensionality reduction and its geometric interpretation, *Annals of Nuclear Energy*, 32(11):1191–1206.

Marwala, T. (2002). Finite element updating using wavelet data and genetic algorithm. *American Institute of Aeronautics and Astronautics, Journal of Aircraft*, 39:709–711.

Marwala, T. (2004). Control of complex systems using Bayesian neural networks and genetic algorithm, *International Journal of Engineering Simulation*, 5, 28–37.

Marwala, T. (2005). The artificial beer taster. *Electricity + Control*, May, 22, Johannesburg: Crowne Publications.

Marwala, T. (2007a). Bayesian training of neural network using genetic programming. *Pattern Recognition Letters*, 28:1452–1458.

Marwala, T. (2007b). *Computational Intelligence for Modelling Complex Systems*. Delhi: Research India Publications.

Marwala, T. (2009). *Computational Intelligence for Missing Data Imputation, Estimation, and Management: Knowledge Optimization Techniques*, Information Science Reference Imprint. New York: IGI Global Publications.

Marwala, T. (2010). *Finite Element Model Updating Using Computational Intelligence Techniques*, London: Springer-Verlag.

Marwala, T., Lagazio, M. (2011). *Militarized Conflict Modeling Using Computational Intelligence*. Heidelberg: Springer. Translated into Chinese by the National Defence Industry Press.

Marwala, T. (2012). *Condition Monitoring Using Computational Intelligence Methods*. Heidelberg: Springer.

Marwala, T. (2013). *Economic Modeling Using Artificial Intelligence Methods*. Heidelberg: Springer.

Marwala, T. (2014). *Artificial Intelligence Techniques for Rational Decision Making*. Heidelberg: Springer.

Marwala, T. (2015). *Causality, Correlation, and Artificial Intelligence for Rational Decision Making*. Singapore: World Scientific.

Marwala, T., Chakraverty, S. (2006). Fault classification in structures with incomplete measured data using autoassociative neural networks and genetic algorithm. *Current Science*, 90:542–548.

Marwala, T., Hurwitz, E. (2017). *Artificial Intelligence and Economic Theory: Skynet in the Market*. Springer.

Marwala, T., Boulkaibet, I., Adhikari, S. (2017). *Probabilistic Finite Element Model Updating Using Bayesian Statistics: Applications to Aeronautical and Mechanical Engineering*. John Wiley & Sons.

McCulloch, W., Pitts, W. (1943). A logical calculus of ideas immanent in nervous activity. *Bulletin of Mathematical Biophysics*, 5(4):115–133.

Michalewicz, Z. (1996). *Genetic Algorithms + Data Structures = Evolution Programs*. 3rd edition, Berlin, Heidelberg, New York: Springer-Verlag.

Milovanović, S., von Sydow, L. (2017). Radial Basis Function generated Finite Differences for option pricing problems. *Computers & Mathematics with Applications*, in press, corrected proof, Available online 1 December 2017.

Mirme, A., Minkkinen, P., Ruuskanen, J. (1996). Behaviour of urban aerosol, black carbon and gaseous pollutants in urban air: Exploratory principal component analysis, *Nucleation and Atmospheric Aerosols*, 1996:423–426.

Mistry, J., Nelwamondo, F.V., Marwala, T. (2009). Investigating demographic influences for HIV classification using Bayesian autoassociative neural networks, In: *Advances in Neuro Information Processing*, 752–759, Berlin: Springer. *Lecture Notes in Computer Science Series*, Vol. 5507.

Mitchell, M. (1996). *An Introduction to Genetic Algorithms*, Cambridge, MA: MIT Press.

Mohammed, A.K., Nelwamondo, F.V., Marwala, T. (2007). Estimation of missing data: Neural networks, principal component analysis and genetic algorithms. In: *Proceedings of the 18th Annual Pattern Recognition Association of South Africa*, CD-Rom.

Nelwamondo, F. V., Marwala, T. (2008). Techniques for handling missing data: Applications to online condition monitoring. *International Journal of Innovative Computing, Information and Control*, 4(6):1507–1526.

Penttilä, A., Martikainen, J., Gritsevich, M., Muinonen, K. (2018). Laboratory spectroscopy of meteorite samples at UV-vis-NIR wavelengths: Analysis and discrimination by principal components analysis. *Journal of Quantitative Spectroscopy and Radiative Transfer*, 206:189–197.

Radovanović, M., Filipović, S., Golušin, V. (2018). Geo-economic approach to energy security measurement — principal component analysis. *Renewable and Sustainable Energy Reviews*, 82, Part 2:1691–1700.

Ravi, V., Pradeepkumar, D., Deb, K. (2017). Financial time series prediction using hybrids of chaos theory, multi-layer perceptron and multi-objective evolutionary algorithms. *Swarm and Evolutionary Computation*, 36:136–149.

Rios, A., Kabuka, M. (1995). Image compression with a dynamic autoassociative neural network. *Mathematical and Computer Modelling*, 21(1–2):159–171.

Sârbu, C., Pop, H.F. (2005). Principal component analysis versus fuzzy principal component analysis. A case study: The quality of danube water (1985–1996), *Talanta*, 65(5):1215–1220.

Schaal, S.C., Ruff, C., Pluijmers, B.I., Pauws, E., Dunaway, D.J. (2017). Characterizing the skull base in craniofacial microsomia using principal component analysis. *International Journal of Oral and Maxillofacial Surgery*, 46(12):1656–1663.

Schmidhuber., J. (1992). Learning complex, extended sequences using the principle of history compression. *Neural Computation*, 4:234–242.

Sherrington, D., Wong, K.Y.M. (1989). Random Boolean networks for autoassociative memory. *Physics Reports*, 184(2–4):293–299.

Shlens, J. (2005). *A Tutorial on Principal Component Analysis*, Systems Neurobiology Laboratory, University of California, San Diego. Available at: http://www.snl.salk.edu/~shlens/pca.pdf

Smith, L.I. (2002). *A Tutorial on Principal Components Analysis*, Computer Science Technical Report, University of Otago Library, New Zealand.

Soengas, J.L., Aldegunde, M. (2002). Energy metabolism of fish brain. *Comparative Biochemistry and Physiology B*, 131(3):271–296.

Thompson, B.B., Marks, R.J., Choi, J.J. (2002). Implicit learning in autoencoder novelty assessment. In: *Proceedings of the IEEE International Joint Conference on Neural Networks*, 3:2878–2883.

Tim, T.N., Marwala, T. (2006). Computational intelligence methods for risk assessment of HIV. In imaging the future medicine. In: *Proceedings of the IFMBE*, 14:3581–3585, Springer-Verlag.

Tseng, H.-E., Chang, C.-C., Lee, S.-C., Huang, Y.-M. (2018). A block-based genetic algorithm for disassembly sequence planning. *Expert Systems with Applications*, 96:492–505.

White, J.G., Southgate, E., Thomson, J.N., Brenner, S. (1986). The structure of the nervous system of the nematode *Caenorhabditis elegans*. *Philosophical Transactions of the Royal Society B*, 314(1165):1–340.

Xie, X., Liu, W.T., Tang, B. (2007). Sinogram Spacebased estimation of moisture transport in marine atmosphere using support vector regression. *Remote Sensing of Environment*, in press, corrected proof. Available online 29 October 2007.

Xie, Y., Xing, Y. (2017). A prediction method for the wax deposition rate based on a radial basis function neural network. *Petroleum*, 3(2):237–241.

Xing, B., Marwala, T. (2018). *Smart Maintenance for Human–Robot Interaction: An Intelligent Search Algorithmic Perspective*. London: Springer.

Yap, J.T., Kao, C.-M, Cooper, M., Chen, C.-T., Wernick, M.N. (1996). Sinogram recovery of dynamic PET using principal component analysis and projections onto convex sets. In: Meyers, R., Cunningham, V., Bailey, D., Jones, T. (eds.), *Quantification of Brain Function Using PET*. San Diego: Academic Press, 109–112.

Zadkarami, M., Shahbazian, M., Salahshoor, K. (2016). Pipeline leakage detection and isolation: An integrated approach of statistical and wavelet feature extraction with multi-layer perceptron neural network (MLPNN). *Journal of Loss Prevention in the Process Industries*, 43:479–487.

Zhao, S., Xu, Y. (2005). Multivariate statistical process monitoring using robust nonlinear principal component analysis. *Tsinghua Science & Technology*, 10(5):582–586.

# Chapter 11

# Evolving Networks

**Abstract.** The idea of evolving biological systems was studied extensively by Charles Darwin. Intelligent systems in artificial intelligence can also be evolved similarly. In this regard, intelligent networks take on new information and evolve them without fully retraining them, and this is called incremental learning. We describe and compare Learn++ and Incremental Learning Using Genetic Algorithm (ILUGA). We successfully apply these techniques on Optical Character Recognition (OCR), wine recognition, financial analysis and condition monitoring.

## 11.1 Introduction

The method of training a strong static intelligent machine for all data is time consuming and expensive. In such circumstances, some of the data that was, hitherto, trained is unavailable because it has been lost or become corrupt (Higgins and Goodman, 1991; Fu and Hsu, 1996; Yamaguchi *et al.*, 1999; Carpenter *et al.*, 1992). This makes it essential to have an intelligent machine that can incrementally evolve to take on fresh data as they become obtainable, and to remember previously trained data (McCloskey and Cohen, 1989). Franco and Bacardit (2016) used large-scale experimental assessment of GPU approaches for evolutionary machine learning whereas Zohdi (2018) used evolutionary machine learning for dynamic thermomechanical modelling of 3D printing processes. de Melo and Banzhaf (2018) used evolutionary computing for automatic feature engineering whereas Azzam *et al.* (2018) applied evolutionary neural networks and support vector machines (SVMs) to model NOx emissions from gas turbines.

Vilakazi and Marwala (2007a) applied the Learn++ and Fuzzy ARTMAP for online incremental learning technique for high-voltage bushing condition monitoring whereas Mohamed *et al.* (2007) applied incremental learning for classification of protein sequences. Mohamed *et al.* (2006) applied fuzzy ARTMAP for multi-class protein sequence classification and a population-based incremental learning approach was used based on genetic algorithm (GA) to microarray gene expression feature selection.

Hulley and Marwala (2007) applied GA-based incremental learning for optimal weight and classifier selection whereas Lunga and Marwala (2006a) applied time series analysis using fractal theory and online ensemble classifiers to model the stock market. Lunga and Marwala (2006b) applied incremental learning method Learn++ for an online forecasting of stock market movement direction whereas Vilakazi and Marwala (2007b) applied incremental learning to bushing condition monitoring. Other successful implementations of incremental learning techniques include in anomaly detection, missing data estimation (Nelwamondo and Marwala, 2007), human–robot interaction (Okada *et al.*, 2009), online handwriting recognition (Almaksour and Anquetil, 2009), predicting human and vehicle motion (Vasquez *et al.*, 2009) and visual learning (Huang *et al.*, 2009).

For a worthy incremental learning algorithm, the intelligent machine needs to be stable but with good plasticity (Grossberg, 1988; Hulley and Marwala, 2007). A totally stable intelligent machine would be able to retain knowledge but will not be able to learn new information. A totally plastic intelligent machine can learn the new information given to it but cannot preserve the previous knowledge. Examples of intelligent machines are SVMs and multi-layer perceptron (MLP) neural networks (Burges, 1998; Bishop, 1995). Stable intelligent machines suffer from the lack of plasticity and are inclined to the catastrophic forgetting phenomenon (French, 1995; Hamker, 2000). Consequently, to completely take advantage of intelligent machine performance, an incremental learning technique is applied to the standard intelligent machine, which will recollect its stability but make it plastic.

Incremental learning was applied to many problems including in economics and mechanical engineering (Jantke,1993; Marwala, 2012, 2013; Xie *et al.*, 2015). The basic form of the incremental learning method is one of keeping all the data, which permits for retraining with all the data. At the other extreme is the training of the data, example by example, in an online learning manner. Approaches using the online learning technique for incremental learning have been used but have not factored all the elements of learning, principally the learning of new information (Polikar *et al.*, 2001; Vilakazi and Marwala, 2007). According to Polikar *et al.* (2001), for an intelligent machine to be incremental, it should fulfil the following criteria (Polikar *et al.*, 2001):

1. Ability to learn new information from the latest data.
2. It should not necessitate the use of original data to train the current intelligent machine.
3. It should retain past knowledge and not experience catastrophic forgetting.
4. It should be able to factor new information.

Learn++ is an incremental learning method introduced by Polikar *et al.* (2000; 2002). The method is based on the AdaBoost, which uses multiple weak intelligent machines to create an incremental learning system. The method has been revised to the Learn++.MT where it has a dynamic weight update for information that has not been used before (Muhlbaier *et al.*, 2004). These approaches have several disadvantages: Learn++ achieves poor results when new information is added; Learn++.MT learns the new information well but gives poor results because the new information is outvoted due to the dynamic weight update.

To handle these drawbacks of Learn++ and Learn++.MT, the Incremental Learning Using Genetic Algorithm (ILUGA) can be used. ILUGA uses intelligent machines evolved using GA, which optimally chooses the weights for all the decisions of the intelligent system.

## 11.2 Machine Learning

In this chapter, we describe SVM and the MLP because they are used in this chapter. The SVM was proposed by Vapnik (1999) and is based on statistical learning theory. It maps the input vectors to a higher dimensional space using mapping functions (Hulley and Marwala, 2007; Nedaie and Najafi, 2018; Peng and Chen, 2018; Kumar And Thakur, 2017). Using the higher dimensional space, an optimal separating hyperplane between the classes is identified. SVMs attempt to identify a classifier $f(x)$ that minimizes the misclassification rate. The classifier is operationalized as $f(x) = \text{sgn}(\mathbf{w} \cdot \mathbf{x} + b)$ where the vector $\mathbf{w}$ is the *kernel trick*. The kernel function maximizes the margin between the hyperplanes by producing a nonlinear decision boundary, which permits an additional separation of the data to create an exact decision boundary. Consequently, the decision of the $\mathbf{w}$ is an optimization problem to identify the optimal separating hyperplane (Scholkopf and Smola, 2002).

Functions that satisfy the Mercer's condition can be used as kernel functions and these include linear, quadratic, radial basis function, polynomial and hyperbolic tangent (Theodoridis and Koutroumbas, 1999).

The MLP is an algorithm inspired by the functioning of the brain where data is propagated from the input to the output by means of network weights and activation functions (Zhang and Wang; 2015; Rynkiewicz, 2012; Rezai *et al.*, 2014) The MLP can have multiple layers and hidden neurons. If the number of hidden neurons is large enough, the MLP can approximate functions of arbitrary complexity. To train the MLP, one needs the data and an optimization technique. In this regard, training of the MLP involves, identifying the network weights by maximizing the ability of the MLP to predict the output given the input data. Methods that have been used to train the MLP include gradient descent, conjugate gradient and scaled conjugate gradient method.

## 11.3  Genetic Algorithm

GA is a population-based stochastic search method that identifies optimal solutions to problems (Dao *et al.*, 2017; Zang *et al.*, 2018; Arakaki and Usberti, 2018). It applies evolutionary biology techniques such as crossover, mutation, reproduction and natural selection (Goldberg, 1989; Mohamed *et al.*, 2006). Cross-over mixes potential design variables together, mutation alters the design variables and reproduction of the new population is based on the principle of the survival of the fittest. The stochastic nature of the algorithm permits it to search in an extensive choice of design variables to identify the global maximum. The GA identifies the best candidates (chromosomes) by evaluating them with the fitness function, which relates the optimization problem with the GA. The GA is implemented through the following steps (Goldberg, 1989; Mohamed *et al.*, 2006; Hulley and Marwala, 2007):

1. Create a population of possible design solutions (chromosomes) for the optimization problem.
2. Calculate the fitness of each of the chromosomes, reject the chromosomes with the lowest fitness and permit only the fittest to go on to the next generation. The rejected chromosomes are substituted by using crossover and mutation.
3. Repeat steps 1 and 2 until the number of generations is reached or a stated fitness level is attained.

## 11.4 Learn++ Method

Learn++ is an incremental learning procedure that was introduced by Polikar and co-workers (Polikar *et al.*, 2000, 2001, 2002; Muhlbaier *et al.*, 2004; Erdem *et al.*, 2005b). It is based on the AdaBoost which utilizes multiple classifiers to permit the system to learn incrementally. We train each classifier using a data subset that is sampled according to a specified distribution. The procedure operates by utilizing many classifiers that are weak learners to provide good accuracy. A weak learner is a classifier that classifies the data with an accuracy of 50%. The weak learners are trained on an isolated subset of the training data and then the classifiers are combined using a weighted majority vote. The weights for the weighted majority vote are selected using the performance of the classifiers on the entire training dataset.

For an individual database $Dk$ that encompasses training series, $S$, where $S$ comprises learning instances and their equivalent classes, Learn++ begins by resetting the weights, $\boldsymbol{w}$, according to a stated distribution $DT$, where $T$ is the number of hypothesis. Initially, the weights are set to be uniform (Polikar *et al.*, 2002), thus giving equal probability for all cases selected for the first training subset and the distribution as (Marwala, 2012):

$$D = \frac{1}{m}. \tag{11.1}$$

Here, $m$ signifies the number of training samples in $S$. The training data are then distributed into training subset, $TR$ and testing subset, $TE$, to guarantee the weakLearn capability. The distribution is then used to choose the training subset $TR$ and testing subset $TE$ from $Sk$. After the training and testing subsets have been chosen, the weakLearn algorithm is applied. The weakLearner is trained using subset $TR$. A hypothesis, $ht$, attained from a weakLearner is tested using both the training and testing subsets to obtain an error (Polikar *et al.*, 2002; Marwala, 2012):

$$\varepsilon_t = \sum_{t:h_i(x_i) \neq y_i} D_t(i). \tag{11.2}$$

The error should be less than 0.5 and a normalized error $\beta_t$ is estimated using (Polikar *et al.*, 2002; Marwala, 2012):

$$B_t = \frac{\varepsilon_t}{1 - \varepsilon_t}. \tag{11.3}$$

If the error is larger than 0.5, the hypothesis is cast-off, and new training and testing subsets are chosen according to a distribution $DT$, and another hypothesis is estimated. All classifiers produced are then joined using weighted majority voting to attain amalgamated hypothesis, $H_t$ (Polikar et al., 2002; Marwala, 2012):

$$H_t = \arg\max_{y \in Y} \sum_{t:h_t(x)=y} \log\left(\frac{1}{\beta_t}\right). \tag{11.4}$$

Weighted majority voting provides higher voting weights to a hypothesis that performs well on the training and testing data subsets. The error of the composite hypothesis is estimated as follows (Polikar et al., 2002; Marwala, 2012):

$$E_t = \sum_{t:H_i(x_i) \neq y_i} D_t(i). \tag{11.5}$$

If the error is greater than 0.5, the present hypothesis is rejected, and the new training and testing data are chosen according to the distribution $DT$. If the error is less than 0.5, then the normalized error of the composite hypothesis is estimated as follows (Polikar et al., 2002; Marwala, 2012):

$$B_t = \frac{E_t}{1 - E_t}. \tag{11.6}$$

The error is used in the distribution update rule, where the weights of the acceptably classified case are reduced, accordingly increasing the weights of the misclassified instances. This confirms that the cases that were misclassified by the current hypothesis have a higher probability of being chosen for the subsequent training set. The distribution update rule is estimated by the following equation (Polikar et al., 2002; Marwala, 2012):

$$w_{t+1} = w_t(i) \times B_t^{1-[\|H_t(x_i) \neq y_i\|]}. \tag{11.7}$$

After the $T$ hypothesis has been produced for each database, the final hypothesis is estimated by combining the hypothesis using weighted majority voting using the following equation (Polikar et al., 2002):

$$H_t = \arg\max_{y \in Y} \sum_{k=1}^{K} \sum_{t:H_t(x)=y} \log\left(\frac{1}{\beta_t}\right). \tag{11.8}$$

The Learn++ algorithm is diagrammatically represented by Figure 11.1 (Vilakazi and Marwala, 2007).

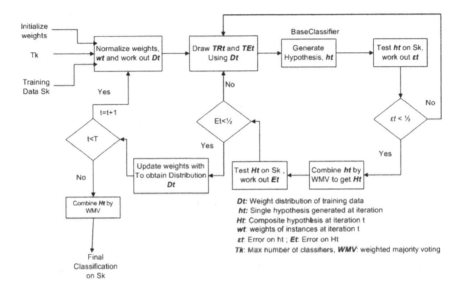

**Figure 11.1** Block diagram of a Learn++ algorithm.

Learn++.MT is an alteration to the Learn++ approach where the weights are dynamically updated (Muhlbaier *et al.*, 2004; Hulley and Marwala, 2007). The dynamic weight update decreases the influence of out-voting new classes as observed in the Learn++ where new classes have a very low accuracy. It applies the procedure that if an ensemble significantly selects a class it has observed previously, then the weights of the ensembles that have not seen the class are reduced (Erdem *et al.*, 2005b). This improvement demonstrates improved accuracies than those of the standard Learn++.

Online learning is suitable for modelling dynamic, non-stationary and time-varying systems where the character of the system in question changes with time. It is also suitable, when the dataset existing is not sufficient and does not entirely describe the system.

Another benefit of online learning is that it is able to embrace new conditions that may be offered by the incoming data. A method is used to approximate the confidence of the algorithm on its own decision. Many hypotheses agreeing on given instances can be viewed as an indication of confidence in the decision proposed. If it is assumed that a total of $T$ hypotheses are generated in $k$ training sessions for a $C$-class problem, then, for any given example, the final classification class, the total vote class $c$ receives is given by (Muhlbaier *et al.*, 2004; Marwala, 2012):

$$\zeta_c = \sum_{t:h_t(x)=c} \Psi_t. \tag{11.9}$$

Here, $\Psi_t$ denotes the voting weights of the $t$th hypothesis $h_t$. Normalizing the votes received by each class can be expressed as follows (Muhlbaier *et al.*, 2004; Marwala, 2012):

$$\lambda_c = \frac{\zeta_c}{\sum_{c=1}^{C} \zeta_c}. \tag{11.10}$$

$\lambda_c$ can be interpreted as a measure of confidence on a scale of 0 to 1 with a high value of $\lambda_c$ showing high confidence in the decision and a low value of $\lambda_c$ showing low confidence in the decision.

## 11.5 Incremental Learning Method Using Genetic Algorithm (ILUGA)

Whereas Learn++ approach uses weak learners to make up a large ensemble of classifiers, the ILUGA approach proposed by Hulley and Marwala (2007) uses strong GA optimized classifiers. In this chapter, ILUGA is used to identify the optimal separating hyperplane by finding the best kernel, soft margin and the voting weights using the GA. ILUGA applies voting mechanism of many ensemble approaches where all the classifiers vote on the class that they predict with the weighted voting mechanism (Kittler *et al.*, 1998). ILUGA permits many classifiers to be trained and the training data for each new classifier that is trained is randomized so that the sections that are used for training and validating respectively will always be different, giving the classifiers new hypothesis on the data. The first step of training for ILUGA is where a strong classifier ensemble is constructed. The strong classifier ensemble consists of binary SVM classifiers to classify the multi class dataset. The training data is randomly divided into three sections namely the training of the classifiers (**Train**), and the two validation sets (**Val1, Val2**). The binary classifiers are trained using the set **Train**, which are then evolved using GA to identify the optimal parameters for the SVM. The variables to be optimized are the kernel functions and the soft margin. The evolution of the classifiers is conducted using the validation results from set **Val1** to regulate the fitness of each of the chromosomes (Figure 11.2).

The second step of training utilizes the strong binary classifier ensemble that was produced in stage one. Each decision of the binary classifiers is allocated with a weight such that each binary classifier has two weights (one for each decision). We evolve the weights using GA, which we assess by using the fitness function. The fitness function evaluates the fitness of the chromosomes (weights) by the percentage correctly classified using weighted majority voting on set **Val2**. The optimization of individual weights makes

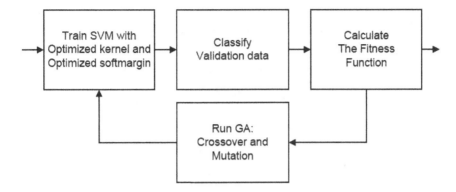

**Figure 11.2**   The optimization of the SVM using GA.

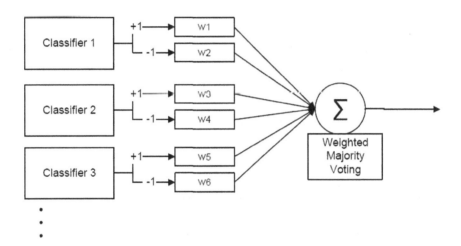

**Figure 11.3**   Voting using unique weights going to the weighted majority vote.

the classification very robust thus eliminating decisions that are incorrectly classified and giving large weightings to correctly classified decisions. This also allows us to correctly classify new classes as they are seen.

We conduct the voting to decide the class that we are classifying. We conduct this using the ensemble of classifiers and their equivalent weights. Initially, we estimate the number of possible votes for each class. Then their number of potential votes divides the weights for all the classes. This gives the new classes that we introduced the same voting power as the classes that we observed before. Then, we input weights into a weighted majority vote as shown in Figure 11.3 where each binary classifier leads to the weighted majority vote, and the predicted class has the highest vote.

When we incrementally train the ILUGA, it necessitates information from the previous classifiers and the weights estimated from previous training. The system then goes through steps one and two of the training, to form the new classifiers and weights, which we add to form the ensemble. All the classifiers then go to vote. The pseudo code is listed below as described by Polikar *et al.* (2002) and Hulley and Marwala (2007).

**Pseudo code:**

*Input*
*Stored binary classifiers*
*Stored weights*
*Stored Classes classified by each binary classifier*
*Number of classifiers to be trained ($m$)*
**Do For** *$k = 1$ to $m$*
*Train strong classifier using set* **Train** *and then optimize the parameters using GA with set* **Val1**
*Optimize the voting weights for each binary decision of the classifier using GA on set* **Val2**
*Add the classifiers and weights to the ensemble*

On classification, we estimate the number of possible votes for each class and then their number of potential votes divides the weights for all the classes. We conduct voting using weighted majority voting to predict a class.

## 11.6  Optical Character Recognition (OCR)

Hulley and Marwala (2007) implemented Learn++.MT and ILUGA to the OCR database (Newman *et al.*, 1998). The OCR data contained ten classes of digits 0–9 and 64 input features. The data was distributed into three parts for the training (**DS1, DS2, DS3**) and one part for the testing (**Test**). Each of the incremental learning approaches were restricted to the number of classifiers permitted. Learn++ and Learn++.MT which were constructed using the SVM were used to train seven classifiers. Using the Learn++ and Learn++.MT, Hulley and Marwala (2007) created five classifiers and ILUGA was used to train two multi-class classifiers per dataset. The training dataset contained 6 of the 10 classes that were to be trained. Classes 4 and 9 were used only in the final training set so that the ability of the system to include new classes was tested. The distribution of the training and testing datasets is given in Table 11.1. The simulations were run many times to get a generalized average and standard deviation. The Learn++, Learn++.MT

Table 11.1   OCR data distribution.

| Class | C0 | C1 | C2 | C3 | C4 | C5 | C6 | C7 | C8 | C9 |
|-------|-----|-----|-----|-----|-----|-----|-----|-----|-----|-----|
| DS1 | 250 | 250 | 250 | 0 | 0 | 250 | 250 | 250 | 0 | 0 |
| DS2 | 150 | 0 | 150 | 250 | 0 | 150 | 0 | 150 | 250 | 0 |
| DS3 | 0 | 150 | 0 | 150 | 400 | 0 | 150 | 0 | 150 | 400 |
| Test | 110 | 114 | 111 | 114 | 113 | 111 | 111 | 113 | 110 | 112 |

Table 11.2   SVMLearn++.MT performance results on OCR database.

| Class | C0 (%) | C1 (%) | C2 (%) | C3 (%) | C4 (%) | C5 (%) | C6 (%) | C7 (%) | C8 (%) | C9 (%) | Gen. (%) | Std. (%) |
|-------|-----|-----|-----|-----|-----|-----|-----|-----|-----|-----|-----|-----|
| DS1 | 99 | 100 | 100 | — | — | 98 | 100 | 99 | — | — | 59 | 0.05 |
| DS2 | 99 | 34 | 99 | 97 | | 93 | 20 | 99 | 60 | | 59 | 0.43 |
| DS3 | 99 | 98 | 95 | 97 | 89 | 53 | 100 | 52 | 95 | 90 | 85 | 0.56 |

Table 11.3   Learn++.MT performance results on OCR database.

| Class | C0 (%) | C1 (%) | C2 (%) | C3 (%) | C4 (%) | C5 (%) | C6 (%) | C7 (%) | C8 (%) | C9 (%) | Gen. (%) | Std. (%) |
|-------|-----|-----|-----|-----|-----|-----|-----|-----|-----|-----|-----|-----|
| DS1 | 95 | 98 | 98 | — | — | 95 | 99 | 100 | — | — | 58 | 0.8 |
| DS2 | 96 | 95 | 99 | 95 | — | 95 | 98 | 100 | 98 | — | 69 | 0.6 |
| DS3 | 67 | 95 | 92 | 98 | 83 | 63 | 98 | 100 | 95 | 96 | 89 | 0.7 |

Table 11.4   ILUGA performance results on OCR database.

| Class | C0 (%) | C1 (%) | C2 (%) | C3 (%) | C4 (%) | C5 (%) | C6 (%) | C7 (%) | C8 (%) | C9 (%) | Gen. (%) | Std. (%) |
|-------|-----|-----|-----|-----|-----|-----|-----|-----|-----|-----|-----|-----|
| DS1 | 100 | 96 | 98 | — | — | 99 | 99 | 100 | — | — | 59 | 0.2 |
| DS2 | 100 | 82 | 98 | 94 | — | 99 | 84 | 99 | 80 | — | 74 | 0.9 |
| DS3 | 92 | 97 | 96 | 92 | 95 | 90 | 99 | 98 | 90 | 83 | 93 | 1 |

and ILUGA were simulated 30 times; SVMLearn++ and SVMLearn++.MT were simulated 20 times.

Results that Hulley and Marwala (2007) observed from Learn++ and SVMlearn++ gave a generalized performance of 81% and 80%, respectively, where classes 3 and 8 performed poorly after the **DS2** of the training data and classes 4 and 9 performed poorly after the **DS3** of the training data. The results that Hulley and Marwala (2007) obtained when using the SVMLearn++.MT, Learn++.MT and ILUGA are in Tables 11.2–11.4, respectively. Rows indicate the classification performance of classes for the full training dataset and the last two columns indicate the average generalized performance (**Gen.**) and the standard deviation (**Std.**) of the generalized performance.

The generalized performance is obtained by testing the classifier on the full dataset and not only the classes trained for that stage. Thus, the generalized performance for sections **DS1** and **DS2** were low. The results of Learn++.MT and SVMLearn++.MT demonstrated that they learn new classes well the first time they were seen, yet using the dynamic weight update, the classes that were performing well before the new data was added were negatively affected. ILUGA did not suffer from catastrophic forgetting when compared to the SVMLearn++.MT and Learn++.MT, and the generalized performance of ILUGA was better by over 4%.

## 11.7  Wine Recognition

Hulley and Marwala (2007) applied Learn++.MT and ILUGA for wine recognition (Newman *et al.*, 1998). The Wine dataset contained three classes with 13 input attributes. Hulley and Marwala (2007) divided the dataset into two training sets (**DS1 and DS2**), a validation set (**Valid.**) and a testing set (**Test**). The distribution of the data is displayed in Table 11.5. Both Learn++.MT and ILUGA were simulated 30 times. They used Learn++.MT to create the optimal number of classifiers to classify the data using the validation set with no upper limit and ILUGA used two multi-class classifiers per section of the training data.

The results and number of classifiers trained per increment of data are shown in Tables 11.6 and 11.7 for Learn++.MT and ILUGA, respectively. These two approaches learn the new classes well with good generalized performance. The generalized performance for the training set **DS1** was low because it was tested on the full testing dataset and not on just the classes that were trained. Both Learn++.MT and ILUGA exhibited good

**Table 11.5**  Wine recognition dataset.

| Class | C1 | C2 | C3 |
|-------|----|----|----|
| DS1   | 26 | 31 | 0  |
| DS2   | 13 | 16 | 32 |
| Valid | 7  | 8  | 5  |
| Test  | 13 | 16 | 11 |

**Table 11.6**  Learn++ MT performance on the wine recognition dataset.

| Class | C1 | C2 | C3 | C4 | Gen. | Std. |
|-------|-----|-----|-----|-----|------|------|
| DS1(5 classifier) | 96% | 96% | — | 70% | 70% | 6% |
| DS2(6 classifier) | 99% | 87% | 90% | 92% | 92% | 5% |

**Table 11.7**  Training and generalization performance of Learn++.

| Database | Class (1) | Class (−1) | Test Performance (%) |
|----------|-----------|------------|----------------------|
| $S_1$ | 132 | 68 | 72 |
| $S_2$ | 125 | 75 | 82 |
| $S_3$ | 163 | 37 | 85 |
| $S_4$ | 104 | 96 | 86 |
| Validate | 143 | 57 | — |

incremental learning ability. ILUGA had only four multi-class classifiers in total, while the Learn++.MT method trained eleven classifiers, making ILUGA able to classify faster with better accuracy than the Learn++.MT.

On the small Wine Dataset, the performance of ILUGA showed marginally better generalized performance and better standard deviation than the Learn++.MT. Nevertheless, with the larger dataset where there were more classes added incrementally, ILUGA performed better with a 4% higher generalized performance than the Learn++.MT. The higher generalized performance was because the classifiers had optimally chosen parameters, and the weights for each decision of the binary classifier used the GA optimization method. This enabled the classifiers to classify the data with very low errors, whereas the Learn++.MT used weak learners. The weights were chosen for a high output accuracy with unobserved data, whereas Learn++.MT chose weights for an overall decision of the classifier, which did not offer the optimal output of the classifier.

Learn++.MT learned the new classes better but the dynamic weight update produced classes that were classified with very high accuracies in prior training to be adversely affected, and the classification of those classes were thus diminished. This is because classes were not trained in a certain ensemble of classifiers and the classes were outvoted because of the dynamic weight update, thereby decreasing the weights of the classifiers. ILUGA, consequently, benefited because there was no dynamic weight update and the weights and classifiers were chosen using an optimization technique with known data.

## 11.8  Financial Analysis

Marwala (2013) examined the daily variations of the Dow Jones Index. The Dow Jones averages are specific in that they are price weighted rather than market capitalization weighted. Their component weightings are influenced only by changes in the stock prices. This is contrary to other indexes' weightings that are impacted by both price changes and changes in the number of shares outstanding (Leung *et al.*, 2000). When the averages are estimated, their values are computed by merely totalling up the constituent stock prices and dividing by the number of constituents. The Dow Jones Industrial Average measures the composite price performance of over 30 highly capitalized stocks trading on the New York Stock Exchange (NYSE). This represents broad industries in the USA. The increasing diversity of financial instruments associated to the Dow Jones Index has expanded the dimension of global investment prospect for both individual and institutional investors. There are two reasons for the success of these index-trading instruments. These are that they are an effective means for investors to hedge against potential market risks and that they generate new profit-making prospects for market investors. Accordingly, it has serious consequences and importance for researchers and practitioners to forecast the direction of the movement of stock prices.

Previous research has investigated the cross-sectional relationship between stock index and macroeconomic variables. Macroeconomic input variables, include term structure of interest rates, short-term interest rate, long-term interest rate, consumer price index, industrial production, government consumption, private consumption and gross domestic product. Marwala (2013) used the closing values of the index as inputs.

He performed one step forward prediction of the index on a daily basis. The output of this prediction model was used as input to the Learn++ algorithm. The Learn++ was used for classification into the correct category that would give an indication of whether the predicted index value is 1 or −1. A value of 1 indicated a positive increase in next day's predicted closing value compared to the previous day's closing value and a −1 indicated a decrease in next day's predicted closing value compared to the previous day's closing value. The second model took the output of the first model as its input in predicting the direction of movement for the index. $Direction_t$ is a categorical variable that indicate the movement direction of the Dow Jones Index at time $t$. If the Dow Jones Index at time $t$ is larger than that at time $t-1$, $Direction_t$ is 1, otherwise, $Direction_t$ is −1.

Model selection was conducted by an empirical evaluation based on the out-of-sample data. The confidence of the algorithm on its own decision was used to evaluate the accuracy of the predicted closing value category. The first experiment implements a one step forward prediction of the next day's stock closing value. After predicting the next day's closing value, this value is fed into a classification model to indicate the direction of movement for the stock prices. The database consisted of 1476 instances of the Dow Jones average closing value during the period from January 2000 to November 2005. 1000 instances were used for training and all the remaining instances were used for validation (Lunga and Marwala, 2006a). The two binary classes were 1, indicating an upward direction of returns in Dow Jones stock, and $-1$ indicating a predicted fall/downward direction of movement for the Dow Jones stock.

Four datasets $S_1$, $S_2$, $S_3$, $S_4$, where each dataset included exactly one quarter of the entire training data, were provided to Learn++ in four training sessions for incremental learning. For each training session $k$ $(k = 1, 2, 3, 4)$, three weak hypotheses were produced by Learn++. Each hypothesis $h_1$, $h_2$ and $h_3$ of the $k$th training session was produced using a training subset $TR_t$ and a testing subset $TE_t$. The WeakLearner was a single hidden layer MLP with 15 hidden layer nodes and 1 output node with an MSE goal of 0.1. The testing set of data consisted of 476 instances that were used for validation purposes. On average, the MLP hypothesis, weakLearner, performed little over 50%, which improved to over 80% when the hypotheses were combined by making use of weighted majority voting. This improvement demonstrated the performance improvement property of Learn++, as inherited from Adaptive Boosting, on a given database. The data distribution and the percentage classification performance are given in Table 11.7 (Lunga and Marwala, 2006b). The performances listed are on the validation data. Table 11.7 gives an actual breakdown of correctly classified and misclassified instances falling into each confidence range after each training session. The trends of the confidence estimates after subsequent training sessions are given in Table 11.8. The desired outcome on the actual confidences are high to very high confidences on correctly classified instances, and low to very low confidences on misclassified instances. The desired outcome on confidence trends increased for correctly classified instances and decreased for misclassified instances as new data was introduced.

The performance shown in Table 11.7 indicates that the algorithm improved its generalization capacity as new data became available. This improvement was modest, though, as majority of the new information was

Table 11.8  Confidence results.

|  |  | VH | H | M | VL | L |
|---|---|---|---|---|---|---|
| Correctly classified | $S_1$ | 96 | 96 | 13 | 15 | 6 |
|  | $S_2$ | 104 | 104 | 22 | 17 | 14 |
|  | $S_3$ | 111 | 111 | 6 | 3 | 39 |
|  | $S_4$ | 101 | 101 | 42 | 12 | 4 |
| Incorrectly classified | $S_1$ | 23 | 7 | 13 | 3 | 8 |
|  | $S_2$ | 27 | 0 | 1 | 3 | 4 |
|  | $S_3$ | 21 | 1 | 2 | 4 | 2 |
|  | $S_4$ | 24 | 0 | 2 | 2 | 0 |

Table 11.9  Confidence trends for Dow Jones.

|  | Increasing Steady | Decreasing |
|---|---|---|
| Correctly classified | 119 | 8 |
| Misclassified | 16 | 24 |

already learnt in the first training session. Table 11.8 indicates that the vast majority of correctly classified instances tended to have very high confidences, with continually improved confidences at consecutive training sessions (Lunga and Marwala, 2006a). While a considerable portion of misclassified instances also had high confidence for this database, the general desired trends of increased confidence on correctly classified instances and decreasing confidence on misclassified ones were notable and dominant, as shown in Table 11.9 (Lunga and Marwala, 2006a).

## 11.9  Condition Monitoring of Transformers

Marwala (2012) as well as Vilakazi and Marwala (2007a & b) used dissolved gas analysis to estimate the faulty gases in the bushing oil. The information from the dissolved gas analysis reflected the states of the transformer and bushing. Ten diagnostic gases were extracted, and these were $CH_4$, $C_2H_6$, $C_2H_4$, $C_2H_2$, $H_2$, CO, $CO_2$, $N_2$, $O_2$ and total dissolved combustible gases. The total dissolved combustible gas was the sum of methane, hydrogen, acetylene, ethane, ethylene and hydrogen. The faulty gases were analysed using the IEEE C57.104 standards.

The first experiment evaluated the incremental capability of the Learn++ algorithm using first level fault diagnosis. This was to classify the presence or the absence of faults in transformer bushings. The data used was from bushing over a period of 2.5 years from bushings in services. The algorithm implemented used 1500 training and 4000 validation instances. Vilakazi and Marwala (2007a) segmented the training data into five databases each with 300 training instances. In each training session, Vilakazi and Marwala (2007a) provided Learn++ with each database and generated 20 hypotheses. The weakLearner used an MLP with 10 input layer neurons, 5 hidden layer neurons and one output layer neuron. To ensure that the technique retained previously learned data, the previous database was tested at each training session.

The first row of Table 11.10 demonstrates the performance of the Learn++ on the training data for different databases. On average, the weakLearner gave 60% classification rate on its training dataset, which improved to 98% when the hypotheses were combined.

These results demonstrate the performance improvement of Learn++ on a single database and indicate that Learn++ did not forget the previously learned information when new data was introduced. The classifiers performances on the testing dataset, steadily increased from 65.7% to 95.8% as new databases became available, demonstrating incremental capability of Learn++.

The second experiment evaluated whether the frameworks could accommodate new classes and the results are in Table 11.11. The faulty data were divided into 1000 training examples and 2000 validation data, which contained all the three classes. The training data were divided into 5 databases, each with 200 training instances. The first and second database contained, training examples of partial discharges and thermal faults.

The data of unknown fault were introduced in training session three. In each training session, Learn++ was provided with each database and 20 hypotheses were generated. The classifiers performances increased from 60% to 95.3% as new classes were introduced in the subsequent training datasets.

Table 11.10 Learn++ for first level online condition monitoring ($S$ = databases).

| Dataset | $S_1$ | $S_2$ | $S_3$ | $S_4$ | $S_5$ |
|---|---|---|---|---|---|
| $S_1$ | 89.5 | 85.8 | 83.0 | 86.9 | 85.3 |
| $S_2$ | — | 91.4 | 94.2 | 93.7 | 92.9 |
| $S_3$ | — | — | 93.2 | 90.1 | 91.4 |
| $S_4$ | — | — | — | 92.2 | 94.5 |
| $S_5$ | — | — | — | — | 98.0 |
| Learn++ Testing (%) | 65.7 | 79.0 | 85.0 | 93.5 | 95.8 |

**Table 11.11**   Performance of Learn++ for second stage bushing condition monitoring.

| Dataset | $S_1$ | $S_2$ | $S_3$ | $S_4$ | $S_5$ |
|---|---|---|---|---|---|
| $S_1$ | 95.0 | 95.2 | 94.6 | 95.7 | 95.1 |
| $S_2$ | — | 96.3 | 96.0 | 96.8 | 95.3 |
| $S_3$ | — | — | 97.0 | 96.4 | 96.5 |
| $S_4$ | — | — | — | 97.8 | 96.8 |
| $S_5$ | — | — | — | — | 99.2 |
| Learn++ Testing (%) | 60.0 | 65.2 | 76.0 | 83.0 | 95.3 |

The final experiment addressed the problem of bushing condition monitoring using MLP network trained using batch learning. This was done to compare the classification rate of Learn++ with that of an MLP.

An MLP with the same set of training examples as Learn++ was trained and the trained MLP was tested with the same validation data as Learn++. This was conducted for the first and second levels of fault classification. In the first level fault diagnosis, the MLP gave classification rate of 97.2% whereas the second level MLP gave a classification rate of 96.0%. This was when the classifier had seen all the fault classes *a priori*. If the classifier had not seen all the fault cases, the performance decreased from 65.7% for database 1% to 30.0% for database 2 to 3 for the first level fault classification.

## 11.10   Conclusions

This chapter studied online techniques for machines to incrementally learn from data. Two types of incremental methods were studied, and these were Learn++ and ILUGA. These methods were successfully used for OCR, wine recognition, financial analysis and condition monitoring.

## References

Almaksour, A., Anquetil, E. (2009). Fast incremental learning strategy driven by confusion reject for online handwriting recognition. In: *Proceedings of the International Conference on Document Analysis and Recognition*, 81–85.

Arakaki, R.K., Usberti, F.L. (2018). Hybrid genetic algorithm for the open capacitated arc routing problem. *Computers & Operations Research*, 90:221–231.

Azzam, M., Awad, M., Zeaiter, J. (2018). Application of evolutionary neural networks and support vector machines to model NOx emissions from gas turbines. *Journal of Environmental Chemical Engineering*, in press, accepted manuscript. Available online 9 January.

Bishop, C.M. (1995). *Neural Networks for Pattern Recognition.* Oxford: Oxford University Press.

Burges, C. (1998). *Data Mining and Knowledge Discovery*, 2:121–167.

Carpenter, G.A., Grossberg, S., Marhuzon, N., Reynolds, J.H., Rosen, D.B. (1992). ARTMAP: A neural network architecture for incremental learning supervised learning of analog multidimensional maps. *IEEE Transactions on Neural Networks*, 3:698–713.

Dao, S.D., Abhary, K., Marian, R. (2017). An innovative framework for designing genetic algorithm structures. *Expert Systems with Applications*, 90:196–208.

de Melo, V.V., Banzhaf, W. (2018). Automatic feature engineering for regression models with machine learning: An evolutionary computation and statistics hybrid. *Information Sciences*, 430–431:287–313.

Erdem, Z., Polikar, R., Gurgen, F., Yumusak, N. (2005a). Reducing the effect of out-voting problem in ensemble based incremental support vector machines. *15th International Conference on Artificial Neural Networks: Lecture Notes in Computer Science*, 3697:607–612.

Erdem, Z., Polikar, R., Gurgen, F., Yumusak, N. (2005b). Ensemble of SVMs for incremental learning. in multiple classifier systems. *6th International Workshop on Multiple Classifier Systems, Springer Lecture Notes in Computer Science*, 246–256.

Franco, M.A., Bacardit, J. (2016). Large-scale experimental evaluation of GPU strategies for evolutionary machine learning. *Information Sciences*, 330:385–402.

French, R. (1999). *Trends in Cognitive Sciences*, 3:128–135.

Fu, L., Hsu, H.H., Principe, J.C. (1996). Incremental backpropagation networks. *IEEE Transactions on Neural Networks*, 7:757–761.

Goldberg, D.E. (1989). *Genetic Algorithms in Search, Optimisation & Machine Learning.* New York: Addison Wesley Publishing Company, Inc.

Grossberg, S. (1988). Nonlinear neural networks: Principles, mechanisms, and architectures. *Neural Networks*, 1(1):17–61.

Hamker, F.H. (2000). Distributed competition in directed attention. In: *Proceedings in Artificial Intelligence*, 9:39–44.

Higgins, C.H., Goodman, R.M. (1991). Incremental learning for rule based neural network. In: *Proceedings of the International Joint Conference on Neural Networks*, 875–880.

Huang, D., Yi, Z., Pu, X. (2009). A new incremental PCA algorithm with application to visual learning and recognition. *Neural Process Letters*, 30:171–185.

Hulley, G., Marwala, T. (2007). Genetic algorithm based incremental learning for optimal weight and classifier selection. In: *Computational Models for Life Sciences. American Institute of Physics Series*, 952:258–267, doi: 10.1063/1.2816630.

Jantke, K. (1993). Types of incremental learning. *AAAI Symposium on Training Issues in Incremental Learning*, 23–25.

Kittler, J., Hatef, M., Duin, R., Matas, J. (1998). On combining classifiers. *IEEE Transactions on Pattern Analysis and Machine Intelligence*, 20:226–238.

Kumar, D., Thakur, M. (2017). All-in-one multicategory least squares nonparallel hyperplanes support vector machine. *Pattern Recognition Letters*, in press, corrected proof. Available online 12 October.

Leung, M., Daouk, H., Chen, A. (2000). Forecasting stock indices: A comparison of classification and level estimation models. *International Journal of Forecasting*, 16:173–190.

Lunga, D., Marwala, T. (2006a). Time series analysis using fractal theory and online ensemble classifiers. *Lecture Notes in Computer Science*, 4304:312–321.

Lunga, D., Marwala, T. (2006b). Online forecasting of stock market movement direction using the improved incremental algorithm. *Lecture Notes in Computer Science*, 4234:440–449.

Marwala, T. (2012). *Condition Monitoring Using Computational Intelligence Methods*. Heidelberg: Springer.

Marwala, T. (2013). *Economic Modeling Using Artificial Intelligence Methods*. Heidelberg: Springer.

McCloskey, M., Cohen, N. (1989). Catastrophic interference connectionist networks: The sequential learning problem. *The Psychology of Learning and Motivatation*, 24:109–164.

Mohamed, S., Rubin, D., Marwala, T. (2006). Multi-class protein sequence classification using fuzzy ARTMAP. In: *Proceedings of the IEEE International Conference on Systems, Man, and Cybernetics*, 1676–1681.

Mohamed, S., Rubin, D., Marwala, T. (2007). Incremental learning for classification of protein sequences. In: *Proceedings of the IEEE International Conference on Neural Networks*, 19–24.

Mohamed, S., Rubin, D., Marwala, T. (2007a). Adaptive GPCR classification based on incremental learning. *SAIEE Africa Research Journal*, 98(3):71–80.

Muhlbaier, M., Topalis, A., Polikar, R. (2004). Learn++.MT: A new approach to incremental learning. *5th International Workshop on Multiple Classifier Systems*, Springer LINS, 3077:52–61.

Nedaie, A., Najafi, A.A. (2018). Support vector machine with Dirichlet feature mapping. *Neural Networks*, 98:87–101.

Nelwamondo, F.V., Marwala, T. (2007). Handling missing data from heteroskedastic and nonstationary data. *Lecture Notes in Computer Science*, 4491:1293–1302.

Newman, C.B.D.J., Hettich, S., Merz, C. (1998). *UCI Repository of Machine Learning Databases, University of California, Irvine, Dept. of Information and Computer Sciences*, Available at: http://www.ics.uci.edu/_mlearn/MLRepository.html.

Okada, S., Kobayashi, Y., Ishibashi, S., Nishida, T. (2009). Incremental learning of gestures for human–robot interaction. *AI & Society*, 25:155–168.

Peng, X., Chen, D. (2018). PTSVRs: Regression models via projection twin support vector machine. *Information Sciences*, 435:1–14.

Polikar, R., Udpa, L., Udpa, S., Honavar, V. (2000). Learn++: An incremental learning algorithm for multilayer perceptrons. In: *Proceedings of IEEE 25th International Conference On Acoustics, Speech and Signal Processing (ICASSP 2000)*, 6:3414–3417.

Polikar, R., Udpa, L., Udpa, S., Honavar, V. (2001). Learn++: An incremental learning algorithm for supervised neural networks. *IEEE Transactions on Systems, Man and Cybernetics, Special Issue on Knowledge Management*, 31:497–508.

Polikar, R., Byorick, J., Krause, S., Marino, A., Moreton, M. (2002). Learn++: A classifier independent incremental learning algorithm for supervised neural networks. In: *Proceedings of International Joint Conference on Neural Networks*, 2:1742–1747.

Rezai, A., Keshavarzi, P., Mahdiy, R. (2014). A novel MLP network implementation in CMOL technology. *Engineering Science and Technology*, 17(3):165–172.

Rynkiewicz, J. (2012). General bound of overfitting for MLP regression models. *Neurocomputing*, 90:106–110.

Scholkopf, B., Smola, A. (2002). *Learning with Kernels*. UK, London: The MIT Press.

Theodoridis, S., Koutroumbas, K. (1999). *Pattern Recognition*, 1st Edition. New York: Academic Press.

Vapnik, V.N. (1999). *The Nature of Statistical Learning Theory*, 2nd Edition. Berlin: Springer.

Vasquez, D., Fraichard, T., Laugier, C. (2009). Growing hidden markov models: An incremental tool for learning and predicting human and vehicle motion. *International Journal of Robot Research*, 28:1486–1506.

Vilakazi, C.B., Marwala, T. (2007). *Lecture Notes in Computer Science*, 4491:1241–1250.

Vilakazi, C.B., Marwala, T. (2007a). Incremental learning and its application to bushing condition monitoring. *Lecture Notes in Computer Science*, 4491:1237–1246.

Vilakazi, C.B., Marwala, T. (2007b). Online incremental learning for high voltage bushing condition monitoring. In: *Proceedings of the International Joint Conference on Neural Networks*, 2521–2526.

Xie, Z., Sun, J., Palade, V., Wang, S., Liu, Y. (2015). Evolutionary sampling: A novel way of machine learning within a probabilistic framework. *Information Sciences*, 299:262–282.

Yamaguchi, K., Yamaguchi, N., Ishii, N. (1999). Incremental learning method with retrieving of interfered patterns. *IEEE Transactions on Neural Networks*, 10: 1351–1365.

Zang, W., Ren, L., Zhang, W., Liu, X. (2018). A cloud model based DNA genetic algorithm for numerical optimization problems. *Future Generation Computer Systems*, 81:465–477.

Zhang, Y., Wang, S. (2015). MLP technique based reinforcement learning control of discrete pure-feedback systems. *Neurocomputing*, 168:401–407.

Zohdi, T.I. (2018). Dynamic thermomechanical modeling and simulation of the design of rapid free-form 3D printing processes with evolutionary machine learning. *Computer Methods in Applied Mechanics and Engineering*, 331:343–362.

Chapter 12

# Causality

**Abstract.** This chapter studies causality, including the Neyman–Rubin, Pearl and Granger causality models. We describe the Neyman–Rubin causal model within the context of missing data estimation framework and directed acyclic graphs. We describe the Granger causality within the context of the identification of the causal relations.

## 12.1 Introduction

Causality has occupied the attention of philosophers for a very long time (Marwala, 2015). Even in the times of Plato and Aristotle, humans have been inquiring why and how they are on this planet, and several answers to these questions entail causality. The premise that a high being or power created the world is the principle of causality. The importance of comprehending causality to fulfil human curiosity and enhance the functioning of society is enormous. For instance, the basis of the medical field is the premise that some medicines cause healing of diseases. To link specific medicines to the curing of diseases requires a good understanding of causality, and if this understanding is not complete, the results of clinical studies are sub-optimal. One example to illustrate this notion is the story that avocado pear was considered dangerous because the causal relation between avocado and cholesterol was poorly understood. However, today we consider avocado good for cholesterol (Marwala, 2013a, 2015).

Causality is often confused with correlation. On understanding causality, it is vital to understand the principle of correlation because within any causal model lies a correlation machine.

## 12.2   Correlation

To understand causality, we ought to explore the concept of correlation. In the *www.dictionary.com* dictionary, correlation is defined as (Marwala, 2015): 'the degree to which two or more attributes or measurements on the same group of elements show a tendency to vary together'. This degree to which variables vary together is quantified as a correlation. Two variables are correlated if their underlying sub-structures are connected. For example, if one was to measure the heart rate and blood pressure of patient John, then these parameters may be correlated primarily because they are measurements from a common sub-structure, and in this case a patient called John.

In Marwala (2015), a concept called a correlation machine was introduced, which is a conventional predictive system that is primarily based on mapping variables to themselves, and this is called the auto-associative network (Kramer, 1992). It is a machine that recreates a complete set of information from a small piece of information. In an example given by Marwala (2015), one can easily complete the following statement if one is familiar with the US President J.F. Kennedy: 'Ask not what your country can do for you but. . . .' In order to achieve this task, the auto-associative memory is used, and it is shown in Figure 12.1. These networks were used in several applications including in novelty detection, image compression (Rios and Kabuka, 1995) and missing data estimation (Marwala, 2009).

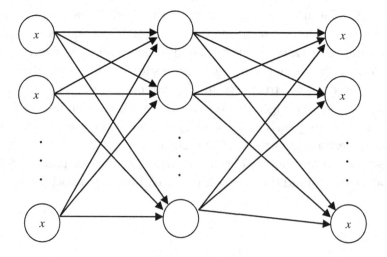

**Figure 12.1**   An auto-associative network.

Examples of the use the auto-associative networks include in pattern recognition (Masuda *et al.*, 2012), for fault detection (Miranda *et al.*, 2012), to reconstruct colour images (Valle *et al.*, 2011), for face recognition (Fernandes *et al.*, 2011), for laser spot recognition (Jeong *et al.*, 2011), in business failure (Chen, 2010) and gaze tracking (Proscevicius *et al.*, 2010). The philosophies governing the auto-associative network are (Marwala, 2009, 2015):

1. Identify a correct model that defines the interrelationships that are seen among the data variables and express the rules that govern the data using the auto-associative memory network.
2. To approximate the unknown variable(s), the correct estimated variable(s) are those that when identified obey all the interrelationships that exist among the data as defined in Step 1 and the rules that govern the data. Then, to ensure that the estimated values obey the interrelationships in the data, an optimization method treats the unknown variable(s) as design variable(s) and the interrelationships among the data and rules that govern the data as the objective to be reached. Therefore, the unknown variable(s) estimation problem is fundamentally an optimization problem where the objective is to estimate unknown variable(s) by ensuring that the rules and interrelationships governing the data are maintained.
3. It is vital to have a good idea of the bounds that govern the unknown variable(s) so as to aid the optimization process.

## 12.3 Causality

The Oxford English dictionary defines causality as 'the relationship between something that happens and the effect it produces' and defines a cause as 'making something' while an effect is defined as 'a change which is a result of an action'. The cause does not necessarily have to be 1D. In an example by Marwala (2015), in a causal relationship between sunlight, minerals, air and water causing the tree to grow, the cause has 4 dimensions (sunlight, minerals, air and water). Marwala (2015) adopted the concept that for one variable to cause another, there must be a flow of information from the cause to the effect. According to Suppes (1970), there are many different types of causes and these are *prima facie* causes, spurious causes, direct causes, supplementary causes, sufficient causes and negative causes.

In Suppes (1970) the event $B$ is the *prima facie* cause of event $A$ if event $A$ happened after event $B$ has happened. Furthermore, the probability of event $B$ happening, $p(B)$, is greater than zero and the probability of event $A$ happening given the fact that event $B$ has happened, $p(A|B)$, is greater than the probability of event $A$ happening, $p(A)$. Spurious cause is the cause of an event in which an earlier cause is the real cause of the event. According to Suppes (1970) 'an event $B_t$ is a spurious cause of $A_t$ if and only if $t' > t''$ exists and that there is a partition $\pi_{t''}$ such that for all elements $C_{t''}$ of $\pi_{t''}$, $t' < t$, $p(B_{t'}) > 0$, $p(A_t|B_{t'}) > p(A_t)$, $p(B_{t'}C_{t''}) > 0$ and $p(A_t|B_{t'}C_{t''}) = p(A_t|C_{t''})$'. Again in Suppes (1970), 'an event $B_{t'}$ is a direct cause of $A_t$ if and only if $B_{t'}$ is a *prima facie* cause of $A_t$ and there is no $t''$ and no partition $\pi_{t''}$ such that for every $C_{t''}$ in $\pi_{t''}$, $t' < t'' < t$, $P(B_{t'}C_{t''}) > 0$ and $p(A_t|B_{t'}C_{t''}) = p(A_t|C_{t''})$'. Supplementary causes are more than one cause supplementing one another to cause an event. Suppes (1970) defines $B_{t'}$ and $C_{t''}$ as supplementary causes of $A_t$ 'if and only if $B_{t'}$ is a *prima facie* cause of $A_t$, $C_{t''}$ is a *prima facie* cause of $A_t$, $p(B_{t'}C_{t''}) > 0$, $p(A|B_{t'}C_{t''}) > \max(p(A_t|B_{t'}), p(A_t|C_{t''})$'. Suppes (1970) defined that '$B_{t'}$ is a sufficient cause of $A_t$ if and only if $B_{t'}$ is a *prima facie* cause of $A_t$ and $p(A_t|B_{t'}) = 1$'. Negative cause is an event that causes another event not to occur. In Suppes (1970) 'the event $B_{t'}$ is a *prima facie* negative cause of event $A_t$ if and only if $t' < t$, $p(B_{t'}) > 0$ and $p(A_t|B_{t'}) < p(A_t)$'.

## 12.4  Theories of Causality

Hume (1896) advanced the following eight principles of causality as described by Marwala (2015):

1. There is a connection between the cause and effect in space and time.
2. The cause must happen before the effect.
3. There should be a continuous connectivity between the cause and effect.
4. The specific cause must always give the identical effect, and the same effect not be obtained from any other event but from the same cause.
5. Where several different objects give the same effect, it ought to be because of some quality that is the same among them.
6. The difference in the effects of two similar events must come from that which they are different.
7. When an object changes its dimensions with the change of its cause, it is a compounded effect from the combination of a number of different effects, which originate from a number of different parts of the cause.
8. An object that occurs for any time in its full exactness without any effect, is not the only cause of that effect but needs to be aided by some other norm which may advance its effect and action.

Studies on the theories and applications of causality include Pećnjak (2011), Paoletti (2011), McBreen (2007), Rohatyn (1975), Rodríguez Sánchez (2004) and Watkins (2004). Granger (1969) reduced the eight causality statements proposed by Hume to three principles and these are that the cause and effect are associated or correlated, that the cause happens before the effect and that the cause and effect are connected.

### 12.4.1 Transmission theory of causality

The transmission theory of causality proposes that causality is a transmission of information from the cause to the effect (Ehring, 1986; Kistler, 1998; Salmon, 1984; Dowe, 1992). For the reason of the transmission of such information from the cause to the effect, there is a correlation between the cause at the time of the transmission of this information and the effect at the time of the arrival of the information. It is because of this reason that whenever correlation is observed, causality is wrongly inferred, and human intuition has evolved such that it has learned to identify causality through correlation. This is because of the human's inability to detect a time lag between a cause and effect, which implies causality.

Marwala (2015) proposed that within any causality model there is a correlation machine. Therefore, if $x$ causes $y$ then $y$ at a later time is necessarily correlated to $x$ at the earlier time.

### 12.4.2 Probability theory of causality

The probability theory of causality states that some classes of causality are probabilistic. This violates the principle advocated by Hume that states that 'the specific cause must at all times give the identical effect, and the same effect should not be obtained from any other event but from the same cause'. Marwala (2015) used an example on whether *HIV causes AIDS*. There is clearly a correlation between HIV and AIDS, but not all people with HIV necessarily develop AIDS. In the deterministic framework, HIV does not cause AIDS, because all people who have HIV will not necessarily develop AIDS. However, in the probabilistic world indeed HIV causes AIDS. Therefore, the probability of getting AIDS given HIV is more than a probability of chance. A generalized causal model is probabilistic with the deterministic version being a special case when the probability is 100%.

Other researchers that studied causal probability are Ten Kate (2010), Schmidtke and Krawczak (2010), Plotnitsky (2009), González Fernández (2005) and Dawid (2004).

### 12.4.3  Projectile theory of causality

Marwala (2015) proposed the projectile theory of causality and this is a generalized version of the transmission theory of causality. Like the transmission theory, it assumes that there is transmission of information from the cause to the effect. However, the transmission of information is with a specific intensity (speed) and configuration (angle). He viewed the transmission of information from the cause to the effect as a projectile. Causal information leaves the point of cause with a certain velocity indicating a specific intensity of the cause. Sometimes it reaches the point of effect, sometimes it falls short or overshoots the target and from this it is possible to build a probability distribution of causation. This theory is illustrated in Figure 12.2 (Marwala, 2015).

### 12.4.4  Causal calculus and structural learning

As described by Marwala (2015), suppose one wanted to find the validity of the hypothesis that HIV causes AIDS. Causal calculus allows us to estimate the interventional probability that a person who is forced to have HIV develops AIDS, which is written as $P(AIDS \,|\, \text{forced}(HIV))$ from the conditional probability $P(AIDS \,|\, HIV)$ using Bayesian networks. When we define this process on a directed acyclic graph (DAG), it is possible to infer causal relationships among variables. More details on this can be found in Pearl (2000), Ortigueira *et al.* (2012), Raginsky (2011) and Pommereau (2004). This causal calculus assumes that the structure that connects variables is in existence. There are cases where the structure does not exist and there is a need to identify this from the observed data. This we can achieve by using the Bayesian networks.

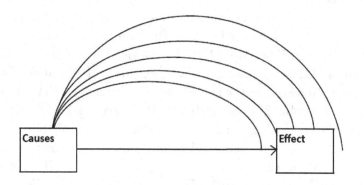

**Figure 12.2**   An illustration of the projectile theory of causality.

## 12.4.5 Granger causality

As described in Marwala (2015), Granger causality is a technique for revealing directed functional connectivity based on time series analysis of causes and effect. Suppose we have variable observations $y_k, y_{k-1}, \ldots, y_1$ and $x_{k-1}, x_{k-2}, \ldots, x_1$, then there is a causal relationship between the variables if when solving the following linear regression problem, the coefficients, $\beta$, are non-zero (Granger, 1969):

$$y_k = \alpha_1 y_1 + \alpha_2 y_2 + \cdots + \alpha_{k-1} y_{k-1} + \beta_1 x_1 + \beta_2 x_2 + \cdots + \beta_{k-1} x_{k-1} + \varepsilon.$$
(12.1)

This relationship can then be generalized to become (Granger, 1969):

$$y_k = f(\alpha_{k-1} y_{k-1}, \ldots, \alpha_1 y_1, \beta_{k-1} x_{k-1}, \ldots, \beta_1 x_1, \varepsilon). \qquad (12.2)$$

Here, $\alpha$ and $\beta$ are hyperparameters, and are non-zero if there is a causal relationship between $x$ and $y$, and $\beta$ is zero if there is no relationship between $x$ and $y$. Successful applications of Granger causality include Candelon *et al.* (2013), Seth *et al.* (2013), Zhao *et al.* (2013), Friston *et al.* (2012) as well as Croux and Reusens (2012).

## 12.4.6 Structural learning

Marwala (2015) described structural learning (SL) as an approach used to identify connections between a set of variables. SL is based on the premise that there are three causal sub-structures that define causal relationships between variables (Wright, 1921) and these are direct and indirect causation ($X \rightarrow Z \rightarrow Y$), common cause confounding ($X \leftarrow Z \rightarrow Y$) and a collider ($X \rightarrow Z \leftarrow Y$). In the direct and indirect causation, $X$ and $Y$ are conditionally dependent and furthermore, $X$ and $Y$ are conditionally independent given $Z$. For the common confounding, $X$ and $Y$ are conditionally dependent and furthermore, $X$ and $Y$ are conditionally independent given $Z$. In the collider, $X$ and $Y$ are independent of one another but are dependent given $Z$. Therefore, we can uniquely identify from cross-sectional data. In SL, we identify relationships between variables using heuristic optimization techniques.

## 12.4.7 Manipulation theory

Manipulation theory (MT) of causality considers causal relationships between causal variable $x$ and effect variable $y$ and considers changes in

$x$ called $\Delta x$ and assesses whether it leads to change in $y(\Delta y)$ in the model $y = f(x)$ (Marwala, 2015). If it does, then there is a causal relationship between $x$ and $y$. If this is not the case, then there is another variable which both $x$ and $y$ depend on. Studies on the MT include works by Baedke (2012), Imai *et al.* (2013), Erisen and Erisen (2012), Silvanto and Pascual-Leone (2012) and Mazlack (2011).

### 12.4.8 Process theory

Process theory (PT) of causality considers the causal relationship between variables $x$ and $y$ and identifies the actual process of causality, not its mirror (Marwala, 2015). Studies on PT include Anderson and Scott (2012), Rodrigo *et al.* (2011), Sia (2007) and Samgin (2007).

### 12.4.9 Counterfactual theory

In counterfactual thinking (CT), given a factual with an antecedent (cause) and a consequence (effect), we alter the antecedent and the new consequence is derived (Byrne, 2005; Lewis, 1973; Miller and Johnson-Laird, 1976; Simon and Rescher, 1966). Marwala (2015) used an example where one intends to test what happens to a headache when aspirin is administered. Then one would observe what happens when one has a headache, and nothing is administered and compare this to when aspirin is administered. In this instance, not administering aspirin is called a factual while administering aspirin is called a counterfactual. Ideally for the efficacy of aspirin to be observed, then not administering aspirin (factual) and administering aspirin (counterfactual) should happen at the same time which is physically impossible. The compromise is for the factual and counterfactual to happen at nearly identical conditions (Byrne and Tasso, 1999; De Vega *et al.*, 2007). Rational counterfactual is a special type of CT proposed by Marwala (2015) and is a counterfactual that maximizes the attainment of the consequence. Directionality counterfactuals give direction and an example given by Marwala (2015) is as follows: if John had moved to London, John would have been wealthy (factual) as opposed to if John had not moved to London, John would have been poor (factual). Additive/subtractive counterfactuals are the types where you add or subtract on the antecedent. Some successful applications of counterfactual theory to model causality include Shpitser (2013), Fillenbaum (1974), Ferguson and Sanford (2008) and Ginsberg (1986).

## 12.4.10 Neyman–Rubin causal model

Marwala (2015) used the theory of counterfactuals to describe the Neyman–Rubin causal (NRC) model (Neyman, 1923; Rubin, 1974, 1977, 1978). The NRC model assumes that for there to be a causal relationship between a decision action to administer a particular action and an effect, then there has to be a difference between the result of administering an action and not administering an action. The difficulty with this procedure is that it is impossible to administer an action on a particular object and not administer an action on the same object at the same time. In the definition derived from the NRC model, the decision of administering an action is called a counterfactual while the decision not to administer an action is called a factual (Rubin, 2005).

Marwala (2015) gave the following example of a NRC model: Suppose we want to establish whether *Muvhale* tree leaves are able to reduce sugar level when ingested. Then we have 100 participants to test this and from each participant we measure the sugar level obtained when the participant has not ingested the leaves ($y_c$) and the sugar level when the participant has ingested the leaves ($y_t$), and these results are represented as in Table 12.1 (Marwala, 2015). In order to complete this causal identification process, the missing data in Table 12.1 needs to be estimated and thus the causality identification process using the NRC model is essentially a missing data estimation problem, and this is a subject of the next section (Rubin, 1978).

To apply the NRC model, we require that a subject treatment and control occur concurrently. This is physically impossible. Accordingly, Rubin (1973) proposed a method called matching to match the control case to its corresponding treatment. Marwala (2009) proposed auto-associative model to estimate missing data.

**Table 12.1**  Results from a study on the impact of administering leaves of Muvhale tree on subjects.

| Subject | $y_c$ | $y_t$ | $\sigma = y_t - y_c$ |
|---------|-------|-------|----------------------|
| Denga   | 3.5   | ?     | ?                    |
| John    | ?     | 5.3   | ?                    |
| Khathu  | 4.2   | ?     | ?                    |
| Mary    | ?     | 5.5   | ?                    |
| Mashudu | ?     | 38    | ?                    |
| Thendo  | 5.9   | ?     | ?                    |

## 12.4.11  Causal calculus

Causal calculus is derived from conditional probability theory and is the idea of approximating interventional probability $(p(y \mid do(x)))$ from conditional probabilities $(p(y \mid x))$ (Rebane and Pearl, 1987; Verma and Pearl, 1990; Pearl and Verma, 1995; Pearl and Dechter, 1996; Pearl, 2000; Marwala, 2015). An example introduced by Judea Pearl is the problem of approximating the probability of cancer given the fact that the subjects are forced to smoke vs. estimating the conditional probability of a person developing cancer given the fact that they smoke. This involves the use of DAGs and Bayesian networks to estimate interventional probability from conditional probabilities. Pearl causal approach is intended to structure the problem so that it becomes easier to distinguish between causality and correlation in relations defined by conditional probabilities.

Pearl causality model uses DAGs. DAG is directed in the sense that it is pointing at a direction, and if we adopt the transmission theory of causality, indicates the direction in which information flows from the cause to the effect (Steinsky, 2003; Xie *et al.*, 2006; Luciani and Stefanini, 2012). DAG is acyclic because it goes from one variable to another rather that from one variable to itself. An illustration of a graph is shown in Figure 12.3 (Marwala, 2015). This graph has variables which are $X$, $Y$, $Z$, $A$ and $P$. It also has arcs whose arrows represent direction. Marwala (2015) viewed these arcs as causal models which can be modelled parametrically as a function, $y = f(x)$, where $x$ happens before 0 $y$, and $x$ and $y$ are connected. Furthermore, there is a flow of information from $x$ to $y$ as represented by the direction of the arc. Each variable may have a parent, and, in this regard, the parent of $Y$ is $X$. Additionally, each variable can have a child and the child of $Y$ is $Z$. Each variable may have an ancestor and the ancestors of $Z$ are $X$ and $Y$. In addition, each variable may have descendants and the descendants of $Z$ are $A$ and $P$. The general idea of the Pearl causality is to estimate

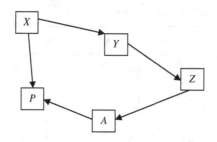

**Figure 12.3**  An illustration of the DAG.

the interventional probability from the conditional probabilities, from the joint probabilities. In Figure 12.3, the interventional probability may be the $p(Y \mid do(X))$ from the conditional probability $p(X, Y, Z, A, P)$.

One principal question we describe is how two variables are related to one another. We express the mathematical relations that describe the data in a DAG as a joint probability function as follows (Marwala, 2015):

$$p(X_1, X_2, \ldots, X_n) = \prod_i^n p(X_i \mid \mathrm{par} X_i). \qquad (12.3)$$

Here, $\prod$ is the product and *par* is the parent. From Equation (12.3), the joint probability in Figure 12.3 is $p(X)p(Y \mid X)p(Z \mid Y)p(A \mid Z)p(P \mid A, X)$. There are three causal sub-structures that define causal relationships between variables and these are direct and indirect causation (Figure 12.4), common cause confounding (Figure 12.5) and a collider (Figure 12.6) (Wright, 1921). In Figure 12.4, $X$ and $Y$ are conditionally dependent. Furthermore, $X$ and $Y$ are conditionally independent given $Z$. The effect of this on causal model is that it intercepts the causal pathway.

In Figure 12.5, $X$ and $Y$ are conditionally dependent. Furthermore, $X$ and $Y$ are conditionally independent given $Z$. Marwala (2015) explained Figure 12.6, by supposing that $X$ represents the fact that it has rained, and $Y$ represents the fact that the sprinkler was on and $Z$ represents the fact

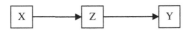

**Figure 12.4**   Direct and indirect causation.

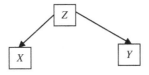

**Figure 12.5**   Common cause confounding.

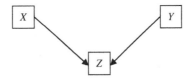

**Figure 12.6**   The collider.

that the grass is wet. The fact that it has rained is independent from the fact that the sprinkler is on. Mathematically, this can be expressed as follows:

$$p(X \mid Y) = p(X) \quad \text{and} \quad p(Y \mid X) = p(Y). \tag{12.4}$$

However, if we know that the grass is wet and that it has rained then this reduces the probability that the sprinkler was on. Therefore, the knowledge of $X$ and $Z$ gives us some information about $Z$. Therefore, for a collider, $X$ and $Y$ are conditionally independent. Furthermore, $X$ and $Y$ are conditionally dependent given $Z$.

In Figures 12.4 and 12.5, $X$ and $Y$ are dependent but are independent given $Z$. They are statistically indistinguishable from cross-sectional data. Figure 12.6 is uniquely identifiable because $X$ and $Y$ are independent but are dependent given $Z$. They, therefore, can be identified from cross-sectional data.

The concept of $d$-separation defines conditions in which a DAG transmits causal information (Pearl and Verma, 1995). Verma and Pearl (1987) demonstrated that the $d$-separation technique can identify independencies from any DAG based on a causal input list. According to Pearl, a path, $p$, is considered $d$-separated by a set of nodes $Z$ if and only if (Marwala, 2015):

1. $p$ has a chain $x \to n \to y$ or a fork $x \leftarrow n \to y$ such that the middle node $n$ is in $Z$ or
2. $p$ contains a collider $x \leftarrow n \to yx \to n \leftarrow y$ such that the middle node $n$ is not in $Z$, and that no descendent of $n$ is in $Z$.
3. A set $Z$ $d$-separates $X$ from $Y$ if and only if $Z$ blocks all paths from $X$ to $Y$.

These rules are depicted in Figure 12.7, where $y$ and $x$ are $d$-separated by $z$, or $x$ and $y$are $d$-separated by a collider while $y$, $p$ and $q$ are $d$-connected.

A back-door adjustment estimates the probability of observing one variable $y$ given variable $x$ by using conditional probabilities that relate variables $x$, $y$ and $z$ where $z$ influences directly $x$ and $y$ (Pearl, 2000). The back-door criterion is in Figure 12.8. A $z$ meets the back-door criterion with respect to variables $x_i$ and $x_j$ in a DAG if none of the variables in $z$ descend from $x_i$ and $z$ $d$-separates or blocks all paths between $x_i$ and $x_j$, which include arrows leading to $x_i$. In Figure 12.6, $x$ $d$-separates all paths from $p$ to $y$, and $x$ does not descend from $p$. The back-door criterion is derived by calculating the joint probability, $p(x, y, z)$ (Doob, 1953; Prohorov, 1969; Billingsley, 1979; Marwala, 2013a):

$$p(x, y, z) = p(z)p(x \mid z)p(y \mid x, z). \tag{12.5}$$

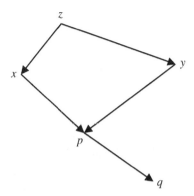

**Figure 12.7**   Illustration of *d*-separation.

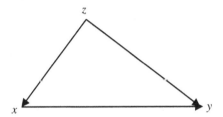

**Figure 12.8**   Illustration of the back-door criterion.

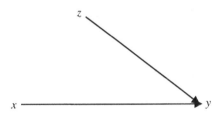

**Figure 12.9**   Illustration of the back-door criterion with an edge eliminated because $x$ is forced to happen.

We can modify Figure 12.8 to form Figure 12.9 by removing the edge between $x$ and $z$ to estimate the causal probability $p(y \mid do(x))$. Equation (12.5) thus becomes (Pearl, 2000; Marwala, 2015):

$$p(do(x), y, z) = p(z)p(y \mid x, z). \qquad (12.6)$$

Rearranging Equation (12.6) becomes (Pearl and Verma, 1995; Marwala, 2015):

$$p(do(x) \mid y, z) = p(z)p(y \mid x, z). \qquad (12.7)$$

We can integrate $z$ in Equation (12.7) to form (Pearl, 2000; Marwala, 2015):

$$p(y \mid do(x)) = \sum_z p(y \mid x, z)p(z). \qquad (12.8)$$

A variable $z$ fulfils the front-door criterion with respect to variables $x_i$ and $x_j$ in a DAG if and only if every directed path from $x_i$ to $x_j$ contains variable $z$ and there is no back-door route from $x_i$ to $z$, and $x_t$ blocks all back-door paths to $x_j$ Pearl (2000). To derive the front-door criterion, we calculate the joint probability $p(x, y, z, u)$ in Figure 12.10 as follows (Doob, 1953; Prohorov, 1969; Billingsley, 1979; Marwala, 2015):

$$p(x, y, z, u) = p(u)p(x \mid u)p(z \mid x)p(y \mid z, u). \qquad (12.9)$$

After intervention, $x = x'$ and we can eliminate the edge between $u$ and $x$ to provide intervention at $x$ given the following mathematical expression (Pearl, 2000; Marwala, 2015):

$$p(do(x), y, z, u) = p(u)p(z \mid x)p(y \mid z, u). \qquad (12.10)$$

Integrating out $z$ and $x'$, the front-door adjustment that satisfies the front-door criterion with respect to $(x, y)$ gives the causal relationship between $x$ and $y$ that can be identified as follows (Pearl, 2000; Marwala, 2015):

$$p(y \mid do(x)) = \sum_z p(z \mid x) \sum_{x'} p(y \mid x', z)p(x'). \qquad (12.11)$$

Pearl (1995) proposed three sets of rules that transform conditional probabilities into interventional calculus. The first one is insertion or deletion of observation and it is based on the concept of $d$-separation. Insertion or

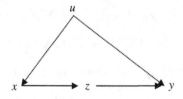

**Figure 12.10**   Illustration of the front-door criterion.

deletion of observation ($d$-separation) does not have any consequences if the variables are conditionally independent. It is expressed as follows (Pearl, 1995; Marwala, 2015):

$$p(y \mid do(x), z, w) = p(y \mid do(x), z), \qquad (12.12)$$

where $(y \amalg z \mid x, w)_{G_{\bar{x}}}$ and this means that Equation (12.12) is only valid when $y$ and $z$ are conditionally independent given $x$ and $z$, and $G_{\overline{X}}$ is the graph obtained from $G$ when the arrows pointing into $x$ are removed. This rule allows us to ignore irrelevant information.

The second rule of do-calculus states that actions and observations can be interchanged if all the back-doors are blocked, and this is expressed as (Pearl, 1995; Marwala, 2015):

$$p(y \mid do(x), do(z), w) = p(y \mid do(x), z, w), \qquad (12.13)$$

where $(y \amalg z \mid x, w)_{G_{\bar{x}z}}$ and thus $y$ and $z$ are conditionally independent given $x$ and $w$, and $G_{\overline{X}\underline{Y}}$ is a graph obtained when all arrows pointing into $x$ and pointing out of $y$ are removed.

The third do-calculus rule is that inserting or deleting of actions after the action, does not change anything and this is expressed as follows (Pearl, 1995; Marwala, 2015):

$$p(y \mid do(x), do(z), w) = p(y \mid do(x), w), \qquad (12.14)$$

where $(y \amalg z \mid x, w)_{G_{\overline{XZ(W)}}}$ and here, $z(w)$ is the set of $z$-nodes that are not ancestors of any $w$-node in $G_{\overline{X}}$.

## 12.4.12 Inductive causation (IC)

This section describes the inductive causation (IC) algorithm. The IC was proposed by Rebane and Pearl (1987) and is summarized as follows (Rebane and Pearl, 1987; Pearl and Verma, 1995; Marwala, 2015):

1. Produce a complete undirected graph connecting every variable with all other variables
2. Test for correlation and then eliminate edges through tests of no or partial correlation
3. Identify the direction of the edges remaining after all the possible correlations tests have eliminated edges with no associations.

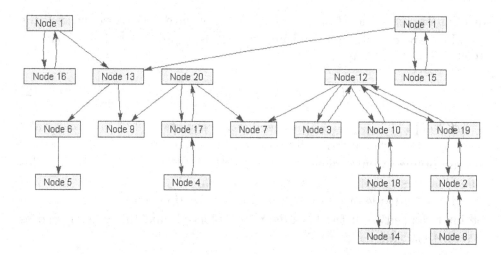

**Figure 12.11**    Results from the implementation of the IC model developed by Li.

Figure 12.11 shows the implementation of the IC algorithm written by Li (Bielza *et al.*, 2011; Marwala, 2015).

## 12.5  How to Detect Causation?

An important question is how we detect causation and how do we measure it. If we are to adopt the transmission model of causation, we could possibly observe information moving from the cause to the effect. However, no one is sure what this information is. Another way to sense causation is to frame a question differently by inquiring how relevant the cause is on the effect rather than asking how the cause is transmitted to the effect. By asking the question on how relevant the cause is on the determination of the effect and ruling out correlation, this can allow one to use relevance determination models such as factor analysis to possibly sense causality.

In his book, Marwala (2015) defined a causal machine, which takes an input vector $(x)$ which is the cause and propagates it into the effect $(y)$. This is represented as follows:

$$y = f(x). \tag{12.15}$$

Here, $f$ is the functional mapping. This equation strictly implies that $y$ is directly obtained from $x$. Of course, this elegant equation is not strictly only applicable to the cause and effect but can still be valid if $x$ and $y$ are correlated. What Marwala argued was that a function structurally assumes a causal model under certain conditions prescribed by Hume (1896) and these are that there should be a flow of information from $x$ to $y$.

## 12.6 Causality and Artificial Intelligence

Artificial Intelligence (AI) is about the construction of intelligent systems with the ability to learn and think (Hopfield, 1982; Marwala, 2009; Marwala and Lagazio, 2011; Cireşan *et al.*, 2012). This chapter links causality with AI. Marwala (2015) proposed neural networks to create models that transmit information from the cause to the effect. Neural network uses neurons to transmit information from the cause to the effect. Different kinds of neural networks include the multi-layer perceptron (MLP) and the radial basis function (RBF) (Chemachema, 2012; Liu *et al.*, 2012; Cañete *et al.*, 2012; Marwala, 2013, 2015).

The MLP has multiple layers of neural units interconnected in a feed-forward configuration (Haykin, 1999; Marwala, 2013a, 2013b). In the MLP, each neuron in a layer is connected to the neurons in the subsequent layer. The MLP is, therefore, a feed-forward neural network model in which the input variables feed-forward to become the effect and thus estimates a relationship between sets of input data (cause) and a set of appropriate output (effect). The MLP was successful in modelling many complex problems (Golzan *et al.*, 2012; Rababaah and Tebekaemi, 2012; Elmannai *et al.*, 2012; Sanz *et al.*, 2012; Marwala, 2010, 2012; PourAsiabi *et al.*, 2012; Culotta *et al.*, 2012; Bachtiar *et al.*, 2011).

Genetic algorithm is an optimization method based on the principles of evolution (Darwin, 1859; Lin *et al.*, 2013; Marwala, 2015). It operates through crossover, mutation and reproduction. Crossover is when two members of the population exchange information to produce an offspring. Mutation is when a member of the population changes aspects of its genes. Reproduction is done through the principles of the survival of the fittest. Genetic algorithm was applied successfully to optimize many complex problems (Lin *et al.*, 2013; Hassan, 2013; Poirier *et al.*, 2013; Wang and Liu, 2013; Darrah *et al.*, 2013; Marwala, 2015).

Particle swarm optimization (PSO) technique is a stochastic, population-based evolutionary global optimization technique inspired by the 'flocking behaviour' of birds (Kennedy and Eberhart, 1995). In the optimization method, birds identifying a roost is akin to identifying an optimal solution.

PSO is governed by group and individual knowledge. PSO has been applied successfully in complex problems (Sermpinis *et al.*, 2013; Abd-Elazim *et al.*, 2013; Zhang *et al.*, 2013a & b; Scriven *et al.*, 2013).

## 12.7  Causality and Rational Decision

Our understanding of causality can be used in decision-making. Correlation fills in the gaps that exist because of the limitation of information in decision-making. Causality in decision-making is especially through causal loops whereby we choose an appropriate cause of action from many possible causes of actions. In rational decision, we choose a decision that maximizes the utility based on relevant information, appropriate logic and optimization of resources (Habermas, 1984; Etzioni, 1988; Marwala, 2015). Simon Herbert proposed the idea of bounded rationality, which prescribes that when making rational decisions, information, logic and efficiency are limited (Simon, 1991; Gigerenzer and Selten, 2002; Marwala, 2015).

Marwala (2015) used the auto-associative network and genetic algorithm to model the antenatal HIV database. The results demonstrated this method performs well. Marwala (2015) used the MLP to identify the causal relationship between interstate conflict variables (causes) and conflict status (effect). Marwala (2015) used the MLP network to extend the Granger causality model to the nonlinear domain. He used this to model chaotic time series. In this regard, $x$ causes $y$ if the past values of $y$ and $x$ predict future values of $y$ better than the past values of $y$ predict future values of $y$. This framework was used to model the causal relationship between the demographic characteristics and HIV infection. Marwala (2015) proposed the PSO and auto-associative neural network to estimate missing data and used this on the beer taster and fault identification problems.

## 12.8  Conclusions

This chapter studied causality. In particular, it explored the Neyman–Rubin, Pearl and Granger causality models. We described the NRC model within the context of missing data estimation framework and directed acyclic graphs. We described the Granger causality within the context of the identification of the causal relations. Applications of these causal models to problems in engineering, HIV and beer tasting were discussed.

# References

Abd-Elazim, S.M., Ali, E.S. (2013). A hybrid particle swarm optimization and bacterial foraging for optimal power system stabilizers design. *International Journal of Electrical Power and Energy Systems*, 46(1):334–341.

Anderson G.L., Scott J. (2012). Toward an intersectional understanding of process causality and social context. *Qualitative Inquiry*, 18(8):674–685.

Bachtiar, L.R., Unsworth, C.P., Newcomb, R.D., Crampin, E.J. (2011). Predicting odorant chemical class from odorant descriptor values with an assembly of multi-layer perceptrons. In: *Proceedings of the Annual International Conference of the IEEE Engineering in Medicine and Biology Society*, EMBS, art. no. 6090755, 2756–2759.

Baedke, J. (2012). Causal explanation beyond the gene: Manipulation and causality in epigenetics. *Theoria*, 27(2):153–174.

Bielza, C., Li, G., Larrañaga, P. (2011). Multi-dimensional classification with Bayesian networks. *International Journal of Approximate Reasoning*, 52:705–727.

Billingsley, P. (1979). *Probability and Measure*. New York: Wiley.

Byrne, R.M.J. (2005). *The Rational Imagination: How People Create Counterfactual Alternatives to Reality*. Cambridge, MA: MIT Press.

Byrne, R.M.J., Tasso, A. (1999). Deductive reasoning with factual, possible, and counterfactual conditionals. *Memory & Cognition*, 27:726–740.

Candelon, B., Joëts, M., Tokpavi, S. (2013). Testing for Granger causality in distribution tails: An application to oil markets integration. *Economic Modelling*, 31(1):276–285.

Cañete, E., Chen, J., Marcos Luque, R., Rubio, B. (2012). NeuralSens: A neural network based framework to allow dynamic adaptation in wireless sensor and actor networks. *Journal of Network and Computer Applications*, 35(1):382–393.

Chemachema, M. (2012). Output feedback direct adaptive neural network control for uncertain SISO nonlinear systems using a fuzzy estimator of the control error. *Neural Networks*, 36:25–34.

Chen, M.-H. (2010). Pattern recognition of business failure by autoassociative neural networks in considering the missing values. *ICS 2010 — International Computer Symposium*, art. no. 5685421, 711–715.

Cireşan, D., Meier, U., Masci, J., Schmidhuber, J. (2012). Multi-column deep neural network for traffic sign classification. *Neural Networks*, 32:333–338.

Croux, C., Reusens, P. (2012). Do stock prices contain predictive power for the future economic activity? A Granger causality analysis in the frequency domain. *Journal of Macroeconomics*, 35:95–103.

Culotta, S., Messineo, A., Messineo, S. (2012). The application of different model of multi-layer perceptrons in the estimation of wind speed. *Advanced Materials Research*, 452–453:690–694.

Darrah, M., Fuller, E., Munasinghe, T., Duling, K., Gautam, M., Wathen, M. (2013). Using genetic algorithms for tasking teams of raven UAVs. *Journal of Intelligent and Robotic Systems: Theory and Applications*, 70(1–4):361–371.

Darwin, C. (1859). *On the Origin of Species by Means of Natural Selection, or the Preservation of Favoured Races in the Struggle for Life*. London: John Murray.

Dawid, A.P. (2004). Probability, causality and the empirical world: A Bayes-de Finetti–Popper–Borel synthesis. *Statistical Science*, 19(1):44–57.

De Vega, M., Urrutia, M., Riffo, B. (2007). Canceling updating in the comprehension of counterfactuals embedded in narrative. *Memory & Cognition*, 35:1410–1421.

Doob, J.L. (1953). *Stochastic Processes*. New York: Wiley.

Dowe, T.P. (1992). Wesley Salmon's process theory of causality and conserved quantity theory. *Philosophy of Science*, 59:195–216.

Ehring, D. (1986). The transference theory of causation. *Synthese*, 67:249–258.

Elmannai, H., Loghmari, M.A., Karray, E., Naceur, M.S. (2012). Nonlinear source separation based on multi-layer perceptron: Application on remote sensing analysis. In: *2nd International Conference on Remote Sensing, Environment and Transportation Engineering. RSETE — Proceedings*, art. no. 6260640.

Erisen, E., Erisen, C. (2012). The effect of social networks on the quality of political thinking. *Political Psychology*, 33(6):839–865.

Etzioni, A. (1988). Normative-affective factors: Towards a new decision-making model. *Journal of Economic Psychology*, 9:125–150.

Ferguson, H.J., Sanford, A.J. (2008). Anomalies in real and counterfactual worlds: An eye-movement investigation. *Journal of Memory Language*, 58:609–626.

Fernandes, B.J.T., Cavalcanti, G.D.C., Ren, T.I. (2011). Autoassociative pyramidal neural network for face verification. In: *Proceedings of the International Joint Conference on Neural Networks*, art. no. 6033417, 1612–1617.

Fillenbaum, S. (1974). Information amplified: Memory for counterfactual conditionals. *Journal of Experimental Psychology*, 102:44–49.

Friston, K., Moran, R., Seth, A.K. (2012). Analysing connectivity with Granger causality and dynamic causal modelling. *Current Opinion in Neurobiology*, 23:172–178.

Gigerenzer, G., Selten, R. (2002). *Bounded Rationality: The Adaptive Toolbox*. London, England: MIT Press.

Ginsberg, M.L. (1986). Counterfactuals. *Artificial Intelligence*, 30:35–79.

Golzan, S.M., Avolio, A., Graham, S.L. (2012). Non-invasive cerebrospinal fluid pressure estimation using multi-layer perceptron neural networks. In: *Proceedings of the Annual International Conference of the IEEE Engineering in Medicine and Biology Society, EMBS*, art. no. 6347185, 5278–5281.

González Fernández, M.P. (2005). Probability and causality in the philosophy of Max Born Logos, 38:241–269.

Granger, C.W.J. (1969). Investigating causal relations by econometric models and cross-spectral methods. *Econometrica*, 37:424–438.

Habermas, J. (1984). *The Theory of Communicative Action Volume 1; Reason and the Rationalization of Society*. Cambridge: Polity Press.

Hassan, M.M. (2013). Optimization of stay cables in cable-stayed bridges using finite element, genetic algorithm, and B-spline combined technique. *Engineering Structures*, 49:643–654.

Haykin, S. (1999). *Neural Networks: A Comprehensive Foundation*, 2nd Edition. New Jersey: Prentice-Hall.

Hopfield, J.J. (1982). Neural networks and physical systems with emergent collective computational abilities. In: *Proceedings of the National Academy of Sciences of the USA*, 79(8):2554–2558.

Hume, D. (1896). (Selby-Bigge, ed.) *A Treatise of Human Nature*. Oxford, UK: Clarendon Press.

Imai, K., Tingley, D., Yamamoto, T. (2013). Experimental designs for identifying causal mechanisms. *Journal of the Royal Statistical Society. Series A: Statistics in Society*, 176(1):5–51.

Jeong, S., Jung, C., Kim, C.-S., Shim, J.H., Lee, M. (2011). Laser spot detection-based computer interface system using autoassociative multilayer perceptron with input-to-output mapping-sensitive error back propagation learning algorithm. *Optical Engineering*, 50(8): art. no. 084302.

Kennedy, J., Eberhart, R.C. (1995). Particle 1 swarm optimization. In: *Proceedings of the IEEE International Joint Conference on Neural Networks*, 4:1942–1948.

Kistler, M. (1998). Reducing causality to transmission. *Erkenntnis*, 48:1–24.

Kramer, M.A. (1992). Autoassociative neural networks. *Computers & Chemical Engineering*, 16(4):313–328.

Lewis, D. (1973). *Counterfactuals*. New Jersey: Blackwell Publishers.

Lin, R.-C., Sir, M.Y., Pasupathy, K.S. (2013). Multi-objective simulation optimization using data envelopment analysis and genetic algorithm: Specific application to determining optimal resource levels in surgical services. *Omega*, 41(5):881–892.

Liu, Q., Guo, Z., Wang, J. (2012). A one-layer recurrent neural network for constrained pseudoconvex optimization and its application for dynamic portfolio optimization. *Neural Networks*, 26:99–109.

Luciani, D., Stefanini, F.M. (2012). Automated interviews on clinical case reports to elicit directed acyclic graphs. *Artificial Intelligence in Medicine*, 55(1):1–11.

Marwala, T. (2009). *Computational Intelligence for Missing Data Imputation, Estimation, and Management: Knowledge Optimization Techniques*, Information Science Reference Imprint. New York. IGI Global Publications.

Marwala, T. (2010). *Finite Element Model Updating Using Computational Intelligence Techniques*. London: Springer-Verlag.

Marwala, T., Lagazio, M. (2011). *Militarized Conflict Modeling Using Computational Intelligence Techniques*. London: Springer-Verlag.

Marwala, T. (2012). *Condition Monitoring Using Computational Intelligence Methods*. London: Springer-Verlag.

Marwala, T. (2013). *Flexibly-bounded Rationality and Marginalization of Irrationality Theories for Decision Making*, arXiv:1306.2025 [cs.AI].

Marwala, T. (2013a). Causality, correlation and artificial intelligence: Implication on policy formulation. *The Thinker*, 49:36–37.

Marwala, T. (2013b). *Economic Modelling Using Artificial Intelligence Methods*. London: Springer-Verlag.

Marwala, T. (2015). *Causality, Correlation, and Artificial Intelligence for Rational Decision Making*. Singapore: World Scientific.

Masuda, K., Fukui, B., Kurihara, K. (2012). A weighting approach for autoassociative memories to maximize the number of correctly stored patterns. In: *Proceedings of the SICE Annual Conference*, art. no. 6318692, 1520–1524.

Mazlack, L.J. (2011). Approximate computational intelligence models and causality in bioinformatics. In: *Proceedings of the 6th IASTED International Conference on Computational Intelligence and Bioinformatics*, CIB 2011, 1–8.

McBreen, B. (2007). Realism and empiricism in Hume's account of causality. *Philosophy*, 82(321):421–436.

Miller, G., Johnson-Laird, P.N. (1976). *Language and Perception*. Cambridge: Cambridge University Press.

Miranda, V., Castro, A.R.G., Lima, S. (2012). Diagnosing faults in power transformers with autoassociative neural networks and mean shift. *IEEE Transactions on Power Delivery*, 27(3): 1350–1357.

Neyman, J. (1923). Sur Les Applications de La Theorie Des Probabilites Aux Experiences Agricoles: Essai Des Principes, Master Thesis (D.M. Dabrowska, and T.P. Speed, Translators.), Excerpts reprinted in English, Statistical Science, Vol. 5, 463–472.

Ortigueira, M.D., Rivero, M., Trujillo, J.J. (2012). The incremental ratio based causal fractional calculus. *International Journal of Bifurcation and Chaos*, 22(4):1–9.

Paoletti, C. (2011). Causes as proximate events: Thomas Brown and the Positivist interpretation of Hume on causality. *Studies in History and Philosophy of Science Part A*, 42(1):37–44.

Pearl, J. (2000). *Causality: Models, Reasoning, and Inference*. Cambridge: Cambridge University Press.

Pearl, J., Dechter, R. (1996). Identifying independencies in causal graphs with feedback. In: *Proceedings of the 12th Annual Conference on Uncertainty in Artificial Intelligence*, San Francisco: Morgan Kaufmann, 420–426.

Pearl, J., Verma, T.S. (1995). A theory of inferred causation. *Studies in Logic and the Foundations of Mathematics*, 134:789–811.

Pećnjak, D. (2011). Freedom of the will, causality and Hume Prolegomena. 10(2): 311–316.

Plotnitsky, A. (2009). Causality and probability in quantum mechanics. *AIP Conference Proceedings*, 1101:150–160.

Poirier, J.D., Vel, S.S., Caccese, V. (2013). Multi-objective optimization of laser-welded steel sandwich panels for static loads using a genetic algorithm. *Engineering Structures*, 49:508–524.

Pommereau, F. (2004). Causal time calculus. *Lecture Notes in Computer Science (Including Subseries Lecture Notes in Artificial Intelligence and Lecture Notes in Bioinformatics)*, 2791:260–272.

PourAsiabi, H., PourAsiabi, H., AmirZadeh, Z., BabaZadeh, M. (2012). Development a multi-layer perceptron artificial neural network model to estimate the Vickers hardness of Mn–Ni–Cu–Mo austempered ductile iron. *Materials and Design*, 35:782–789.

Prohorov, Y.V. Rozanov, Yu.A. (1969). *Probability Theory, Basic Concepts. Limit Theorems, Random Processes*. Berlin, Heidelberg: Springer.

Proscevicius, T., Raudonis, V., Kairys, A., Lipnickas, A., Simutis, R. (2010). Autoassociative gaze tracking system based on artificial intelligence. *Elektronika ir Elektrotechnika*, 5:67–72.

Rababaah, A.R., Tebekaemi, E. (2012). Electric load monitoring of residential buildings using goodness of fit and multi-layer perceptron neural networks. *CSAE 2012 — Proceedings, 2012 IEEE International Conference on Computer Science and Automation Engineering*, 2:733–737.

Raginsky, M. (2011). Directed information and Pearl's causal calculus. *2011 49th Annual Allerton Conference on Communication, Control, and Computing*, Allerton 2011, art. no. 6120270, 958–965.

Rebane, G., Pearl, J. (1987). The recovery of causal poly-trees from statistical data. In: *Proceedings, 3rd Workshop on Uncertainty in AI*, Seattle, WA, 222–228.

Rios, A., Kabuka, M. (1995). Image compression with a dynamic autoassociative neural network. *Mathematical and Computer Modelling*, 21(1–2), 159–171.

Rodrigo, M., Liberos, A., Guillem, M.S., Millet, J., Climent, A.M. (2011). Causality relation map: A novel methodology for the identification of hierarchical fibrillatory processes. *Computers in Cardiology*, 38:173–176.

Rodríguez Sánchez, R.A. (2004). Knowledge and causality in the thinking of David Hume. *Pensamiento*, 60(226):145–161.

Rohatyn, D.A. (1975). Kant, hume and causality journal for general philosophy of science. *Zeitschrift für Allgemeine Wissenschaftstheorie*, 6(1):34–36.

Rubin, D.B. (1973). Matching to remove bias in observational studies. *Biometrics*, 29(1):159–183.

Rubin, D.B. (1974). Estimating causal effects of treatments in randomized and nonrandomized studies. *Journal of Educational Psychology*, 66(5):688–701.

Rubin, D.B. (1977). Assignment to treatment group on the basis of a covariate. *Journal of Educational Statistics*, 2:1–26.

Rubin, D.B. (1978). Bayesian inference for causal effects: The role of randomization. *The Annals of Statistics*, 6:34–58.

Rubin, D.B. (2005). Causal inference using potential outcomes. *Journal of the American Statistical Association*, 100(469):2005.

Salmon, W. (1984). *Scientific Explanation and the Causal Structure of the World*. Princeton: University Press.

Samgin, A.L. (2007). On an application of the causality principle to the theory of ion transport processes. *Journal of Physics and Chemistry of Solids*, 68(8):1561–1565.

Sanz, J., Perera, R., Huerta C. (2012). Gear dynamics monitoring using discrete wavelet transformation and multi-layer perceptron neural networks. *Applied Soft Computing Journal*, 12(9):2867–2878.

Schmidtke, J., Krawczak, M. (2010). Psychomotor developmental delay and epilepsy in an offspring of father-daughter incest: Quantification of the causality probability. *International Journal of Legal Medicine*, 124(5):449–450.

Scriven, I., Lu, J., Lewis, A. (2013). Electronic enclosure design using distributed particle swarm optimization. *Engineering Optimization*, 45(2):167–183.

Sermpinis, G., Theofilatos, K., Karathanasopoulos, A., Georgopoulos, E.F., Dunis, C. (2013). Forecasting foreign exchange rates with adaptive neural networks using radial-basis functions and particle swarm optimization. *European Journal of Operational Research*, 225(3):528–540.

Seth, A.K., Chorley, P., Barnett, L.C. (2013). Granger causality analysis of fMRI BOLD signals is invariant to hemodynamic convolution but not downsampling. *NeuroImage*, 65:540–555.

Shpitser, I. (2013). Counterfactual graphical models for longitudinal mediation analysis with unobserved confounding. *Cognitive Science*, 37:1011–1035.

Sia, S. (2007). Creative synthesis: A process interpretation of causality. *Philosophia*, 36(2):213–221.

Silvanto, J., Pascual-Leone, A. (2012). Why the assessment of causality in brain-behavior relations requires brain stimulation. *Journal of Cognitive Neuroscience*, 24(4):775–777.

Simon, H. (1991). Bounded rationality and organizational learning. *Organization Science*, 2(1):125–134.

Simon, H., Rescher, N. (1966). Cause and counterfactual. *Philosophy of Science*, 33:323–40.

Steinsky, B. (2003). Enumeration of labelled chain graphs and labelled essential directed acyclic graphs, *Discrete Mathematics*, 270(1–3):267–278.

Suppes, P. (1970). *A Probabilistic Theory of Causality*. Amsterdam: North-Holland Publishing Company.

Ten Kate, L.P. (2010). Psychomotor developmental delay and epilepsy in an offspring of father-daughter incest: Quantification of the causality probability. *International Journal of Legal Medicine*, 124(6):667–668.

Valle, M.E., Grande, Vicente D.M. (2011). Some experimental results on sparsely connected autoassociative morphological memories for the reconstruction of color images corrupted by either impulsive or Gaussian noise. In: *Proceedings of the International Joint Conference on Neural Networks*, art. no. 6033232, 275–282.

Verma, T.S., Pearl, J. (1987). Causal Networks: Semantics and Expressiveness. In: *Proceedings of the Fourth Conference on Uncertainty*.

Verma, T., Pearl, J. (1990). Equivalence and synthesis of causal models. In: *Proceedings of the Sixth Conference on Uncertainty in Artificial Intelligence*. Cambridge, MA, 220–227.

Wang, S., Liu, M. (2013). A genetic algorithm for two-stage no-wait hybrid flow shop scheduling problem. *Computers and Operations Research*, 40(4):1064–1075.

Watkins, E. (2004). Kant's model of causality: Causal powers, laws, and Kant's reply to Hume. *Journal of the History of Philosophy*, 42(4):449–488.

Wright, S. (1921). Correlation and causation. *Journal of Agricultural Research*, 7(3): 557–585.

Xie, X., Geng, Z., Zhao, Q. (2006). Decomposition of structural learning about directed acyclic graphs. *Artificial Intelligence*, 170(4–5):422–439.

Zhang, Y., Gallipoli, D., Augarde, C. (2013a). Parameter identification for elasto-plastic modelling of unsaturated soils from pressuremeter tests by parallel modified particle swarm optimization. *Computers and Geotechnics*, 48:293–303.

Zhang, Y., Gong, D.-W., Zhang, J.-H. (2013b). Robot path planning in uncertain environment using multi-objective particle swarm optimization. *Neurocomputing*, 103:172–185.

Zhao, Y., Billings, S.A., Wei, H., He, F., Sarrigiannis, P.G. (2013). A new NARX-based Granger linear and nonlinear casual influence detection method with applications to EEG data. *Journal of Neuroscience Methods*, 212(1):79–86.

# Chapter 13

# Gaussian Mixture Models

**Abstract.** This chapter describes the Gaussian mixture models (GMMs) to model complex data. GMM is a technique which uses a mixture of Gaussian distributions to model the data using the mean vector and covariance matrix. To train the GMM, the expected maximization technique is employed. The GMMs are used for condition monitoring problems.

## 13.1 Introduction

Gaussian mixture models (GMMs) are methods for modelling data that are based on a mixture of Gaussian distributions (Nelwamondo and Marwala, 2006; Nelwamondo, 2008; Miya *et al.*, 2008). In this regard, they are in general formulated as a function of the data that is being modelled, the mean vector and the covariance matrix. Training GMMs entail estimating the mean vector and the covariance matrix in the presence of unobserved classes of the data. To train the GMMs, the expectation maximization (EM) algorithm is used.

Marwala *et al.* (2007) and Nelwamondo *et al.* (2006) used the GMMs and extracted features to classify bearing faults. The results showed that GMM performed well and was computationally efficient. Chen *et al.* (2004) successfully used the GMMs and Karhunen–Loeve transform for speaker identification. Choi *et al.* (2004) successfully used a GMM through principal component analysis (PCA) and discriminant analysis for process monitoring. Liu *et al.* (2018a) successfully used the GMM for monitoring multi-phase batch processes whereas Ji *et al.* (2017) used GMM and rough sets successfully for image segmentation. Kim *et al.* (2017) successfully used the GMM for 3 degree of freedom orientations whereas Ma *et al.* (2018) successfully used GMMs for the root cause diagnosis of faults in industrial multimode processes. Susan and Sharma (2017) successfully used the Gaussian mixture entropy model for texture defect detection whereas Kayabol and Kutluk

(2016) successfully used GMMs for Bayesian classification of hyperspectral images.

The second leg of the GMM is the estimation of the latent variables, mean and covariance, and this is done using the EM algorithm (Dempster *et al.*, 1977; Neal and Hinton, 1998; Wang *et al.*, 2007; Marwala, 2009). The EM algorithm operates by alternating between two steps, and these are the expectation and maximization steps until convergence. Bordes *et al.* (2007) successfully applied the EM algorithm to image reconstruction and observed 10% accuracy. Cai *et al.* (1997) successfully applied the EM algorithm to missing data estimation whereas Han *et al.* (2008) combined the EM algorithm with Laplace technique and applied successfully this combined framework to modelling economic data. Ingrassia and Rocci (2007) successfully generalized the EM algorithm to semi-parametric mixture models and observed that the proposed method was simple to implement and was computationally efficient. Kauermann *et al.* (2007) successfully used the EM algorithm to recognize polymorphism in pharmacokinetic/pharmacodynamic phenotypes. The computational load of the EM algorithm was improved and used for brain tissue segmentation. Other successful implementations of the EM algorithm include in binary text classification (Park *et al.*, 2007). Reche-Lopez *et al.* (2018) applied the EM algorithm for binaural lateral localization of multiple sources in real environments whereas Ranjan *et al.* (2016) successfully used the EM algorithm for robust Gaussian process modelling. Dou *et al.* (2016) successfully applied the EM algorithm for estimation whereas Maaziz and Kharfouchi (2018) used the EM algorithm for parameter estimation of Markov switching bilinear model.

Other improvements and applications of the EM algorithm include accelerating computational speed by Patel *et al.* (2007), in semantic segmentation (Li *et al.*, 2018), for spatio-temporal disease mapping (Lee *et al.*, 2017), for robust identification of nonlinear errors-in-variables systems (Guo *et al.*, 2017), to estimate the Bernstein copula (Dou *et al.*, 2016) and to estimate multiple sound sources with data and model uncertainties.

## 13.2  Gaussian Mixture Models

When the random variable $x$ is Gaussian, it can be expressed using the following probability distribution function (Bishop, 2006):

$$p(x) = \frac{1}{\sigma\sqrt{2\pi}} e^{-(x-\mu)^2/2\sigma^2}. \tag{13.1}$$

Here, $p(x)$ represents the probability distribution function of $x$, $\sigma$ is the standard deviation and $\mu$ is the mean. This expression can be simplified as follows (Day, 1969; Bishop, 2006):

$$p(x) = N(x, \mu, \sigma). \tag{13.2}$$

Here, $N$ represents normal or Gaussian distribution. For a given set of random numbers of $x$, one might desire to estimate the probability distribution. This is done by estimating the mean and the standard deviation of the random variable. Suppose $X$ is represented as $x_1, x_2, \ldots, x_n$, then this can be mathematically expressed as follows (Day, 1969; Bishop, 2006):

$$
\begin{aligned}
p(x_{1\ldots n}) &= N(x_1, \mu, \sigma^2) \times N(x_2, \mu, \sigma^2) \times \cdots \times N(x_n, \mu, \sigma^2) \\
&= \prod_{i=1}^{n} N(x_i, \mu, \sigma^2) \\
&= \prod_{i=1}^{n} \frac{1}{\sigma\sqrt{2\pi}} e^{-(x_i - \mu)^2 / 2\sigma^2}.
\end{aligned}
\tag{13.3}
$$

The aim here is to identify the parameters $\mu$ and $\sigma$ such that given $X$, the probability distribution function is maximized. This means we ought to identify the probability distribution function that best represents the observations $X$. This is done by calculating the log-likelihood of Equation (13.3) and differentiating it as a function of $\mu$. The log-likelihood is thus written as follows (Day, 1969; Bishop, 2006):

$$\ln p(x_{1\ldots n}) = \sum_{i=1}^{n} \ln\left(\frac{1}{\sigma\sqrt{2\pi}}\right) - \frac{1}{2\sigma^2}(x_i - \mu)^2. \tag{13.4}$$

The differential of the log-likelihood with respect to $\mu$ is written as follows (Day, 1969; Bishop, 2006):

$$\frac{d}{d\mu}(\ln p(x_{1\ldots n})) = \sum_{i=1}^{n} \frac{1}{\sigma^2}(x_i - \mu). \tag{13.5}$$

Equating Equation (13.5) to zero we obtain the following (Day, 1969; Bishop, 2006):

$$\sum_{i=1}^{n} \frac{1}{\sigma^2}(x_i - \mu) = 0. \tag{13.6}$$

This gives the following expression (Day, 1969; Bishop, 2006):

$$\mu_{ML} = \frac{1}{N} \sum_{i=1}^{N} x_i. \tag{13.7}$$

Similarly:

$$\frac{d}{d\sigma}(\ln p(x_{1...n})) = 0. \tag{13.8}$$

Equation (13.8) gives (Day, 1969; Bishop, 2006):

$$\sigma_{ML}^2 = \frac{1}{N}\sum_{i=1}^{N}(x_i - \mu_{ML})^2. \tag{13.9}$$

What is described above is only valid when $X$ is scalar. If, however, $X$ is a vector and is represented as $\boldsymbol{x}_1, \boldsymbol{x}_2, \ldots, \boldsymbol{x}_n$ then the probability of the observed data is represented as follows (Day, 1969; Bishop, 2006):

$$P(X = \mathbf{x}_j) = \frac{1}{(2\pi)^{m/2}\|\Sigma\|^{1/2}}\exp\left[-\frac{1}{2}(\mathbf{x}_j - \boldsymbol{\mu}_i)^T\sum_i^{-1}(\mathbf{x}_j - \boldsymbol{\mu}_i)\right]. \tag{13.10}$$

Here, the $\boldsymbol{\mu}$ and $\mathbf{x}$ are vectors and $\sum$ is the covariance matrix. The covariance matrix is a diagonal matrix whose eigenvalues characterize the relative elongation of the data. If the data $X$ is from one class, then we can maximize the log-likelihood function to obtain the following (Day, 1969; Bishop, 2006):

$$\mu_{ML} = \frac{1}{n}\sum_{j=1}^{n}x_n, \tag{13.11}$$

$$\sum_{ML} = \frac{1}{n}\sum_{j=1}^{n}(\mathbf{x}_j - \boldsymbol{\mu}_{ML})(\mathbf{x}_j - \boldsymbol{\mu}_{ML})^T. \tag{13.12}$$

What we have described thus far is valid for data from a single variable. In order to expand this to more than one class, the GMM is used (Bryc, 1995). The GMM is characterized by four parameters and these are expressed as follows (Day, 1969; Bishop, 2006):

$$\lambda = \left\{\mathbf{x}, \boldsymbol{\mu}_k, \sum_k, c_k\right\}. \tag{13.13}$$

Here, $\mathbf{x}, \boldsymbol{\mu}_k, \sum_k$ and $c_k$ are vectors of the observed data, mean and covariance, and the corresponding class, respectively. We write a mixture of Gaussians using a superposition of $K$ Gaussian densities as follows (Day, 1969; Bishop, 2006):

$$p(\mathbf{x}|\lambda) = \sum_{k=1}^{K}\pi_k N\left(\mathbf{x}|\boldsymbol{\mu}_k, \sum_k\right). \tag{13.14}$$

Here, $\pi_k$, is the mixing coefficient and $N$ is a Gaussian distribution. The sum of the parameters $\pi_k$ must be one, and each parameter must be greater or equal to zero, and this is mathematically represented as follows (Day, 1969; Bishop, 2006):

$$\forall k : \pi_k \geq 0 \quad \sum_{k=1}^{K} \pi_k = 1. \tag{13.15}$$

Estimating the values of the model, i.e. means and covariances, of each class given the observed data cannot be determined analytically but is accomplished numerically through the use of the maximum-likelihood method. We estimate the maximum-likelihood of a GMM from a distribution function and as follows (Day, 1969; Bishop, 2006):

$$\ln p(\mathbf{x}|\lambda) = \ln \sum_{n=1}^{N} \sum_{k=1}^{K} \pi_k N\left(\mathbf{x}_n | \boldsymbol{\mu}_k, \sum_k\right). \tag{13.16}$$

Here, $N$ is the number of data training instances, and the number of classes is $K$, and the means and covariances of the model are calculated using the EM algorithm. The EM algorithm finds the parameters that increase the likelihood of the cluster from the given data. The probability of a class given the observation is given as follows (Day, 1969; Bishop, 2006):

$$p(Y = k|\mathbf{x}_j) \propto \frac{1}{(2\pi)^{\frac{m}{2}} \|\Sigma\|^{\frac{1}{2}}} \left[-\frac{1}{2}(\mathbf{x}_j - \boldsymbol{\mu}_k)^T (\mathbf{x}_j - \boldsymbol{\mu}_k)\right] p(Y = k). \tag{13.17}$$

We write this for multiple classes as follows (Day, 1969; Bishop, 2006):

$$\prod_{j=1}^{m} p(\mathbf{x}_j) = \prod_{j=1}^{n} \sum_{k=1}^{K} p(\mathbf{x}_j, Y = k)$$

$$= \prod_{j=1}^{n} \sum_{k=1}^{K} \frac{1}{(2\pi)^{\frac{m}{2}} \|\Sigma\|^{\frac{1}{2}}} \left[-\frac{1}{2}(\mathbf{x}_j - \boldsymbol{\mu}_k)^T (\mathbf{x}_j - \boldsymbol{\mu}_k)\right] p(Y = k).$$

$$\tag{13.18}$$

## 13.3 EM Algorithm

The EM algorithm is an optimization technique where the design variables are classified into two parts i.e. latent and parameter variables. In the EM algorithm, the maximum-likelihood estimation of the parameter vector is iteratively identified by repeating the expectation and the maximization steps (Little and Rubin, 1987; Marwala, 2009). The objective of the problem to be optimized can be written as follows (Dempster *et al.*, 1977):

$$\arg\max_{\lambda} \ln \prod_{j} \sum_{k=1}^{K} p(Y_j = k, \mathbf{x}_j \,|\, \lambda) = \sum_{j} \ln \sum_{k=1}^{K} p(Y_j = k, \mathbf{x}_j \,|\, \lambda). \quad (13.19)$$

The design variables are written as follows:

$$\lambda = \left\{ \mu_K^{(t)}, \mu_K^{(t)}, \ldots, \mu_K^{(t)}, \sum_{1}^{(t)}, \sum_{2}^{(t)}, \ldots, \sum_{K}^{(t)}, p_1^{(t)}, p_2^{(t)}, \ldots, p_K^{(t)} \right\}. \quad (13.20)$$

*The expectation E-step:* In the presence of a set of parameter estimates, for example. a mean vector and covariance matrix for a multivariate normal distribution, the E-step estimates the conditional expectation of the complete-data log-likelihood given the observed data and the parameter estimates. This is represented mathematically as follows (Little and Rubin, 2000; Marwala, 2009):

$$\arg\max_{\lambda} \prod_{j} p(x_j) = \arg\max \prod_{j} \sum_{k=1}^{K} p(Y_j = k, x_j). \quad (13.21)$$

In the E-step therefore, the unobserved class may be estimated conditioned on the observed values using the last values as follows (Little and Rubin, 1987; Marwala, 2009):

$$P(Y_j = k | \mathbf{x}_j, \lambda_t) = \frac{P(Y_j = k, \mathbf{x}_j | \lambda_t)}{P(\mathbf{x}_j | \lambda_t)}$$

$$= \frac{P(\mathbf{x}_j | Y_j = k, \lambda_t) P(Y_j = k | \lambda_t)}{\sum_{k=1}^{n} P(\{\mathbf{x}_j | Y_j = k, \lambda_t) P(Y_j = k | \lambda_t)}$$

$$\propto p_k^{(t)} p\left(\mathbf{x}_j | \mu_k^{(t)}, \sum_{k}^{(t)}\right). \quad (13.22)$$

*The maximization M-step:* The M-step identifies the parameter estimates that maximize the complete-data log-likelihood from the E-step given a complete-data log-likelihood. This is represented as follows (Little and Rubin, 1987; Marwala, 2009):

$$\lambda = \arg\max_{\lambda} \sum_{j} \sum_{k} p(Y_j, \lambda) \ln p(Y_j = k, x_j | \lambda). \quad (13.23)$$

In the M-step, the expected value of the log-likelihood of the joint event needs to be maximized as follows (Dempster *et al.*, 1977):

$$\boldsymbol{\lambda}_{t+1} = \arg\max_{\lambda} \sum_{j=1}^{n} \sum_{k=1}^{K} P(Y_j = k | \mathbf{x}_j, \boldsymbol{\lambda}_t) \ln P(Y_j = k, \mathbf{x}_j | \boldsymbol{\lambda}_t). \qquad (13.24)$$

These steps are iterated until convergence. We thus use the following expressions (Dempster *et al.*, 1977):

$$\mu_k^{(t+1)} = \frac{\sum_j P(Y_j = k | \mathbf{x}_j, \boldsymbol{\lambda}_t) \mathbf{x}_j}{\sum_j P(Y_j = k | \mathbf{x}_j, \boldsymbol{\lambda}_t)}. \qquad (13.25)$$

$$\sum_k^{(t+1)} = \frac{\sum_j P(Y_j = k | \mathbf{x}_j, \boldsymbol{\lambda}_t) \left( \mathbf{x}_j - \mu_k^{(t+1)} \right) \left( \mathbf{x}_j - \mu_k^{(t+1)} \right)^T}{\sum_j P(Y_j = k | \mathbf{x}_j, \boldsymbol{\lambda}_t)}. \qquad (13.26)$$

$$p_k^{(t+1)} = \frac{\sum_j P(Y_j = k | \mathbf{x}_j, \boldsymbol{\lambda}_t)}{m}. \qquad (13.27)$$

## 13.4 Condition Monitoring: Transformer Bushings

Miya *et al.* (2008) used data collected from the dissolved gas analysis (DGA) tests according to IEEEc57.104, IEC60599 and production rates methods. Combustible and non-combustible gases, which were $CH_4$, $C_2H_6$, $C_2H_4$, $C_2H_2$, $H_2$, CO, $CO_2$, $N_2$, $O_2$ and TDCG, were acquired for each experiment. The state of these gases describes the condition of the bushing. The status of the bushing condition for a given pattern is described with a zero for no fault and one for a fault.

The data was normalized to facilitate the application of the methods described. To side-step under-fitting and over-fitting, data was partitioned into three equal sets; training, validating and testing data. Each set had 11,704 instances. Out of the training instances, 1,000 balanced patterns (500 faulty and 500 non-faulty) were used when developing base classifiers in order to prevent the network from being biased and also from memorizing the training data.

The GMM which was optimized using the EM algorithm was constructed. The GMM maximizes the likelihood of detecting the probable output cluster for a given testing data. Two stages were embarked upon and these were the detection and diagnosis stages. Detection identifies margins set by faulty gases whereas diagnosis evaluates the concentration of the instance of gases and identifies the most probable fault to be associated with the given instance. The GMM detected faults with the accuracy of 88% and diagnosed with the rate of 86%.

## 13.5  Condition Monitoring: Cylindrical Shells

Marwala *et al.* (2005) used the GMM to experimentally validate and compare the procedure to the multi-layer perceptron (MLP). Marwala performed the experiment on a population of cylinders by Marwala (2001), divided each cylinder into three equal sub-structures, and introduced holes of 10–15 mm in diameter at the centres of the sub-structures to simulate faults. Types of faults were classified as [000], indicating that there are no faults in any of the three sub-structures, [100], [010] and [001] indicating one hole in sub-structures 1, 2 or 3, respectively. The third type of fault was a two-fault scenario, where holes were located in two of the three sub-structures and these were [110], [101], and [011], and [111] indicates faults are located in all three sub-structures. The PCA was used to reduce the dimension of the input data. The data was used for the MLP training and the MLP architecture contained 10 input units, 8 hidden units and 3 output units. The results obtained are shown in Table 13.1. These results show that the MLP classifies fault cases to the accuracy of 88%. GMM architecture on the other hand used a diagonal covariance matrix with 3 centres. Table 13.2 shows that the GMM gives an accuracy of 98%. The GMM outperformed the MLP.

**Table 13.1**  The confusion matrix obtained when the MLP network is used for fault classification: Vertical: Actual, Horizontal: Predicted.

|        | [000] | [100] | [010] | [001] | [110] | [101] | [011] | [111] |
|--------|-------|-------|-------|-------|-------|-------|-------|-------|
| [000]  | 39    | 0     | 0     | 0     | 0     | 0     | 0     | 0     |
| [100]  | 0     | 3     | 0     | 0     | 0     | 0     | 0     | 0     |
| [010]  | 0     | 0     | 3     | 0     | 0     | 0     | 0     | 0     |
| [001]  | 0     | 0     | 0     | 3     | 0     | 0     | 0     | 6     |
| [110]  | 0     | 0     | 0     | 0     | 3     | 1     | 0     | 0     |
| [000]  | 0     | 0     | 0     | 0     | 0     | 2     | 0     | 0     |
| [100]  | 0     | 0     | 0     | 0     | 0     | 0     | 3     | 4     |
| [010]  | 0     | 0     | 0     | 0     | 0     | 0     | 0     | 29    |

**Table 13.2**   The confusion matrix obtained when the GMM network is used for fault classification: Vertical: Actual, Horizontal: Predicted.

|        | [000] | [100] | [010] | [001] | [110] | [101] | [011] | [111] |
|--------|-------|-------|-------|-------|-------|-------|-------|-------|
| [000]  | 39    | 0     | 0     | 0     | 0     | 0     | 0     | 0     |
| [100]  | 0     | 3     | 0     | 0     | 0     | 0     | 0     | 0     |
| [010]  | 0     | 0     | 3     | 0     | 0     | 0     | 0     | 0     |
| [001]  | 0     | 0     | 0     | 3     | 0     | 0     | 0     | 1     |
| [110]  | 0     | 0     | 0     | 0     | 3     | 0     | 0     | 1     |
| [000]  | 0     | 0     | 0     | 0     | 0     | 3     | 0     | 0     |
| [100]  | 0     | 0     | 0     | 0     | 0     | 0     | 3     | 2     |
| [010]  | 0     | 0     | 0     | 0     | 0     | 0     | 0     | 35    |

## 13.6   Condition Monitoring: Bearings

Nelwamondo *et al.* (2006) used the variations in vibration signals to detect faults in rotating machineries. A bearing functioning under normal and flawless conditions yields less vibration than when it has defects. Causes of these variants in vibration of rotating systems include mass unbalance around the centre of rotation. This mass unbalance produces sinusoidal force (Nelwamondo *et al.*, 2006; Peng *et al.*, 2005). A bearing defect produces an impulsive force (Ocak and Loparo, 2004; Wang and Kootsookos, 1998). Vibrations from the inner raceway, outer raceway and rolling element faults produce spectra with different frequency components whose magnitudes can be used to determine the condition of the bearing (Nelwamondo *et al.*, 2006).

Normally, the rolling element bearing comprises of two concentric rings named the inner and outer raceway and are shown in Figure 13.1 (Nelwamondo *et al.*, 2006). Additionally, the bearing comprises a set of rolling elements that run in the tracts of these raceways. There is a number of standard shapes of the rolling elements such as the ball, cylindrical roller, tapered roller, needle rollers, symmetrical and unsymmetrical barrel roller (Nikolaou and Antoniadis, 2002).

There were three faults that Nelwamondo *et al.* (2006) studied and these were the inner raceway fault, outer raceway fault and the rolling element fault. A bearing fault increases the rotational friction of the rotor. Each fault generates vibration spectra with unique frequency components, which are a linear function of the running speed (Ericsson *et al.*, 2004). The two-raceway frequencies are also linear functions of the number of balls. The motor bearing condition monitoring systems were implemented by analysing the

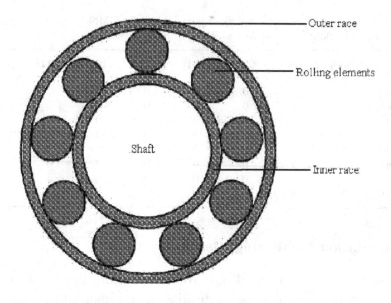

**Figure 13.1**    A typical ball bearing.

vibration signal of all the bearing faults. The vibration signal was produced by the impact pulse generated when a ball roller hit a defect in the raceways or each and every time the defect in the ball hit the raceways (Li *et al.*, 2000). Various features were extracted from vibration signals of bearing elements. These vibration data were analysed using fractal analysis, Mel-frequency cepstral coefficients (MFCC) and kurtosis.

Fractal dimensions have been used quite successfully in many applications such as image processing (Zhang and Zhao, 2006) and financial forecasting (Marwala and Lunga, 2006). Motor bearing vibrations are usually periodic movements with some degree of turbulence. To detect different bearing faults, we extract these nonlinear turbulence features. The nonlinear turbulence features of the bearing signal can be quantified using fractal model (Maragos and Sun, 1993; Maragos and Potamianos, 1999).

On fractal modelling, the issue of the fractal dimension is important. One such fractal dimension of compact planar set is called the Hausdorff dimension and its values lie between one and two (Maragos and Potamianos, 1999). Its disadvantage is that it is a mathematical concept but difficult to compute. Other methods that estimate this dimension include the Minkowski Bouligand dimension and Box-counting dimension (Maragos and Potamianos, 1999). Nelwamondo *et al.* (2006) used the Box-Counting dimension to approximate the fractal dimension. The Box-counting dimension is attained by dividing the plane with a square grid and the number of squares that intersect the plane (Falconer, 1952).

The fractal dimension discussed is a global measure and does not represent all the fractal characteristics of the vibration signal (Wang *et al.*, 2000; Ma and Zhai, 2018; Zhokh, 2018). To overcome this problem, the Multi-scale fractal dimension (MFD) was proposed. The MFD of the vibration signal is attained by calculating the dimensions over a small-time window by allocating the bearing vibration signal into $K$ frames, and then setting $K$ maximum computation resolutions (Wang *et al.*, 2000).

The MFCC is a kind of wavelet computation in which frequency scales are located on a linear scale for frequencies less than 1 kHz and on a log scale for frequencies above 1 kHz (Ocak and Loparo, 2004). The complex cepstral coefficients obtained from this scale are called the MFCC. The MFCC contains both time and frequency information of the signal and they are used for feature extraction. MFCC were used in speech recognition and can handle dynamic features because they extract both linear and nonlinear properties of the signal. MFCC is useful for feature extraction in vibration signals as vibrations contain both linear and nonlinear features. The MFCC is implemented by following these steps (Nelwamondo *et al.*, 2006):

- Compute the Fourier Transform (FFT) of the signal.
- Perform Mel-frequency wrapping.
- Convert the logarithmic Mel spectrum back to the time domain to obtain the MFCC.

This MFCC is then used to represent the character of the signal.

There is a necessity to handle occasional spiking of vibration data and in this regard, we use the kurtosis. Kurtosis analysis of vibration data has been successfully used in condition monitoring by El-Wardany *et al.* (1996). The success of kurtosis in vibration signals is because vibration signals of a system under stress or having defects differ from those of a normal system. The sharpness or spiking of the vibration signal changes when there are defects in the system. Kurtosis is a measure of the sharpness of the peak and is the normalized fourth-order central moment of a signal (Purushothama *et al.*, 2005; Nelwamondo *et al.*, 2006; Liu *et al.*, 2018a; Mohanty *et al.*, 2018). The kurtosis identifies transients and spontaneous events within vibration signals (Altman and Mathew, 2001).

The first stage in the fault detection involves feature extraction (McClintic *et al.*, 2000). The signal is pre-processed by dividing the vibration signals into segments of equal lengths. After pre-processing, features are extracted using the Box-counting MFD, MFCC and kurtosis. Nelwamondo *et al.* (2006) divided the vibration data into segments, each five revolutions long and extracted the MFCC from each frame of the signal. The extracted MFCC formed a matrix of size $n \times 14$ where $n$ was the number of MFCC features extracted and 14 was the number of frames within a particular segment. Fractal and kurtosis features were extracted from each segment.

Relevant features were extracted, and the reference models used to classify faults were built and applied to classify the fault conditions. The features used with the GMM were reduced to a lower dimension using the PCA. The PCA is a non-parametric technique that extracts relevant information from any complex data. The PCA reduces the dimensionality of the data while preserving vital information, by removing variables with high correlation and using the least number of uncorrelated variables called principal components. The PCA simplifies the data and makes the training of GMM computationally efficient (Jolliffe, 1986; Bai *et al.*, 2017; Fuentes-García *et al.*, 2018). The process of reducing dimensionality using the PCA is done using these steps (Jolliffe, 1986):

- Estimate the covariance matrix of the input data.
- Estimate the eigenvalues and eigenvectors of the covariance matrix.
- Keep the largest eigenvalues and the matching eigenvectors that cover at least 80% of the variance of the data.
- Project the original data into the reserved eigenvectors to create reduced input data.

The design of the proposed structure consisted of two major steps after vibration signal measurement and these were pre-processing with feature extraction and classification. Nelwamondo *et al.* (2006) calculated the probability of the feature vector given the previously constructed fault model to diagnose the motor. The GMM with maximum probability then determined the bearing condition. The investigation was based on the data obtained from Case Western Reserve University (Anonymous, 2009).

The GMM architecture used the diagonal covariance matrix with three centres because this de-correlate the feature vectors. The first investigation studied the effectiveness of the time domain fractal dimension based feature extraction using vibration signal. Using optimum GMM architecture together with MFD, Nelwamondo *et al.* (2006) obtained the confusion matrix for different bearing faults and this is shown in Table 13.3.

Nelwamondo *et al.* (2006) additionally investigated the use of MFCC with the GMM. They obtained the results in Table 13.4.

**Table 13.3**   The confusion matrix for the GMM classifier used with Fractal features Horizontal: Predicted, Vertical: Actual.

|         | Normal | Inner | Outer | Ball |
|---------|--------|-------|-------|------|
| **Normal** | 100    | 0     | 0     | 0    |
| **Inner**  | 0      | 100   | 0     | 0    |
| **Outer**  | 0      | 0     | 100   | 0    |
| **Ball**   | 1.8    | 1     | 0     | 98.2 |

**Table 13.4**   The confusion matrix for the GMM with MFCC features.

|         | Normal | Inner | Outer | Ball |
|---------|--------|-------|-------|------|
| **Normal** | 86.6   | 0     | 0     | 13   |
| **Inner**  | 0      | 96.6  | 3.3   | 0    |
| **Outer**  | 0      | 0     | 100   | 0    |
| **Ball**   | 3.7    | 1.8   | 0     | 94   |

**Table 13.5**   Summary of classification results.

|                  | Accuracy (%) |
|------------------|--------------|
| Fractals         | 99           |
| MFCC             | 94           |
| MFCC + Kurtosis  | 99           |

When Nelwamondo *et al.* (2006) added the kurtosis values to the MFCC, an improvement of about 5% was obtained for the GMM. MFD features were capable of obtaining a 100% classification on their own, and as a result, there was no need to add the kurtosis features. Overall, the results are summarized in Table 13.5

## 13.7 Conclusions

This chapter described the GMMs. GMMs are models that model data in terms of means and covariance of the data. Once the means and covariances of the data are known and their respective classes, it is possible to determine the likelihood of a given observation to be associated with the class that best represents it. Sometimes, one does not necessarily know the class in which the data was sampled from and thereby making the optimization process to have design variables which are means, covariance and classes in which they belong. The EM technique was studied and it is used to estimate the means, covariance and the class of data. The EM works by alternating between the expectation and maximization steps. The GMMs are applied for fault identification of cylindrical shells, bearing and transformer bushings. The results obtained indicated that the GMM algorithm is able to identify faults satisfactorily.

## References

Anonymous (2009). Bearing Data Centre, Case Western Reserve University, Available at: https://csegroups.case.edu/bearingdatacenter/pages/welcome-case-western-reserve-university-bearing-data-center-website. Accessed on 17 October 2009.

Altman, J., Mathew, J. (2001). Multiple band-pass autoregressive demodulation for rolling element bearing fault diagnosis. *Mechanical Systems and Signal Processing*, 15(5): 963–997.

Bai, X., Gao, N., Zhang, Z., Zhang, D. (2017). 3D palmprint identification combining blocked ST and PCA. *Pattern Recognition Letters*, 100:89–95.

Bishop, C. (2006). *Pattern Recognition and Machine Learning*. New York: Springer.

Bordes, L., Chauveau, D., Vandekerkhove, P. (2007). Comparison of ML–EM algorithm and ART for reconstruction of gas hold-up profile in a bubble column. *Chemical Engineering Journal*, 130(2–3):135–145.

Bryc, W. (1995). *The Normal Distribution: Characterizations with Applications*. Springer-Verlag.

Cai, X., Zhang, N., Venayagamoorthy, G.K., Wunsch II, D.C. (2004). Time series prediction with recurrent neural networks using a hybrid PSO-EA algorithm. *IEEE International Conference on Neural Networks — Conference Proceedings*, 2:1647–1652.

Chen, C.T., Chen, C., Hou, C. (2004). Speaker identification using hybrid Karhunen–Loeve transform and Gaussian mixture model approach. *Pattern Recognition*, 37(5): 1073–1075.

Choi, S.W., Park, J.H., Lee, I. (2004). Process monitoring using a Gaussian mixture model via principal component analysis and discriminant analysis. *Computers & Chemical Engineering*, 28(8):1377–1387.

Day, N.E. (1969). Estimating the components of a mixture of normal distributions. *Biometrika*, 56:463–474.

Dempster, A.P., Laird, N.M., Rubin, D.B. (1977). Maximum likelihood for incomplete data via the EM algorithm. B39:1–38.

Dou, X., Kuriki, S., Lin, G.D., Richards, D. (2016). EM algorithms for estimating the Bernstein copula. *Computational Statistics & Data Analysis*, 93:228–245.

El-Wardany, T.I., Gao, D., Elbestawi, M.A. (1996). Tool condition monitoring in drilling using vibration signature analysis. *International Journal of Machine Tools & Manufacture*, 36:687–711.

Ericsson, S., Grip, N., Johansson, E., Persson, L.E., Sjöberg, R., Strömberg, J.O. (2004). Towards automatic detection of local bearing defects in rotating machines. *Mechanical Systems and Signal Processing*, 19:509–535.

Falconer, K. (1952). *Fractal Geometry, Mathematical Foundations and Application*. New York: John Wiley.

Fuentes-García, M., Maciá-Fernández, G., Camacho, J. (2018). Evaluation of diagnosis methods in PCA-based multivariate statistical process control. *Chemometrics and Intelligent Laboratory Systems*, 172:194–210.

Guo, F., Hariprasad, K., Huang, B., Ding, Y.S. (2017). Robust identification for nonlinear errors-in-variables systems using the EM algorithm. *Journal of Process Control*, 54:129–137.

Han, H., Ko, Y., Seo, J. (2008). Stacked Laplace-EM algorithm for duration models with time-varying and random effects. *Computational Statistics & Data Analysis*, 52(5):2514–2528.

Ingrassia, S., Rocci, R. (2007). A stochastic EM algorithm for a semiparametric mixture model. *Computational Statistics & Data Analysis*, 51(11):5429–5443.

Ji, Z., Huang, Y., Xia, Y., Zheng, Y. (2017). A robust modified Gaussian mixture model with rough set for image segmentation. *Neurocomputing*, 266:550–565.

Jolliffe, I.T. (1986). *Principal Component Analysis*. New York: Springer-Verlag.

Kauermann, G., Xu, R., Vaida, F. (2007). Nonlinear random effects mixture models: Maximum likelihood estimation via the EM algorithm. *Computational Statistics & Data Analysis*, 51(12): 6614 6623.

Kayabol, K., Kutluk, S. (2016). Bayesian classification of hyperspectral images using spatially-varying Gaussian mixture model. *Digital Signal Processing*, 59:106–114.

Kim, S., Haschke, R., Ritter, H. (2017). Gaussian mixture model for 3-DoF orientations. *Robotics and Autonomous Systems*, 87:28–37.

Lee, J.S.W., Nguyen, P., Brown, P.E., Stafford, J., Saint-Jacques, N. (2017). A local EM algorithm for spatio-temporal disease mapping with aggregated data. *Spatial Statistics*, 21, Part A: 75–95.

Li, B., Chow, M.Y., Tipsuwan, Y., Hung, J.C. (2000). Neural-network-based motor rolling bearing fault diagnosis. *IEEE Transactions on Industrial Electronics*, 47: 1060–1068.

Li, Y., Liu, Y., Liu, G., Zhai, D., Guo, M. (2018). Weakly supervised semantic segmentation based on EM algorithm with localization clues. *Neurocomputing*, 275: 2574–2587.

Little, R.J.A., Rubin, D.B. (1987). *Statistical Analysis with Missing Data*. New York: John Wiley.

Little, R.J.A., Rubin, D.B. (2000). *Statistical Analysis with Missing Data*, 2nd Edition. New York: John Wiley.

Liu, J., Liu, T., Chen, J. (2018a). Sequential local-based Gaussian mixture model for monitoring multiphase batch processes. *Chemical Engineering Science*, 181:101–113.

Liu, S., Hou, S., He, K., Yang, W. (2018b). L-Kurtosis and its application for fault detection of rolling element bearings. *Measurement*, 116:523–532.

Ma, L., Dong, J., Peng, K. (2018). Root cause diagnosis of quality-related faults in industrial multimode processes using robust Gaussian mixture model and transfer entropy. *Neurocomputing*, 285:60–73.

Ma, Y.-J., Zhai, M.-Y. (2018). Fractal and multi-fractal features of the broadband power line communication signals. *Computers & Electrical Engineering*, in press, corrected proof. Available online 7 February.

Maaziz, M., Kharfouchi, S. (2018). Parameter estimation of Markov switching bilinear model using the (EM) algorithm. *Journal of Statistical Planning and Inference*, 192:35–44.

Maragos, P., Sun, F.K. (1993). Measuring the fractal dimension of signals: Morphological covers and iterative optimization. *IEEE Transaction on Signal Processing*, 41:108–121.

Maragos, P., Potamianos, A. (1999). Fractal dimensions of speech sounds: Computation and application to automatic speech recognition. *Journal of the Acoustical Society of America*, 1925–1932.

Marwala, T. (2001). Fault Identification Using Neural Networks and Vibration Data. PhD Thesis, University of Cambridge, Cambridge, UK.

Marwala, T. (2009), *Computational Intelligence for Missing Data Imputation, Estimation, and Management: Knowledge Optimization Techniques*, Information Science Reference Imprint. New York: IGI Global Publications

Marwala, T., Chakraverty, S., Mahola, U. (2005). Neural networks and support vector machines for fault identification in cylinders. In: *Proceedings of International Symposium on Neural Networks and Soft Computing in Structural Engineering*, Krakow, Poland.

Marwala, T. Mahola, U., Chakraverty, S. (2007). Fault classification in cylinders using multi-layer perceptrons, support vector machines and Gaussian mixture models. *Computer Assisted Mechanics and Engineering Sciences*, 14(2):307–316.

Marwala, T., Mahola, U., Nelwamondo, F. (2006). Hidden Markov models and Gaussian mixture models for bearing fault detection using fractals. In: *Proceedings of the IEEE International Joint Conference on Neural Networks*, BC, Canada, 5876–5881.

McClintic, K., Lebold, M., Maynard, K., Byington, C., Campbell, R. (2000). Residual and difference feature analysis with transitional gearbox data, In: *Proceedings of the 54th Meeting of the Society for Machinery Failure Prevention Technology*, Virginia Beach, 635–645.

Miya, W.S., Mpanza, L.J., Nelwamondo, F.V., Marwala, T. (2008). Condition monitoring of oil-impregnated paper bushings using extension neural network, Gaussian mixture models and hidden Markov models. In: *Proceedings of the IEEE International Conference on Man, Systems and Cybernetics*, 1954–1959.

Mohanty, V., McKinnon, E.T., Helpern, J.A., Jensen, J.H. (2018). Comparison of cumulant expansion and q-space imaging estimates for diffusional kurtosis in brain. *Magnetic Resonance Imaging*, 48:80–88.

Neal, R., Hinton, G. (1998). A view of the EM algorithm that justifies incremental, sparse, and other variants. In: Jordan, M. (ed.), *Learning in Graphical Models*, Netherlands, Dordrecht: Kluwer Academic Press.

Nelwamondo, F.V. (2008). Computational Intelligence Techniques for Missing Data Imputation. PhD Thesis, University of the Witwatersrand.

Nelwamondo, F.V., Marwala, T. (2006). Fault detection using Gaussian mixture models, Mel-frequency Cepstral coefficient and kurtosis. In: *Proceedings of the IEEE International Conference on Systems. Man and Cybernetics*, Taiwan, 290–295.

Nelwamondo, F.V., Marwala, T., Mahola, U. (2006). Early Classifications of bearing faults using Hidden Markov models, Gaussian mixture models, Mel-frequency Cepstral coefficients and fractals. *International Journal of Innovative Computing, Information and Control*, 2(6):1281–1299.

Nikolaou, N.G., Antoniadis, L.A. (2002). Rolling element bearing fault diagnosis using wavelet packets. *NDT&E International*, 35:197–205.

Ocak, H., Loparo, K.A. (2004). Estimation of the running speed and bearing defect frequencies of an induction motor from vibration data. *Mechanical Systems and Signal Processing*, 18: 515–533.

Park, J., Qian, G.Q., Jun, Y. (2007). Using the revised EM algorithm to remove noisy data for improving the one-against-the-rest method in binary text classification. *Information Processing & Management*, 43(5):1281–1293.

Patel, A.K., Patwardhan, A.W., Thorat, B.N. (2007). Acceleration schemes with application to the EM algorithm. *Computational Statistics & Data Analysis*, 51(8):3689–3702.

Peng, Z.K., Tse, P.W., Chu, F.L. (2005). A comparison study of improved Hilbert-Huang transform and wavelet transform: Application to fault diagnosis for rolling bearing. *Mechanical Systems and Signal Processing*, 19:974–988.

Purushothama, V., Narayanana, S., Suryanarayana, Prasad, A.N. (2005). Multi-fault diagnosis of rolling bearing elements using wavelet analysis and Hidden Markov model based fault recognition. *NDT&E International*, 38:654–664.

Ranjan, R., Huang, B., Fatehi, A. (2016). Robust Gaussian process modeling using EM algorithm. *Journal of Process Control*, 42:125–136.

Reche-Lopez, P., Perez-Lorenzo, J.M., Rivas, F., Viciana-Abad, R. (2018). Binaural lateral localization of multiple sources in real environments using a kurtosis-driven split-EM algorithm. *Engineering Applications of Artificial Intelligence*, 69:137–146.

Susan, S., Sharma, M. (2017). Automatic texture defect detection using Gaussian mixture entropy modeling. *Neurocomputing*, 239:232–237.

Wang, F., Zheng, F., Wu, W. (2000). A C/V segmentation for Madarian speech based on multi-scale fractal dimension. In: *Proccedings of the International Conference on Spoken Language Processing*, 4:648651.

Wang, X., Schumitzky, A., D'Argenio, D.Z. (2007). Constrained monotone EM algorithms for finite mixture of multivariate Gaussians. *Computational Statistics & Data Analysis*, 51(11): 5339–5351.

Wang, Y.F., Kootsookos, P.J. (1998). Modeling of low shaft speed bearing faults for condition monitoring. *Mechanical Systems and Signal Processing*, 12:415–426.

Zhang, Z., Zhao, Y. (2006). Improving the performance of fractal image coding. *International Journal of Innovative Computing, Information and Control*, 2:387–398.

Zhokh, A., Trypolskyi, A., Strizhak, P. (2018). Relationship between the anomalous diffusion and the fractal dimension of the environment. *Chemical Physics*, 503: 71–76.

# Chapter 14

# Hidden Markov Models

**Abstract.** This chapter studies the theory and applications of the hidden Markov Model (HMM). The HMM is a model that is based on the theory of the Markov chain. The HMM is compared to the Gaussian mixture model (GMM), which is based on the Gaussian approximation of the data. The HMM is compared to the GMM on condition monitoring of bearings. Furthermore, the HMM is applied for speaker recognition.

## 14.1 Introduction

The hidden Markov model (HMM) is a statistical Markov model that assumes the Markov process with states that are hidden and, therefore, unobservable (Marwala, 2012). In a Markov model, the state is observable, and therefore we only estimate the transition probabilities. The HMM is thus a stochastic signal model and is referred to as probabilistic functions of Markov chains (Rabiner, 1989; Marwala, 2012). The HMM has been typically applied to speech recognition systems. In the HMM, the observation is a probabilistic function of the state and, therefore, the model is a stochastic process that is not observable (Rabiner, 1989; Marwala, 2012). However, this process is only observed via an additional stochastic process that generates the sequence.

Boutros and Liang (2011) used discrete HMM for detection and diagnosis of bearing and cutting tool faults whereas Wong and Lee (2010) successfully used the HMM for fault detection in the shell-and-tube heat exchanger. Lee *et al.* (2010) used the HMM for online degradation assessment and adaptive fault detection of multiple failure modes whereas Calefati *et al.* (2006) successfully used the HMM for machine faults detection and forecasting in gearboxes. Zhou and Wang (2005) successfully used the HMM and the principal component analysis (PCA) for online fault detection and diagnosis in industrial processes whereas Menon *et al.* (2003) successfully used the HMM for fault detection and diagnosis in turbine engines. The HMM for fault detection in dynamic systems was applied. Recent successful applications of the HMM include for laughter facial expression (Çakmak and Dutoit, 2018), handwriting recognition (Samanta *et al.*, 2018), for temporal data clustering (Yang and Jiang, 2018), protein fold recognition (Lyons *et al.*, 2016) and for molecule data analysis (Sgouralis and Pressé, 2017).

## 14.2 Hidden Markov Models

HMMs were introduced in the 1960s and were first applied to speech processing (Baker, 1973; Jelinek, 1976). The HMM were applied to various applications such as in machine tool monitoring (Owsley *et al.*, 1997), speech recognition (Wang *et al.*, 2000; Suleiman *et al.*, 2017), fault detection (Purushothama *et al.*, 2005; Zhang *et al.*, 1998; Darong *et al.*, 2018), text mining (Kang *et al.*, 2018), fraud detection (Robinson and Aria, 2018) and anomaly detection. HMM is a stochastic method based on the principles of Markov processes (Rabiner, 1989). A Markov chain is a random process of discrete-valued variables that consist of a number of states. These states are connected by transition probabilities, each with a related probability and each state has a related observation. The transition from one state to another depends only on the current state and not on the previous states (Hayes, 2013; Bremaud, 2013; Gagniuc, 2017).

One type of a Markov chain is by using the Markov Chain Monte Carlo (MCMC) simulation (Marwala, 2012). In the MCMC method, we consider a system whose evolution is represented by a stochastic process consisting of random variables $\{x_1, x_2, x_3, \ldots, x_i\}$. A random variable $x_i$ is at state $x$ at discrete time $i$. The assembly of all possible states that all random variables can be in is a *state space*. If the probability that the system is in state $x_{i+1}$ at time $i + 1$ completely depends on its location at state $x_i$ at time $i$, then the random variables $\{x_1, x_2, x_3, \ldots, x_i\}$ are characterized as a Markov chain. For the MCMC method, we transit between the states by adding a random noise to the current state (Bishop, 1995; Marwala, 2010, 2012). When we reach the current state, we either accept or reject using the Metropolis algorithm (Metropolis *et al.*, 1953).

The Metropolis algorithm has been used widely in statistical mechanics. Bazavov *et al.* (2009) successfully used the Metropolis algorithm for protein simulation. Other successful uses of the Metropolis algorithms include for nuclear power plants (Sacco *et al.*, 2008), to simulate protein chains (Tiana *et al.*, 2007), to predict free Co–Pt nano-clusters (Moskovkin and Hou, 2007), for swarm control (Chamie and Açıkmeşe, 2018), quantification of stream flows (Wang *et al.*, 2017) and for energy modelling (Nakade and Biswas, 2012). Therefore, on sampling a stochastic process using the MCMC random variables $\{x_1, x_2, x_3, \ldots, x_i\}$, we introduce random changes to $x$ and accept or reject this using Metropolis *et al.* (1953) criterion (Marwala, 2009, 2010). Rodina *et al.* (2010) applied the MCMC to estimate renal disease, whereas Drugan and Thierens (2010) developed evolutionary MCMC. Applications of the MCMC include for subset simulation (Papaioannou *et al.*, 2015), in the real estate market (Gargallo *et al.*, 2017), for modelling terrorist activities (White and Porter, 2014), for wind power modelling (Almutairi *et al.*, 2016) and for scene analysis (Liu *et al.*, 2015).

In the HMM, the sequence of states is not observable and, therefore, it is called HMM (Ertunc *et al.*, 2001). The illustration for an HMM with a discrete output probability distribution is given by the following equation (Baum and Petrie, 1966; Baum *et al.*, 1970; Blasiak and Rangwala, 2011):

$$\lambda = \{A, B, \pi\}. \tag{14.1}$$

Here, $\lambda$ is the model, $A = \{a_{ij}\}$, $B = \{b_{ij}(k)\}$ and $\pi = \pi_i$ is a transition probability distribution. These parameters of a given state, $S_i$, are defined as (Baum and Petrie, 1966; Nelwamondo *et al.*, 2006a):

$$a_{ij} = P(q_{t+1} = S_j \,|\, q_t = S_i) \quad ,1 \le i,\ j \le N, \tag{14.2}$$

$$b_{ij}(k) = P(o_k \,|\, q_t = S_i), \quad 1 \le j \le N,\ 1 \le k \le M, \tag{14.3}$$

$$\pi_i = P(q_1 = S_i), \quad 1 \le i \le N. \tag{14.4}$$

Here, $q_t$ is the state at time $t$ and $N$ symbolizes the number of states. Additionally, $o_k$ is the $k$th observation and $M$ is the number of discrete observations. The HMM is therefore a finite state machine which changes state at every time unit. There are three kinds of HMM and these are the left-to-right model, the two-parallel left-to-right model and the ergodic model. The three models are shown in Figures 14.1–14.3 (Ertunc *et al.*, 2001).

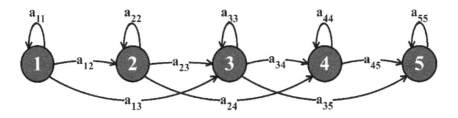

**Figure 14.1**   Left-to-right HMM.

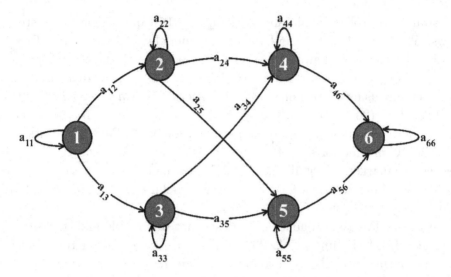

**Figure 14.2**   Parallel left-to-right HMM.

The left-to-right model has the characteristics that the subsequent state index is at all times greater or equal to the current state index. This model is known as the left-to-right since the transition states travel from the left to the right direction. The two-parallel left-to-right model is similar to the left-to-right model despite the fact that there are two parallel paths. The ergodic model conversely shows a property that the transition from any state to any other state is conducted in a finite number of steps (Ertunc *et al.*, 2001). Among these three kinds, the left-to-right is frequently used and investigated.

There are three HMM problems to be solved. The first is to evaluate the probability of the observation sequence, $O = o_1, o_2, \ldots, o_T$, of visible states produced by model $\lambda$. The probability is estimated as follows (Baum and Petrie, 1966; Nelwamondo *et al.*, 2006a):

$$P(O, \lambda) = \sum_{\text{all } S} \pi_{S_0} \prod_{t=0}^{T=1} a_{S_y S_{t+1}} b_{S_{t+1}}(O_{S_{t+1}}). \tag{14.5}$$

This is done using the forward–backward algorithm. The forward procedure is described below. Setting the following (Baum and Petrie, 1966; Nelwamondo *et al.*, 2006a):

$$\alpha_i(t) = P(O_1 = o_1, O_2 = o_2, \ldots, O_t = o_t, X_t = i | \lambda). \tag{14.6}$$

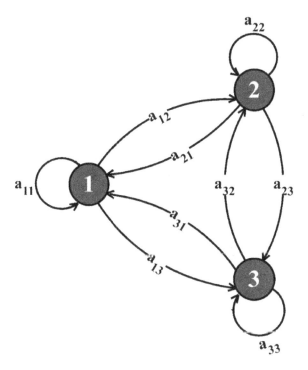

**Figure 14.3** The ergodic HMM.

This means the probability of observing the sequence $o_1, o_2, \ldots, o_t$ to be at state $i$ in time $t$ can be estimated repeatably as follows:

$$\alpha_1 = \pi_i b_i(o_1), \tag{14.7}$$

and

$$\alpha_i(t+1) = b_i(o_{i+1}) \sum_{j=1}^{N} \alpha_j(t) a_{ji}. \tag{14.8}$$

The backward procedure is started by letting (Mitra and Date, 2010; Puengnim *et al.*, 2010):

$$\beta_i(t) = P(O_{t+1} = o_{t+1}, \ldots, O_T = o_T | X_t = i, \lambda). \tag{14.9}$$

And this is the probability of ending an incomplete sequence $o_{t+1}, o_2, \ldots, o_T$ given the initial state $i$ at time $t$. We therefore can estimate the following (Tai *et al.*, 2009; Mitra and Date, 2010; Puengnim *et al.*, 2010):

$$\beta_i(T) = 1, \tag{14.10}$$

and

$$\beta_i(t) = \sum_{j=1}^{N} \beta_j(t+1) a_{ij} b_j(o_{t+1}). \tag{14.11}$$

The next step is to perform an update using Bayes' theorem (Zellner, 2007; Loh, 2016; Alendal *et al.*, 2017):

$$\gamma_i(t) = P(X_t = i \mid O, \lambda),$$
$$= \frac{P(X_t = i \mid O, \lambda)}{P(O \mid \gamma)},$$
$$= \frac{\alpha_i(t) \beta_i(t)}{\sum_{j=1}^{N} \alpha_j(t) \beta_j(t)}. \tag{14.12}$$

This is a probability of being in state $i$ at time $t$ given the observed sequence $O$ and the parameter $\lambda$. The probability of being in state $i$ and $j$ at times $t$ and $t+1$ given the observed sequence $O$ and parameters $\lambda$ can be written as follows (Tai *et al.*, 2009; Mitra and Date, 2010; Puengnim *et al.*, 2010):

$$\xi_{ij}(t) = P(X_t = i, X_{t+1} = j \mid O, \lambda),$$
$$= \frac{P(X_t = i \mid O, \lambda)}{P(O \mid \gamma)},$$
$$= \frac{\alpha_i(t) a_{ij}(t+1) \beta_j(t+1) b_j(o_{t+1})}{\sum_{i=1}^{N} \sum_{j=1}^{N} \alpha_i(t) a_{ij} \beta_j(t+1) b_j(o_{t+1})}. \tag{14.13}$$

The parameters of the HMM can thus be estimated as follows (Tai *et al.*, 2009; Mitra and Date, 2010; Puengnim *et al.*, 2010):

$$\pi_i^* = \gamma_i(1), \tag{14.14}$$

$$a_{ij}^* = \frac{\sum_{t=1}^{T-1} \xi_{ij}(t)}{\sum_{t=1}^{T-1} \gamma_i(t)}, \tag{14.15}$$

$$b_{ij}^*(v_k) = \frac{\sum_{t=1}^{T} 1_{o_t = v_k} \gamma_i(t)}{\sum_{t=1}^{T} \gamma_i(t)}, \tag{14.16}$$

and here,

$$1_{o_t = v_k} = \begin{cases} 1 & \text{if } o_t = v_k, \\ 0 & \text{otherwise.} \end{cases}$$

These steps are recurred until convergence. In summary, the training of the HMM are conducted as follows (Baum, 1972; Rabiner, 1989):

1. Randomly choose a set of initial parameters $\lambda_t = \{A, B, \pi\}$.

2. Approximate the parameters using Equations (14.14)–(14.16) (Tai *et al.*, 2009).
3. Let $A = a^*_{ij}$, $B = b^*_{ij}(v_k)$ and $\pi = \pi^*_i$.
4. Let $\lambda_{t+1} = \{A, B, \pi\}$.
5. If convergence criteria are met then end otherwise let $\lambda_t = \lambda_{t+1}$, $\lambda = \bar{\lambda}$ and go to Step 2.

The HMM is in this chapter compared to the Gaussian mixture model (GMM) which was described in detail in Chapter 13. GMM has been successful in many pattern recognition applications such as in speech and face recognition. GMM have performed better than HMM in text independent speaker recognition (Reynolds *et al.*, 2000). Other successes of GMM include in face recognition (Cardinaux *et al.*, 2003), to estimate autoregressive models (Wang *et al.*, 2018), for Hindi speech recognition (Maurya *et al.*, 2018), for online handwriting recognition (Mandal *et al.*, 2018), for writer identification (Christlein *et al.*, 2017) and for modelling political stability (Uddin *et al.*, 2017). One advantage of using the GMM is that it is computationally inexpensive. The GMM works by creating a model of each class based on the means and covariance of the data. To increase accuracy of the model, a weighted sum of the Gaussians is used with each Gaussian comprising of a mean and a covariance, and therefore a mixture of components. Training of the GMM is fast and it estimates the mean and covariance parameters from the training data (Wang *et al.*, 2002; Meng *et al.*, 2004). The training procedure estimates the model parameters from a set of observations and we normally use the Expectation Maximization (EM) algorithm (Reynolds *et al.*, 2000; Ding and Song, 2016; Hu *et al.*, 2017; Huang and Chen, 2017; Yu *et al.*, 2018). The EM algorithm maximizes the expected log-likelihood of the complete data given the partially observed data.

## 14.3 Condition Monitoring: Motor Bearing Faults

This section describes the application of the HMM for condition monitoring of bearings (Nelwamondo *et al.*, 2006a; Marwala, 2012). This condition-monitoring framework is based on vibration measurement data. Most rolling bearings contain two concentric rings, and these are the inner and outer raceway (Li *et al.*, 2000; Marwala, 2012). These bearings contain rolling elements that run in the tracts of the raceways. There are different kinds of standard shapes of the rolling elements including the ball, cylindrical roller, needle roller, symmetrical and unsymmetrical barrel roller (Nelwamondo *et al.*, 2006a; Marwala, 2012).

This chapter studies three types of faults and these are the inner raceway, outer raceway and the rolling element faults. Bearing faults increase rotational friction of the rotor and each fault shows vibration spectra with distinctive frequency components (Nelwamondo *et al.*, 2006a; Marwala, 2012). These frequency components are a linear function of the running speed. Furthermore, the two raceway frequencies are linear functions of the number of balls. The motor bearing condition monitoring systems analyse vibration signals of the bearing faults. Vibration signals produced was using the impact pulse generated when a ball roller knocks a defect in the raceways or when the defect in the ball knocks the raceways (Li *et al.*, 2000; Nelwamondo *et al.*, 2006a; Marwala, 2012).

Nelwamondo *et al.* (2006a) proposed a motor bearing fault detection and diagnosis system shown in Figure 14.4. The system has two major stages after the acquisition of vibration data and these are the pre-processing and classification stages. The first stage of the fault identification system, depicted in Figure 14.5, is the signal pre-processing and feature extraction. Faults cause changes in the vibration of structures.

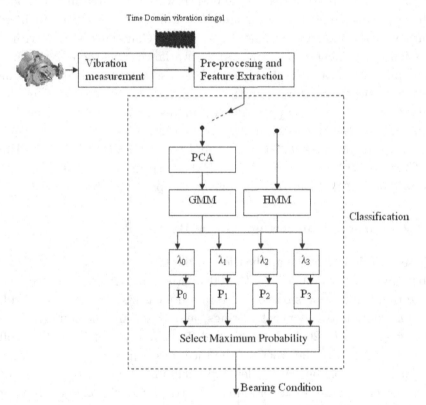

**Figure 14.4**    Motor bearing fault identification system.

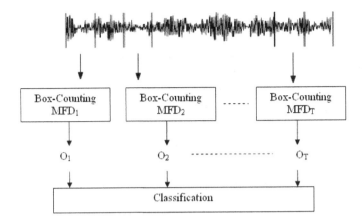

**Figure 14.5** Pre-processing and feature extraction of vibration data.

Moosavian *et al.* (2017) observed the effect of piston scratching fault on the vibration data of the IC engine whereas Xue and Howard (2018) successfully used the torsional vibration data to detect faults in gear. Khadersab and Shivakumar (2018) observed the impact of vibration data on bearing faults. Feng *et al.* (2016) successfully used vibration data for fault identification bearings whereas Dolenc *et al.* (2016) successfully used vibration data for bearing fault identification.

Therefore, it is evident that the information on the condition of the structure is in the vibration data (McClintic *et al.*, 2000). In this chapter, data was pre-processed by distributing the vibration data into $T$ windows of equal lengths. After the pre-processing of data, features were extracted using the Box-counting multiscale fractal dynamics (MFD). This forms the observation sequence for the GMM and HMM classifiers.

Due to the huge disparities in the vibration data, it was difficult to perform direct comparison of the signals. Therefore, nonlinear pattern classification approaches were used to classify different bearing faults. The features extracted were used as inputs to the classification stage. The performance of the GMM and the HMM classifiers were compared. For the GMM classifier, the PCA, was used to reduce the dimension of the data (Jolliffe, 1986; Liu *et al.*, 2018). The PCA data transformation is based on the eigenvalue analysis and is as follows (Jolliffe, 1986):

- Estimate the covariance matrix of the input data.
- Estimate the eigenvalues and eigenvectors of the covariance matrix.
- Reserve the largest eigenvalues and their respective eigenvectors.
- Project the original data into the reduced eigenvectors.

Fault identification of the motor bearing is attained by estimating the probability of the feature vector, given the fault model. The GMM or HMM with maximum probability identifies the bearing condition. The vibration data used was gathered at Rockwell Science Centre (Loparo, 2006). Single point faults of diameters of 7 mils, 14 mils and 21 mils (1 mil = 0.001 inches) were introduced individually at the inner raceway, rolling element and outer raceway. The experiments were executed for each fault diameter and repeated for two load conditions, and these were 1 and 2 horsepower, and data was gathered.

The appropriate HMM classifier was a 2 state model with diagonal covariance matrix with 10 Gaussian mixtures. The GMM classifier had a diagonal covariance matrix with 3 centres (Maragos and Potamianos, 1999). Nelwamondo *et al.* (2006a) measured the effectiveness of the time domain fractal dimension of vibration signal and this is shown in Figure 14.6.

Nelwamondo *et al.* (2006a) used the HMM and GMM classifiers and the results are in Table 14.1. The HMM outperformed the GMM classifier, with 100% and 99.2% classification for HMM and GMM, respectively.

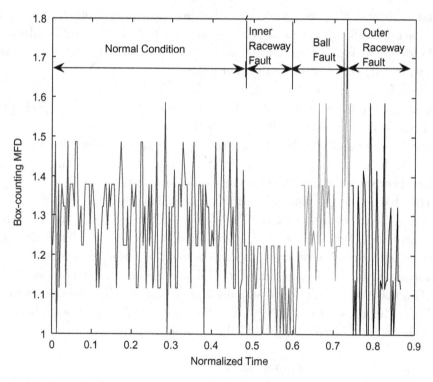

**Figure 14.6**  MFD feature extraction of the normal, inner, outer and ball fault of a vibration signal.

**Table 14.1**  The classification rate for different loads and fault diameters for both the GMM and HMM classifier.

| | 7 mils | | 14 mils | | 21 mils | |
|---|---|---|---|---|---|---|
| **Load** | **HMM (%)** | **GMM (%)** | **HMM (%)** | **GMM (%)** | **HMM (%)** | **GMM (%)** |
| 1 | 100 | 99.2 | 100 | 98.7 | 100 | 99 |
| 2 | 100 | 99 | 100 | 99.1 | 100 | 99 |

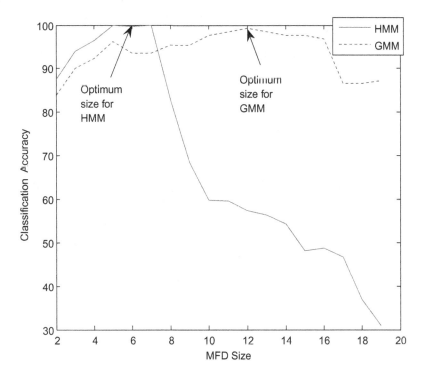

**Figure 14.7**  The graph of the change classification rate with change in MFD size.

It also demonstrates that changing the bearing load or diameter does not significantly change the classification rate.

Figure 14.7 shows the MFD feature vector which extracts the bearing fault specific information. It should be noted that these features are only for the first second of the vibration signal. This figure shows that the feature extraction technique extracted the fault specific features which classified different bearing faults. It shows that the GMM had an optimum MFD size of 13 whereas the HMM had the optimum size of 5.

The results of the comparison between the GMM and HMM on classifying the different bearing faults showed that the HMM outperformed the GMM classifier. The HMM was computationally more expensive than the GMM.

## 14.4 Speaker Recognition

Nelwamondo *et al.* (2006b) applied the HMM to a database consisting of 20 speakers with 50% being females with different South African indigenous accents that were drawn from 11 different official languages. Each of the 20 speakers was made to state the word '*password*' 40 times. The speech signals were recorded at a sampling frequency of 16 kHz in a controlled environment. The speech signals were taken in sittings that were at least a week apart to capture speakers' moods and tones. The signals were pre-processed using the Mel-Frequency Cestrum Coefficients (MFCC) with Box-counting dimension, as well as the MFCC with Minkowski–Bouligand dimension (Falconer, 1990; Zheng *et al.*, 2001). Twenty of the 40 signals from 10 speakers were used for training and the other twenty signals were used for validating the speaker identification rate. All 40 signals from the rest of the 10 speakers were used to test for impostor rejection rate. The HMM speaker recognition system is as implemented by Nelwamondo *et al.* (2006b) and is shown in Figure 14.8. Here, a speech is recorded, and it is pre-processed using the MFCC with Box-counting and Minkowski–Bouligand dimensions. The data is decoded using the HMM and this is compared to the data in the stored template, and based on this, the speaker is identified.

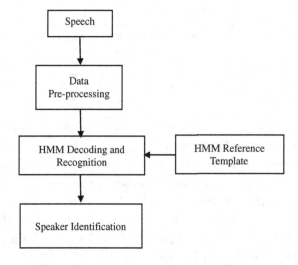

**Figure 14.8**    The HMM speaker recognition system.

**Table 14.2** Identification rates for different feature extractions and different merging techniques.

| | 84.5 % | | | | | |
| | MFCC with Box-counting Dimension | | | MFCC with Minkowski–Bouligand Dimension | | |
| Baseline | V | W | U | V | W | U |
|---|---|---|---|---|---|---|
| 2-band | — | 84.8 | 98.3 | — | 84.8 | 96.7 |
| 4-band | 98.3 | 98.3 | 96.7 | 96.7 | 98.3 | 95.67 |
| 7-band | 99.3 | 99.2 | 84.78 | 98.3 | 98.3 | 84.3 |

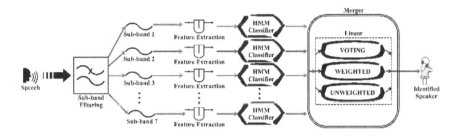

**Figure 14.9** The speech recognition system.

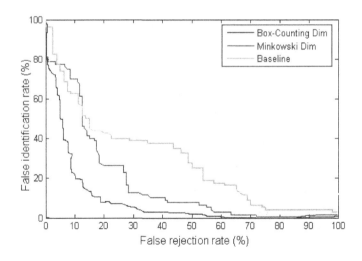

**Figure 14.10** Probability distributions of false identification and false rejection rates.

Table 14.2 summarizes the experimental results. The letters V, W and U summarize the Voting, Weighted and Unweighted mergers, respectively. The V, W and U system is illustrated in Figure 14.9 and more information on this is in Nelwamondo *et al.* (2006b). Table 14.2 shows the identification rates

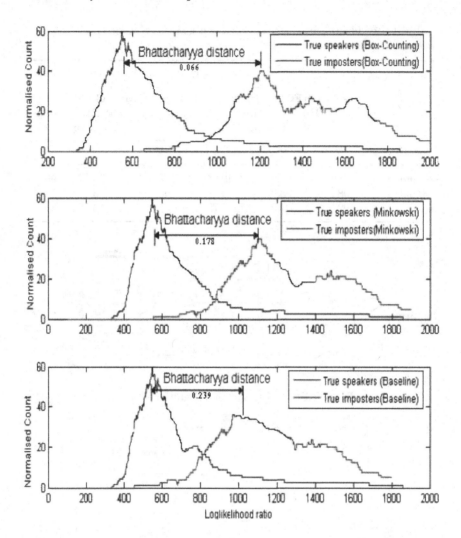

**Figure 14.11**    Separation between the impostors and enrolled speakers.

obtained from the HMM-based recognizer (Nelwamondo *et al.*, 2006b) and it shows that the identification rates of the proposed framework outperform the conventional speaker identification recognizer with more than 10% identification difference.

Figure 14.10 demonstrates the detection error trade-off of the system. It shows that decreasing the false acceptance rate increases the false rejection rate. This figure shows that the minimum false identification rates for the proposed framework with both Box-counting and Minkowski–Bouligand dimensions were 8% and 11.5%, respectively. The false rejection rate was 19% for the proposed framework with Box-counting dimension and 27.2%

with Minkowski–Bouligand dimension. The Minkowski–Bouligand feature extraction underperformed compared to the Box-counting method, which performed the baseline recognizer. Figure 14.11 shows that there is a clear decision boundary between impostors and speakers as quantified by the Bhattacharyya distance (Bhattacharyya, 1943).

The proposed framework with Box-counting was found to have the smallest Bhattacharyya distance of 0.0662 as shown in Figure 14.11. This Bhattacharyya distance difference means this framework is more reliable as the occurrence of misidentification is minimized. The reason for this is that the distributions of enrolled speakers and that of impostors are more separable as illustrated by Figure 14.11.

## 14.5  Conclusions

HMM was used for fault identification in bearings. The HMM was compared to the GMM. The results showed that the HMM classifier performed better than the GMM classifier with HMM giving 100% and GMM 99.2% classification rate. The HMM classifier was found to be computationally more expensive to train than the GMM classifier. The HMM was applied for speaker recognition of 20 people with 11 different accents corresponding to South Africa's official languages. The results obtained showed that the proposed system was able to recognize speakers at best with an accuracy of 99.3% using the MFCC with Box-counting dimension and 98.3% using the MFCC with Minkowski–Bouligand dimension.

## References

Alendal, G., Blackford, J., Chen, B., Avlesen, H., Omar, A. (2017). Using Bayes theorem to quantify and reduce uncertainties when monitoring varying marine environments for indications of a leak. *Energy Procedia*, 114:3607–3612.

Almutairi, A., Ahmed, M.H., Salama, M.M.A. (2016). Use of MCMC to incorporate a wind power model for the evaluation of generating capacity adequacy. *Electric Power Systems Research*, 133:63–70.

Baker, J.K. (1973). Machine-aided Labeling of Connected Speech. In: *Working Papers in Speech Recognition XI*, Technical Reports, Computer Science Department, Carnegie-Mellon University, Pittsburgh, PA.

Baum, L.E., Petrie, T., Soules, G., Weiss, N. (1970). A maximization technique occurring in the statistical analysis of probabilistic functions of Markov chains. *The Annals of Mathematical Statistics*, 41:164.

Baum, L.E., Petrie, T. (1966). Statistical inference for probabilistic functions of finite state Markov chains. *The Annals of Mathematical Statistics*, 37(6):1554–1563.

Bazavov, A., Berg, B.A., Zhou, H. (2009). Application of biased metropolis algorithms: From protons to proteins. *Mathematics and Computers in Simulation*, doi: 10.1016/j.matcom.2009.05.005.

Baum, L. (1972). An inequality and associated maximization techniques in statistical estimation for probabilistic function of Markov processes. *Inequality*, 3:1–8.

Bhattacharyya, A. (1943). On a measure of divergence between two statistical populations defined by their probability distributions. *Bulletin of the Calcutta Mathematical Society*, 35:99–109.

Bishop, C.M. (1995). *Neural Networks for Pattern Recognition*. London: Oxford.

Blasiak, S., Rangwala, H. (2011). A hidden Markov model variant for sequence classification. *IJCAI Proceedings-International Joint Conference on Artificial Intelligence*, 22:1192.

Boutros, T., Liang, M. (2011). Detection and diagnosis of bearing and cutting tool faults using hidden markov models. *Mechanical Systems and Signal Process*, 25:2102–2124.

Bremaud, P. (2013). *Markov Chains: Gibbs Fields, Monte Carlo Simulation, and Queues*. Berlin, Heidelberg, Germany: Springer Science & Business Media.

Calefati, P., Amico, B., Lacasella, A., Muraca, E., Zuo, M.J. (2006). Machinery faults detection and forecasting using hidden Markov models. In: *Proceedings of the 8th Biennial ASME Conference on Engineering System Devices and Analytics*, 895–901.

Çakmak, H., Dutoit. T. (2018). HMM-based generation of laughter facial expression. *Speech Communication*, 98:28–41.

Cardinaux, F., Cardinaux, C., Marcel, S. (2003). *Comparison of MLP and GMM Classifiers for Face Verification on XM2VTS*, Springer-Verlag GmbH, 2688:911–920.

Chamie, M.E., Açıkmeşe, B. (2018). Safe Metropolis–Hastings algorithm and its application to swarm control. *Systems & Control Letters*, 111:40–48.

Christlein, V., Bernecker, D., Hönig, F., Maier, A., Angelopoulou, E. (2017). Writer identification using GMM supervectors and exemplar-SVMs. *Pattern Recognition*, 63:258–267.

Darong, H., Lanyan, K., Xiaoyan, C., Ling, Z., Bo, M. (2018). Fault diagnosis for the motor drive system of urban transit based on improved hidden Markov model. *Microelectronics Reliability*, 82:179–189.

Ding, W., Song, P.X.-K. (2016). EM algorithm in Gaussian copula with missing data. *Computational Statistics & Data Analysis*, 101:1–11.

Dolenc, B., Boškoski, P., Juričić, Đ. (2016). Distributed bearing fault diagnosis based on vibration analysis. *Mechanical Systems and Signal Processing*, 66–67:521–532.

Drugan, M.M., Thierens, D. (2010). Recombination operators and selection strategies for evolutionary Markov Chain Monte Carlo algorithms. *Evolutionary Intelligence*, 3:79–101.

Ertunc, H.M., Loparo, K.A., Ocak, H. (2001). Tool wear condition monitoring in drilling operations using hidden Markov models. *International Journal of Machine Tools & Manufacture*, 41:1363–1384.

Falconer, K. (1990). *Fractal Geometry: Mathematical Foundations and Applications*. Chichester: John Wiley, pp. 38–47.

Feng, Z., Ma, H., Zuo, M.J. (2016). Vibration signal models for fault diagnosis of planet bearings. *Journal of Sound and Vibration*, 370:372–393.

Gagniuc, P.A. (2017). *Markov Chains: From Theory to Implementation and Experimentation*. New Jersey: John Wiley & Sons.

Gargallo, P., Miguel, J.A., Salvador, M.J. (2017). MCMC Bayesian spatial filtering for hedonic models in real estate markets. *Spatial Statistics*, 22, Part 1:47–67.

Hayes, B. (2013). First links in the Markov chain. *American Scientist.* 101(2):92–96.

Hu, H., Yao, W., Wu, Y. (2017). The robust EM-type algorithms for log-concave mixtures of regression models. *Computational Statistics & Data Analysis,* 111: 14–26.

Huang, W., Chen, Y. (2017). The multiset EM algorithm. *Statistics & Probability Letters,* 126:41–48.

Jelinek, F. (1976). Continuous Speech Recognition by Statistical Methods. In: *Proceedings of the IEEE,* 64(4):532–556.

Jolliffe, I.T. (1986). *Principal Component Analysis.* Springer-Verlag, New York.

Kang, M., Ahn, J., Lee, K. (2018). Opinion mining using ensemble text Hidden Markov Models for text classification. *Expert Systems with Applications,* 94:218–227.

Khadersab, A., Shivakumar, S. (2018). Vibration analysis techniques for rotating machinery and its effect on bearing faults. *Procedia Manufacturing,* 20:247–252.

Lee, S., Li, L., Ni, J. (2010). Online degradation assessment and adaptive fault detection using modified hidden Markov model. *Journal of Manufacturing Science and Engineering,* 132:0210101-02101011.

Li, B., Chow, M.Y., Tipsuwan, Y., Hung, J.C. (2000). Neural-network-based motor rolling bearing fault diagnosis. *IEEE Transactions on Industrial Electronics,* 47:1060–1068.

Liu, Z., Chen, D., Wurm, K.M., von Wichert, G. (2015). Table-top scene analysis using knowledge-supervised MCMC. *Robotics and Computer-Integrated Manufacturing,* 33:110–123.

Liu, Y., Zhao, S., Wang, Q., Gao, Q. (2018). Learning more distinctive representation by enhanced PCA network. *Neurocomputing,* 275:924–931.

Loh, H. (2016). The converse of a theorem by Bayer and Stillman. *Advances in Applied Mathematics,* 80:62–69.

Loparo K.A. (2006). Bearing Data Center Seeded Fault Test Data, Available at: https://csegroups.case.edu/bearingdatacenter/pages/download-data-file. Accessed on 01 June 2006.

Lyons, J., Paliwal, K.K., Dehzangi, A., Heffernan, R., Sharma, A. (2016). Protein fold recognition using HMM–HMM alignment and dynamic programming. *Journal of Theoretical Biology,* 393:67–74.

Mandal, S., Prasanna, S.R.M., Sundaram, S. (2018). GMM posterior features for improving online handwriting recognition. *Expert Systems with Applications,* 97:421–433.

Maragos, P., Potamianos, A. (1999). Fractal dimensions of speech sounds: Computation and application to automatic speech recognition. *Journal of the Acoustic Society of America,* 105:1925–1932.

Marwala, T. (2009). *Computational Intelligence for Missing Data Imputation, Estimation and Management: Knowledge Optimization Techniques.* New York: IGI Global Publications.

Marwala, T. (2010). *Finite Element Model Updating Using Computational Intelligence Techniques.* London: Springer-Verlag.

Marwala, T. (2012). *Condition Monitoring Using Computational Intelligence Methods.* Heidelberg: Springer.

Maurya, A., Kumar, D., Agarwal, R.K. (2018). Speaker recognition for Hindi speech signal using MFCC–GMM Approach. *Procedia Computer Science,* 125:880–887.

McClintic, K., Lebold, M., Maynard, K., Byington, C., Campbell, R. (2000). Residual and difference feature analysis with transitional gearbox data. In: *Proceedings of the 54th Meeting of the Society for Machinery Failure Prevention Technology,* 635–645.

Meng, L., Frei, M.G., Osorio, I., Strang, G., Nguyen, T.Q. (2004). Gaussian mixture models of ECoG signal features for improved detection of epileptic seizures. *Medical Engineering & Physics*, 26:379–393.

Menon, S., Kim, K., Uluyol, O., Nwadiogbu, E.O. (2003). Incipient fault detection and diagnosis in turbine engines using hidden Markov models. *American Society of Mechanical Engineering, International Gas Turbine Institute*, Turbo Expo (Publication), IGTI:493–500.

Metropolis, N., Rosenbluth, A., Rosenbluth, M. (1953). A. Teller, and E. Teller, equation of state calculations by fast computing machines. *The Journal of Chemical Physics*, 21:1087–1092.

Mitra, S., Date, P. (2010). Regime switching volatility calibration by the Baum–Welch method. *Journal of Computational and Applied Mathematics*, 234(12):3243–3260.

Moosavian, A., Najafi, G., Ghobadian, B., Mirsalim, M. (2017). The effect of piston scratching fault on the vibration behavior of an IC engine. *Applied Acoustics*, 126:91–100.

Moskovkin, P., Hou, M. (2007). Metropolis Monte Carlo predictions of free Co–Pt nanoclusters. *Journal of Alloys and Compounds*, 434–435:550–554.

Nakade, A., Biswas, S. (2012). Effect of increasing the energy gap between the two lowest energy states on the mixing time of the Metropolis algorithm. *Information Processing Letters*, 112(23):922–927.

Nelwamondo, F.V., Marwala, T., Mahola, U. (2006a). Early classifications of bearing faults using hidden Markov models, Gaussian mixture models, Mel-frequency Cepstral coefficients and fractals. *International Journal of Innovative Computing, Information and Control*, 2(6):1281–1299.

Nelwamondo, F.V., Mahola, U., Marwala, T. (2006b). Multi-scale fractal dimension for speaker identification. In: *Proceedings of the 8th WSEAS International Conference on Automatic Control, Modeling and Simulation*, Prague, Czech Republic, March 12–14, 81–86.

Owsley, L.M.D., Atlas, L.E., Bernard, G.D. (1997). Self-organizing feature maps and hidden Markov models for machine tool monitoring. *IEEE Transactions on Signal Processing*, 45(11):2787–2798.

Papaioannou, I., Betz, W., Zwirglmaier, K., Straub, D. (2015). MCMC algorithms for Subset Simulation. *Probabilistic Engineering Mechanics*, 41:89–103.

Puengnim, A., Thomas, N., Tourneret, J.-Y., Vidal, J. (2010). Classification of linear and non-linear modulations using the Baum–Welch algorithm and MCMC methods. *Signal Processing*, 90(12):3242–3255.

Purushothama, V., Narayanana, S., Suryanarayana, Prasad, A.N. (2005). Multi-fault diagnosis of rolling bearing elements using wavelet analysis and hidden Markov model based fault recognition. *NDT&E International*, 38:654–664.

Rabiner, L.R. (1989). A tutorial on hidden Markov models and selected applications in speech recognition. *Proceedings of IEEE*, 77(2):257–286.

Reynolds, D.A., Quatieri, T.F., Dunn, R.B. (2000). Speaker verification using adapted Gaussian mixture models. *Digital Signal Processing*, 10:19–41.

Robinson, W.N., Aria, A. (2018). Sequential fraud detection for prepaid cards using hidden Markov model divergence. *Expert Systems with Applications*, 91:235–251.

Rodina, A., Bliznakova, K., Pallikarakis, N. (2010). End stage renal disease patients' projections using Markov Chain Monte Carlo simulation. In: *Proceedings of IFMBE*, 796–779.

Sacco, W.F., Lapa, C.M.F., Pereira, C.M.N.A., Filho, H.A. (2008). A Metropolis algorithm applied to a nuclear power plant auxiliary feedwater system surveillance tests policy optimization. *Progress in Nuclear Energy*, 50:15–21.

Samanta, O., Roy, An., Parui, S.K., Bhattacharya, U. (2018). An HMM framework based on spherical-linear features for online cursive handwriting recognition. *Information Sciences*, 441:133–151.

Sgouralis, I., Pressé, S. (2017). An Introduction to infinite HMMs for single-molecule data analysis. *Biophysical Journal*, 112(10):2021–2029.

Suleiman, D., Awajan, A., Etaiwi, W.A. (2017). The use of Hidden Markov Model in natural ARABIC language processing: A survey. *Procedia Computer Science*, 113:240–247.

Tai, A.H., Ching, W.K., Chan, L.Y. (2009). Detection of machine failure: Hidden Markov Model approach. *Computers and Industrial Engineering*, 57:608–619.

Tiana, G., Sutto, L., Broglia, R.A. (2007). Use of the metropolis algorithm to simulate the dynamics of protein chains. *Physica A*, 380:241–249.

Uddin, M.A., Ali, M.H., Masih, M. (2017). Political stability and growth: An application of dynamic GMM and quantile regression. *Economic Modelling*, 64:610–625.

Wang, F., Zheng, F., Wu, W. (2000). A C/V segmentation for Mandarian speech based on multi-scale fractal dimension. In: *Proceedings of the International Conference on Spoken Language Processing*, 4:648–651.

Wang, J., Wang, J., Weng, Y. (2002). Chip design of MFCC extraction for speech recognition, Integration. *The VLSI Journal*, 32:111–131.

Wang, W., Lee, L.-F., Bao, Y. (2018). GMM estimation of the spatial autoregressive model in a system of interrelated networks. *Regional Science and Urban Economics*, 69:167–198.

Wang, H., Wang, C., Wang, Y., Gao, X., Yu, C. (2017). Bayesian forecasting and uncertainty quantifying of stream flows using Metropolis–Hastings Markov Chain Monte Carlo algorithm. *Journal of Hydrology*, 549:476–483.

White, G., Porter, M.D. (2014). GPU accelerated MCMC for modeling terrorist activity. *Computational Statistics & Data Analysis*, 71:643–651.

Wong, W.C., Lee, J.H. (2010). Fault detection and diagnosis using hidden Markov disturbance models. *Industrial and Engineering Chemistry Research*, 49:7901–7908.

Xue, S., Howard, I. (2018). Torsional vibration signal analysis as a diagnostic tool for planetary gear fault detection. *Mechanical Systems and Signal Processing*, 100:706–728.

Yang, Y., Jiang, J. (2018). Bi-weighted ensemble via HMM-based approaches for temporal data clustering. *Pattern Recognition*, 76:391–403.

Yu, J., Chaomurilige, C., Yang, M.-S. (2018). On convergence and parameter selection of the EM and DA-EM algorithms for Gaussian mixtures. *Pattern Recognition*, 77:188–203.

Zellner, A. (2007). Generalizing the standard product rule of probability theory and Bayes's Theorem. *Journal of Econometrics*, 138(1):14–23.

Zhang, Y., Li, X.R., Zhou, K. (1998). A fault detection and diagnosis approach based on hidden Markov chain model. In: *Proceedings of the American Control Conference*, Philadelphia, 2012–2016.

Zheng, F., Zhang, G., Song, Z. (2001). Comparison of different implementations of MFCC. *Journal of Computer Science & Technology*, 16(6):582–589.

Zhou, S.Y., Wang, S.Q. (2005). On-line fault detection and diagnosis in industrial processes using hidden Markov model. *Developments in Chemical Engineering and Mineral Processing*, 13:397–406.

Chapter 15

# Reinforcement Learning

**Abstract.** This chapter uses reinforcement learning and neural networks to study the effects of social learning in the training of game playing agents as well as the concept of computer bluffing. It uses the reinforcement learning method of TD-lambda. Agents that use the reinforcement learning algorithms are trained in a social context instead of a self-play environment. This mimics the way in which players of games such as scrabble, Lerpa and chess mentor each other in their clubs. The social learning trained agents exhibit better playing experience than self-play agents. It was observed that an agent can learn to bluff its opponents, with the action demonstrating not an 'illogical' action but instead an act of maximizing returns through an effective statistical optimization.

## 15.1 Introduction

Intelligent agents that play board games have been a focus in machine learning and artificial intelligence (AI) (Wooldridge, 2002; Hurwitz and Marwala, 2007a; Marivate *et al.* 2008a; Marwala and Hurwitz, 2009). These agents are trained on how to play games and learn from either previous games or by playing against themselves (Hurwitz, 2007; Schaeffer, 2001; Marivate *et al.*, 2008). The disadvantage of agents that learn from playing against themselves is that they do not always capture all the dynamics of a game or variations in opponent's strategy. Therefore, self-play (S-P) agents have a propensity to perform below par against opponents that they have not encountered before. To remedy this, game designers have presented the ability to save a large database of hitherto played games (Morehead *et al.*, 2001; Hurwitz and Marwala, 2005; Marivate and Marwala, 2008b). Therefore, agents have databases of saved games that they can access, and this requires large memory as games increase their state sizes. Furthermore, this increases computational complexity, as searches within the databases are required to identify the best moves. Researchers have extensively used reinforcement learning in multiple domains including in developing game playing agents (Sutton, 1988; Sutton and Barto, 1998; Marivate, 2009; Hurwitz and Marwala, 2007b). A problem that arises with S-P and reinforcement learning is the inability to model large state board, and Marivate (2009) examined the training of agents in social settings contrary to S-P and monitored the consequences of this on the overall performance of the different agents created. The game playing agents are rational and, therefore, attempt to maximize their utility, which we define as performance, and have no explicit knowledge of how other agents in the social group are performing.

Furthermore, many card games involve an element of bluffing; simulating and fully comprehending bluffing is one of the most difficult endeavours for game designers (Lelouche and Doublait, 1992; Holm, 2010). The whole process of bluffing depends on performing an assignment that is unexpected, and the opponents misunderstand it. To produce an artificial intelligent agent that can bluff, we initially build an agent that can learn. The agent should learn the inherent nature of the game it is playing and trends emerging from its opponent's behaviour because bluffing is only probable when one can expect the opponent's reactions to one's own actions.

## 15.2  Reinforcement Learning: TD-Lambda

An intelligent agent is a computer system/program that resides in some environment and autonomously and adaptively performs actions in that environment. We learn by interacting with one another and obtain reward or punishment after performing an action. This is different from supervised learning where we have cases with inputs $x$ and outputs $y$ and we learn the function:

$$y = f(x, w). \tag{15.1}$$

Here, $x$ is a vector of multiple inputs, $y$ is a vector of multiple outputs and $w$ are the network weights. The learning algorithm approximates the weights. Reinforcement learning is unsupervised, and an agent located in an environment learns by interacting with the environment, and we use the feedback from the environment to reinforce attributes or eliminate attributes. We execute actions in the environment, and effects of the actions are perceived using sensors or receptors. The agent gets a reward or punishment

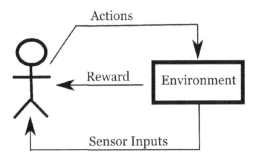

**Figure 15.1**   Reinforcement learning framework.

given the change the action has made in the environment. This reward can be extrinsic (from the environment) or intrinsic (from within the agent). Figure 15.1 illustrates the reinforcement framework (Marivate, 2009; Marivate and Marwala, 2008a).

Reinforcement learning has been applied successfully in areas such as in robotics (Leottau *et al.*, 2018), in stealth technology (Mendonça *et al.*, 2018), in financial trading (Pendharkar and Cusatis, 2018), in behavioural studies (Frankenhuis *et al.*, 2018) and in embedding virtual network (Yao *et al.*, 2018). Reinforcement learning uses the Markov Decision Problem (MDP) (Sutton, 1988; Sutton and Barto, 1998). The MDP consists of the following variables (Marivate and Marwala, 2008a; Sutton, 1988; Sutton and Barto, 1998):

$S$: possible states
$s$: current state
$s'$: subsequent state
$\Lambda$: possible actions of an agent
$a$: current action selected by the agent
$R$: Reward given $(R(s), (R(s, a), R(s, a, s'))$
$P(s' \mid s, a)$: transitional probability

The transitional probability $(P(s' \mid s, a))$ is the probability of moving from one state to another state $(s')$ given an action $(a)$ and a current state $(s)$. An agent makes a decision on the best actions and we call this the policy $(\pi)$ of the agent. The policy maps a state to a specific action $(a = \pi(s))$. The transitional probabilities of an environment are unknown and thus in reinforcement learning, the challenge is how to model an environment's dynamics within the agent. To achieve this, we introduce the concept of the value of a state in the form of value function and action value functions. These functions evaluate the policy that the agent is taking and the value function $V_\pi$, is (Marivate and Marwala, 2008a; Sutton, 1988; Sutton and Barto, 1998):

$$V_\pi(s) = E_\pi \left[ \sum_{k=0}^{\infty} \gamma^k r_k \mid s_0 = s \right]. \tag{15.2}$$

This is the expected value $(E)$ of the summation of the discounted $(\gamma)$ reward $(r)$ of all possible future states given that the agent is executing a policy $\pi$ given that we are starting at the current state. The policy $(\pi)$ are the mappings of state to actions (Sutton, 1988; Sutton and Barto, 1998; Marivate and Marwala, 2008a):

$$V_\pi(s) \leftarrow V_\pi(s) + \alpha(r + \gamma V_\pi(\acute{s}) - V_\pi(s)). \tag{15.3}$$

We can write the action-value function as follows (Sutton, 1988; Sutton and Barto, 1998; Marivate and Marwala, 2008a):

$$Q_\pi(s,a) = E_\pi \left[ \sum_{k=0}^{\infty} \gamma^k r_{k+1} \mid s_0 = s, a_0 = a \right]. \tag{15.4}$$

Here, $Q(s,a)$ takes into account the current state and the current action. We maximize Equations (15.3) and (15.4) using an optimal policy $\pi^*$ resulting in higher rewards. To identify the policy that maximizes the value function or action-value function, we use dynamic programming through the application of the Bellman Optimality equation (Bellman, 1954; Batsekas, 2000; Nelwamondo *et al.*, 2013). To learn in reinforcement learning from a system without the complete model of the system, then the agent needs to learn through experience. The agent thus must interact and identify an optimal policy. The learning algorithm used was the TD-lambda algorithm (Sutton, 1988; Sutton and Barto, 1998; Marivate and Marwala, 2008a). We apply the algorithm to the action-value function in Equation (15.4), and it allows the agents to initially explore and then exploit more and explore less. This study used the action-value functions with a table structure and it combines dynamic programming with Monte Carlo method (Bellman, 1954; Batsekas, 2000; Sutton, 1988; Sutton and Barto, 1998). The algorithm implemented is as follows (Bellman, 1954; Batsekas, 2000; Sutton, 1988;

Sutton and Barto, 1998; Marivate and Marwala, 2008a):

Initialize $V(s)$ randomly and set $e(s) = 0$
Repeat
Initialize $s$
Repeat (for each step)
$\qquad a \leftarrow$ action with policy $\pi$ and state $s$
$\qquad$ Take action $a$, observe reward $R$, and move to the next state $s'$
$$\delta \leftarrow \gamma V(s') - V(s)$$
$$e(s) \leftarrow e(s) + 1$$
$\qquad$ For all $s$
$$V(s) \leftarrow V(s) + \alpha \delta e(s)$$
$$e(s) \leftarrow \gamma \lambda e(s)$$
$$e(s) \leftarrow s'$$
Until end

Here, $e(s)$ is the eligibility trace of a certain state (Sutton, 1992). Therefore, if a state repeats itself, its update factored into account a higher significance conditional on how recent the previous occurrence was. For selecting the actions and permitting exploration and exploitation, actions were selected using and epsilon greedy distribution, which is, expressed as follows (Sutton, 1988; Sutton and Barto, 1998; Marivate and Marwala, 2008a)

$$P(s, a_i) = \begin{cases} 1 - \varepsilon + \dfrac{\varepsilon}{\lceil A \rceil} & \text{if } a_i = \underset{a' \in A}{\arg\max}\, Q(s, a'), \\ \dfrac{\varepsilon}{\lceil A \rceil} & \text{otherwise.} \end{cases} \tag{15.5}$$

The agent selects a random action with probability $\varepsilon$ and implements a greedy action with probability $1 - \varepsilon$. This ensures that the agents at first are more probably exploring but later on, $\varepsilon$ decreases and the agents begin to exploit using the knowledge gained through the undergone experience.

## 15.3 Game Theory

Another area to be understood in this chapter is game theory. Game theory consists of players, set of actions (strategy) and a pay-off function (Villena and Villena, 2004; Ross, 2006; van den Brink *et al.*, 2008; Hodgson and Huang, 2012; Marwala, 2013). Game theory has been successfully applied in areas such as in economics (van den Brink *et al.*, 2008), land procurement

(Hui and Bao, 2013), auction (Laffont, 1997), the hotel industry (Wei et al., 2012), labour market (Roth, 2002), facial recognition (Roy and Kamel, 2012), medicine (McFadden et al., 2012) and computer science (Papadimitriou, 2001). Recent successful applications of game theory include to study competition in the banking industry (Khanizad and Montazer, 2018), to improve protection in chemical plants (Zhang et al., 2018), to study sustainability of supply chains (Babu and Mohan, 2018), to study network security (Christin, 2011; Lee et al., 2018) and to model patients recovery after surgery (Castellanos et al., 2018).

John von Neumann identified the best strategy in a game as the one that guarantees maximum possible outcome even if your competition know what choice you will make. John Nash introduced the Nash equilibrium, which states that the best strategy for a rational player is that every player's move should be the best response to the other players' move.

In game theory, a two-player game is easy to handle but multiple player games are difficult to deal with. A computational technique was developed to handle multiple player games, and this is the multi-agent system, which is discussed in the next section.

## 15.4 Multi-agent Systems

A multi-agent system is a system with many agents. An agent is an entity such as a software, which is autonomous, perceives its environment and acts on its environment, is intelligent, and operates autonomously in that environment (Russell and Norvig, 2003; Franklin and Graesser, 1996; Kasabov, 1998; Marwala, 2013). According to Kasabov (1998) agents are autonomous, flexible, reactive, proactive, social and are able to control. Marwala (2013) used swarm intelligence to explain the working of a multi-agent system. More details on swarm intelligence are in Marwala (2009), Marwala (2010), Marwala and Lagazio (2011) and Marwala (2012). Successful applications of multi-agent system include in modelling HIV (Teweldemedhin et al., 2004), for traffic light control (Abdoos et al., 2011), safety assessment (Stroeve et al., 2013) and in energy consumption studies (Montoya and Ovalle, 2013). Recent applications of multi-agent systems include robotics (Shahabpoor et al., 2018), in migration studies (Fu and Hao, 2018), to simulate earthmoving operations (Jabri and Zayed, 2017), for program design (Lawlor and McGirr, 2017), diffusion of electric vehicles (Kangur et al., 2017), and studying mobility (El-Amine et al., 2017). An illustration of the multi-agent system is in Figure 15.2.

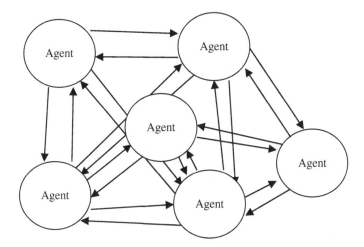

**Figure 15.2**  Illustration of a multi-agent system.

## 15.5 Modelling the Game of Lerpa

Hurwitz and Marwala (2007a) modelled the game of Lerpa using intelligent agent Multi-agent modelling (MAM). We play the game of *Lerpa* with a standard deck of cards, except that not all of the 8s, 9s and 10s are on the deck (Morehead *et al.*, 2001; Schaeffer, 2001). As described by Hurwitz and Marwala (2007a) the cards are valued from greatest to the least-valued, from the ace down to 2, except that we value 7 higher than a king, but lower than an ace. This makes 7 the second most valuable card in a suit. At the end of dealing the hand, the dealer has the choice of *dealing himself in*. This means flipping his last card, which is unseen until this point, over and this declares the *trump suit*. If the player clccts not to do this, then the player flips the next card in the deck to identify the trump suit. Notwithstanding, once trumps are identified, the players then one by one, moving clockwise from the dealer's left, elect whether or not to play the hand (to *knock*), or to drop out of the hand, known as *folding*. If the dealer has *dealt himself in*, he is then required to play the hand. When all players have selected the players that have chosen to play, then a player plays the hand with the player to the dealer's left playing the first card. After we play this card, players should then play *in suit*. In suit means if we play a heart, other players must play a heart if they have one. If other players do not have the suit, they may play a trump, which wins the trick except if another player plays a higher trump. The highest card played wins the trick, with all trumps valued higher than any other card. The winner of the trick leads the first card in the next trick.

At any time, if a player has the Ace of trumps and can play it, he is then required to do so. The true risk in the game comes from the betting.

At the start of the round, the dealer pays the table of whatever the basic betting denomination is, known as 'chips'. When the hand is completed, we divide the chips proportionately between the winners. In this way if one wins two tricks, one receives two thirds of what is in the pot. Nevertheless, if one stays in, but does not win any tricks, he is *Lerpa'd*, and is required to match what was in the pot for the next hand, effectively costing him the pot. The evaluation of this risk determines the true skill in *Lerpa*.

Careful reflection regarding how we structure the system should be considered because the consequences of these decisions can result in unintentional assumptions made by the system created. Bearing this in mind, Hurwitz (2007) and Hurwitz and Marwala (2007a) designed the Lerpa Multi-Agent System (MAS) to permit the maximum amount of freedom to the system, and the agents within, while also permitting for generalization and swift convergence to allow the intelligent agents to interact unconstrained by human assumptions.

Hurwitz and Marwala (2007a) used four players and each of these players interacted with each other indirectly, by interacting directly with the *table*, a shared environment. Over the course of a single hand, an agent makes three decisions, at each step of the game and these are: (1) to play the hand or drop (*knock* or *fold*), (2) to decide which card to play first and (3) decide on the card to play second.

Because there is no decision to be taken at the final card, the hand is said to be effectively finished from the agent's perspective after it has played its second card. Using the TD-lambda algorithm (Sutton, 1989), each agent updates its own neural network at each step, using its own predictions as a reward function and receiving a true reward after its final decision is concluded.

With each agent effected as explained, the agents interact with one another in their shared environment, and continue to learn from each interaction and its result. Each hand played is an independent, stochastic event and consequently only the information about the current hand is available to the agent that draws on its own experience to draw deductions not from previous hands. We make several decisions to use the agent AI effectively and efficiently. We choose the type of learning to use as well as the neural network architecture (Marwala, 2009). We should pay particular attention to the design of the inputs to the neural network, as these govern the information an agent has at any given time. This also defines what assumptions, the agent, if any, indirectly makes. Finally, this determines the dimensionality of the network and this affects the learning rate of the network.

To design the input step of the agent's neural network, it is important to establish all that the network may need to know at any given decision-making stage. We structure all inputs as binary-encoded inputs. On making its first decision, the agent requires to know its own cards, which agents have stayed in or folded, and which agents are still to decide (Miller *et al.*, 1990; Hurwitz, 2007). It is required for the agent to be able to establish which particular agents have taken their particular actions, as this will permit an agent to learn a specific opponent's features, a task that is difficult to achieve if it can only see a number of players in or out. Likewise, the agent's own cards must be specified completely, ensuring the agent to reach its own conclusions about each card's relative value. It is also essential to inform the agent which suit is labelled the trumps suit, but a more neat method has been identified to handle that information. The first information needed by the network are players who called, players in or folded and a hand.

We require to clearly define the agent's hand, and the solution is to encode the cards precisely, i.e. 4 suits, and 10 numbers in each suit, giving 40 possibilities for each card. A fast preview of the number of choices accessible demonstrates that a raw encoding style offers a significant problem of dimensionality. This is because an encoded hand is one of the $40^3$ possible hands and we can choose only $^{40}P_3$ hands, as we cannot repeat any cards. However, the raw encoding structure actually allows for repeated cards and therefore $40^3$ choices are available. Only a single deck of cards is used and therefore no card can ever be repeated in a hand. Using this principle, reliable ordering of the hand implies that the base dimensionality of the hand is substantially reduced because it is a combination of cards that are represented instead of permutations. The number of combinations represented is therefore $^{40}C_3$. This apparently small change from $^nP_r$ to $^nC_r$ decreases the dimensionality of the representation by a factor of r!, and is a factor of 6. Additionally, it is not optimal to represent the cards, as discrete suits because the game places no specific value on any suit by its own accord but by the feature of which suit is the trump suit. Consequently, an alternative encoding scheme was established, rating the 'suits' based on what the agent has at hand, rather than four random suits. The suits are encoded as being in one of these groups (Hurwitz, 2007; Hurwitz and Marwala, 2007a, 2007b): Trump suit; Suit agent has multiple cards in (not trumps); Suit in agent's highest singleton; Suit in agent's second-highest singleton; and Suit in agent's third-highest singleton.

This facilitates an efficient depiction of the agent's hand, significantly improving the dimensionality of the inputs, and therefore the learning rate of the agents. We encoded these five options in a binary setup, to ensure stability, and therefore three binary inputs are essential to denote the suits. To denote the card's number, ten discrete values must be denoted, therefore necessitating four binary inputs to denote the card's value. Therefore, seven binary inputs, four representing suits and three representing numbers denote cards in an agent's hand.

The key issues are that cards that have already been played are required to identify the correct next card to play and that knowledge of who has won a trick is important. The maximum number of cards that is played prior to a decision is seven, and because the table after a card is played is used to estimate and update the network, eight played cards are required to be characterized. Nevertheless, simply using the accessible encoding technique is not automatically the most efficient technique. The actual values of the cards played are not essential, only relative values with respect to the cards in the agent's hand. Therefore, Hurwitz (2007) as well as Hurwitz and Marwala (2007a) characterized the values as follows, with respect to the cards in the same suit in the agent's hand:

- Higher than the card/cards in the agent's hand.
- Higher than the agent's second-highest card.
- Higher than the agent's third-highest card.
- Lower than any of the agent's cards.
- Member of a void suit (number is immaterial).

In addition, another suit is therefore pertinent for illustration of the played cards and this is the void suit. The void suit is a suit in which the agent has no cards. Finally, it is essential to handle the special case of the Ace of trumps because its unique rules imply that strategies are possible to develop based on whether it has been played yet. The current six suits only necessitate three binary inputs to represent, and the six number groupings, therefore, reduce the value depictions from four binary inputs to three binary inputs. This reduces the dimensionality of the input system.

With inputs specified, the agent has the information required to reach its own conclusions and produce its own strategies, without humans making its assumptions. With the inputs now stated, we can design the hidden and output layers. The output neurons represent the prediction $P$ that the network is estimating (Sutton, 1989). A single hand has one of five possible outcomes to be determined. Hurwitz (2007) as well as Hurwitz and Marwala

(2007a) identified these possible outcomes as:

- The agent wins all three tricks, winning 3 chips.
- The agent wins two tricks, winning 2 chips.
- The agent wins one trick, winning 1 chip.
- The agent wins zero tricks, losing 3 chips.
- The agent elects to fold, winning no tricks, but losing no chips.

This is understood as a set of choices, namely $[-3\ 0\ 1\ 2\ 3]$. Although it may appear attractive to output this as one continuous output, there are two persuasive explanations for dividing these into binary outputs, and these are to optimize stability and that because these are discrete, continuous representation covers the impossible range of $[-3\ 0]$.

After identifying its own predictor, the agent is capacitated to make decisions when playing and these decisions are reached by estimating the return of the resulting condition arising from each choice it can take. The $\varepsilon$-greedy policy is then applied to establish whether the agent will select the most optimal option, or whether it will evaluate the result of the less interesting result. Therefore, the agent is able to balance exploration vs. exploitation.

With each agent applied and interacting with each other as explained earlier in the chapter, we can utilize the multi-agent model to analyse a particular game and develop strategies to solve the game for different situations. Hurwitz and Marwala (2007a) surmised that only when agents know how to play a particular hand, they could then start to outplay and possibly bluff each other.

For the model to have any legitimacy, it is important to determine that the agents learn as they were designed. To authenticate agents learning, Hurwitz and Marwala (2007a) produced a single intelligent agent, and placed it at the table with three 'stupid' agents. These 'stupid' agents constantly stayed in the game, and acted randomly whenever required to make a decision. The results demonstrated convincingly that the intelligent agent soon learned to perform better than its opponents did.

The agents Randy, Roderick and Ronald used random decision-making, whereas AIden had the TD-lambda AI system installed (Hurwitz and Marwala, 2007a). The results were averaged over 40 hands, so that they were more viewable, and to permit for the random nature of cards being dealt. Hurwitz and Marwala (2007a) observed that AIden consistently performed better than its counterparts performed and continued to learn the game as it played. In the learning stage of the aforementioned intelligent agent, a fascinating and rather instructive problem arose. It was observed that when the agent was initially learning, it did not continue to learn but it rapidly determined that it was losing chips and decided to not continue to play, thereby keeping its chips.

Hurwitz and Marwala (2007b) observed that AIden rapidly decided that the risks were significant, and did not play any hands initially. After forty hands, AIden decided to play a few hands, and when it performed badly, got scared off permanently. This was because of the penalizing nature of the game. This is because poor play results in the loss of three chips. A coward agent is not useful, and therefore we give it courage to play and learn the game. To achieve this, one choice is to increase the value of $\varepsilon$ for the $\varepsilon$-greedy policy, but this renders the agent to be similar to a random player with no intelligence. A robust solution was to compel the agent to play when it knew nothing, until it was prepared to play. This was achieved by compelling AIden to play the first 200 hands it came across.

We optimized several parameters to improve agents learning and these were the learning-rate $\alpha$, the memory parameter $\lambda$ and the exploration parameter $\varepsilon$. The multi-agent system offered an ideal environment for this test, because four different parameter combinations were tested competitively. Through letting different agents to different combinations and permitting them to play against each other for a prolonged period of time (number of hands), it was possible to iteratively identify the parameter combinations that attained the optimum learning parameters (Hurwitz and Marwala, 2007a). We used the optimal parameters for the rest of the MAM. Hurwitz and Marwala (2007a) observed that the moment the dominant agent began to lose, it adapted its play to remain competitive with inferior opponents. The parameters that gave the most optimum results were $\alpha = 0.1$, $\lambda = 0.1$ and $\varepsilon = 0.01$. Even though, the $\varepsilon$ value was not surprising, the relatively low $\alpha$ and $\lambda$ values were not intuitive. What they amounted to was a degree of temperance, because higher values meant a great deal of learning from any given hand. This effectively meant over-reacting even though they may have played well and simply encountered bad luck. The results indicated that the rewards obtained by intelligent agents were far better than those obtained by the random agents were. Hurwitz and Marwala (2007a), furthermore, observed that agents learnt far better when playing against intelligent opponents and this quality is in human competitive learning. The agents with better experience tended to fold bad hands, and therefore lost far fewer chips than the intelligent agent playing against unpredictable opponents. To establish whether the agents adapt to each other, they were offered pre-dealt hands, and were required to play them against each other repetitively. The results demonstrated how an agent learned from its own blunder and once sure of it, altered its play and thereby adapting to better results.

Hurwitz and Marwala (2007b) showed that the agents successfully learned to play the game and to adapt to each other's play to maximize their own rewards. These agents were used to analyse and solve the game. Because the game had a non-trivial degree of complexity, we solved circumstances within the game by viewing each situation as a sub-game of the overall game. The first and most obvious type of analysis was the static analysis where all of the hands were pre-dealt. We stabilized this system when the results converged and therefore all agents were content to play the hand out in the same manner. A bluff is an action, typically in the setting of a card game that falsifies one's cards with the goal of letting one's opponents to drop theirs. There are two views on bluffing and these are that bluffing is a psychological phenomenon whereas the other claims that a bluff is a purely statistical act. Hurwitz and Marwala (2007a) observed that the intelligent agents learn to bluff.

## 15.6 Modelling of Tic–Tac–Toe

Marivate and Marwala (2008a, 2008b) applied reinforcement learning in the tic–tac–toe game. In reinforcement learning, agents learn to play games by playing games against themselves for a large amount of iterations (Kaelbling *et al.*, 1996; Moscato, 1999; Hurwitz, 2007; Marivate and Marwala, 2008a). Therefore, agents learn from the experiences that they produce. Players of such board games such as chess, Scrabble and checkers tutor each other in their clubs (Sandholm and Crites, 1996; Marivate and Marwala, 2008a). In social learning, there are vital features that an object/being should possess to be capable of learning and these are (Bandura, 1986; Marivate, 2009):

- Paying attention to the observations
- Remembering observations
- Reproducing behaviour
- Demonstrating what they have learnt

Therefore, learning by seeing comprises four processes: attention, retention, production and motivation. In reinforcement learning, we extend this to playing a game and observing state transitions, recalling what actions have occurred, trying a different action if the previous one was unsuccessful and then being rewarded if it leads to a terminal state. Furthermore, an agent then perceives what an opponent does. Vygotsky (1978) discussed the concept, which entails that in a social setting, an agent learns more from another agent that has more experience or is at the same level. This is also in chess clubs where we pair members to train stronger players or peers.

We introduce the non-stationary playing environment by placing agents as opponents in the learning step (Sandholm and Crites, 1996; Marivate and Marwala, 2008a). If the opponent is an intelligent software, a reinforcement-learning agent learns a strategy or policy that optimally beats the opponent (Pieter *et al.*, 2006; Marivate and Marwala, 2008a). This increases the probability of producing agents that know how to beat specific opponents' strategy and have a wider knowledge of a state space.

Human beings play and learn board games in social groups where players teach each other. To mimic a social learning setting like this, Marivate and Marwala (2008a) created multiple agents where they gave each agent its own identity through different initialization parameters. These agents had the equivalent learning algorithm but different initialization choices. We used two training structures to train the agents and these were the Swiss and a Round Robin system (Okulicz *et al.*, 2007). In the Swiss structure, we pair agents to play one round of a game, which is a full episode and when we complete this, there is either a winner or a loser or is a draw. We initialized agents positioned in the initial population and in the first iteration, we placed them in two sub-classes, which were winning agents and losing agents. In the second iteration and the rest of the game, agents play games against each other. A winning agent competes against a losing agent. After a game, the winner is located in the winner agent list and the losing agent in the losing agent list. This gives us a simulation of a mentor and a learner. Rounds are played, and the procedure of coupling losers and winners is repeated until the maximum number of rounds is attained. The focus is to get agents to be paired with players that have better experience.

In a round robin setting, each agent plays against the other and there is no dividing of the group to winners and losers. After a round of playing, the player competes against the next player until reaching the maximum number of games. Another agent produced is the S-P agent, which learns by only playing against itself. It plays a move as one player, and then plays another move as the other player and is able to benchmark how well the social agents fair against conventional S-P learning.

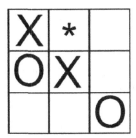

**Figure 15.3**   An illustration of the Tic–Tac–Toe.

The Tic–Tac–Toe is a 3 × 3 board game where two players place pieces on the board trying to connect three of their own pieces in a row (Cyber, 2008). The illustration of this is in Figure 15.3.

If two good players play a game of Tic–Tac–Toe, it should end with a draw (Schaeffer, 2001; Marivate and Marwala, 2008a). We modelled the game with reinforcement learning and observed that agents take 50000 learning episodes to be competent at a beginner level (Mannen, 2003).

We used reinforcement learning to model the game, which was represented by 10 state variables. Nine of the variables had three different values which denoted positions on the board. Each place on the board can either be empty or has a nought or cross. The tenth state is the player supposed to play. The model also keeps track of which actions are available to an agent in a certain state. Therefore, an illegal move such as placing a piece on a board area that already has a piece is not possible. When an agent wins a game, it is rewarded with a reward of 1.0. When the agent loses it then gets a reward of −1.0. When there is a draw, the agent gets a reward of 0.0. For all other game states that are not completed the reward is 0.0.

The games were managed by a game controller who allocates who has to play next and keeps track of game statistics such as wins, test results and how many times each agent has played games. It also matches winners and losers and thus implements the social frameworks. The agents were initialized with different learning parameters. Therefore, the agents play against non-stationary opponents to stimulate the emergence of more robust agents. The opponent's policies change and therefore, a learner adjusts its policy to play against more than one stationary opponent.

Two tests were produced for the agents. The first test was to assess how well the agents pick the correct actions in given test states. The Tic–Tac–Toe board was setup with pieces already on it and there was only one correct move that can be made. There were 10 test boards with different levels of difficulty. The agents were given one try at each board. Some boards had to reach a terminal state whereas in others the agent had to choose an action that resulted in forcing a draw in the game. There were 5 easy boards, 2 intermediate boards and 3 hard boards. The easy boards tested if the agent observed states that made them win.

The second test allowed to play with all the other agents. We recorded the wins, losses and draws. The agents played 5000 games against each other. We applied this to the best-modified Swiss agents and S-P agents. We built agents with different population sizes. The first size was 4, then 6 and then 8. We tested each of these 5 different times with the board test and then 5 times with the play test.

Marivate and Marwala (2008a) tested the procedure for different agent populations and the results for the modified Swiss structure are in Figure 15.4.

The results demonstrated that the S-P agent got 4 moves correct while the best Swiss social agent in the 4 population (SO4) got 5, while the one in the 6 (SO6) got 6 correct. This implies that the S-P agent played at a beginner level while the SO6 played at an intermediate level compared to the other agents. The other test was with the Round Robin Structure and we show the results in Figure 15.5 (Marivate and Marwala, 2008a).

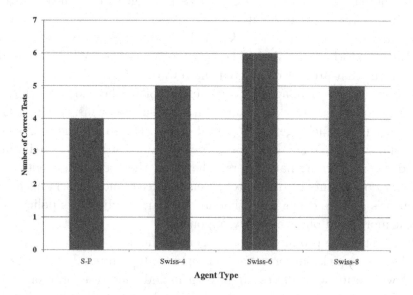

**Figure 15.4**   Board test results S-P vs. Swiss self play.

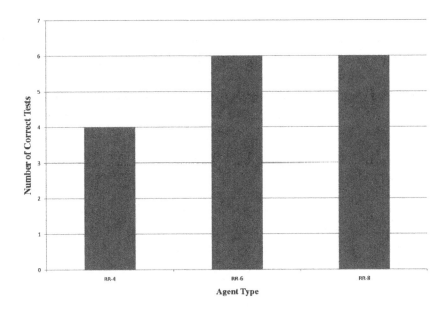

**Figure 15.5** Round Robin agent performance.

**Table 15.1** Average Swiss social agent play test.

|        | S-P   | SO1   | SO2   | SO3   | SO4   |
|--------|-------|-------|-------|-------|-------|
| **S-P**  | 0     | 3049  | 3041  | 3028  | 3046  |
| **SO1**  | 3084  | 0     | 3058  | 3077  | 3089  |
| **SO2**  | 3024  | 3034  | 0     | 3063  | 3080  |
| **SO3**  | 3060  | 3059  | 2995  | 0     | 3047  |
| **SO4**  | 3037  | 3063  | 3028  | 3022  | 0     |

Additional comment from the social agents is that as more and more agents (>8) are utilized in the population, there is an increase in the number of intermediary agents in one generation. This is more apparent with the Swiss tournament setting compared to the Round Robin structure. We tested both structures with 16 and 32 agent-sized populations. When the populations were increased with the modified Swiss structure, a number of intermediate agents emerged. In some steps, up to 6 intermediate agents emerged. With the Round Robin structure, 2 intermediate playing agents emerged. Introducing multiple different agents as opponents in the training stages, created agents that were better than the S-P agent.

We conducted the play test on the Swiss Structure social agents and the results are in Table 15.1.

The agents played 5000 games against each other. This table has 4 social agents and one S-P agent. The S-P agent is the best agent kept during initialization and training of the agents. The table shows that the S-P agent won 3041 games against SO2, while SO1 won 3084 games. This shows that when an agent starts a game first, they are more likely to win. The agents on average won over 60% of the games they started first. The social agents on average beat the S-P agents 50 times or more.

## 15.7  Conclusions

This chapter introduced reinforcement learning, game theory and multi-agent system. These techniques were applied to model the game of Lerpa as well as the game of Tic–Tac–Toe. When implemented, reinforcement learning was able to model these two problems well. It was observed that it is possible to model an agent to be able to bluff.

## References

Abdoos, M., Mozayani, N., Bazzan, A.L.C. (2011). Traffic light control in non-stationary environments based on multi agent Q-learning. In: *Proceedings of the IEEE Conference on Intelligence Transportation Systems*, 1580–1585.

Babu, S., Mohan, U. (2018). An integrated approach to evaluating sustainability in supply chains using evolutionary game theory. *Computers & Operations Research*, 89:269–283.

Bandura, A. (1986). *Social Learning Theory*. Englewood Cliffs, NJ: Prentice Hall.

Bellman, R. (1954). The theory of dynamic programming. *Bulletin of the American Mathematical Society*, 60(6):503–516.

Bertsekas, D.P. (2000). *Dynamic Programming and Optimal Control*, 2nd Edition. Athena Scientific.

Castellanos, S.A., Buentello, G., Gutierrez-Meza, D., Forgues, A., Suliburk, J.W. (2018). Use of game theory to model patient engagement after surgery: A qualitative analysis. *Journal of Surgical Research*, 221:69–76.

Christin, N. (2011). Network Security Games: Combining game theory, behavioral economics and network measurements. *Lecture Notes in Computer Science*, 7037:4–6.

Cyber, O. (2018). Tic–Tac–Toe. Available at: http://www.cyberoculus.com/tic-tac-toe.asp. Accessed on 8 February 2018.

El-Amine, S., Galland, S., Yasar, A-U-H., Koukam, A. (2017). Towards agent based modeling for mobility behavior shift. *Procedia Computer Science*, 109:949–954.

Frankenhuis, W.E., Panchanathan, K., Barto, A.G. (2018). Enriching behavioral ecology with reinforcement learning methods. *Behavioural Processes*, in press, corrected proof, Available online 13 February 2018.

Franklin, S., Graesser, A. (1996). Is it an Agent, or just a Program? A taxonomy for autonomous agents. In: *Proceedings of the Third International Workshop on Agent Theories, Architectures, and Languages*, 21–35.

Fu, Z., Hao, L. (2018). Agent-based modeling of China's rural–urban migration and social network structure. *Physica A*, 490:1061–1075.

Hodgson, G.M., Huang, K. (2012). Evolutionary game theory and evolutionary economics: are they different species? *Journal of Evolutionary Economics*, 22:345–366.

Holm, H.J. (2010). Truth and lie detection in bluffing. *Journal of Economic Behavior & Organization*, 76(2):318–324.

Hui, E.C.M., Bao, H. (2013). The logic behind conflicts in land acquisitions in contemporary china: A framework based upon game theory. *Land Use Policy*, 30: 373–380.

Hurwitz, E., Marwala, T. (2005). Optimising reinforcement learning for neural networks. In: *Proceedings of the 6th Annual European on Intelligent Games and Simulation*, Leicester, UK, 13–18.

Hurwitz, E., Marwala, T. (2007a). Learning to bluff: A multi-agent approach. *IEEE International Conference on Systems, Man and Cybernetics*, Montreal, Canada, 1188–1193.

Hurwitz, E., Marwala, T. (2007b). Multi-agent modeling of interaction-based card games. In: *Proceedings of the 3rd International North American Conference on Intelligent Games and Simulation*, University of Florida, USA, 23–28.

Hurwitz, E. (2007). Multi-Agent Modelling using Intelligent Agents in Competative Games. Master Thesis, Johannesburg, South Africa: University of the Witwatersrand.

Jabri, A., Zayed, T. (2017). Agent-based modeling and simulation of earthmoving operations. *Automation in Construction*, 81:210–223.

Kaelbling, L., Littman, M., Moore, A. (1996). Reinforcement learning: A survey. *Journal of Artificial Intelligence Research*, 4:237–285.

Kangur, A., Jager, W., Verbrugge, R., Bockarjova, M. (2017). An agent-based model for diffusion of electric vehicles. *Journal of Environmental Psychology*, 52:166–182.

Kasabov, N. (1998). Introduction: Hybrid intelligent adaptive systems. *International Journal of Intelligent System*, 6:453–454.

Khanizad, R., Montazer, G. (2018). Participation against competition in banking markets based on cooperative game theory. *The Journal of Finance and Data Science*, 4(1):16–28.

Laffont, J.-J. (1997). Game theory and empirical economics: The case of auction data. *European Economic Review*, 41:1–35.

Lawlor, J.A., McGirr, S. (2017). Agent-based modeling as a tool for program design and evaluation. *Evaluation and Program Planning*, 65:131–138.

Lee, S., Kim, S., Choi, K., Shon, T. (2018). Game theory-based security vulnerability quantification for social internet of things. *Future Generation Computer Systems*, 82:752–760.

Lelouche, R., Doublait, S. (1992). Qualitative reasoning with bluff and beliefs in a multi-actor environment. *International Journal of Man-Machine Studies*, 36(2):149–165.

Leottau, D.L., Ruiz-del-Solar, J., Babuška, R. (2018). Decentralized reinforcement learning of robot behaviors. *Artificial Intelligence*, 256:130–159.

Mannen, H. (2003). Learning to Play Chess Using Reinforcement Learning with Database Games. Master Thesis, Utrecht University.

Marivate, V.N., Nelwamondo, V.F., Marwala, T. (2008). Investigation into the use of autoencoder neural networks, principal component analysis and support vector regression in estimating missing HIV data. In: *Proceedings of the 17th World Congress of The International Federation of Automatic Control*, Seoul, Korea, July 6–11, 682–689.

Marivate, V.N., Marwala, T. (2008b). Social learning methods in board game agents. In: *Proceedings of the IEEE Symposium on Computational Intelligence and Games*, Australia, 323–328.

Marivate, V.N. (2009). Investigation into the Effect of Social Learning in Reinforcement Learning Board Game Playing Agents. Master Thesis, University of the Witwatersrand.

Marivate, V., Ssali, G., Marwala, T. (2008a). An intelligent multi-agent recommender system for human capacity building. In: *Proceedings of the 14th IEEE Mediterranean Electrotechnical Conference*, 909–915.

Marwala, T., Hurwitz, E. (2009). *A Multi-agent Approach to Bluffing. Multiagent Systems*, Salman A. Mohd Noh Karsiti, M.N. (eds.), I-Tech, Vienna, Austria, pp. 233–246.

Marwala, T. (2009). *Computational Intelligence for Missing Data Imputation, Estimation and Management: Knowledge Optimization Techniques*. New York: IGI Global Publications.

Marwala, T. (2010). *Finite Element Model Updating Using Computational Intelligence Techniques*. London: Springer-Verlag.

Marwala, T. (2013). *Economic Modeling Using Artificial Intelligence Methods*. Heidelberg: Springer.

Marwala, T. (2012). *Condition Monitoring Using Computational Intelligence Methods*. London: Springer-Verlag.

Marwala, T., De Wilde, P., Correia, L., Mariano, P., Ribeiro, R., Abramov, V., Szirbik, N., Goossenaerts, J. (2001). Scalability and optimisation of a committee of agents using genetic algorithm. In: *Proceedings of the 2001 International Symposium on Soft Computing and Intelligent System for Industry*, arxiv: 0705.1757.

Marwala, T., Lagazio, M. (2011). *Militarized Conflict Modeling Using Computational Intelligence Techniques*. London: Springer-Verlag.

McFadden, D.W., Tsai, M., Kadry, B., Souba, W.W. (2012). Game theory: Applications for surgeons and the operating room environment. *Surgery*, 152:915–922.

Mendonça, M.R.F., Bernardino, H.S., Neto, R.F. (2018). Reinforcement learning with optimized reward function for stealth applications. *Entertainment Computing*, 25:37–47.

Miller, W.T., Sutton, R.S., Werbos, P.J. (1990). *Neural Networks for Control*. London, UK: MIT Press.

Montoya, A., Ovalle, D. (2013). Energy consumption by deploying a reactive multi-agent system inside wireless sensor networks. *Lecture Notes in Electrical Engineering*, 152:925–934.

Morehead, A.H., Mott-Smith, G., Morehead, P.D. (2001). *Hoyle's Rules of Games*, 3rd revised and updated edition. Signet book.

Moscato, P. (1999). Memetic algorithms: A short introduction. *McGraw-Hill'S Advanced Topics in Computer Science Series*, 219–234.

Nelwamondo, F.V, Golding, D., Marwala, T. (2013). A dynamic programming approach to missing data estimation using neural networks. *Information Sciences*, 277, 49–58.

Okulicz, E., Vialle, W., Verenikina, I. (2007). The development of expertise within a community of practice of scrabble players. *Learning and Socio-Cultural Theory: Exploring Modern Vygotskian Perspectives International Workshop*, Vol. 1.

Papadimitriou, C.H. (2001). Game theory and mathematical economics: A theoretical computer scientist's introduction. In: *Proceedings of the Annual Symposium on Foundations of Computer Science*, 4–8.

Pendharkar, P.C., Cusatis, P. (2018). Trading financial indices with reinforcement Learning Agents. *Expert Systems with Applications*, in press, accepted manuscript. Available online 6 March 2018.

Pieter, J.H., Tuyls, K., Panait, L., Luke, S., La Poutré, J. (2006). An overview of cooperative and competitive multiagent learning. In: *Learning and Adaption in Multi-Agent Systems*, Vol. 3898/2006, Anonymous Berlin/Heidelberg: Springer, 1–46.

Ross, D. (2006). Evolutionary game theory and the normative theory of institutional design: Binmore and behavioral economics. *Politics, Philosophy & Economics*, 5:51–79.

Roth, A.E. (2002). The economist as engineer: Game theory, experimentation, and computation as tools for design economics. *Econometrica*, 70:1341–1378

Roy, K., Kamel, M.S. (2012). Facial expression recognition using game theory. *Lecture Notes in Computer Science*, 7477:139–150.

Russell, S.J., Norvig, P. (2003). *Artificial Intelligence: A Modern Approach*. Upper Saddle River, New Jersey.

Sandholm, T., Crites, R. H. (1996). On multiagent Q-learning in a semicompetitive domain. In: *Proceedings of the Workshop on Adaption and Learning in Multi-Agent Systems*, 191–205.

Schaeffer, J. (2001). A Gamut of Games. *AI Magazine*, 22:29–46.

Shahabpoor, E., Pavic, A., Racic, V. (2018). Identification of walking human model using agent-based modelling. *Mechanical Systems and Signal Processing*, 103:352–367.

Stroeve, S.H., Blom, H.A.P., Bakker, G.J. (2013). Contrasting safety assessments of a runway incursion scenario: Event sequence analysis versus multi-agent dynamic risk modelling. *Reliability Engineering and System Safety*, 109:133–149.

Sutton, R.S. (1992). *Reinforcement Learning*. Boston: Kluwer Academic Publishers, p. 171.

Sutton, R.S., Barto, A.G. (1998). *Reinforcement Learning: An Introduction*, 1st Edition. Cambridge, MA: MIT Press.

Sutton, R.S. (1988). Learning to predict by the methods of temporal differences. *Machine Learning*, 3:9–44.

Teweldemedhin, E., Marwala, T., Mueller, C. (2004). Agent-based modelling: A case study in HIV epidemic. In: *Proceedings of the 4th International Conference on Hybrid Intelligent System*, 154–159.

van den Brink, R., van der Laan, G., Vasil'ev, V. (2008). Extreme points of two digraph polytopes: Description and applications in economics and game theory. *Journal of Mathematical Economical Economics*, 44:1114–1125.

Villena, M.G., Villena, M.J. (2004). Evolutionary game theory and thorstein veblen's evolutionary economics: Is EGT Veblenian? *Journal of Econom Issues*, 38:585–610.

Vygotsky, L.S. (1978). *The Development of Higher Psychological Process*. Cambridge, MA: Harvard University Press.

Wei, X., Qu, H., Ma, E. (2012). Decisive mechanism of organizational citizenship behavior in the hotel industry — An application of economic game theory. *International Journal of Hospitality Management*, 31:1244–1253.

Wooldridge, M.J. (2002). *Introduction to Multiagent Systems*. New York, NY: John Wiley & Sons, Inc.

Yao, H., Chen, X., Li, M., Zhang, P., Wang, L. (2018). A novel reinforcement learning algorithm for virtual network embedding. *Neurocomputing*, 284:1–9.

Zhang, L., Reniers, G., Chen, B., Qiu, X. (2018). Integrating the API SRA methodology and game theory for improving chemical plant protection. *Journal of Loss Prevention in the Process Industries*, 51:8–16.

# Chapter 16

# Conclusion Remarks

**Abstract.** This chapter gives a summary of the topics that were discussed in this book. These include machine-learning methods such as neural networks, support vector machines and granular methods such as fuzzy logic and rough sets. It also describes advanced topics such as reinforcement learning, causality and evolving machines. This chapter then describes some of the philosophical and practical implications of deployment of artificial intelligence in all areas of our lives.

## 16.1 Summary of the Book

This book studied the multi-layer perceptron (MLP) neural network, its architecture and the way to train the MLP (Marwala, 2007, 2009; Marwala and Lagazio, 2011; Xing and Marwala, 2018a). Furthermore, this book studied how the MLP was applied for both regression and classification problems. The MLP was then used to classify mechanical faults and steam generator and to model interest rate and interstate conflict.

This book also studied the theory and applications of the radial basis function (RBF) (Marwala, 2013, 2014; Xing and Marwala, 2018b). This book studied two approaches to train the RBF. The first was the combination of the $K$-means clustering algorithm and the pseudo-inverse methods. The second was the Expectation Maximization (EM) algorithm. The RBF was applied to model inflation, steam generator, interstate conflict and caller behaviour classification.

This book also introduced the automatic relevance determination (ARD). This is a technique for ranking input variables in the order of their importance on predicting the output. The theory of regularization is the foundation of formulation of the ARD, and we assign each input its own regularization coefficient. The book applied the ARD to rank inputs in interstate conflict model and an inflation model.

This book also studied the Bayesian approach to neural networks. The consequence of the Bayesian formulation of neural networks is the concept of the posterior probability function (Marwala, 2015; Marwala *et al.*, 2017). It describes various methods for estimating the posterior probability function using the Hybrid Monte Carlo, Shadow Hybrid Monte Carlo and Separable Shadow Hybrid Monte Carlo. It applied the Bayesian network to classification of interstate conflict.

This book also studied the support vector machine (SVM) and how it is implemented for both classification and regression problems (Vapnik, 1998). The book applied the SVM to classify interstate conflict and to model a steam generator.

This book studied the theories and applications of fuzzy logic and neuro-fuzzy systems (Zadeh, 1965; Takagi and Sugeno, 1985). It studied the transparency in the Takagi–Sugeno neuro-fuzzy model. In this book, the fuzzy logic and Takagi–Sugeno neuro-fuzzy model were applied to model a steam generator and in the prediction of interstate conflict.

This book studied rough set theory (Crossingham, 2007; Crossingham and Marwala, 2007). In particular, it studied the concept of rough sets discretization and introduced neuro-rough sets (NRS). The NRS is based on rough sets and the MLP. The NRS was applied to model HIV and interstate conflict.

This book examined the hybrid of machines for both classification and regression (Perrone and Cooper, 1993). The hybrid approach is more accurate than the individual methods if the individual methods are not correlated. The hybrid method was applied for fault classification in mechanical systems and caller behaviour classification.

This book introduced the auto-associative network to predict missing data (Anishchenko and Treves, 2006). It used two approaches for a missing data system based on auto-associative network. These were the combination of the MLP and the principal component analysis as well as the auto-associative network trained using the MLP and RBF. These approaches were implemented using genetic algorithm and were tested on modelling HIV as well as a beer taster.

This book studied the idea of evolving biological systems of Charles Darwin on building evolving intelligent systems in Artificial Intelligence (AI) (Marwala, 2010, 2014). Intelligent networks take new information and evolve them without fully retraining them, and this is called incremental learning. Learn++ and Incremental Learning Using Genetic Algorithm (ILUGA) were applied on the Optical Character Recognition (OCR), wine recognition, financial analysis and condition monitoring data.

This book studied causality, the Neyman–Rubin, Pearl and Granger causality models. It described the Neyman–Rubin causal model within the context of missing data estimation framework and directed acyclic graphs. It described the Granger causality within the context of the identification of the causal relations.

This book discussed the theory and applications of the Gaussian mixture models (GMM). The GMM was applied to condition monitoring.

This book studied the hidden Markov Models (HMMs) and applied them to the problems of condition monitoring and speech recognition (Nelwamondo *et al.*, 2006).

This book studied reinforcement learning and multi-agent systems (MAS) (Sutton, 1992; Sutton and Barto, 1998). In particular, it studied the TD-lambda algorithm. The MAM and TD-lambda algorithm were applied to model the games of Lerpa and Tic–Tac–Toe.

## 16.2  Implications of Artificial Intelligence

AI is changing many aspects of our lives. Factories are being automated at an astonishing rate using intelligent robots (Xing and Marwala, 2018b). Self-driving will more and more become common. One area that is also changing very fast because of intelligent machines is the financial markets. For example, the company Amazon has collected so much information about customers and suppliers that this is changing the very concept of the law of demand and supply. The law of demand and supply is a basic law of economic trade. It describes the relationship between price and quantity of goods for buyers and sellers. This relationship for the buyer is called a demand curve and for the sellers, the supply curve. The point at which the suppliers are willing to supply a specified quantity of goods and services which are the same as those that the customers are willing to buy is called equilibrium. Marwala and Hurwitz (2017) observed that the advent of AI allows the opportunity for individualized demand and supply curves to be produced and reduces the degree of arbitrage in the market and, consequently, brings a certain degree of fairness into the market, and thus bringing more efficiency in the economy. Furthermore, the advent of AI results in individualized pricing models.

AI also has an impact on what is called the theory of rational choice (Marwala and Hurwitz, 2017). Rational choice assumes that people make decisions by maximizing their utility. This requires the use of all the information available, and, consideration of all the options available to select a rational choice. AI makes the expectations of the future to be more consistent. This implies that AI reduces the biases and the variances of the error of the predictions. AI thus makes decisions that are more rational and, thus, the marketplace becomes more rational.

Rational decision-making comprises of utilizing imperfect and incomplete information, with an intelligent machine, i.e. human brain, which is unable to maximize utility. Because life is not perfect, and we make decisions although the information is incomplete and imperfect, these decisions are rationally limited. This is what Nobel Prize Laureate Herbert Simon called bounded rationality (Simon, 1957, 1991). Advances in AI and improvements of computational power due to Moore's law expand the bounds of rationality in decision-making (Marwala and Hurwitz, 2017).

Behavioural economics is the type of economics that factors human behaviour (Kahneman, 2011; Kahneman and Tversky, 1979). Some of these behavioural traits are the inability of human beings to think statistically, called heuristics and biases, the concept of anchoring, availability effect, substituting effect, optimism and loss aversion effect, framing effect, sunk costs and prospect theory. The advent of AI at the least reduces all these effects (Marwala and Hurwitz, 2007).

Frequently, when human beings make decisions, one human agent has more information than the other and this phenomenon is called information asymmetry. Information asymmetry distorts the markets and this idea won Akerlof, Stiglitz and Spence a Nobel Prize (Akerlof, 1970; Spence, 1973; Stiglitz, 1974). Advances in AI signalling and screening are easier to achieve. AI agents reduce the degree of information asymmetry and makes markets more efficient. AI agents reduce the volume of trades in the market because asymmetry of information facilitates trade because it creates arbitrage.

Game theory has been applied widely in economics, social sciences and politics. In game theory, agents with rules interact to obtain pay-off at Nash equilibrium (Nash, 1950; Marwala and Hurwitz, 2017). The advent of AI led to intelligent multi-agent games.

The efficient market hypothesis has facilitated the formation of financial models based on share price movements. Marwala and Hurwitz (2017) explored the impact of AI on the efficient market hypothesis and concluded that advances in AI make markets more efficient.

In game theory, players use rules and pay-off and they interact until Nash equilibrium is reached. Mechanism design is the inverse of game theory as the end-state is known, and the goal is to identify the rules and pay-off function that lead to the desired end-state being achieved. AI is able to make mechanism design easier to implement (Marwala and Hurwitz, 2017).

Portfolio theory is rooted in statistical models based on Brownian motion. The use of AI to portfolio theory has far-reaching consequences. AI methods permit us to model price movements with much greater accuracy than the random-walk nature of the original Markowitz model (Markowitz, 1952; Marwala and Hurwitz, 2017). Moreover, optimizing a portfolio is performed with greater optimality and efficiency using evolutionary computation while still staying true to the original goals and conceptions of portfolio theory.

Rational counterfactuals is a concept of identifying a counterfactual from the factual (whether perceived or real), and knowledge of the laws that govern the relationships between the antecedent and the consequent, that maximizes the attainment of the desired consequent (Marwala and Hurwitz, 2017). In counterfactual thinking, factual statements like: 'The country Venda was not financially prudent and consequently its finances are in tatters', and with its counterfactual being: 'The country Venda was financially prudent and consequently its finances are in good shape'. To construct rational counterfactuals, AI techniques are applied.

# References

Akerlof, G.A. (1970). The market for 'lemons': Quality uncertainty and the market mechanism. *Quarterly Journal of Economics*, 84(3):488–500.

Anishchenko, A., Treves, A. (2006). Autoassociative memory retrieval and spontaneous activity bumps in small-world networks of integrate-and-fire neurons. *Journal of Physiology*, 100(4):225–236.

Crossingham, B. (2007). Rough Set Partitioning Using Computational Intelligence Approach. Master Thesis, University of the Witwatersrand, Johannesburg.

Crossingham, B., Marwala, T. (2007). Using optimisation techniques to granulise rough set partitions. In: *Proceedings of International Symposium on Competitional Models of Life Sciences*, 952:248–257.

Kahneman, K. (2011). *Thinking, Fast and Slow.* Macmillan.

Kahneman, D., Tversky, A. (1979). Prospect theory: An analysis of decision under risk. *Econometrica*, 47(2):263.

Markowitz, H.M. (1952). Portfolio selection. *The Journal of Finance*, 7(1):77–91.

Marwala, T. (2007). *Computational Intelligence for Modelling Complex Systems.* Delhi: Research India Publications.

Marwala T. (2009). *Computational Intelligence for Missing Data Imputation, Estimation, and Management: Knowledge Optimization Techniques,* Information Science Reference Imprint. New York, USA: IGI Global Publications.

Marwala, T. (2010). *Finite Element Model Updating Using Computational Intelligence Techniques.* London: Springer-Verlag.

Marwala, T. (2012). *Condition Monitoring Using Computational Intelligence Methods.* Heidelberg: Springer.

Marwala, T. (2013). *Economic Modeling Using Artificial Intelligence Methods.* Heidelberg: Springer.

Marwala, T. (2014). *Artificial Intelligence Techniques for Rational Decision Making.* Berlin, Heidelberg: Springer.

Marwala, T. (2015). *Causality, Correlation, and Artificial Intelligence for Rational Decision Making.* Singapore: World Scientific.

Marwala, T., Hurwitz, E. (2017). *Artificial Intelligence and Economic Theory: Skynet in the Market.* Springer.

Marwala, T., Lagazio, M. (2011). *Militarized Conflict Modeling Using Computational Intelligence.* Heidelberg: Springer.

Marwala, T., Boulkaibet, I., Adhikari S. (2017). *Probabilistic Finite Element Model Updating Using Bayesian Statistics: Applications to Aeronautical and Mechanical Engineering.* London: John Wiley & Sons.

Nash, J.F. (1950). Non-Cooperative Games. PhD Thesis. Princeton University.

Nelwamondo, F.V., Marwala, T., Mahola, U. (2006). Early Classifications of bearing faults using hidden Markov models, Gaussian mixture models, Mel-frequency Cepstral coefficients and fractals. *International Journal of Innovative Computing, Information and Control,* 2(6):1281–1299.

Perrone, M.P., Cooper, L.N. (1993). When networks disagree: Ensemble methods for hybrid neural networks. In: Mammone R.J. (ed.), *Artificial Neural Networks for Speech and Vision.* London: Chapman and Hall.

Simon, H. (1957). A behavioral model of rational choice, in *Models of Man, Social and Rational: Mathematical Essays on Rational Human Behavior in a Social Setting.* New York: Wiley.

Simon, H. (1991). Bounded rationality and organizational learning. *Organization Science,* 2(1):125–134.

Spence, M. (1973). Job market signaling. *Quarterly Journal of Economics.* The MIT Press, 87(3):355–374.

Stiglitz, J.E. (1974). Incentives and risk sharing in sharecropping. *Review of Economic Studies,* Oxford Journals, 41(2):219–255.

Sutton, R.S. (1992). *Reinforcement Learning.* Boston: Kluwer Academic Publishers, p. 171.

Sutton, R.S., Barto, A.G. (1998). *Reinforcement Learning: An Introduction,* 1st Edition. Cambridge, MA: MIT Press.

Takagi, T., Sugeno, M. (1985). Fuzzy identification of systems and its applications to modeling and control. *Information and Control, IEEE Transactions on Systems, Man, and Cybernetics,* 15:116–132.

Vapnik, V. (1998). *Statistical Learning Theory.* New York: Wiley-Interscience.

Xing, B., Marwala, T. (2018a). *Smart Computing in Crowdfunding.* London: CRC Press.

Xing, B., Marwala, T. (2018b). *Smart Maintenance for Human–Robot Interaction: An Intelligent Search Algorithmic Perspective.* London: Springer.

Zadeh, L.A. (1965). Fuzzy sets. *Information and Control,* 8:338–353.

# Index

Printed in the United States
By Bookmasters